Agnes Baldwin Alexander
Hand of the Cause of God

Agnes Baldwin Alexander
Hand of the Cause of God

Earl Redman and Duane Troxel

GEORGE RONALD
OXFORD

George Ronald, Publisher
Oxford
www.grbooks.com

A catalogue record for this book is available from the British Library

ISBN 978-0-85398-647-8

Cover photograph taken by John Schwerin, May 1965,
in Agnes Alexander's apartment in Kyoto, Japan

Cover design: Steiner Graphics

CONTENTS

Acknowledgements   x

1   Who is Agnes Alexander?   1

2   Christianity, Politics and Conquest   6

3   Agnes Baldwin Alexander: The Early Years   11
    The episode of the cake – The University of California, Berkeley –
    Camp Azalea – Berkeley, California and Oberlin University, Ohio
    – Back in Hawaii

4   A Life-Changing Adventure: 1900–1901   25
    Across America and Europe to Rome – An encounter with destiny –
    Back to Hawaii

5   Spreading the Bahá'í Faith in Hawaii: 1902–1913   40
    Helen, Edwin and Ella Goodall's visit, and Elizabeth Muther's
    declaration – Kanichi Yamamoto – Slow growth of the Bahá'í
    community – Agnes goes to Alaska – 'Abdu'l-Bahá and Ada Whitney
    – A love interest for Agnes, and teaching work – George and Ruth
    Augur – Abby Frances Johnson – Ella Louise Rowland – Mason
    Remey and Howard Struven – Organizing the Hawaiian Bahá'ís –
    'Abdu'l-Bahá in North America – Mason Remey's second visit

6   Beginning the Great Adventure: 1913   71
    An interest in Japan – The journey to Italy – War breaks out in
    Europe

7   The Japanese Adventure: 1914–1917   83
    Arrival in Japan – Beginning the life of a pioneer in Tokyo –
    Vasily Eroshenko – Teaching contacts – Kikutaro Fukuta: The
    first Japanese Bahá'í – Martha Root in Japan – George and Ruth
    Augur arrive – The coronation and a Hiroshima visit – Back in
    Tokyo – The importance of Esperanto – A Japanese contribution

for the Mashriqu'l-Adhkár in Chicago – Daiun Inouye, a Buddhist priest – Vasily leaves Japan – Tokujiro Torii – Back in Tokyo – Ichi Kamichika: A woman imprisoned – Two Tablets from the Master – Yuri Mochizuki: The first Japanese woman to accept the Faith

8   Two Years in America: 1917–1919   116
    California – The National Bahá'í Convention – The travels of Agnes

9   Return to Japan: 1919–1921   127
    The power of prayer – Where to live? – A devastating fire – Recovery – Three schoolgirls – Karuizawa – Connecting with China – Star of the East –'In short, it has a long description, but I mention it briefly'

10 Korea, China and Japan's Great Earthquake: 1921–1923   153
    Back in Tokyo – The Passing of 'Abdu'l-Bahá – The Guardian's first letter to Japan – The doll project – China to the forefront – New Bahá'ís and visitors – Martha Root returns – The Great Earthquake – China

11 Back in Hawaii: 1924–1927   190
    Maui, Hawaii and Kauai – Orcella Rexford, Orol Platt and Valera Allen – Planning another return to Japan – Hawaiian activities – Return to Japan

12 Japan and China: 1928–1933   203
    A problem with Communism – Opportunities and the Guardian's encouragement – The ascent of Mt. Fuji – Continuing efforts – Martha Root returns – California connections – Keith Ransom-Kehler visits Japan – Home visits – The first Local Spiritual Assembly in Japan – Visiting Hokkaido – Translation of Bahá'u'lláh and the New Era *into Japanese – A call to Hawaii*

13 Hawaii and America: 1933–1935   242
    Maui – North American National Bahá'í Convention – Looking toward Japan, again

14 Back to Japan: 1935–1936   251
    Bahá'u'lláh and the New Era *in Japanese Braille – Problems and possibilities – An army mutiny and the seeds of war – Visiting Fujita's mother – The Guardian encourages steadfastness*

15 Pilgrimage: 1937   261
    Preparations for pilgrimage – Departure for the Holy Land – Agnes's
    pilgrimage – Travels through Europe – America

16 Hawaii and America: 1939–1949   285
    1939 National Convention – The passing of Martha Root – The
    passing of May Maxwell – Writing the history of the Cause in
    Japan and Hawaii – Back in Hawaii – Full drafts of the histories
    are completed – New directions – Travelling across America in the
    Second Seven Year Plan – Hawaii and America

17 Back in Japan, Again: 1950–1957   312
    Rebuilding the Japanese Bahá'í community – Agnes returns to Japan
    – Activities of Ahmad Sohrab's Caravan of the East – Where to
    live? – The Holy Year and Ten Year Crusade – Michitoshi Zenimoto
    – Two Intercontinental Teaching Conferences – Auxiliary Board
    member – A trip to Taiwan

18 Hand of the Cause of God: 1957–1965   337
    The passing of Shoghi Effendi – Moving forward without the
    Guardian – The travels of a Hand – Hawaii elects First National
    Spiritual Assembly

19 The Last Years: 1965–1971   366
    Confined to a bed in Japan – The last years – The passing of Agnes
    Alexander – A life well lived

Appendix: May Maxwell – A Tribute, *by Agnes Alexander*   380

Bibliography   389

Notes and References   393

Index   419

About the Authors

DEDICATION

This book is dedicated to the memory of Dr Odmaa Dugersuren, MD (1957–2019).

Dr Dugersuren was a Mongolian Baháʼí, embracing the Cause of Baháʼuʼlláh about the year 2000. During the last decade of her life, she devoted herself to an archival project of the National Spiritual Assembly of the Baháʼís of the United States to digitally preserve the priceless audiovisual heritage of the Baháʼí Faith. In a letter to her shortly before her passing the Assembly wrote:

> Gratitude fills our hearts whenever we contemplate the significant service you rendered this Assembly and the entire American Baháʼí community through the patient, meticulous, and highly skilled efforts you devoted to our Heritage Project. Thanks to your work, vast in scope and of immense import, thousands of unique and precious audio and video files, photographic images, and documents are now preserved for future generations in enduring digital form. Taken together, they constitute a priceless legacy to present and future historians, researchers, writers, and artists.
>
> Be sure your generous, wholehearted, and unselfish service will never be forgotten and will long inspire us to warmest admiration and affection.
>
> With our deepest love,
> *National Spiritual Assembly of the Baháʼís of the United States*

ACKNOWLEDGEMENTS

Most of the material used to write this book comes from the 40 years of research by Duane K. Troxel in the Hawaiian and American National Bahá'í Archives, and from Agnes's own publications, *History of the Bahá'í Faith in Japan* and *Forty Years of the Baha'i Cause in Hawaii*. Unless otherwise attributed, material cited in the reference section comes from Duane's large collection of letters and documents, including many of the letters from the Guardian.

John Schwerin, who knew Agnes in Japan after her accident, connected us with Michitoshi Zenimoto and Ruth Suzuki, both of whom knew Agnes very well. Michitoshi contributed the intimate story of how he became a Bahá'í through Agnes's efforts and added other bits and pieces. Ruth Suzuki (née Baldridge) was Agnes's nurse for two years after 1965 and she shared her experiences. Elahe Vahdat Young contributed a beautiful story of seeing Agnes in her final days.

Melina Rajaei very helpfully searched the Hawaiian Bahá'í Archives for letters about Agnes's trip to Alaska in 1905.

Chris Cholas, Keith Munro, Michael V. Day and Neda Najibi reviewed all or parts of the manuscript at various stages and offered helpful suggestions.

My thanks also go to Christine Boyett for her editorial efforts to make sure this book and its references were completely accurate. It was undoubtedly a challenge for a first time George Ronald editor with over a thousand endnotes, but she rose to the challenge and I am indebted to her careful eye.

As always, my wife Sharon O'Toole was a constant source of encouragement and proofreading help. She patiently put up with me constantly bouncing ideas and questions off her and provided much good advice about the organization and readability of the bits I struggled with.

Earl Redman

WHO IS AGNES ALEXANDER?

Agnes Alexander was born and raised in the Hawaiian Islands, the daughter and granddaughter of some of the first Christian missionaries to the islands. She became the first Hawaiian Bahá'í and one of the first to teach the Faith in Hawaii, Japan, Korea and China. She also wrote the first histories of the Bahá'í Faith for both Hawaii and Japan at the Guardian's request. She was educated in the Faith by one of its foremost scholars, Mírzá Abu'l-Faḍl, as well as some of its most enlightened followers, such as May Bolles (Maxwell), Emogene Hoagg, Laura Dreyfus-Barney, Lua and Edward Getsinger, William Hoar, Ethel Rosenberg and Ali-Kuli Khan. Her close friends included Ella Cooper and Louise Bosch, and she travelled through China and Japan with Martha Root.

Despite all her amazing achievements, Agnes remained a very humble person. Her philosophy was summed up in a statement she made at the first Hawaiian National Convention in 1964: 'God uses those who are nothing; and if you are something He cannot use you.' Her humility was further illustrated in a letter sent to Duane Troxel from a Bahá'í friend in 1981:

Last night Mr Dale Allen came to visit me. I showed him a letter from dear Agnes Alexander. He read it and praised her, then told me that in 1925 his mother (Mrs Valera Fisher Allen) sat next to Agnes at a Bahá'í conference in Hawaii. Years afterwards she told Dale, 'Agnes gave a talk and then read the Master's Tablet addressed to herself. But she did not read it all and I saw that there were words of praise from the Beloved Master to Agnes. I said to her, "You did not read all the words of the Master, May I read them aloud to the friends?" She replied, "It is not necessary or important." Then I asked, "May I then see the Tablet just for myself?" Agnes said, "I think there is no need."' This was Agnes Alexander's nature. She was very humble. She was never one to push herself forward. It was for this reason that she never said, 'I am appointed a Hand of the Cause,' until sick in Tokyo in 1965, she dictated her last letter to all the friends in the Pacific area and quoted the Guardian's cable of 1957 concerning her elevation to the station of a Hand of the Cause.[1]

Agnes is best known for her prolonged efforts to establish the Bahá'í Faith in Japan as well as her unstinting work as a Hand of the Cause. 'Abdu'l-Bahá had first mentioned the need to take the Faith to Japan as early as 1903.[2] Five years later, in a letter to Howard MacNutt, 'Abdu'l-Bahá wrote, 'A trip of the believers of God to the Orient is of the utmost importance and it will become the cause of great connection between the two regions.' Mason Remey and Howard Struven were the first Bahá'ís to go to Japan, doing so in 1909 on their around-the-world teaching trip. When they met 'Abdu'l-Bahá in the Holy Land, He told them:

> Blessed results will appear from the Holy Cause established in that land. I have sent your letter regarding the work in Japan to Mr. McNutt in New York, that he may spread the word for some of the American Bahá'ís to go to Japan, and there serve and teach in the Cause. It is very good for teachers to travel, and, through the love of God, give life to the people. American Bahá'ís should go to Oriental countries as teachers.[3]

Mason and Howard were followed by travel-teachers Mme Aurelia Bethlen in 1911 and Hippolyte and Laura Dreyfus-Barney in 1914. Hawaiian Bahá'í George Augur pioneered to Japan in late 1914 and was followed by Agnes and his wife, Ruth, the same year. Ultimately, Agnes lived for a total of 30 years in Japan between 1914 and 1967.

Agnes lived a life of complete servitude to the Faith of Bahá'u'lláh. A suggestion from 'Abdu'l-Bahá or Shoghi Effendi she considered to be a divine order. She lived by her inspirations, which she felt to be whisperings of the divine spirit and, in everything, her guideline was, 'if God wills'. She received 13 Tablets from 'Abdu'l-Bahá and at least 94 letters from Shoghi Effendi, not counting cablegrams. Age did not slow her down. At the age of 83, she served on the Local Spiritual Assembly of Kyoto, the Regional Spiritual Assembly of North East Asia and as a Hand of the Cause of God.

Hands of the Cause of God occupy a high station in Bahá'u'lláh's Revelation. They are special people, devoted to the Cause and possessing deep knowledge of it, who could only be appointed by the Centre of the Bahá'í Faith: Bahá'u'lláh, 'Abdu'l-Bahá or Shoghi Effendi. In Bahá'u'lláh's Book of Laws, the *Kitáb-i-Aqdas*, they are called the 'learned ones in Bahá' and 'charged with various duties, especially those of protecting and propagating His Faith'.[4] 'Abdu'l-Bahá defined them as those '(pillars) of the Cause of God that have diffused widely the Divine Fragrances, declared His Proofs, proclaimed His Faith, published abroad His Law, detached themselves from all things but Him, stood for righteousness in this world, and kindled the Fire of the Love of God in the very hearts and souls of His servants'.[5] The work of the Hands of the Cause was apparently not just for this physical world because many were appointed after they ascended into the spiritual worlds.

Shoghi Effendi called the Hands of the Cause the 'Chief Stewards of Bahá'u'lláh's embryonic World Commonwealth, who have been invested by the unerring Pen of the Center of His Covenant with the dual function of guarding over the security, and of insuring the propagation, of His Father's Faith'.[6] Between 1951 and 1957, Shoghi Effendi appointed 32 outstanding living Bahá'ís to this position. The 81-year-old Agnes Alexander, who replaced the Irish Hand George Townshend upon his passing, was one of them. Six months after her appointment, the Guardian ascended to the Abhá Kingdom and Agnes found herself one of those Shoghi Effendi had named as the 'Chief Stewards' of the Bahá'í Faith and in charge of guiding the Bahá'í world to the completion of the world-embracing Ten Year Crusade and the election of the Universal House of Justice.

I was in the middle of working on a book about Howard Colby and Mabel Rice-Wray Ives when Duane Troxel, who was of great assistance for my two volumes about Shoghi Effendi and the book on the Knights of Bahá'u'lláh, asked if I would be interested in writing a book on Hand of the Cause of God Agnes Baldwin Alexander. Writing about a Hand of the Cause was daunting and I was initially quite reluctant to tackle the task of writing about such a significant person. Duane, however, was very persuasive – this book is the proof – and the more I explored the materials he had collected, the more fascinating Agnes became.

Raised in privilege as part of a ruling class, she dedicated her life to uplifting the spiritual lives of the Japanese, and particularly the blind Japanese. It became a challenge to see if I could write a book about a Hand of the Cause.

It was a paragraph from one of the *Tablets of the Divine Plan*, written by 'Abdu'l-Bahá in April 1916, that actually resulted in my writing this book. Up to April 1916, Agnes had brought a handful of people into the Faith in Hawaii and they had brought in a few others so that there was a community of about a dozen Bahá'ís. She had been in Japan for almost a year and a half and her teaching efforts had raised up a single Japanese Bahá'í. But 'Abdu'l-Bahá wrote of her having an amazing station:

> At this time, in the Hawaiian Islands, through the efforts of Miss Alexander, a number of souls have reached the shore of the sea of faith! Consider ye, what happiness, what joy is this! I declare by the Lord of Hosts that had this respected daughter founded an empire, that empire would not have been so great! For this sovereignty is eternal sovereignty and this glory is everlasting glory. [7]

He also mentioned May Maxwell and Alma Knobloch in those same Tablets. And He mentioned Agnes Alexander twice.

Duane initially met Hand of the Cause Agnes Alexander at the first Hawaiian National Bahá'í Convention in 1964 when she represented the Universal House of Justice, and then visited her in 1968 after she had returned to Hawaii following her long years in Japan. Six years later, Agnes's book about the history of the Bahá'í Faith in Hawaii was published and Duane wrote his first short biography about her. He became the Archivist for the Hawaiian Bahá'í community in 1980 and wrote about her life in a booklet titled *Eighty Golden Years: 1901–1981*, a history of the Faith in Hawaii to that time. [8] In 1984, the University of Hawaii published a book about Hawaii's famous women and Duane contributed her biography for that. He was then asked to write a three-part biography about her for the *Bahá'í News* that was published in 1983. He had been collecting information about her for 40 years and decided that it was time to try to get a book out of it, so in August 2016, Duane sent me over 12,000 files – letters, files, photographs, audio and video interviews and a host of other materials – about Agnes.

Trying to understand who Agnes Baldwin Alexander was becomes much clearer when reading the Guardian's first letters to the Bahá'ís of Japan on 26 January 1922. Quoting the words of 'Abdu'l-Bahá, Shoghi Effendi wrote:

> 'Japan will turn ablaze! Japan is endowed with a most remarkable capacity for the spread of the Cause of God! Japan, with (another country whose name He stated but bade us conceal it for the present) will take the lead in the spiritual reawakening of peoples and nations that the world shall soon witness!' On another occasion, – how vividly I recall it! – as He reclined on His chair, with eyes closed with bodily fatigue, He waved His hand and uttered vigorously and cheerfully these words in the presence of His friends: – 'Here we are seated calm, quiet and inactive, but the Hand of the Unseen is ever active and triumphant in lands, even as distant as Japan!'9

Agnes Alexander was moved by the Hand of the Unseen, willingly and with her full cooperation.

2

CHRISTIANITY, POLITICS AND CONQUEST

Agnes Baldwin Alexander was born on 21 July 1875 in a house named 'Maluhia', which is Hawaiian for tranquillity, quiet or harmony, in Makiki Heights not far above Waikiki Beach. She was the granddaughter of Protestant missionaries whose descendants became some of the most important, powerful and wealthy people in the islands.

The first Europeans to encounter the Hawaiian Islands were Captain James Cook and his crew in 1778. Cook decided to name the cluster of isolated volcanic landmasses the Sandwich Islands in honour of another Englishman, and he was killed by the Hawaiians the following year. By the time the missionaries first arrived in 1820, Hawaii was in a state of change. King Kamehameha had united all the islands into a single kingdom, but that unification, along with the increasing presence of foreigners, initiated great changes. The old idols the people had worshipped had been destroyed, thus diminishing the power of the priests. Into this partial vacuum came Christianity. Kamehameha had died a year before the first missionaries arrived and his successors were more and more influenced by the white newcomers.[1]

Agnes's story begins in June 1831 with the arrival of Rev. Dr Dwight and Charlotte Baldwin, after a sea voyage of 161 days from Boston, in the fourth company of missionaries sent out to Hawaii by the American Board of Commissioners for Foreign Missions. This great project began in 1820, when the first missionaries arrived in the islands. The Baldwins spent a short while on the Big Island (Hawaii) and eventually settled at Lahaina on the island of Maui and began their life's work of bringing Christianity to the Hawaiian people. Dr Baldwin was also a physician and the only doctor for the islands of Maui, Molokai and Lanai. The Baldwins had eight children: David, Abigail (Abby), Mary, Charles, Douglas, Henry, Emily and Harriet. Abigail married William De Witt Alexander and became Agnes's mother.[2]

William De Witt Alexander's parents had been in the fifth company of missionaries who arrived in Honolulu in May 1832. His father, William Patterson Alexander, had been appointed as a missionary in November 1830, and his immediate reaction was:

It produces very solemn reflections. Now unless God prevent by his providence, I am going to the heathen to spend my life in telling them of Jesus (a thing for which I have often prayed). It will be a trial to leave my friends and country; but 'if any man love father or mother more than me, he is not worthy of me.' I do love them, but I feel in my heart I can gladly bid them farewell. I may meet with sore trials on pagan ground; the rude barbarian may imbrue his hands in my blood . . .³

William's paternalistic attitude and ignorance of Hawaiian culture was fairly typical of those who went forth to save the Hawaiians from their un-Christian existence.

Before leaving the United States, William was told that to be a missionary, he had to be married. Some behind the scenes matchmaking resulted in William meeting Mary Ann McKinney and marrying her on 25 October.⁴ One month after their marriage, the new couple boarded their ship. Agnes told of her grandparents' journey to Hawaii:

With God's light upon their foreheads, with earth's hoards beneath their feet, and earth's self-denials thronging on their pathway indiscreet – so they sailed to bear the message of good-will forevermore to the tribes that dwelt in darkness on a distant island shore . . .

In the fifth company of missionaries sent to the Hawaiian Islands were my father's parents, Rev. and Mrs. William Patterson Alexander. They were in a party of nine bridal couples, all young people in their twenties . . . On November 26, 1831, they set sail from New Bedford, Massachusetts, on a small whaling ship of three hundred and fifty tons.

Equipped for whaling, the passenger accommodations were very meager. The cabin, which was used as an eating, sleeping and sitting room, was so small that only one half the company could be seated at a time. The furniture consisted of two chairs and boxes and trunks. Their sleeping accommodations are thus described: 'Half the missionaries had to take berth in the cabin where four berths, each suitable for one person, and separated only by a curtain, had to do services for two each. Some had to be stowed away in temporary berths on the side of the dismal after-cabin, which was crowded with a confusion of boxes, casks and kegs . . .'

After a voyage of one hundred and eighty-six days, Honolulu was reached in May, 1832.[5]

The Alexanders had nine children: William De Witt (Agnes's father), James, Samuel, Henry, Mary Jane, Ann, Emily, Charles Hodge and Ellen.

The missionaries set up the first printing press in the islands, created an alphabet for the Hawaiian language and opened schools. During their first decade in the islands, they established 900 schools, staffed with native teachers, who were educating almost 45,000 pupils.[6] Within a quarter century, 80% of the Hawaiians could read. But the diseases brought in by the foreign visitors and settlers decimated the Hawaiian population, reducing it from about 300,000, when Captain Cook had first landed on the islands in 1778, to 57,000 by 1866.[7]

Though the missionaries were initially spiritually oriented, other white arrivals were not, and soon making money became a strong motive throughout the islands for both the white newcomers and the Hawaiians. This money motive also affected some of the missionaries. As early as 1836, the focus of some of the missionaries had changed, bringing about the accusation that 'some of the number who went forth to those heathen islands to save souls by their teaching and preaching, remained there to put away their missionary character and assume the part of amateur statesmen, much occupied thereafter in secular matters, and not altogether foregoing such secular honours as their connection with that small state could bestow'.[8]

All land in the islands belonged to the King when the foreign invasion began, but that began to change in 1846 when some land was offered for sale. The white settlers wanted to own land and they had pushed the King to allow the private ownership of land. They achieved their goal in 1850 and by 1886, the whites owned most of the available land.[9] The first generation of missionaries were not immune from this passion to own land, and many of their sons fully embraced it, some acquiring huge land holdings and becoming more businessmen than missionaries.[10]

With public land becoming available for purchase, sugar companies began a dramatic expansion. This brought about two major changes. First, the Big Five sugar companies, who dominated the industry in the islands, imported large numbers of Chinese, Filipino and Japanese workers for their operations, and second, the second generation of the missionary families became very involved in the sugar business. Two of the Big Five sugar companies, Alexander & Baldwin and Castle & Cook, were run by the children of missionaries. The result was that these missionary children became the 'inner elite within the oligarchy' of white businessmen.[11]

The white businessmen realized that they could never dominate and have their own way unless the powers of the King were curtailed. Understanding what was happening, King Kalakaua tried to reverse the white power grab in the 1870s and 1880s, but the whites organized their own army, ostensibly to be in the service of the King. In reality, the army was designed to force the King to relinquish most of his power, and in 1887, he was given no choice but to acquiesce. The result was the creation of a House of Nobles whose members had to meet certain income and property minimums, which few Hawaiians could do. The Chinese and Japanese were not allowed to vote, therefore the House of Nobles was dominated by white businessmen and missionaries. Hawaiians could vote, but the House of Nobles became 'the voice' of the whites and had the power to overrule the popular vote.

It all came to a head in January 1893:

The word *pilikia* (trouble) was on the lips of hundreds of Hawaiians on the evening of January 16, 1893, as they peeked from behind doors and around corners, watching American sailors arrogantly parade two light cannon through the virtually empty streets of Honolulu. By prearrangement with a small group of resident Americans, and with the full support of the American Minister to the Independent Kingdom of Hawaii, the visiting bluejackets were quartered in the vacant building known as Arion Hall, directly across the street from the government building and only a short distance from the palace.

Queen Liliuokalani protested the landing, but the American occupation of Hawaii was beyond her control. Early the next afternoon, the local revolutionaries seized the government building, demanded the Queen's abdication, and declared martial law. The United States government, through its Minister, gave immediate diplomatic recognition to the rebel group, which then proclaimed the abrogation of the monarchy, forced the resignation of the sorrowful but dignified Queen, and launched the American flag where the Hawaiian pennant had flown . . .

Capitalism replaced feudalism, and oligarchy supplanted monarchy.[12]

American President Grover Cleveland demanded that Queen Liliuokalani be restored to her throne, but Governor Stanford Dole refused. The next year, Dole was elected President of the new Republic of Hawaii.[13]

Thus did the Hawaiians lose control of their islands. By 1895, 70% of the key government officials were related to the missionaries. This elite group of missionaries and businessmen, comprising just 5% of the total population, had as their goal the control of Hawaii. They 'lived in stately mansions surrounded by royal palms in the hills of Honolulu, or in large sprawling houses set on manicured lawns in rural areas . . . The girls, if they married at all, were expected to choose only [whites] of their own class. To improve their prospects, they were frequently sent off to the best Eastern schools . . . As women of gentle breeding, they were not expected to pursue careers, though there were exceptions.'[14]

As explained in Lawrence H. Fuch's book *Hawaii Pono*:

The men and women who ruled Hawaii for four decades after annexation grew up in families that not only assumed the right to rule, but also assumed that wealth and power brought certain obligations. The haole [white] missionary families especially felt a sense of community obligation through private charity. If there was little justice in Hawaii at the turn of the century, there was much charity. This sentiment, best known in Hawaii by the word paternalism, had two major sources: the first was the missionary conscience, and the second was the receptivity of the Hawaiians. The missionary conscience produced a considerable uneasiness among many haoles in their relationships with Hawaiians. A common sense of obligation to the natives stemmed from a knowledge that no matter how strong the missionaries' self-conception as the natural custodians of the Islands, they were intruders in the eyes of many Hawaiians.[15]

This was the world that Agnes Baldwin Alexander was born into, one of privilege and chaos.

3

AGNES BALDWIN ALEXANDER

THE EARLY YEARS

Into the chaos of power struggle and cultural clash, Agnes Baldwin Alexander was born on 21 July 1875, the fifth child of William De Witt and Abigail Alexander. She had three brothers: William, born in 1861; Arthur, born in 1863; Henry, born in 1868; and a sister, Mary, born in 1874.

Agnes was not Agnes for the first month or so of her life. On 16 August, her father wrote to his father about their naming conundrum:

Dear Father,
The little baby is a very contented happy child, cries very seldom, wakes up generally but once in the night, & has a good appetite. She has bright eyes of a dark blue color, & regular features, but has a rather scanty development of hair on top of her head at present . . .

No name has yet been decided on for the last arrival. I have had the name 'Emily' running in my head for some time past, but Abbie [Abigail] is 'Kanalua' [uncertain] about it.

I have proposed Kate, and Ellen Julia & Agnes & Alice, etc, family names, at least on my Mother's side.

I made out a list of Bible women as, Sarah, Rachel, Rebecca, Deborah, Hannah, Bath Sheba, Dorcas, Eunice, Huldah, etc, but they did not take. Have you any suggestions to offer?
WD Alexander[1]

The name Agnes obviously was not her father's first choice, but we do not know whether it was her grandfather or her mother who christened her Agnes.

Agnes grew up fairly isolated from the power struggles between the

11

white settlers and the Hawaiian government. Her father may have been actively involved in what was happening at that time, but Agnes as a child, and as a girl, was probably quite cocooned. The missionaries formed a society within a society and Agnes spent most of her childhood happily associating with the children of other missionaries and the power elite. It was a life of comfort. She travelled extensively, visiting her Baldwin relatives on Maui and making trips to California. The Alexanders lived in a large, two-storey house surrounded by gardens.

In 1883, she began attending the Punahou Preparatory School, which had been established for the children of the Protestant missionaries[2] and where 'the children of the favored [whites] in Hawaii received a superior education through high school from well-trained mainland teachers'. The Punahou School was the oldest preparatory school west of the Rocky Mountains. Hawaiian children had their own schools.[3]

One of Agnes's best friends at this time was Ada Whitney. Unlike most of Agnes's friends, Ada was of mixed race, being one eighth Black, and had been adopted by Mary and John Morgan Whitney in California. Ada lived just a block from Agnes and they both went to the Punahou School and spent a lot of time together. In July 1883, eight-year-old Agnes wrote to her brother, Henry, that 'Mama and Willie have gone downtown shopping. I wish I could see you. Three of Biddie's chicking [chickens] are dead. I read to Mama almost every morning. Mary and I went down to the Whitney's to play with Ada.'[4]

In the handwritten letter, all of Agnes's 'S's are backwards. Agnes apparently also had peculiar speech abnormalities. In 1879, her father collected these letter transpositions, finding that she changed 'd's to 'g's (dress to guess), 'r's into 'l's (rice into lice).[5]

In 1886, Agnes, Mary, Henry and their mother spent the summer in Oakland, California, staying from early April until late September. Agnes wrote to her father about going to Woodward's Gardens, a combination amusement park, zoo, museum and aquarium. She highlighted the monkeys, who had a cat in their cage, the bears and alligators. She also wrote that 'I could just as soon live here as Honolulu,' and that everyone had the whooping cough except Henry.[6] In September, Agnes wrote to her father that her brother Willie had got a job running a street car.[7]

Agnes was a good letter writer and kept in touch with her brothers as they began to leave home and make their own way in life. On

5 February 1888, she wrote to her brother Willie that both she and Mary were going to the Punahou school, though Mary was in the 'big Punahou School'. She also informed her brother that she had six cats and their mother had 21 canaries. She wrote that 'We have a Chinese man to work in the yard and a native woman in the house; her name is Kealoha . . . We have a nice new piano, it has a lovely tone. Mary and I are both taking music lessons.' The Chinese man was both cook and gardener. For Chinese New Year, he gave Agnes 'a lot of candied fruits, and lichee nuts. They gave me a Chinese wax doll.'[8] A few months later, she wrote to another brother, Arthur:

> Aunt Em[ily] has invited mama, Mary and me to go to Maui and spend August.
>
> I suppose you remember the little Makiki church above us. Well every Sunday afternoon Papa, Henry, Mary and I go up there and teach Sunday School. Mary and I teach a class of little Chinese children and Henry teaches some grown Chinese men. Some of the children are very cunning.
>
> July 30th. Next week on Tuesday we all go to Maui excepting Henry. We will go to Aunt Helen Alexander's first and then to Aunt Em Baldwin's. Papa is only going to stay with us one week.[9]

All during this time, Agnes said that she 'loved and wished to serve Christ, but His life seemed far away from me, and I always felt that something was lacking, that I had never been reborn'. She noted that the family gathered each morning for prayers and her father read from the Bible and she later wrote: 'Once when listening to him read from the Revelation of St. John, I had thought the words were beautiful, but wondered whether I would understand them when I died. Little did I then know that while on earth they would become clear to me, for Baha'u'llah had unsealed the meanings of all the Holy Scriptures.'[10] But this was still in the future for the teenage school girl.

In the year 1890, King Kalakaua died and Liliuokalani became Queen. For Agnes, all this meant was some holiday time and a visit to the palace, as she told her brother Henry: 'Yesterday the Charleston came in bringing the remains of the King. We had a half holiday yesterday and today a whole holiday. This morning Mary and I went down with the Punahou scholars and saw the Kings remains at the palace. We all marched in two by two at the front gate and went out at the back.' The next thing she told her brother was that 'Last Christmas I went up to Maui to spend my vacation at Aunt Annie's. While I was there Aunt Annie cut me some bangs. Mamma had been wanting me to have some for quite a while and we thought we would surprise her.'[11] Politics and power struggles were of no interest to the 14-year-old missionary's daughter. Later in the summer, Agnes told Henry: 'This afternoon I took a ride on "Koko", as Arthur has named a colt, to the base-ball grounds . . . Cousin Clar Gregory has been giving Mary and I painting lessons. I have painted some mangoes and started a taro plant.'[12]

Agnes spent the Christmas/New Year holiday on Maui. In a letter to her mother, she wrote:

> Yesterday when Miss Cushman and I came down from Olinda it rained steady from the time we left Makawao until we got to Haiku. We had a splendid time at Olinda. I went up Monday morning and Miss Cushman came up Wednesday morning. She went up to the top of the mountain Thursday and saw the sun rise. I did not go because Aunt Annie thought my horse would not stand the trip. The folks that did go up said they had to wait half an hour for the sun to rise, and they nearly froze, but when it did rise it was beautiful . . .
>
> I feel sleepy this morning because I did not get much sleep at Olinda. We stayed up one night until 1:45, and then on New Year's night we stayed up until the New Year came in. Just as the clock struck twelve we made a terrible noise, ringing bells, blowing whistles, etc.[13]

Makawao was up on the side of Haleakala volcano at an elevation of about 1,575 feet (480 metres). Olinda was a mile further up the mountain, while Haiku is much lower down to the north and not far from the coast.

The next year, 1891, Agnes spent the summer on Maui. Both she and Mary took the steamer and were 'dreadfully seasick'. Much of her letter to her mother was about the tooth brush and saddle she forgot to bring. The two sisters spent much of their month on Maui going between Olinda, Haiku and Paia, visiting their aunts and uncles.[14] Paia was on the coast not far from the present airport. The girls returned to Honolulu in mid-September.

Upon her return, Agnes had to go straight into school. Her mother was still in Maui and Agnes wrote about her courses: 'I have taken Geometry & Phisiology. I've only have French once a week now so that I thought you would not mind if I took it, even though they say she gives lessons long enough to last for five days . . .' She also noted that: 'My eyes hurt quite badly after school now but Mrs Whitney had me bath them in hot salt water and they feel ever so much better now.' This was the beginning of a long-term eye problem.[15]

Agnes complained on 26 September that she was unable to get the mail from the steamer because it had to be fumigated for five hours on account of the cholera in the United States. A few weeks later, ships arriving from America were still having to be quarantined. The great excitement on 18 October was that: 'Last night a man pointed a pistol at Robert Wilcox and stories go around that he had been shot. The man was caught and it was found he was drunk.'[16]

In 1893, Agnes again spent the summer on Maui, going back and forth between Olinda, high on the side of Haleakala volcano, and Haiku, lower down. She was apparently not a good sea voyager, because she wrote that 'I was quite sick coming up, although it was not very rough.' Agnes enjoyed what was called the Literary, a literary club. One night, 'It was an evening in Ireland and was very good. There were a great many Honolulu folks.'[17] Later, she wrote to her mother saying that:

The Literary was on Tuesday night and as Cousin Clar wanted me to be in some of the tableaux I had to be down on Monday night to rehearse. Ben [a Baldwin cousin] and Mrs Gray, Winnie [another Baldwin cousin] and all went down to the Paia depot to rehearse in what they called the 'spring wagon'. It was a wagon with a seat put in the back. May and I sang all the way down, but coming home the winds blew in our faces and so we kept our mouths shut. The next night Mr Andrews let Ben have his double carriage to go in. The Literary was given in order to raise money to buy a piano for the church. I hear they raised $117.[18]

The house at Olinda had a telephone, but on 11 August it was out of order, meaning that they could not make calls with it. But it was still very useful for another rather mischievous pastime: 'The telephone up here has been out of order so that we cannot use it, but we have great fun listening to other people talking. I've found out all the news, and what is going on below us.'[19]

Haleakala volcano, at 10,023 feet (3,055 metres), was quite a tourist attraction with its volcanic features and amazing sunrise viewing from the summit. Many people made the trek by horse. Agnes recounted the passage of one group of tourists who went through Olinda: 'Last Tuesday [three ladies] stopped in here on their way up the mountain. They had a tent and a guide with them, and expected to camp out down in the crater, but the guide did not seem to know much about the way down into the crater, so Uncle Dwight went along with them. We expect them back either today or tomorrow.'[20]

Agnes stayed on Maui until late in September, but was back in late November. On 27 November came the big news that Queen Liliuoka-lani was to be restored to her throne by order of President Cleveland:

> Saturday afternoon I went down to Aunt Annie's to play tennis and found everybody in great excitement as the Kinan had brought the news up that it had been recommended that the Queen be restored. Everybody here is in a great excitement, and I guess that in Hono-lulu the excitement must be immense. Yesterday before and after church little groups of people were collected around, all talking politics as hard as they could.[21]

Agnes's letter showed no further interest in such political shenanigans and she continued writing about what she called the Literary and the goings and comings of her Baldwin and Alexander relatives.

Agnes was back in school in January 1894. In a letter to her sister Mary, she wrote, 'I have just been going to school a month and three days, and enjoy it very much. My studies this term are French, Geol-ogy, and Rheutoric [Rhetoric] . . . I [have been] taking singing lessons of Miss Paten. I like her real well. She says I have quite a remarkable tongue and I have had no trouble from the first about keeping it down . . . We have drawing every Thursday and we have lots of fun in it. The 2nd year and the 4th year have it together.'[22]

The episode of the cake

In April, Agnes described 'the episode of the cake'. Mrs Sorenson had sent the family a cake one day. After spending a week at Waikiki, Agnes and a few others had walked home while some of the girls had gone to church. Agnes wrote:

> We had it [the cake] carefully put away in the safe while we were outside. We heard the other girls saying that now was their chance while we were away to get the cake and eat it up so we immediately sent Mamie McKinley in as a scout to try and get ahead of them. She had a narrow escape of being caught and had to hide in the bathtub with her cake until the other girls had given up the search. We then went around to the other side of the house and Mamie climbed in the window and hid the cake in a bureau drawer. After that we all went in and showed ourselves at which there was a great row to know what had become of the cake. We did not get to bed until about 12 o'clock that night, and after all the lights were out there were a great many ghosts prowling around, but at least the cake was safely hid in the stove by our side. The next morning when I was getting breakfast, Kate came in and asked me why I did not light the stove. I did not think anything about the cake then but later we found it was gone and that Kate's trunk was locked. While Kate was in bathing that morning Etta found the key and got the cake safely locked up in her bureau drawer. That evening we cut it up into little pieces and brought it out, when each one told their part in the hiding of it.[23]

Agnes's sister Mary moved to Oakland, California, in 1894, and Agnes had hoped to go and visit her. This didn't work out and she ended up in Hilo on the island of Hawaii. In a letter to Mary, Agnes wrote:

> I can imagine your surprise when you read the heading of this letter. I would have written you before about my coming up here, if there had been any definite plan, but I really did not know for sure that I was coming until a few days before. I wanted awfully to be with you next year and was not very enthusiastic about coming up here for that reason but Papa did not think I could go to the States this year,

and so he said I had better come up here and then you see I can see the volcano before I go to the States. Erdy [Baldwin] had said when he was in Honolulu that Willie would like either you or I to come up and visit her & so Papa wrote and asked him if he would take me for a boarder if I came. He answered that they would be very glad to have me make them a little visit, & so here I am . . . [24]

In mid-September, Agnes described her trip to Hilo:

Hilo I think is the prettiest place I was ever in. Of course the town itself is not pretty but the suburbs. The road to the volcano is too grand for description, and Olaa, Erdy's and Willie's place is about the prettiest place on the road. I enjoyed being with Willie, he is so lively, and we kept on the go nearly all the time. One night we started at 8:30 P.M. for Olaa which is 16 miles [26 km] from Hilo [on the road to the volcano]. Erdy and I went in a brake, with a horse that had been out at pasture for three years. Willie and Miss Broadwell, Willie's sister-in-law's sister, went on horseback. We got to Olaa at 2:30 in the morning & then went to bed and got up the next morning at 10 o'clock. Miss B had promised to be back in time for dinner, so we started off again at 1:30, arriving at Hilo about 6 o'clock. The night we went up it was full moon and the woods were beautiful, but it poured and I think we were all pretty tired by the time we got to Olaa. [25]

Agnes graduated from Oahu College, the high school end of the Punahou School, on 24 June 1895. She was one of just seven graduates, which included her best friend Ada Whitney. All the graduates delivered essays they had written. Agnes's essay was titled 'Our Poor Relations' and was about showing kindness to animals. Her mother wrote:

Agnes graduating dress of Japanese silk, was simple and pretty. I presume Agnes will write you of the graduating exercises. They took place last Thursday evening, and passed off well. The [Central Union] church was beautifully decorated for the occasion. The house was full, as it always is on those occasions. Agnes did well, I received many compliments. Was pronounced 'good', and all speak of how well she read it [her essay]. One of our neighbors told me she had heard it praised more than any other essay. Bouquets were numerous . . . She had nine bouquets of carnations. I am glad to have Agnes through school, and I hope she will rest now for a while.[26]

The University of California, Berkeley

Near the end of 1895, Agnes enrolled at the University of California at Berkeley. In January, she had two problems. One was to buy a watch and the other was her eyes. In a letter to her father, she wrote about both:

> I took Uncle Charlie's watch into Oakland the other day to see if I could get it changed for a ladies watch and they would allow me $4 on it. They have Waltham and Elgin watches in gold filled cases for $16, and I could get one for $11 by trading. I did not know as I wanted to spend that much but Arthur thinks it is better to get a good watch, while getting one as a cheap one never lasts. These watches are guaranteed for 20 years and are the very best make. The same works in a silver case would be $2 less, but the man said the gold filled was so much better that it paid. My idea was to get a cheap little silver watch but I haven't decided what to do yet. If I do get one I want to pay for it out of my own money.[27]

The eye problem was much more serious; she was having vision problems, particularly with reading, which caused headaches:

> I went to the optician yesterday and he said he had spoken of my case to some oculist and he thought he was doing exactly right. He said I had better keep on practicing with prisms for six months and then if my eyes were no better I could have the muscles clipped, but he said he would only do that as a last resort. My eyes are so much better now, I mean I can use much stronger prisms now and keep them together though they don't feel very good and he says they will not until they get straightened out . . .[28]

Of this eye problem, Dr Sarah Sabour-Pickett has written that 'it sounds like she had some form of eye muscle weakness, something that in technical terms is called an eye "phoria". In appearance, it would have looked like her eyes were not aligned. The prisms were used as exercises to strengthen the muscles. It is not usually something that improves with age; in fact, it is more likely to get more difficult to overcome as time goes on, particularly for small detailed tasks.'[29] The problem grew worse over time and she finally had to have the over-strong eye muscles clipped three years later.

Agnes was busy in classes by February 1896. She wrote that 'I have commenced my work in the University and enjoy it very much. I have only put my name down for Botany and French for credit, but have been visiting Prof. le Conte's Geology and can visit any of the other classes I want.' She also joined a Gymnasium. Her health had long been rather delicate and she decided to see what exercising could do: 'Tomorrow I am going into the Gymnasium. I got in by paying $2.50 for my examination. I think I will enjoy it very much though the hours are just at noon time, making it rather inconvenient . . . Feb 6. At noon time I went to the Gymnasium though I didn't do hardly anything today. Mr Bagee showed me some exercises I am to do.'[30] Agnes wrote that she had 'gained 10 lbs since I have been here and hope to gain 10 more. I am learning how to make bread. Have made several loaves myself.'[31]

On subsequent visits, Agnes had been very limited in what they would allow her to do because of her frailness. She wrote: 'I am going over to the Gym in about a half an hour. I enjoy it ever so much and have not been the least bit lame from my exercising. I hope to learn to play basketball today. They have not let me play before because they were afraid I would get lame, but I guess my muscles have got pretty tough from riding horseback.'[32]

By May, Agnes was debating what to do after the summer vacation. She wrote to her parents and told them: 'If Papa wants me to stay here next year I should think it would be much less expensive for me to live there [at the university]. I enjoy the university and there are so many advantages in it, especially as I can attend the lectures in any of the classes as a visitor. I think all the instructors in the University are superior minds. I want to stay at the University next year, & want to devote myself more to study than I have done this year.'[33]

Camp Azalea

In July, Agnes joined a group of her cousins led by her Aunt Mary and Uncle Rev. James Alexander to Camp Azalea for five weeks in the

*Agnes Alexander, born at the Alexander family
home 'Maluhia' in Honolulu, 21 July 1875*

Agnes at about age 5

At Waikiki Beach, about 1883. Agnes is seated front row, far right

Agnes, Henry and Mary Charlotte Alexander, about 1884, Honolulu

Agnes at about age 10

The Alexander family home on Punahou Street in Honolulu. The family gave it the Hawaiian name 'Maluhia', meaning peace, stillness, safety or security

Agnes, about 1895, wearing a straw boater

Punahou School Graduating Class of 1895. Left to right, back row: Ada Whitney (Agnes's best friend), Mattie Richardson, Agnes Alexander, Lillian Hapai; seated: Charlotte Hall, President Hosmer, Edward Woodward, Mabel Sorenson

Agnes, second from right, enjoys summertime at Camp Azalea, California, 1896. The camp is within walking distance of sequoia trees

1896 Agnes (left) inside a tree trunk at Camp Azalea

Agnes, second from left, receives 'Aloha'. This photograph dates from the late 1890s or very early 1900s. Agnes is either leaving or arriving by ship at Honolulu Harbour

mountains near Healdsburg, about 50 miles (80 km) north of Oakland. Little did Agnes realize how important this area would become in the future. Just ten miles (16 km) up the road, a summer camp for Bahá'ís called Geyserville would be established in 1927 and Agnes would spend a lot of time there.

At first, Agnes wasn't all that impressed by Camp Azalea:

> The mosquitoes are frightful here in the afternoons. They have nearly devoured me. They bit me worse than anyone else. It is either because I am so fat or because the mosquitoes are different from those we have at home.
>
> It has been real hot here the last few days, and we have sat down at the brook most of the time. Tonight we are going to have a big bon-fire down by the brook.
>
> Yesterday all the girls went into the brook for a bath. The place is only large enough to swim out fifteen strokes, but it was lots of fun to swim again . . .
>
> We don't do very much here but lounge around the camp and go out walking.[34]

On the 21st July, her birthday, one of the girls told Agnes that it was an eventful day for her. Agnes countered that:

> it wasn't. I didn't like being such an old maid. Afterwards the girls all pounded me twenty-one times. I thought that would be the last, but just as we finished lunch, they brought a beautiful birthday cake covered with frosting and decorated with the figures 21 made out of frosting mixed with wild blackberry juice. Around the cake was a wreath of azalea blossoms and ferns. And on top of it were four scrolls of bark with little verses on, composed by Aunt Mary and Mrs Summer . . . [35]

At the end of it all, Agnes admitted that she had 'had a lovely time out camping . . . We had a beautiful camping place and lived and slept out doors in hammocks. Aunt Mary took her cook and we had a stove brought up and we had a very enjoyable time . . . I just had a good time and as I had nothing else to do, planned mischief and played tricks on Edgar until my brain was exhausted.'[36]

Berkeley, California and Oberlin University, Ohio

When Agnes returned to Berkeley for classes, her eyes began to give her some serious problems. At first, she found herself putting off letter writing because her eyes hurt. After having been in classes for just a short time, she wrote to her father:

> I have been so disappointed about my work this year. I thought if I stayed here another year I would do so much work either in the University or take a kindergarten course, but my eyes are not any better so that I just cannot study much or read. I registered for English and Entomology, but I had to give up the laboratory work in En[tomology] as it hurt my eyes. I worked one afternoon dissecting a grasshopper. I was very sorry to give it up though I still attend the lectures once a week.[37]

Her cousin Kate loaned Agnes a bicycle. They took a few short rides before Agnes felt up to something longer. On 20 September, she felt strong enough for a longer ride and went out around Berkeley. She wrote that 'The only trouble in riding here in Berkeley is that there is so much up and down hill,' though she noted that 'I never give up though when I get started up a hill until I reach the top.'

In the same letter, Agnes wrote about meeting the 'Whitney party' at the dock, which included Ethel Whitney and Agnes's best friend Ada. This was the beginning of a new direction for Agnes. The Whitneys lived near Oberlin University in Ohio and Ada was living with them and going to school there. Ethel suggested that Agnes go to Oberlin and live with them and attend the university for a semester. It sounded like a good idea to Agnes: 'I told her I had no objections for there is nothing I would enjoy more than a real cold winter.'[38]

Agnes apparently spent parts of 1897 and 1898 at Oberlin University. Unfortunately, there is little correspondence from that time to tell us what she did except that on 18 June 1898, she sailed up the Hudson River from New York, through Albany to get to Oberlin, New York. She also had one of her eyes operated on 13 August and the other operated on ten days later. The operations, probably to shorten some of her eye muscles, apparently resolved her vision problems because she never again complained about them. Not until her old age did she wear glasses.

Back in Hawaii

Her mother's journal for 14 September 1898 reads: 'Two whistles, just before 6 o'clock this morning announced the Moana off Koko Head. We all sprang from our beds – the carriage was ordered & William & Willie soon started for town in it. About eight it came back with our dear Mary & Agnes & their Aunt Mary Alexander. The girls were looking so well.'[39] For the next two academic years, 1898 and 1900, Agnes was an instructor at the Oahu College (Punahao). The only other information available is a newspaper story about the YMCA giving a luncheon for 300 men at which Agnes assisted in serving the meal.[40]

Agnes's mother also records a visit by Helen Goodall on 1 December 1898. She wrote that she 'Called with Agnes on a Mrs. Goodall at the Hawaiian Hotel. She arrived by the Belgic from Berkeley last Friday & brought a letter of introduction to me from Mary Alexander.' On 23 December, Abigail took Helen Goodall to hear a band play at the Queen Emma Hall and introduced her to some of the women there. Abigail called on Helen several more times during her visit. On 13 January, Abigail, Mary and Agnes had lunch with Helen at the Howe Hotel. They visited her one last time the next day, shortly before Helen sailed for China and Japan.[41]

Helen Goodall had only heard of the Bahá'í Faith the year before and at the time of this visit, her daughter, Ella, was on her way to meet 'Abdu'l-Bahá with the first Western pilgrims who travelled with Phoebe Hearst. Ella would later become an important correspondent and friend of Agnes's. Obviously, either Helen didn't speak much about the Faith or Agnes and her mother didn't understand what she offered them. Helen passed through Honolulu on her return on 10 March 1899, but they were not able to see her because some passengers on board had smallpox and no one on the ship was permitted to disembark. The Alexanders were only able to wave their handkerchiefs to Helen from the dock.[42]

Two days later, William, Abigail and Agnes went to see the funeral procession for Princess Kaiulani. Abigail wrote, 'The procession was one of the longest royal ones that we have had here, but the display of kahilis was not as fine as some previous ones.'[43] The kahili was a symbol of the Hawaiian chiefs and the noble houses and was made using the long bones of an enemy king and decorated with feathers.

On 11 April 1899, Mary and Abigail left Hawaii so that Mary could spend a year in Italy. On the way, they visited Helen Goodall several times in San Francisco. [44]

4

A LIFE-CHANGING ADVENTURE

1900–1901

Across America and Europe to Rome

In the early spring of 1900, without consulting Agnes, her father, William De Witt, proposed that Agnes join the Whitney family on a trip to Europe. Emily Whitney was initially dubious because of Agnes's delicate health, but thought she might be able to: 'If she does not attempt all the sightseeing, but will be content to take in part, and stays quietly at the hotel while the Whitney's go sightseeing part of the time. I do not see how she could go. The time on the steamer would be a rest, and a change of scene . . .; it seems as if it would help her . . . to go with such kind and congenial friends.' Emily's husband, Henry, offered to assist financially.[1]

Agnes's mother, Abigail, too, was worried about Agnes going on such a long trip. In her journal, she wrote: 'A letter from Em[ily] this morning urging Agnes' going with the Whitney's & . . . bro. Henry offering to help financially, opened the subject again. It first came up last week Saturday, the Whitneys proposing that Agnes go with them on a trip to Europe. It was to be such a rushing trip, we thought Agnes hardly strong enough for it, & about decided that she better not go.' The next day, she wrote that 'all friends urge Agnes' going, & we are beginning preparations for it'.[2]

While these consultations were going on, Agnes was kept in the dark. When it was settled, her father told Agnes that the Whitneys were going to Europe and that he wanted her to go with them. Agnes was quite surprised and felt unprepared for such a journey, but her father insisted, saying, 'Go while you are young and prepare after your return.' On 5 May, just a week later, Agnes and the Whitneys left Honolulu on a trip that, for Agnes, was to last for 19 months and would change her life completely.

The trip did not start very well for Agnes. Her health evidently forced her to stay on the west coast of America while the Whitneys continued to Europe. She rejoined them in Europe, but only for a short time, before her father wrote and urged her to go to Rome to meet some cousins.[3] William De Witt Alexander, a second-generation missionary descendant who was strongly Christian, therefore, was directly responsible for Agnes ending up in Rome where, for her, the unimaginable was to happen.

Following her father's wish, Agnes went from Paris to Rome travelling with the Bentley family. Mr and Mrs Bentley and their son were visiting Rome from Freeport, Illinois, where his business was making pianos. They befriended Agnes while she was on her way to Europe. The party stopped in Lucerne, Milan and Genoa on the way. Agnes wrote:

> Lucerne was beautiful in its autumn foliage and snow-capped mts. We had a perfect Sunday there. The Bentleys went up the Rigi, but I stayed below and enjoyed myself. The next morning we went to see the beautiful bijou a second time and then started on our day's journey through the St Gothard Pass. We were going through the mts all day long and reached Milan at 10 o'clock at night. Who do you suppose I met there at the hotel the next morning? J. L. Wood! He is on his way around the world . . . He was jolly and social and I enjoyed seeing him. Our hotel in Milan was near by the cathedral so I had the chance of seeing it a great many times. Milan was my first glimpse of Italy and I fell in love with it.[4]

Agnes arrived in the 'Eternal' city on 1 November 1900. Settling into a *pension* (a small hotel), she wrote to her sister, Mary, 'Can you believe I am really here! I can hardly believe it myself. We arrived night before last at midnight.'

Agnes got together with her cousins, Imogene and Hale Ferreri, the children of Agnes's aunt Ellen and Uncle Giulio Ferreri. She wrote that they were 'exceedingly kind' to her and she saw them nearly every day. Imogene took Agnes to the Vatican, and Hale took her to Castel Sant'Angelo.[5] They both took her to see the Raphael tapestries, the Baths of Diocletian, the Church of St Clements, and the Colosseum. She had a great time with them, writing:

On Saturday morning Cousins Hale and Imogene both went out with me and we had a jolly time. Cousin Hale has a very jolly side as well as a serious one. He said he thought I was too sober and I think he did me a world of good. Imogene said she giggled for two days after we went through the Mamertime Prison and saw where St Paul was imprisoned, and many of the martyrs, then we went out to the [Temple of] Saturn museum . . .

Tuesday was Hale's birthday and Mrs Benton had a little reception in the afternoon. In the morning I wandered off by myself and had a jolly time. I went to the Church of St Maria del Popolo and saw some beautiful paintings . . . and Hilda's Tower . . .

Yesterday morning I went to the 'Rag Fair' or the sale they have every Wed morning of old Roman curios. I saw many tempting things, but did not invest in anything . . . And yesterday afternoon I went with some girls from here to the Medici Gardens and the Pineio to hear the band play . . .

I am sorry you were worried about me in London. Don't worry again for I am sure all will come out right.[6]

We don't know why her parents were worried about her in London.

One morning when Agnes came down for breakfast, Mr Bentley told her that Italy was suddenly at war with America:

I am just getting over a scare. I came downstairs intending to go out and look up the Bentons, when I reached the library, where I am now writing, Mr. Bentley said 'You had better not go out, Italy has declared war with America.' I was startled and he said 'didn't you hear the men crying in the streets.' I said yes, but I thought they were rag peddlers, or something of that sort. He said 'Did you ever hear rag peddlers cry so loud and fiercely?' I began to think I never had after all. I was awfully frightened but it all turned out to be a hoax. Mr. Bentley said he and the boy who was with him had decided they would try and scare the first one who came in and I happened to be the victim, and a pretty good one.[7]

On 19 November, Agnes wrote to her mother complaining that she hadn't received a single letter since she had left Paris three weeks before, noting that 'I will not dare leave Rome until I do get letters and know when I can get money. I have enough to last me sometime here, but not enough to get home unless I should start right off. Papa seemed so anxious to have me see Italy, I thought it would be a mistake to go home when I had the chance to come.'

Agnes was worried about money because she planned to leave Rome on 20 December, though she was thinking of visiting Venice on the way home. She wrote: 'If I go back this winter (which I expect to do) I would like to study in Chicago.' Those plans, though, were subject to change.[8]

An encounter with destiny

What happened next would have been a great surprise to Agnes's missionary father, had he known that it was at his instigation that it was able to occur. The story needs to continue with Agnes's own words:

One day in the dining room of the 'pension' where I was staying in Rome, some people sitting across the long table attracted me. So strong was the magnet which drew me to them, that I gazed at them until ashamed. They seemed to have a happiness which was different from others. Later I learned that they were Mrs. Charlotte Dixon and her two daughters [Louise and Eleanor], who were returning to the United States after a visit with the Master in 'Akka. The happiness which I had seen in their faces was a reflection from 'Akka. A few days after, while sitting in the parlor, I overheard them in conversation with a lady who had heard of the Cause in Paris. Little did I comprehend what they were talking about, but my heart was stirred, and the realization came to me that it was the Truth. The next day I met Mrs. Dixon in the elevator. Taking her hand, I asked if she would tell me what it was she had. With a radiant smile, she invited me to meet her after dinner in the back parlor. That evening as I sat listening to her, my heart was touched and tears came to my eyes. She gave me a prayer copied in longhand, for printed Baha'i literature was then very scarce. The prayer seemed to answer all the longings of my heart. After that we met for three successive evenings. She was endeavoring to prepare me for something which was to come, but did not tell me of the Coming of the Promised One. In those early days of the Cause in America, the Baha'i Message was considered too great to be conveyed at once. As teachers were few,

28

God revealed His Message in strange and wonderful ways. The third evening after meeting with Mrs. Dixon, when I retired to my room, sleep did not come. That night an overwhelming realization came to me, which was neither a dream nor vision, that Christ had come on the earth. All night I waited, unable to close my eyes. When morning came, I met Mrs. Dixon as she came from breakfast, and together we entered my room. There I turned to her and said, 'Christ is on this earth!' She replied, 'Yes, I can see by your face that you know it.'[9]

'And, of course', she later said, 'it was in God's plan.'[10] 'Abdu'l-Bahá had told Charlotte to only give 'this Water of Life' to the spiritually thirsty ones and:

she did not – it wasn't in God's Plan that she should tell me. She did not tell me of 'Abdu'l-Bahá in the prison. But she tried to prepare me. And the third evening after I had talked to her, they were going to leave the next morning, I never closed my eyes that night. And it came to me. It wasn't a dream, and it wasn't a vision, but it was a great illumination, inspiration, that Christ had come again to this earth. You see, Christ, in the Bible, said many times, 'I will come again,' and that He had come. [11]

Charlotte Dixon was a widowed school teacher who had been given an inheritance and with that money had taken herself and her daughters to meet 'Abdu'l-Bahá. They had spent nine days with 'Abdu'l-Bahá in 'Akká and were consequently illuminated and magnetic, to use Agnes's terms. It was an absolutely amazing week.

So it was that on 26 November 1900, Agnes Baldwin Alexander accepted the Manifestation of God for this age, Bahá'u'lláh. But she wrote: 'My first thought was of guilt, that I did not pray except when in trouble and did not even have a Bible with me. How could I have Him see me, I thought. At noon that day Mrs. Dixon and her daughters left Rome. Before she left, she gave me a letter to sign declaring my belief that the Promised One had come.'[12]

In her excitement, Agnes had to tell others about her great discovery, but all she had was a hand-written prayer and a copy of the Arabic *Hidden Words*, which she said she 'could not understand' and put aside. She wrote that 'I was young and innocent and I had to go through a test'.

Then I was left alone for three months with only one prayer and God to guide me. In order to grow I had to be tested. The following Sunday with my cousins I attended their church. After the service I felt impelled to go to the Pastor and tell him I had something I wished to tell him. He invited me into his study where I told him that Christ was on the earth in Akka, Syria. This was all I knew. Then he opened his Bible and read passages to me in order to correct me. I could not then answer him, but left the church with the resolve not to speak [to] anyone, for in my heart I knew it was the Truth and I could pray.[13]

When Agnes left the church, she said to herself,

Everyone will have a different opinion. God is the only Teacher. And I can pray, and I can read the Bible. And then I went and bought a little Bible.

And then, day by day, I would pray first, and then I would open the Bible . . . And little by little it became illumined, because both in the Old Testament, Malachi, and the New Testament, in Revelations, it says that the book is sealed until the time – and the time had been worked out [as] 1844 in several different ways – the date 1844, when the Bahá'í Faith first began in the world.[14]

When Charlotte Dixon left, she gave Agnes the addresses of several Bahá'ís and it was to this list that she now turned. The closest Bahá'í on the list was May Bolles in Paris, so, 'From the depths of my longing heart I wrote asking if she could tell me more of the wonderful Message.'[15] At the beginning of February, Agnes received a reply:

My precious Sister!

Praise be to God that He has enlightened your heart in these wonderful days of the Coming of His Kingdom, and that He has in His Mercy guided you to the Truth.

Please God we may soon welcome you in our midst in Paris and that you may then receive the full Revelation, and much help and instruction. In the meantime, I send you the enclosed pamphlets, Tablets and prayers, which by the Grace of God will illumine your understanding and fill you with the Breath of Life. I also enclose my photograph of our Great and Glorious Lord, which was given to me when I made the pilgrimage to 'Akka, at the foot of Mount Carmel, the New Holy Jerusalem.

My Lord appeared to me in a vision twice, two years before I heard the Great Message, and when, by the great bounty of God, and without regard to my unworthiness, I was permitted to be among the first Americans to visit 'Akaa [sic] – I beheld my dear Lord, I know Him by my visions. The picture I send you of Him was taken about twenty years ago and does not give any adequate idea of His Greatness, Majesty and Power, which are beyond any words to describe – while His wonderful unspeakable love and kindness to everyone is unlike anything we have ever known or dreamed of! Since that time my whole life has been devoted to His service, to teaching and spreading the Cause of God.

I feel by your beautiful letter that God has chosen you to be a servant in His blessed Vineyard, and that you will be greatly blessed.

I am longing with great love to see you, to greet you in the Truth, that you may enter with your brothers and sisters in this city into the full joy and peace.

As to the writings concerning this great religion, they are now being translated slowly from the Arabic and Persian, and each year diffuses more widely the teachings and knowledge, for we are the pioneers and are believers in the most wonderful time of His Appearance.

Read Isaiah, which contains wonderful prophecies of these the 'latter days', 'the end of the world', which means the end of the power of evil – for this is the dawn of the Most Great Peace, the 'Day of God', which is not followed by the night, and already the Sun of Truth has risen and is shining from the zenith.

One thing, dearest spiritual sister, I would say to you. Although the fire of love of God is burning in your heart, and you are longing to spread the glad tidings, be very careful – for every soul is not ripe – and our dear Lord has told us never to give to drink of this pure water of life, but to the thirsty. I know just how you feel, for I was just so myself, but I quickly learned that the Truth is a Spirit which only God can impart, and when it is IN US then it is imparted through us, for we are nothing – God is all – the Wonderful, the Mighty. He is sufficient for everything.

I do not know if dear Mrs. Dixon gave you the prayers. We

should learn them by heart and say them two or three times daily, then we grow spiritually with great power and rapidity, for these prayers are unlike any others; they are from God himself.

May God shower upon you His greatest blessings and confirm you in the Glorious Truth.

I am your loving and devoted sister in the love and service of our Lord.[16]

The letter had reached Agnes while she was in Venice, where she spent six weeks. She travelled alone to Paris, leaving Venice in mid-February 1901, travelling first to Florence, Italy. She described the journey when writing to her parents on 14 March:

I have arrived safely after a journey of 36 hrs. It is the first time I have traveled in Europe at night, but I got along very comfortably. There were only two of us in the coach so we could both lie down. I got rather tired of the custom house officials, not that they gave me any trouble but I had to go through it three times in coming down from Venice here. First in going into Switzerland then Germany and lastly France.[17]

Arriving in Paris, Agnes initially stayed in the Hotel Britannique,[18] where she had stayed the previous summer. The first meeting with May began on the doorstep of her apartment. Agnes rang the bell and a woman opened it. The woman was May's mother, and she was a bit surprised when Agnes, mistakenly thinking she was May, immediately threw her arms around her in joy.[19] The mother then went and got the daughter:

The first meeting with the beloved May Bolles is one of the most pre-cious memories of my life. She was then a frail young woman filled with a consuming love which the Master said was divine. It was this heavenly love which brought the friends together and united all the hearts. From that day May Bolles became my spiritual mother and through all the years her tender love was a guiding star in my life . . .

May had been chosen by God to be the spiritual Mother and first Bahá'í to introduce the Faith to the Latin people. In Paris she had become the spiritual mother of a group of believers, among them French and Americans, some of whom were students of art and architecture. The weekly meetings were held in the studio of Mr. Charles Mason Remey. Accompanying May I attended my first Bahá'í meeting. As I entered the room someone asked: 'Is she a Bahá'í?'. The reply: 'Look at her face!'. As I looked around the room I saw the same look of peace and light on the faces. They had found their Lord and were at rest. Before the meeting began May retired to a room to pray. There before a photograph of the Master she knelt with her forehead on the floor. In that moment I knelt with her and turned in prayer to the Master. Such an atmosphere of pure light pervaded the meetings that one was transported, as it were, from the world of man to that of God. In the spiritual light of those meetings all questions vanished. One of the Paris believers, Berthalin Lexow wrote of that time: 'We were a little group of about twenty in Paris but there was such a strong feeling of unity among us we had so much love for one another which made us as one.'

May was born with great force and energy. She told me that in order that God might use her energies for His service, she had first to be laid low, and was ill on her bed and couch for two and a half years before she heard from Lua the Message in 1898. Then her whole being became alive with the love of her Lord and service to Him never relaxing until her last earthly moment was spent.[20]

In a letter home, she told her father that he should turn in her resignation to the Punahou School so that they would be able to find another teacher. Justifying her resignation, she wrote that 'I know without a doubt that I haven't the health for the work, and would break down if I should try to undertake it.' Then she hinted at her new life: 'I know the Lord has other work for me to do . . . I am very happy here. I have such good friends in Paris, and God watches over me. I know He will bring me safely home for He has work for me to do.'[21] Her 'good friends' were May Bolles and the Bahá'ís. Agnes, who was worried about being healthy enough to teach school, would have been very surprised at the challenges she would overcome in the future.

For the next three and a half months, Agnes basked in the presence of Bahá'ís who were returning from visiting 'Abdu'l-Bahá:

Among them were two from the Paris group, Monsieur Henri and Charles Mason Remey. Shortly after I reached Paris I met the latter who had just returned from his first visit to the Master. When he told me of his experiences in 'Akka, I felt as though I were transported to another world. Other pilgrims from America were Mrs. Emogene Hoagg, Mrs. Helen Ellis Cowles [sic], who was a cousin of May Bolles, also Laura Barney, Lua and Dr. Getsinger and Mrs. William H. Hoar. On her way to England was Miss Ethel Rosenberg. Later 'Ali Kuli Khan arrived on his way to America. Filled with love and light which the Master ignited in them, the pilgrims told of His wonderful, satisfying teachings. One of the Paris believers wrote: 'Those who return from that White City by the sea are indeed filled with manifest light and when they speak of the Holy Place tears come to their eyes and they seem full of a new life and energy, and there is a restful, convincing peace about them which all feel who come in contact with them.'

Some of the pilgrims shared notes which they had taken from the Master's talks. These I eagerly copied and studied. The greatest blessing of all was the coming of the saintly 'Abu'l-Fadl and his interpreter, Anton Haddad. At the request of 'Abdu'l-Baha he came to teach the friends in Paris before proceeding to America. Frail in appearance and small of stature, he was the most gentle and humble person I have ever met. When he was told that I was from Honolulu and would return there to teach the Cause, he said to me, 'Always remember the words of Daniel, "They that turn many to righteousness shall shine as the stars forever and ever." If in the future there are five believers in the Hawaiian Islands, you will have done a great work.' He also said that I should have faith like Peter.

It was a great bounty from God that I was permitted to be taught by him. Every day he gave the believers a lesson, which was interpreted by Anton Haddad into English, on the proofs of a prophet and Bible interpretations. I was staying then in a small 'pension' on rue d'assas in the Latin Quarter, not far from the apartment where May Bolles and her mother and brother lived. When Lua and Dr. Getsinger arrived from Palestine, they came to stay there. Later Laura Barney joined us and lastly, Mr. W. H. Hoar.

It was the only time that I had the bounty of meeting the beloved Lua. She gave me some treasures from 'Akka, one of which was a Baha'i ringstone blessed by 'Abdu'l-Baha.[22]

Other than the vaguest of hints, Agnes's letters home give no indication that anything had changed. Writing to one of her brothers, she told him:

> I am quite a girl of the world now. Some Germans [sic] ladies were astonished this morn to hear I had been traveling around alone, but really I have met nothing but kindness everywhere. I enjoyed Venice so much. It is an ideal spot. Rome, Florence and Venice are each so interesting in themselves, and yet they are each entirely different. I am so glad there is no exposition here now. Paris seems quite different and I enjoy it. [I] never want to see another exposition. The trouble was it was so perfectly immense. One tried to see it all and consequently saw very little of anything, and spent lots of money and strength.[23]

The 'exposition' was the 1900 World's Fair, held that year in Paris. Between April and November, almost 50 million people came to Paris to see all the excitement. Agnes had arrived on her first trip to Paris in October 1900.

In another letter to her sister Mary, the spiritual revelations she was discovering were hidden under the mundane. She wrote about buying a 'silk waist' at the Bon Marché, that she had seen Dr and Mrs Day (from Hawaii) and that she had received a letter from Ada. She also said that she was planning to buy a new dress there in Paris because 'it is probably once in a lifetime I can have the chance then I will be ready to accept any invitation without saying I haven't anything to wear'.[24] She wrote not a word about her new life.

Agnes mentioned Clarence Smith in a couple of her letters home, but only to mention that she had heard from him or was expecting him. Clarence was also from Hawaii and his relatives had been missionaries. What Agnes didn't tell her parents was that she had introduced him to the Bahá'í Faith:

> While with him one day I felt urged to tell him the Good News, but fearing he would not understand, I kept delaying. At last, just as we were about to part, I felt that if I did not speak I would die, and said abruptly, 'Christ has come!' The next day he came to see me. The power of the spirit had been so great when I spoke the day

before that he had believed at once. He said that when he returned to his room that day he felt frightened. Afterwards he attended the Baha'i meeting where he met May Bolles and experienced the heavenly atmosphere of those meetings. 'Abu'l-Fadl remarked how great was the power in the Cause, that in a few months I had a spiritual child.[25]

In mid-April 1901, Agnes wrote to tell her parents that she thought 'it is best for me to stay here for another month at least now. Now is the time for me to get all I can, then when I go home I can settle down & be of use to others. I never enjoyed life so much before as I do now. It is glorious to be living.'[26] Little did they know the reason she wanted to stay was to be with the Bahá'ís and learn about the Faith.

In June, after three and a half months, the feeling that it was time to return to Hawaii began increasing until she finally packed to go home. The day before she was to leave, Anton Haddad knocked at her door and handed her a Tablet from 'Abdu'l-Bahá that he had translated for her. This Tablet, the first of 13 she was to receive from Him, read:

> O thou maid-servant of God!
>
> The tongues have spoken of thy attraction to God and the pens testified of thy burning by the fire of the love of God. Indeed the heart of 'Abdu'l-Baha approveth of this, because it feeleth its heat from this distant and Blessed Spot.
>
> O maid-servant of God! By God, the Truth, the Spirit of Christ from the Supreme Concourse doth in every time and aspect announce to thee this great good news. Be, therefore, a divine bird, proceed to thy native country, spread the wings of sanctity over those spots and sing and chant and celebrate the name of thy Lord, that thou mayest gladden the Supreme Concourse and make the seeking souls hasten unto thee as the moths hasten to the lamp, and thus illumine that distant country by the light of God.
>
> Upon thee be salutations and praise.[27]

Any doubts she had had about going home were instantly vanquished by 'Abdu'l-Bahá's direction. This was the first of several times when Agnes was inspired to do something which was confirmed by either 'Abdu'l-Bahá or Shoghi Effendi after she had already acted on that inspiration.

Back to Hawaii

Agnes left Paris with William Hoar and went to London and then Portland, Maine. As she sailed away, May Bolles sent her a letter:

Allah'u'Abha!

My Darling!

It is Sunday and you are on the great sea, on your way to work in God's beautiful vineyard.

Oh! my little girl – my sweet gentle Agnes, only God knows how I love you – how the image of your pure face as it was that last night with its radiant look of happiness and peace – is graven on my heart.

As I think of you, dear heart – a great pure love wells up in me – a love that will follow you, bless you and watch over you with devout prayers all my life. I have thanked God over and over again that the Blessed Tablet reached you in time – so that wherever you go henceforth, you can feel that Our Great, Our Beloved Lord (may my soul be sacrificed to the dust of His Holy Feet!) has set His Eternal Seal upon you – has accepted you for His own – and that He will move you – guide you, strengthen you and uphold you – and surround you by His incomparable love – and His irresistible Protection.

This was the thought that consoled and upheld me that night after you had gone – when my tender little bird had flown from the nest of her Mother! I thought, she is His Divine Bird now – and has flown away to seek her Eternal Nest in His Bosom . . .

God bless you – bless you, my darling – and grant that all the pure beauty of your soul may continue to unfold in His Light. I greet you from the depths of my heart in His Blessed Name.

Allah'u'Abha!

Your humble sister and mother

May Bolles. [28]

Mason Remey had told Agnes about Sarah Farmer's Green Acre, which at that time was a budding Baháʼí summer school. When Agnes arrived in Portland, Maine, she stored her baggage then took a streetcar to Eliot, Maine, and from there was directed to Sarah Farmer's home, called Bittersweet. Agnes wrote:

I was welcomed by dear Baha'i sisters who were so happy to meet a new child in the Faith. It was a heavenly meeting and they asked me to come and stay with them, so, procuring my baggage, I returned to 'Bittersweet', Miss Farmer's home. Later my father wrote me that he and my mother were coming to the United States and advised me to remain in Green Acre for the summer, as I could then return with them to Honolulu. Thus, in God's plan, my stay lengthened into two months, and I came to know intimately some of the glorious believers in the Cause, among whom was 'Sister Louise', as she was then called, now Mrs. John D. Bosch of Geyserville, California, who was helping in the home. She took me into her loving heart, a love which was unchanged throughout the years, and brought us together to work in His Cause after her marriage to Mr. Bosch.

The beloved sister, Mrs. Charlotte Dixon, and her two daughters, whom God used to attract me to the Cause in Rome, Italy, came to Green Acre, where we had a joyous reunion. Among the dear believers whom I came to know was Mother Beecher, whose granddaughter, Mrs. Dorothy Baker, has become a lighted lamp in the Cause. When I left Green Acre, I had the privilege of staying for three weeks in an apartment in New York where Mother Beecher made a home for two other friends.[29]

What Agnes was experiencing was completely unknown to her parents. Her mother wrote in her journal: 'We had a good letter from Agnes dated Eliot, Maine, July 16th & 19th. She seemed to be enjoying her stay with nice people.' In a letter written on 8 August, she told her parents about what was happening at Green Acre:

In Greenacre I met people and heard many lectures which have been a great help to me. There are lectures there every morning & every afternoon.

One day a professor from Hampton came up with a colored quartette & an Indian & African speaker. They both were very interesting, especially the Indian.

Col. Pratt of the Indian School lectured one day & another day Miss Dean of the African or 'Black American' Industrial School in Manassas, Virginia.

I should like to tell you more of what they said. At any rate we all feel that universal peace among nations must come & is coming. The means we have of traveling, telegraphy, etc. are all helping to do it. Sometime when the right time comes, there will be but one language & one God . . . Why not all brothers.[30]

Agnes was educating her parents about the Bahá'í Faith.

Agnes stayed with Sarah Farmer until the autumn when she joined her parents, who had arrived in San Francisco from Honolulu on 22 September, then travelled across the country to meet her. While travelling back to California, the Alexander party passed through Chicago on 26 November. Meeting some Bahá'ís there, Agnes told them that it was her first spiritual birthday and they revealed to her that the same day was the Day of the Covenant. [31]

The Alexanders travelled together as far as San Francisco. Arriving there, they found that they could not get passage for Agnes on the same steamer her parents were booked on. This was not a problem for Agnes, because while she remained in Oakland, she met Helen Goodall and her daughter Ella, soon to become the first Bahá'í visitors to Hawaii.

5

SPREADING THE BAHÁ'Í FAITH IN HAWAII

1902–1913

Agnes arrived back in Honolulu on 26 December 1901. As the steamer approached her home town, she wrote: 'Strange feelings came over me as the steamer on which I voyaged to Honolulu neared the shore, for alone I was to stand there, the first Baha'i to touch that soil.'[1] Two months later, Clarence Smith also returned to Hawaii and suddenly there were two Bahá'ís in the islands.

Agnes was eager to share the Revelation of Bahá'u'lláh, but it was difficult. She spent a lot of time with her sister Mary after her return, but Mary was not interested. From the few bits and pieces Agnes had told her parents about the principles of the Bahá'í Faith and her conspicuous happiness, her relatives began getting suspicious of what had happened on her long trip. For the most part, she relied on her actions to teach:

> Among my relatives a rumor had spread that I had taken up some strange belief. I had then to show through my life, and not by words, the great happiness that had come into my life. My sister said to me, 'We all know you are happy and contented and if it helps you, it must be good.' As she was satisfied in her Christian Faith, she did not seek more. My father told the uncle, through whose gift I had gone to Europe, that the trip had been my salvation. He did not, however, in his lifetime come to realize the truth of the Revelation of Baha'u'llah. My friends also recognized the change that had come in my life.[2]

Agnes's mother's journal recorded only the mundane notes that 'Mary & Agnes go to an "At Home" at Mrs Chas. Athertons,' 'Mary and Agnes go to an afternoon tea up Pacific Heights,' and 'Mary and Agnes went to a "Polypiper" party at Maude's [Baldwin] this p.m.'[3]

Helen, Edwin and Ella Goodall's visit, and Elizabeth Muther's declaration

Agnes and Clarence were not the only two Bahá'ís for long because in April 1902, Helen Goodall, her husband Edwin, and her daughter Ella became the first Bahá'í visitors to Hawaii. Ella, who is better known by her later married name Ella Cooper (married in 1905), had been part of the first Western pilgrimage to 'Abdu'l-Bahá in 1899 and was able to share with Agnes her unique experiences with the Master. On 8 April, Agnes's mother, Abigail, wrote in her journal, 'This evening William, Agnes & myself went to the hotel reception. Many were there, & . . . We met there Mr. & Mrs Goodall of Oakland, & their daughter.' On 18 April, Mrs Alexander wrote, 'Mary & Agnes went this afternoon to a party given by Mrs. W.[illiam] O.[wens] Smith for Miss [Ella] Goodall up Pacific Heights. There were about twelve young ladies.'⁴ Abigail made no mention of any spiritual matters.

But another woman did show interest in spiritual matters. While there, Helen and Ella met Elizabeth Muther, who had been Clarence Smith's governess. Elizabeth wrote that she had received her first letter about the Faith from Clarence in 1901. In a letter she later wrote to Ella, she described what happened in Honolulu:

A little later Agnes returned to Honolulu, and shortly after Clarence Smith followed, and then we began to meet once a week. Occasionally we met in some home but generally out of doors . . . Clarence had met Mrs. Goodall at her home in Oakland, Calif, and when he heard of her arrival in Honolulu he wanted me to call on her with him, for he felt if I called and heard her speak of the Cause, that I would be convinced of its being God's Truth and would become a believer in the teachings. I told Clarence that he would have to call without me because I saw no reason for my forcing myself upon dear Mrs. Goodall, especially as she came for a restful time with her husband. So he called without me, but I suppose he told Mrs. Goodall what I had said for a note soon arrived from this dear lady inviting me to call on her, – that she had heard of me and wanted to meet me, – and have a little talk together, – and could I come at a certain time. Of course I could not refuse to call after receiving that sweet note.

Mrs. Goodall received me so cordially and the love that beamed upon me through her luminous eyes drove away all embarrassment, and I opened my heart to her at once. She said that she was so glad to hear I was interested in the Bahá'í Teachings, – but, I explained, that while I enjoyed reading the 'tracts' and pamphlets I had received from Clarence, I had accepted the teachings of Jesus and was trying to be a Christian and felt I would be disloyal to Christ to accept the teaching of anyone else, whereupon she showed me that both were really the <u>same</u>, that the Bahá'í Teachings were the fulfilment of all that Christ had given to the people so long ago . . .

Then she said, 'Now, when you go to your room tonight, <u>pray earnestly</u> that God will show you if these Bahá'í Teachings are His Truth, and He <u>will</u> show you, then open the 'Hidden Words' and read them with an open mind and heart.' I was prepared for a <u>long struggle</u>, but found when I read only a few pages, everything seems so clear, so full of meaning, so luminous!

It is very hard to explain, but it seemed to me that I was being shown God's plan for the saving of His children from sin and sorrow, from all that defiles their nature, and by His Wonderful Love and Mercy . . . He was drawing us to Himself . . . forgetting my surroundings and everything, I called out aloud, 'This is God's Truth!' Then I wondered if I had awakened the sleepers downstairs . . . but all seemed quiet. I then realized that what your blessed Mother had said was true, – God had shown me that the Bahá'í Teachings were and are God's Truth.[5]

Where four months previously, Hawaii had been devoid of Bahá'ís, now there were three: Agnes, Clarence and Elizabeth.

In early 1903, Agnes received her second Tablet from the Master. She had obviously been attempting to gently teach the Faith to her family and relatives. Agnes also must have begged for something that became her great desire throughout her life – to be empty and void of thoughts of the material world:

O thou bird warbling in the Garden of the Love of God!

Thank God that He has illumined thy insight, led thee unto the Fire glowing in the tree of man, caused thee to utter His Praise among the creatures, and guided certain women to whom thou spoke the Word of God.

O maid-servant of God, verily thy Lord lighteth the lamp of Love in the heart of whomsoever He chooseth. This is indeed the great happiness. He confirmeth him in the service of the Supreme Vineyard.

I pray God to confirm the relatives in attaining to the Brilliant Light, to let the Lights of Insight shine forth to the hearts and sights, to aid thy friends in being illumined by the Light of El Baha and fed from the Heavenly Table, and to make thee empty, void from the thoughts of the life of this world, and filled with the Love of thy Lord, ready for His service, uttering His Praise and demonstrating with proofs the appearance of the Kingdom of God.[6]

Agnes wanted to share her great treasure with her long-time best friend, Ada. Agnes wrote:

I had longed to share my joy with my dearest childhood friend. God prepared her heart so that when I told her that a Prophet had come again to the earth, she burst into tears and said, 'It is Christ! I have been thinking of His coming all this week.' She became filled with the love of her Lord and wrote many beautiful letters expressing the joy she had found. In one of these she wrote: 'I know I am with Him in soul sometimes for all is so clear that I am then so happy. His sweet face is before me so often . . . I am so truly with Him now. Oh, such love and sweetness in His face!' Then her husband became the test of her life and objected to her connection with the Cause. As she conceded to his wishes and ceased to meet with the believers or read the Baha'i writings, saying she must be silent and patient, her faith began to weaken.[7]

During the spring and summer of 1902, Agnes's mother, Abigail, recorded her daughter's activities in her personal journal. Agnes's spiritual activities were apparently invisible to her mother:

Sat. Ap. 19th Agnes went to Ewa this p.m. to stay over Sunday.

Sat. Ap. 26th Agnes spent the day on a picnic up P valley with Mr. Frank Cooke, his daughter & Annie [Ann Elizabeth Alexander Dickey]. They came home soaked with rain.

Sat. May 24th This p.m. William & I, also the girls [Mary] Charlotte & Agnes went to a matinee – the play was 'Julius Caesar.'

Agnes & I went to a tea this p.m. at the Kamehameha School – four miles ride on the electric cars from here. We had a pleasant time."

Thurs. June 5th Call with Agnes this morning on Aunt Em [Mrs. Emily Whitney (Alexander) Baldwin] & Maud (Baldwin) Cooke] at Waikiki. – they are at W.R. Castle's place. Then called on Martha Waterhouses's [Martha (Alexander) & John Waterhouse].

Sund. June 15th Mary & Agnes went to Luahaha this afternoon – Mrs. Chas. Cooke had invited them to come up & spend the night. Tomorrow is Mary's [Mary Charlotte Alexander, Agnes' sister] last day of teaching – then a long vacation.

Thurs. June 26th Mary & Agnes, cousin Kate, Miss Downing & three gentlemen went surf riding this p.m. & then took their supper at the park – picnic fashion.

Sat. July 5th Agnes went to Pearl city this morning to stay at Dr. Whitney's [Ada's father] a while.

Thurs. July 10th This morning Agnes went with Jeanette Rice to Pearl City to stay until tomorrow.

Thurs. July 17th Mary & Agnes have gone to Luakaha by invitation from Mrs. Chas. Cooke, to stay until Saturday morning.

On July 19th the girls came home & "Agnes had a bathing party at Waikiki."

Thurs. Aug. 7th Mary & Agnes plan to leave that same day [Aug. 12] for Maui, to visit cousin Claire Lindsay.[8]

During the summer of 1902, Agnes and Elizabeth Muther carried the Faith to Maui:

Miss Muther gave the Message to Clarence Smith's eldest sister. She did not awaken . . . I was guided to give the Message to a dear aunt. After having told her the Good News, when I returned to visit her a second time, I wrote Miss Muther, October 13, 1902: 'Aunt Annie seemed so happy to see me and was so eager to hear more of our Glorious News. I had three beautiful talks with her. She said, "Oh, if I could believe it was Christ!" But she can't quite comprehend it all yet . . . After I had my first talk with her, Uncle Charley [Baldwin] returned from a trip. He told Aunt that when he was at Mrs. Shaw's, she wanted him to read a letter she had received from a cousin in Canada telling her how she had received the Message . . . Aunt Annie was so interested she wrote and asked if it could be sent to her, that she had already heard of the Message.'

My dear aunt wrote to the Master asking Him some questions. I also wrote Him and supplicated Him for a Tablet for her and also for a young man there to whom I had given the Message. 'Abdu'l-Baha poured out His great bounty to us in four Tablets which I received in Honolulu on February 20, 1903, through Mrs. Helen S. Goodall. Two of these Tablets were addressed to my aunt. One was in answer to the questions she asked the Master, and the other fulfilled my request for a Tablet for her. In the latter He wrote: *'Listen to the servant of God, Agnes.'* The third Tablet was addressed to the young man for whom I had supplicated a Tablet and the fourth one was to me. In answer to her questions, the Master wrote my aunt:

O thou who are advancing toward God!

Know verily that the reign of Jesus was a spiritual Reign – penetrative in the hearts and the spirits and not over the bodies, rocks and earth.

The fetters which Christ put to Satan's neck meant the breaking of his power, the hindering of his dominion and the dispersing of his assemblage through the power of Inspiration and Revelation. But as to those who deprive themselves of the spiritual Table and of the Fragrance of the Spirit of God, they are dead and devoid of Life. There is no immortality for them in this world nor in the Kingdom of God.

As to the sincere believers, verily they rejoice in the garden of the Mercy of their Lord, are glad, associate with one another and praise God for this bountiful blessing.

O maidservant of God, verily the life of the world is a dream. Neither itself nor its happiness is of any important station, but the great happiness is after the departure unto the Supreme Friend, entrance into the Paradise of Immortality and the Sublime Garden at the time of meeting and beholding.[9]

Neither Aunt Annie nor the young man accepted the Faith.

Kanichi Yamamoto

Elizabeth Muther quickly became a good Bahá'í teacher. William Owen and Abby Smith, Clarence Smith's parents, employed a 23-year-old Japanese gardener named Kanichi Yamamoto at this time. Moto, as he was known, had left his home in Yamaguchi, Japan with the goal of going to America. He stopped in Hawaii for a time and found work with the Smiths. Living in the Smith home was Elizabeth and, since Moto spoke very little English, she helped him learn the language.[10]

Elizabeth was drawn to Moto. Before she became a Bahá'í, Elizabeth 'had many a little talk with him about the Christian life which he has been trying to live under great difficulties, such a consistent Christian life as has made me feel ashamed of my own weak efforts in the same direction.'[11] After becoming a Bahá'í in April 1902, she felt that she should share the message with Moto and on 8 September of that year, she did:

After I became a believer I felt that sometime I might tell Moto. I thought of him on Maui and prayed that his heart might be prepared to receive the Truth. Soon after I returned I felt that I ought to speak to him. Although it was a little difficult to give him the Message because of his imperfect knowledge of English, yet God helped me so that he understands perfectly and is rejoicing in the knowledge of His Truth. I have just had a little talk with him and he told me how happy he was and that he expects to write his letter to the Master this evening. He seems fearful lest something may happen to the Master before his letter may reach Him. He thanked me with so much feeling this evening for telling him this good news and I feel that he will be a power for good among the Japanese here. He has a very even temper and winning disposition and seems to have many devoted friends, but as he told me before I went to Maui, 'but my friends not Christian. Oh, Miss Muther, very hard when your friends not Christian – this is very lonely when only you Christian and you cannot talk to friends about be Christian, they do not want to hear.' Now he has received the Message and I thought this evening from the joy expressed in his face, as well as his words of gratitude for the Truth of God, that he must have forgotten everything but to rejoice in God. 'Oh Miss Muther, I am so happy!' he said in parting, 'and I can only say, Oh God! How hast Thou honored me to have made me Thy servant!'[12]

Moto tried to write his letter to 'Abdu'l-Bahá, but his English was just too poor. After several attempts, 'He felt that he could not write in English, so I told him that I thought it would be all right for him to write in Japanese. I was sure the Master would understand the spirit of his letter.'[13] When the letter written in Japanese arrived in 'Akká, 'Abdu'l-Bahá showed it to Yúnis Khán, one of His secretaries:

> The Master mused, 'Well now, you do not know Japanese.'
> 'No, Beloved', I volunteered. 'I hardly know English.'
> 'So, what are we to do with this letter?' He remarked, smiling.
> I bowed, and in my heart proposed, 'The same thing you do with other letters.'
> 'Very well then,' He said, 'We will rely on the Blessed Beauty and will write him a reply.'[14]

The answer was just what Moto wanted:

> O thou who art attracted by the Word of God to the Kingdom of God!
> Turn with the whole of thy being to God, forget aught else save God, and supplicate God to make thee a sign of guidance in the midst of people who are veiled from God, perchance they may be guided to the Orb of all horizons, enter the Kingdom of Harmony, drink of the cup of the love of God, rejoice at the manifestation of the Kingdom of God, taste the delight of the mention of God and

shelter themselves in the shadow of the Tree of Life in the midst of the Paradise of God.

This beseemeth the believers; this is the qualification of the sincere; this is the path of the knowers; and this is the utmost aim of the faithful. Exert thy utmost power that thou mayest share this great bounty. [15]

Moto left Honolulu in March of 1903 and served in the home of Helen Goodall in Oakland, California. He received further Tablets from the Master; one which he received while there read, 'O thou who art the single one of Japan and the unique one of the extreme Orient!'[16] He was still there when 'Abdu'l-Bahá visited in 1912 and was able to both serve the Master and organize a meeting with the Japanese in the city for Him.

Slow growth of the Bahá'í community

The second Bahá'í visitor to Hawaii was Anna Bailey, the sister of Abby Smith. She came in the spring of 1903. Anna had learned of the Faith from Helen Goodall, her neighbour in California, a year before. She was surprised to find out that her nephew, Clarence Smith, had already become a Bahá'í. While in Honolulu, Anna went with Agnes, Elizabeth, Clarence and Moto to Pacific Heights and took a photo of the first Bahá'í group in the Pacific Ocean region.[17]

During 1904, Agnes continued her normal activities as well as her Bahá'í ones. Agnes's mother again recorded her everyday activities through the summer:

Sat. June 25th This evening we all went to Ada Whitney's wedding. Agnes & Harriet Austin were bridesmaids. It was a small private wedding – (all present numbering about twenty six), but a very pleasant one.

Wed. Aug 3rd Agnes & I were invited to Okindita to stay until Saturday with Martha W[aterhouse] I could not go – Agnes went, driving up in Martha's buggy.

Sat. Aug. 6th Agnes returned from Okindita this p.m.

Mond. Aug. 8th Agnes left this evening on the Nevadan for Maui to visit cousins Clair, Lindsay & May Murdock. We went down to see her off.

Mond. Aug. 29th Rec. a letter from Agnes – she says she will come home next Saturday – Sept. 3rd.

Frid. Sept 9th Mary, Agnes, the two Thayer girls & Edith Alex. went to Waikiki for a bath & supper. They reported a 'splendid time'.[18]

In late 1904, Elizabeth introduced the Faith to Alice Otis, the soloist at the Central Union Church. Alice went to Oakland late in the year and met Helen Goodall. Upon her return to Honolulu in late 1905, she became a Bahá'í and opened her home for weekly Bahá'í meetings, the first gathering place for the Honolulu Bahá'ís.

On 20 December, Agnes's father wrote that Agnes and Mary were 'enjoying a well-earned vacation' from their teaching duties at the Punahou School. A month later, he wrote, 'My daughter Agnes, resigned her position at Punahou at the Christmas vacation on account of her health . . . Since then she has been steadily improving in health.'[19]

Agnes goes to Alaska

On 21 June 1905, Agnes boarded the steamer *Manchuria* and sailed to San Francisco for a holiday. Two of her trunks were misplaced at some point. One was found after three days and the other after nine. During July, she sailed to Alaska and visited Ketchikan, Wrangell, Tonka (Petersburg), Juneau, Treadwell, Skagway, Whitehorse, Haines, Hunter's Bay, Killinore (Angoon) and Sitka. This made her the first Bahá'í to visit Alaska, though she was there as a tourist. Since her letters were to her parents, she made no mention of any discussions she may have had about the Bahá'í Faith.

Agnes arrived at her first Alaskan port, Ketchikan, in bad weather and wrote nothing about it in her letters. After that first day, she enjoyed nine straight days of beautiful weather, something quite uncommon in Southeast Alaska. Arriving in Wrangell, she met the minister of the People's Church, who gave Agnes and some of the other passengers a tour of the small town. She noted that he 'showed us the totems & explained them. We saw more totems there than any place.'[20]

From Wrangell, the steamer continued to Tonka, a fish cannery at what is now known as Petersburg. She wrote: 'The Indian women are always ready with the bundles to open up as soon as a steamer arrives. Some of the baskets are beautiful but I have invested little, though most of the people on board have bought a great many. The Indian women make their money in the summer out of the tourists evidently. There are boats now about every two days.'[21]

The steamer arrived in Juneau in the middle of the night. The next morning, Agnes went out to see the sights. Her first stop was the Tread-well gold mine, one of the largest in the world at that time. The mine was interesting, but 'The noise of the machinery though was so great that I didn't stay long'.[22] At that time, the various ore-crushing mills contained 880 stamps, each weighing 1,000 pounds, that smashed down on the gold-bearing rock 96 times per minute.[23] She described Juneau as a small town, 'picturesque by situation. Has fine stores, a high school, etc. The tax on saloons . . . all goes to the schools so that the scholars do not even pay for their books. They have nine teachers in the High School.'[24]

The next day, Agnes arrived in Skagway. She was not impressed with the seven-year-old town created by the Klondike gold rush of 1898: 'Skagway was not as green & picturesque as the other stops we had made. It is a dead place now. It has been burnt out several times.'[25] After a quick tour of the town, Agnes and a few other passengers rode the train over White Pass to Whitehorse in the Yukon. Returning from Whitehorse, she met her Aunt Mary,[26] who joined her on the ship.[27]

In Haines, Agnes visited a village adjacent to an army fort. She noted, 'The long days here have given us a chance to sightsee, but it has been pretty strenuous keeping such late hours, & through the day one does not want to miss any of the scenery.'[28] The next morning, they arrived at Funter Bay on Admiralty Island and visited the 'Klinget Can-nery', where they watched

> men bringing in scows of salmon. They catch 20,000 salmon a day. I can readily believe it from what I saw. They say this cannery paid $75,000 clear profit last year. We saw Chinese & Indians working side by side. The owners of the canneries do not live in Alaska &

employ very few laborers from there. They bring most of their labor with them for the season & so do no practical benefit to Alaska. [29]

Later the same day, the steamer stopped in Killisnoo, now known as Angoon. The Tlingit village canned fish and produced fish oil. Agnes was told that it would be a very smelly place, but because she had a cold, she could not smell anything. In the evening, passengers from the steamer heard the head of the Salvation Army speak. Agnes wrote, 'There were two white girls & two men & the rest about eight were Indian men & women. Everyone remarked how different these Indians looked in contrast to the others. Each one spoke in turn & they gave beautiful testimonies. Some of the Indians spoke beautiful English & an Indian woman interpreted for a couple of them.'[30]

The steamer next stopped in the old Russian capital of Sitka, but only for two hours. She was able to see totems, the largest she saw on the trip, and the Russian Orthodox Church. The Bishop of Alaska boarded the steamer in Sitka and gave the passengers a talk about Alaska. After returning to Funter Bay to load salmon, the ship went to the Taku Glacier, where the crew loaded small icebergs.

After a second stop in Juneau, the steamer again visited Wrangell, where Agnes met some family friends who were sailing on another steamer. The ship then sailed for Victoria and Seattle, arriving in the latter on 27 July. Agnes returned to Honolulu on 18 October.[31]

'Abdu'l-Bahá and Ada Whitney

Agnes wrote a letter to 'Abdu'l-Bahá on 30 December 1907, which for some reason she never sent, pleading to be made 'empty and void' of all thoughts of the material world, something she greatly desired her whole life and which the Master had emphasized in His second Tablet to her in 1903:

Thou knowest all my life how very faulty it is. I pray thee oh Abdul Baha to cleanse my life and show me how it may all be used for Thy Services. If it were the Will of God I would ask for health, but if not God's Will, make me content to work to all my ability that Thy glorious Cause may be spread in these Islands, and as my noble grandfather sacrificed all for Christ's Cause, may I with the spirit sacrifice all in this Glorious Day.

What my life is to be is in God's keeping and may I only be led as God would have me – 'to be empty and void from the thoughts of this life, ready for His Service, uttering His praise and demonstrating with proofs the appearance of its Kingdom of God.'[32]

In the letter, Agnes also asked that Ada be enabled to arise and attract others to the Faith. For a year, Ada's husband had forbidden her to either receive or read any Bahá'í literature. At this point, he had relented and said that she could read Bahá'í material 'on her trembling plea that it would make her a better wife and mother'.[33]

Agnes asked 'Abdu'l-Bahá to 'Bless my house and may Thy Light shine into my dear father's soul and give him peace.'[34] Her father had not shown any interest in the Bahá'í Faith, though he had apparently not given Agnes much trouble over it. It wasn't until the end of 1909 that he began to oppose the Faith.

In early 1908, Agnes received a letter from Ada. According to Agnes, Ada's husband 'became the test of her life and objected to her connection with the Cause. As she conceded to his wishes and ceased to meet with the believers or read the Baha'i writings, saying she must be silent and patient, her faith began to weaken.'[35] At this time Ada was still strongly attached to the Faith. In February, she wrote:

We must change completely when we become a Bahai, so in God's great love He will change me, I know He will; change so that even you may marvel at what God has done. How I hope and pray it may be so! Then we can laugh and rejoice together over our own happiness in God . . .

Such wonderful things have happened to me since I last saw you. God has already changed me, dear, so wonderfully, though I so hope and long for a fuller, greater change that I feel as though I had just put the fraction of my foot over the threshold into His Kingdom. My pen cannot write fast enough nor can I anyway tell you all the Lord has done for me. Whereas I was blind, now I can see; whereas I was deaf, now I hear; whereas I was dead, now I live. And such wonderful things I see and such sweet music I hear and such life I have received, Agnes, I begin to tell you. O chant and sing and praise to our God and to His Glory, Baha'u'llah, for the wonders He can perform. How glad I am that I have you dear, dear friend, who guided me so long, so patiently and against such odds to show me what I have only just seen. Thank God my doubts did not turn you, but that you were steadfast and faithful and true and loving and patient. Dear girl, I love you as I never did before.

Surely you need no longer pull me along, but we will run this race hand in hand to the glory of God; run, Agnes, we will run, for with such joy and knowledge, faith and love before us to gain we can no longer walk. Come, dear friend, take my hand now and let us run and run and yet never be weary for the source of all strength will be continually flowing through us.[36]

These heartfelt sentiments were said in anguish as her husband slowly pulled her away from the Faith. She did not leave the Faith so much as her husband smothered the flame in her heart.

A love interest for Agnes, and teaching work

Agnes met a man named William Wallis sometime in 1908 and was very attracted to him. In the only reference found about him in her letters, Agnes wrote on 25 August 1908 to Elizabeth Muther stating that 'I have not seen Mr. Wallis since our happy day at Wahiawa. May God help us to give some real joy to his soul.'[37] This interest evidently developed into a full romance and Agnes wrote to 'Abdu'l-Bahá about whether to marry him. In September 1909, Agnes received a Tablet from Him which responded to her question about marriage and to her great desire to be empty and void of worldly attachments:

O thou seeker of the Kingdom!

Thy letter was received. I prayed at the Court of Holiness to deliver thee from the darkness of the attachment to this world, enlighten thee by the Divine Illumination and purify the mirror of thy heart, so that the Rays of the Sun of Truth may shine therein.

Permission is granted thee to marry Mr. W..... W...., but thou must try with heart and soul to guide him and cause him to enter under the Shade of the Covenant and Testament, so that ye may become united as one soul in two bodies and be engaged in the service of the Kingdom.[38]

Agnes was apparently unable to bring Mr Wallis into the Faith and she never did marry.

These middle years of the first decade of the twentieth century were quiet ones for the Bahá'ís. Agnes's presence is not very conspicuous in the historical record. She had brought Ada Whitney into the Faith, but her attempts to interest her family in her momentous discovery had failed, with the exception of her Aunt Annie Dickey, whose interest proved to be transient. Elizabeth Muther was more successful in bringing people into the Faith, such as Moto and Alice Otis. In November 1908, Agnes wrote:

> God's Spirit is moving in these little island spots and His love is spreading. Though we can only number three acknowledged Bahais [Agnes, Elizabeth and Ada], still a number are greatly attracted. Of the three acknowledged Bahais, one is deprived at present of all intercourse and literature relating to the Cause . . . Every Friday we two Bahais meet with others who are interested. We commence our meeting with a silent prayer and repeating the Greatest Name nine times and end in the same way.[39]

The few Bahá'ís in Honolulu were trying to learn how to teach the Faith and were struggling to create a spiritual atmosphere at their meetings with seekers. At one of these meetings, there was evidently some sort of disunity. Agnes poured her heart out to Elizabeth in an undated letter:

> I want so much to talk to you & I will have to talk on paper. You stood nobly by me yesterday and there was something from that meeting that I took away with me and still have in my heart, something more than I have ever taken away from a Honolulu meeting. But dearest this is only the <u>beginning</u>, where we should have been years ago, so now we must make the double effort to gain what we have lost & strive <u>each</u> time that the spirit will be <u>more</u> manifest then the time before. This is the one great aim of my heart & I can not rest until it is accomplished. We want Abdul Baha's spirit more than anything else, and that is the <u>only</u> thing that will bring the other dear ladies to see the Real Sight. When <u>that Spirit</u> is manifested through the quiet of our meeting, it will take hold of their hearts in a way that they cannot resist.[40]

In the same letter, Agnes writes about Genevra Coombs, who at that time was studying the Faith:

> To show how eager Mrs Coombs is, she came around to see me last evening, to talk about our meetings, which evidently have been deep on her heart. She said she didn't care any more for parties. She said again to me that I must be the leader, then she proposed that after we sang & prayed (silent) we say in unison, 'Give me knowledge, faith & love'. She also wishes we could have a time for just Bible study, where each one brought their Bible. That also was in my heart and I wanted to propose it, so God must be leading us all. She said, 'If I had the time for it, I can give up everything for this'. God seems to be answering my dissatisfied feeling by giving me just the work I have longed to do. [41]

The few Honolulu Bahá'ís were trying to come up with some format for their meetings that would best encourage the seeking souls. Agnes wrote:

> So much depends on our love for each other, dearest, & I so long to have our little meetings like those of Paris where only perfect love abounded & no one thought of interrupting, but all faces were radiant & reflected one from the other the love of Abdul-Baha. Through the calmness & silence of the Believers, Abdul-Baha was present . . . The whole world was forgotten in the great love that was felt by everyone.
>
> <u>Now</u> is the time for us to arise to real service & establish such a meeting. Abdul Baha showers His unbounded love on us and how little it is for us in return to try and do His bidding . . .
>
> Dear Mrs Coombs felt this so deeply & has so strived to have the meetings silent, and if we are to help her & Mrs Augur to see the Real Sight we must do our utmost, and do it only in love for our Master, because we wish to please Him.
>
> I feel especially strongly about it because I met Mrs. Coombs in the car last week and in a loving way she told me how she & Mrs. Augur felt, that the meeting was not what it should be and she said they felt we must have silence . . .
>
> Let us pray earnestly before entering the meeting that God will

help us to do His Will. Abdul-Baha says, while Tablets are being read, we must remain silent & only speak with the permission of all present. So let us look for God's Spirit & not interrupt because we think it has been read before & that something was not stated right, for after all the great & important matter is the meeting with God. All little things will be straightened out if God is with us.[42]

Genevra Coombs evidently became a Bahá'í through the meetings for she was later mentioned in a letter written by Corinne True.

George and Ruth Augur

Growth of the Faith in Hawaii was up and down. Within the first year, Agnes, Clarence Smith, Elizabeth Muther and Moto had become Bahá'ís. Then Moto left in the spring of 1903 and Clarence left two years later, in the summer of 1905. Alice Otis came into the community in late 1905, leaving in 1907. While Alice was in the community and holding weekly Bahá'í firesides at her home, her sister, Ruth Augur, began to attend the Bahá'í meetings, though more out of a general interest, as she said that she was happy as a Christian. But it was not too long before Ruth became a Bahá'í. When Alice left Hawaii in 1907, Ruth and her husband, George, offered their home for the weekly meetings and as a home for the Bahá'í library.

George Augur was a homeopathic physician who was not as quick as his wife to recognize the truth of the Bahá'í Faith, but when he did, he had a 'rare spiritual insight in his comprehension of the station of 'Abdu'l-Baha and his love for Him'. George began writing to 'Abdu'l-Bahá in early 1909 and one of His replies encouraged him to pioneer to Japan (see next chapter). George did so in May 1914 and stayed for ten months before returning to Honolulu. The following year, both George and Ruth moved to Japan.[43]

Abby Frances Johnson

The next person to accept Bahá'u'lláh was introduced to the Faith by Elizabeth. This was Abby Frances Johnson, born on Kauai to missionaries Rev. and Mrs Edward Johnson.

[Frances] accepted the Baha'i Message with great joy when she heard of it from Miss Muther. Her home was at Pearl City, and there the friends would gather for joyous Feasts, especially on Naw Ruz, when she gave the Feast for many years until she was called to a Higher Life. With loving enthusiasm she would serve the friends of the best she could give, after which all enjoyed reading Tablets and Prayers and singing together. Thus the day was spent in love and unity, the friends going together by train from Honolulu. Miss Muther wrote of these Feasts, June 20, 1911, 'I always feel uplifted whenever I go to dear Frances'. She is a dear beautiful soul, so faithful and true.'[44]

In a letter she wrote in February 1909, Agnes described a Feast they had celebrated at Miss Johnson's home:

Frances met us and threw her loving arms around each one in succession she was so radiant, she is a wonder! I think her faith and love are strong enough to turn the world. I asked Frances if she would not like to write to 'Abdu'l-Baha. She replied she had been thinking of it but did not know just what to say – she thought she would say, "Abdu'l-Baha, I am coming to Thee as a little child.' Not long after this Miss Johnson wrote the Master and gave me the letter to send to Him. Then on April 1, 1909, she wrote me: 'I must tell you that I am not at all satisfied with the letter I gave you – I might have said much more – I might have told the Master how my eyes have been opened – how much more wonderful everything seems – how much better I understand God's mighty power, infinite love and His Bounteous care. Agnes, sometimes the world seems filled with the Glory of God – I tell you, it is worth all the rest of my life just to have one day of this knowledge and foretaste of what is before us.'[45]

'Abdu'l-Bahá cautioned Frances to remain 'firm and steadfast':

O thou maidservant of God!
      Thank thou God that thou hast attained to that which thou hast been yearning for. Thou didst see the Kingdom established upon the apex of the world and didst behold the Heavenly Rays. Be thou thankful to Miss Muther who imparted to thee the Glad Tidings of the appearance of the Kingdom and guided thee to the

Fountainhead of Eternal Life. Supplicate thou to the Lord of Hosts so that He may open the doors of knowledge and wisdom, make thee the cause of the guidance of multitudes of people and suffer thee to become a spiritual physician healing the sick hearts with the antidotes of Divine Guidance. But the Magnet which attracts the outpourings of God is firmness and steadfastness. Shouldst thou remain firm and steadfast in the befitting manner, thou shalt attain to all these bounties.[46]

Ella Louise Rowland

In 1909, Agnes's teaching efforts bore fruit when a childhood friend, Ella Louise Rowland, accepted the Faith of Bahá'u'lláh. Ella wrote about her encounter with Agnes and the Faith:

You may be interested to know that from the first moment of my hearing the Glad Tidings of the coming of the Manifestation of God there were no doubts in my heart or mind, and whatever questions arose were from the desire to investigate and study, not only for myself, but rather that I might have something of value to share with humanity everywhere. The location of Hawaii being in the nature of a world center where various nationalities mingled in work and in everyday activities of both spiritual and material progress, the idea of brotherhood and the realization of our dependence each upon the other was so early implanted in my life that I scarcely knew when it became evident to my consciousness, so it was but a step to grasp the significance of the Revelation of this New Day, and I only wish that I had shown earlier in life the hunger which my soul held for the Baha'i Teachings when my life-long friend, Miss Agnes Alexander, shared them with me.[47]

Ella and her daughter, Virginia, were faithful Bahá'ís for the rest of their lives. Such was the bond between Ella and 'Abdu'l-Bahá, that in late November 1921, while she was in church, she wrote, 'I was suddenly overcome by the beauty of the music and expressions so that I burst into tears and fled for home.' That was the day 'Abdu'l-Bahá ascended.[48]

Margaret Knudsen and Meta Sutherland also became Bahá'ís in 1909.

Mason Remey and Howard Struven

In August 1909, Agnes received a letter from Gertrude Buikema in Chicago announcing that Mason Remey and Howard Struven would be visiting Honolulu. She wrote:

> He told us a little about his trip to Persia last year and then mentioned their plans for the trip they are now taking. In speaking of the places they expect to visit, he mentioned Honolulu . . . I know their visit will mean much to the dear ones in Honolulu, who, I am sure, are hungry to see and hear one who has labored so long and faithfully in the Cause and who, I understand, has had the privilege of visiting Abdul-Baha four times. Agnes, I hope your dear father will have an opportunity to meet these young men.[49]

The two Bahá'ís were on a globe-encircling teaching trip that had begun in Washington DC and would ultimately encompass Hawaii, Japan, Shanghai, Burma, Mandalay, India and Europe, with a stop-over in Haifa to see the Master. The men arrived in Honolulu on 23 November and stayed for three weeks. Their ship docked in the early morning and they were met by Agnes, Frances Johnson, Mrs Leyland, George and Ruth Augur, Ella Rowland and a few others.

Mason, Howard and eleven Bahá'ís went to the Augurs' home. Mason wrote:

> At eleven o'clock that morning a meeting was held at the house of Dr. and Mrs. Augur. All the Baha'is were there and we had a delightful time reading the Holy Teaching and talking. A short time before our visit, Mrs. Cooper from San Francisco visited the islands and that helped Agnes Alexander with the work there but there were a number who had come into the movement after her visit and to them we were the first Baha'is from a far that they had ever met.[50]

Their first lecture on the Bahá'í Faith was given in Agnes's home. At first, Agnes was unable to find a large enough room to host the meeting, but then she went to Ruth Augur's home and the two of them prayed for God's assistance: 'The guidance came to me to ask my father's permission to hold the meeting in the 'lanai' (open room) in our home.

Through God's assistance, he gave his consent.'[51] Mason wrote:

> At 2 o'clock in the afternoon Agnes Alexander had a meeting at her house. About fifty or sixty people assembled there on the 'lanai' a large open out-of-door room of a type peculiar to the Hawaiian Islands. Up until that moment we had not made up our minds whether or not we would remain the three weeks but this meeting proved so successful and the interest was so genuine and the people so apparently pleased with everything that we decided then and there that we should remain in order to follow up the work.
>
> Agnes Alexander's family were descended from the old missionary stock that migrated to the Hawaiian Islands in early days, their traditions were a sectarian nature and they naturally were not in sympathy with Agnes' work. Nevertheless, her father had allowed her to have this gathering at his home. Neither he nor Mrs. Alexander were present. There was a newspaperman there who took down practically everything that we said. After the meeting in order to enlighten the reporter we called at his office gave him further information about the Baha'i Cause. The next morning there appeared a glowing account of this meeting which had been held at the home of Professor Alexander and while the article didn't say much, there was a certain inference that Professor Alexander through his hospitality indirectly endorsed a movement.[52]

This was a moment of truth for Agnes's father, William De Witt. Agnes wrote:

> Although my dear father gave his consent that I could hold the meeting in his home, he had not realized at the time what it meant. When the newspaper article appeared about the Baha'i lecture, it caused a crisis which in reality strengthened the Cause. From that time the hospitality of Honolulu was extended to the visitors and Mr. Remey was invited to speak on the Cause in many homes where groups of friends gathered to hear him.[53]

A public meeting was held in the Young Hotel on 29 November where Mason and Howard presented the history and teachings of the Faith to an audience of 75.[54] This was the first public talk ever given on the

Faith in Hawaii. Agnes's father, William De Witt, had not bothered her much about her involvement in the Bahá'í Cause up to this point, but having public talks on the upstart cult was more than he could accept. Mason wrote that the talk

> was too much for the old professor. In the next morning's paper he wrote an article entitled, 'What the Baha'i movement really is', bringing to bear all the arguments that the missionaries in Persia were accustomed to bringing against our people. The article showed that he had devoted a great deal of time and effort to do this study of the Baha'i teaching, not with the idea of the finding any good in it but with the idea of was refuting and condemning it. His article was written in a very mild tone but full of subtlety.[55]

William De Witt sent his letter to the *Honolulu Commercial Advertiser* and tried to explain 'What the "Bahai" Movement Really Is'. Much of his article, though correct in some details, relied completely on the writings of Professor E. G. Browne and the Count de Gobineau. Though Browne actually met Bahá'u'lláh and was highly impressed by Him, his sympathies lay more with Mírzá Yahyá, Bahá'u'lláh's half-brother who attempted to poison Bahá'u'lláh and take over leadership of the Faith. His other source was a book written by Gobineau. Gobineau was highly attracted to the Báb, but his book about Him was commonly inaccurate and described His teachings in such a way that others would interpret as 'pantheistic', the idea that God is in everything and that everything is God. He has also been called the 'father of racism'.[56] These were the only books William De Witt apparently used to write his own article.

After giving a brief history of the split of Islam into the Sunni and Shi'i sects, William De Witt described the 'Sufi mystical philosophy' as an offshoot of Shi'i Islam and 'Babism' as 'Sufism directed into a more practical channel'. The Báb's book, the *Bayán*, he called 'a system of Pantheism tinctured by additions from Gnostic and other sources'. The end of his article focused strongly on the supposed overthrow of the designated successor to the Báb, Mírzá Yahyá, by Bahá'u'lláh, and concluded by stating that:

> As soon as Baha [Bahá'u'lláh] was firmly established in his new

authority, he proceeded to make use of it to abrogate, change and develop the Babite doctrines. His chief aim seems to have been to do away with irksome and unpractical regulations to conciliate Christians and Jews, to diminish the Mohammedan features of Babism, and thus to render it more palatable to western converts. This policy seems to have been highly successful.[57]

William De Witt ended his article by mentioning the 'mosque' being built in Chicago.

Mason and Howard responded to the article a few days later, writing: 'The followers of the Bahai teaching read with interest the scholarly account of the early days of the movement . . . To those familiar with this teaching, however, it was quite evident that the author had had access only to certain literature which dealt but imperfectly with the earliest phase of the teaching.' The article went on to note that: 'As in the early days Christianity was for a time misunderstood and supposed to be a Jewish sect, so in the early days of the present day movement, it was misunderstood and supposed by many to be a sect of Islam.' The article ended with the address of the Bahá'í Publishing Trust in Chicago for those who might be interested in more accurate information. Out of deference to Agnes, Mason and Howard let that be their final word in print.

The visiting Bahá'ís gave two addresses at the Kilohana Art League about the Faith, as well as talks at the homes of Augusta Graham, Mrs Walker, Mrs Dwight Baldwin and Mrs Steer. The *Hawaiian Star* reported: 'The Bahai movement has gained great ground and people of prominence and of all religions have approved its creed as comprising the best of every belief.'[58] Mason gave three talks at the New Thought Center and the Oahu Prison.[59] Mason and Howard also went to Pearl Harbor to meet some friends of Mason's father, who had been an admiral in the Navy. There they held a small meeting and were able to stay overnight in a place found by Frances Johnson; a place with a significant population of mosquitos. Though they slept under mosquito nets, Howard had rolled up against his net and the biting pests took advantage of the opportunity. In the morning, his well-bitten arm looked like it had been burned.[60]

In the *Honolulu Evening Bulletin*, a story about Mason and Howard noted that:

For the past seven or eight years Bahaism has been in our midst, although the general public may not have been aware of the fact. So active has the campaign been conducted during the past few weeks that meetings have been held at the Young Hotel, the Kilohana Art League and at the homes of several prominent people of the city. Of all the forty-six cities that Prof. Remey and Mr Struven have visited during the past six months, they have found more response to Bahaism in Honolulu . . . As so many local people are in sympathy with the movement it has apparently come to stay.[61]

Mason noted that of all the Bahá'ís he met in Hawaii, only one was a man: Dr George Augur. A photo taken in the Auger backyard includes George and Ruth Augur, Agnes Alexander, Ella and Virginia Rowland, Frances Johnson, Elizabeth Muther, Genevra Coombs, Mrs Sutherland (the Augurs' maid), Mason and Howard.

Mason and Howard left Honolulu on 14 December. Mason wrote, 'All the Baha'i friends and many others whom we had met, came to the dock bringing garlands of flowers and fruit and the like for us. We had these garlands draped around our necks until almost covered our persons. Mrs. Swansea, I remember sent us a basket of fruit . . . The dozen pineapples, many "hands" of bananas and several other kinds of fruits.'[62]

Organizing the Hawaiian Bahá'ís

On 16 February 1910, Sigurd Russell arrived in Honolulu. He had met both Agnes and Clarence Smith in Paris in 1901 and had visited 'Abdu'l-Bahá in both 1901 and 1904. Sigurd remained in Hawaii for several months and returned for a second visit in 1911.[63]

On 1 March, Agnes reported to Albert Windust that 'a dozen' Bahá'ís were present to listen to the pilgrim notes of Louise Waite, who had visited the Master in 1909.[64]

The visit of Mason and Howard spurred the Hawaiian Bahá'í community into an effort to organize themselves. On 1 April 1910, the fledgling Bahá'í community held the first of what they called bimonthly 'business meetings' in the home of George and Ruth Augur to consult about teaching the Faith in the islands. The Bahá'ís began their first regular evening firesides in January 1911, also in the Augur home.[65]

Mary Coonradt began attending Bahá'í meetings in 1910 and soon became a Bahá'í. She remained in the community until her passing in 1916.[66] Adeline Mary White also found the Faith in 1910 through her sister, Meta Sutherland, and the teaching efforts of Frances Johnson. She and her husband were able to meet 'Abdu'l-Bahá in San Francisco in 1912.[67] During these years, teaching efforts were obviously being focused on white women. Dr Augur was the only man in the Bahá'í community. Native Hawaiians had been completely overlooked up to this point. The first native Hawaiian Bahá'í, Mary Fantom, wouldn't come into the Faith for over a dozen years.

On 9 August 1910, Aurelia Bethlen, a Bahá'í from Hungary, spent a few hours in Honolulu with the Bahá'ís at the Augur home. The *Honolulu Star* announced her visit with some very unusual headlines, reading 'Countess will come to save Honolulu' and 'Hopes to redeem entire world and predicts the Millennium not later than 1915'. The story called her a 'Hungarian missionary in America for Bahaism'.[68]

Agnes missed Aurelia's visit because she spent much of July and August on the island of Hawaii. On 11 August, she described visiting Kilauea volcano, which was erupting at the time and which chased her away with its smoke. Before being smoked out, she had gone down into the crater for an up-close view of the eruption. Nine days later, Agnes made a second trek down into the volcano: 'Tuesday night a party of us who had not seen the crater since the change, were greatly excited. [We] girls went down to stay until the sunrise. Mrs. Lyman lent us a horse and donkey which Miss Bever and I rode while Ruth Shaw and Miss Morton walked . . . It was after 12 p.m. when we arrived at the brink of the crater.'[69]

Agnes had been working with Jessie Turner on a book called *How to Use Hawaiian Fruits,* which was published in 1910. It was basically a cookbook filled with recipes for using Hawaii's native fruits, such as avocados, bananas, breadfruit, coconuts, figs, grapes, guava, mango, papaya, pineapple, taro, tamarind, watermelon and other things.

The Honolulu 'Bahá'í Assembly' began a more 'structured approach' to their organization and on 11 January 1911 they elected officers and appointed committees. For the calendar year of 1911, the officers and committee members were:[70]

Chairman	Miss Agnes B. Alexander
Recording Secretary	Mrs. E. A. Rowland
Foreign Correspondent	Miss Elizabeth Muther

Treasurer	Dr. George J. Augur
Librarian	Mrs. Ruth Augur
Committee on Letters	
Chairman	Miss Elizabeth Muther
Committee on Health	
Chairman	Mrs. W. M. Graham
Committee on Teaching, Meetings, Subjects	
Chairman	Miss Agnes B. Alexander
Committee on Calendar	
Chairman	Mrs. W. M. Graham

Mr. Shaw, Miss Fletcher, Mrs. Rowland – assistants

It appears that most of the Bahá'ís in the community were given a position.

In April 1911, C. Fisher Langier published an article in the *Paradise of the Pacific Weekly* in which he looked at the religious philosophy of one whom some called a 'heathen'. He defended it because he appreciated the truth:

If I might impose further on your valuable space I should fain submit to your readers an extract from the religious philosophy of a 'heathen' who wrote about the same time as Mrs. Eddy [Mary Baker Eddy, founder of Christian Science] flourished, one Abbas Effendi of Persia. His exposition of the relation of God to man, and of man to his fellow-man, is illuminating, forceful, pointed, and appeals alike to our reason and our emotions.

I quote from 'The Arena' of November, 1904: 'The Beha'i conception of the Supreme Being is not a personality, but an Essence, an all-pervading Force or Power, frequently referred to as Love, or Truth, or Life. "God" is pure essence and cannot be said to be anywhere or in any place. God is Infinite, and, as terms are finite, the nature of God cannot be expressed in terms. But as man must form and express a conception of God in some way he calls God "Love" or "Truth", because these are the highest things he knows. Life is eternal; so men, to express God's Infinity, say that God is 'Life'. But these things in themselves are not God. God is the source of all things that are made, and all things that are, are mirrors reflecting his Glory . . . Self-consciousness follows from the association of spirit evolving these powers with individual forms. These centres of emotion, intelligence, reason and self-consciousness are capable, in due course, of union with, or transfer to, the pure Absolute Essence, whereby the ultimate end of the evolutionary process is attained. The life of men is a single Divine emanation. They should therefore hold to each other the closest relation of sympathy, love, and brotherhood . . . Any other attitude on the part of the human consciousness must cause disharmony between man and God, must, in fact, constitute an insuperable barrier to man's Divine possibilities. Each man is bound up with his fellows. Their welfare should be his concern no less than his own.'

Here we have a message from a 'heathen' that, differ from him as we may, presents an orderly, rational, reasoned and inspiring theme. Compared with Mrs. Eddy's science, it is as in marked contrast as day with night.

I have written at this length for no other reason than this: that I appreciate Truth, Righteousness and Justice above all things, as I believe the nature of every normal man and woman.[71]

There was another article in the *Pacific Weekly* in September that put the Bahá'í Faith in a positive light, and it was too much for Agnes's father, William De Witt Alexander. On 9 October, he wrote to Rev W. Ferrier that 'I was sorry to read in the "Pacific" of September 20th, 1911, a misleading article on "Religious Reform in Persia" probably based on misinformation furnished by the interested party. I take liberty to enclose a brief sketch of the sect, which I wrote for a local paper, when a couple of its emissaries were here on a proselyting tour.' He then listed his references, including Rev. H. H. Jessup, long a devout enemy of the Cause. He continued:

The Bahaites extremely dislike to have the history of their sect, or their esoteric doctrines and practices made public . . .

It is certain that Baha-Ullah claimed and was considered by his followers to be an incarnation or, to use their own term, a 'manifestation' of God. He is generally spoken of as the 'Blessed Perfection'. His son Abbas, permits himself to be worshiped by American women, who believe him to be a reincarnation of Jesus Christ . . .

I am interested to know whether there is to be a perpetual series of incarnations in his family, like those of the Grand Lama of Tibet. His disciples in America speak of him as 'Our Lord'.

It is essentially at bottom a Mohammedan sect, and bears the marks of its origin among the Persian Sufis or mystics. Its members revere Mohammed as a prophet of God, and put the Koran on a par with the Bible. They regard Arabic as a sacred language, employing Arabic phrases in their ritual, and Arabic names for the nineteen months and festal days . . . Their incessant repetition of the declaration of the Unity of God is a Mohammedan characteristic, although their conception of him is pantheistic. The bombastic dialect affected by them is derived from the Persian Sufis.

Bahaism aims at superintending Christianity, whose cardinal doctrines it rejects, and at becoming the World-religion of the future by virtue of fine phrases about Peace, toleration and universal brotherhood, all borrowed by them from the religion which it proposed to supplant. It ignores, or like the Hindoo philosophers, denies the existence of sin, as a positive thing, and the need of redemption. But, as Dr. Warschauer says, 'Only a religion which generates the moral stimulus for the extermination of sin and evil, is fitted to be a world-religion.' Long after Bahaism shall have died out, Jesus Christ will be Lord of all.[72]

Even though William Alexander had an expert on the Bahá'í Faith living in his own house, his own daughter, he obviously did not consult with her about the history, principles or beliefs of the Bahá'í Faith.

Late in 1911, the Honolulu 'Bahá'í Assembly' published what they called the Unity Calendar. This calendar had a quotation from the Bahá'í Writings for every day of the year for 1912, along with photographs of Hawaiian scenes. Profits from the sale of the calendar were to be given to the Bahá'í Temple Fund. Two articles in the *Honolulu Advertiser* described it:

The latest calendar – so late that the year had to begin before it was dry from the presses, is the Unity Calendar. The cause for delay was the epidemic of dengue in the press rooms of the Advertiser which made work impossible for many of the employees for many days just during the busy season.

There are twenty pages with thirty pictures of the most interesting and best places in Hawaii. For each day there is a sound, comforting sentiment, which will help you live a day out with a good thought in your head. It is called 'Unity' because everyone having one of these calendars in any part of the world will be united in thought each day with others having the calendar.

If everyone in Honolulu could, or would, read the saying for each day with all of his townspeople, we would have a 'United Honolulu' that would make living more than worthwhile:

The Unity idea is based upon the request that, 'In order that 'Abdu'l-Baha and his Light Bearers . . . and their friends may unite each day in reading the same words, this calendar is lovingly sent forth by the Baha'i Assembly of Honolulu.'[73]

Unfortunately, the person who took charge of the calendar's printing inserted some of their own words, thus creating a huge test for the Bahá'ís. The Bahá'ís overcame the difficulty by remembering the words of 'Abdu'l-Bahá that through love a wrong could right itself. Unity was maintained within the community, but calendar sales only covered the costs of printing.[74]

'Abdu'l-Bahá in North America

The great excitement in 1912 was 'Abdu'l-Bahá's travels through North America. Elizabeth Muther went to the Bahá'í Temple Unity Convention in May and was able to meet the Master. His response on meeting this Hawaiian Bahá'í was to say, 'From afar! From afar! I entertain the greatest love for them (Honolulu friends) because they are so far away, but yet they have promulgated the Word of God there. They have heard it from afar, therefore I am attached to them and bear my greetings to all of them.' When He arrived in San Francisco in September, the Honolulu Bahá'ís sent Him a cable, begging Him to come to the Islands. Adeline White and her husband travelled to San Francisco and met 'Abdu'l-Bahá on 7 October, where He gave Adeline His answer to their petition:

You have taken great trouble. You have come a long way. You are very welcome. How are the friends of God in Honolulu? Are there many?

Answer: There are about fifteen.

*Agnes Baldwin Alexander in
December 1901. Photograph
taken in Oakland, California,
shortly before she returned home as
Hawaii's first Bahá'í*

*May Bolles, circa 1902: '. . . the first
meeting with the beloved May Bolles
is one of the precious memories of my
life. From that day she became my
spiritual mother, and through all the
years her tender mother love has been
a guiding star in my life . . .'*

Gathering of Bahá'ís in New York City, 1901. Seated, left to right: Howard MacNutt, Agnes Alexander (age 26), three unidentified women, Anton Haddad, William Hoar, Arthur Dodge

Hawaii's first Bahá'í group,
Pacific Heights, 25 April
1903. Left to right: Kanichi
Yamamoto, Elizabeth
Muther, Mrs W. H. (Anna)
Bailey (from Oakland),
Agnes Alexander

Agnes as bridesmaid, probably at her best friend Ada Whitney's wedding in Honolulu in 1904

Agnes taught at her alma mater for a number of years before giving it up entirely. She's shown here with some of her Punahou students in about 1905

Agnes with her parents Professor William De Witt and Abigail Alexander on the lanai of the Alexander family home on Punahou Street in Honolulu, about 1910

Mary and Agnes Alexander at the Baldwin Sugar Plantation on Maui, about 1912. From childhood the Alexander and Baldwin children visited each other on neighbour islands in Hawaii

'Abdu'l-Bahá sent Howard Struven (standing far left) and Mason Remey (standing centre) on a global teaching trip. They landed in Honolulu in November 1909 and stayed for three weeks. Left to right, seated: Ruth Augur, Agnes, Virginia Rowland (little girl), Abbey Frances Johnson, Elizabeth Muther (first to declare in Hawaii); second row: Mrs Augur's maid, Mrs Coombs, Mr Fletcher of New York City, Meta Sutherland, Ella Rowland, George Augur

Honolulu Bahá'ís with Howard Struven and Mason Remey aboard ship in Honolulu Harbour in 1909. Left to right, standing: Elizabeth Muther, Howard Struven, Ella Rowland, Mrs Harvey, Mason Remey, Mrs Thayer, Mrs Fletcher of New York City; seated: Abbey Frances Johnson, Virginia Rowland and Agnes Alexander

Agnes with her family. Left to right: Abigail Baldwin Alexander, William De Witt Alexander, Agnes Baldwin Alexander, Arthur Chambers Alexander, Mary Elizabeth Alexander, William D. Alexander. Her brother Henry E. M. Alexander predeceased her other siblings. Photograph probably taken on the occasion of Agnes's parents 50th wedding anniversary in 1910

Very good. How long does it take to come here?

Answer: Six days.

But we have come from a more distant point. We have traversed an arc to see you.

Mrs. White: Are you going to Honolulu?

'Abdu'l-Baha: There is no time to go to Honolulu. I desire to go there and see the friends, and from there to go to Japan, China, India, but I have not the time. It is a long time since I left the Holy Land. You have come and it is just the same. You are representative of the rest.

How are the friends? Are they attracted? Are they severed? Are they rejoicing? Inasmuch as they are living where they are, they should be much attracted. They are situated so far from the Holy Land, they should be very much attracted. The fact is they have capacity, and that is why they became believers. Evidently they are endowed with capacity. If they were not they would not be so united. It is good to be so far away on an island, and yet be near in the spirit, because places that are far from the Lamp, their traces and rays are not so visible. In places surrounding the Lamp, the light is more evident. When a place is far from the Lamp, it must be like a clear mirror to reflect. It must have a clear surface to reveal the light of the Sun. Were it not for the polished surface of the mirror, it could not reflect the Sun. This is the evidence of the purity of your hearts. Thus the Light of His love is evident and manifest in you, therefore, it is my hope that you will develop extraordinary qualities, that blessed souls may appear, that good souls may appear, that souls like unto angels, free from every fetter, every distant thought, having only the thoughts of His Holiness Baha'u'llah; no thoughts, no desires but these. You should not be fettered. Day and night be aflame with the Light of the love of Baha'u'llah. You are very welcome, you have come from afar.[75]

In March 1912, one of Agnes's correspondents was an English Bahá'í, Dorothy Hodgson. On the 16th of that month, Dorothy was in Paris and went to greet the Master for the Hawaiian Bahá'ís. Upon mentioning Honolulu, 'Abdu'l-Bahá told her to 'Take a pencil and write'. He then dictated this Tablet:

Convey to the friends of Honolulu my utmost greetings and love. Ever do I supplicate on their behalf at the Threshold of El Abha and beg for their confirmation and assistance. May God grant them firmness in His Cause! May they ever remain steadfast in the Covenant and Testament. If ever any person secretly desires to shake their faith in the Covenant and Testament, they must remain firm and know of certainty that the person has evil intentions. They must listen to the words of whomsoever calls the people to the Covenant, and they must know that if anyone desires to shake their faith, that he is a stranger of Baha'u'llah, because such a person thinks of sowing seeds of division in the Cause of God, aiming to scatter the Baha'i unity, so in the meanwhile he may propagate his own selfish desires.[76]

Mason Remey's second visit

At the end of May, Agnes received a letter from Mason Remey in which he wrote, 'The Master has just instructed me to lose no time in going to your shores. I will be with you in July.' Mason and George Latimer arrived in Honolulu as he said and stayed until 14 September.[77]

6

BEGINNING THE GREAT ADVENTURE

1913

Suddenly, Japan came to the forefront in the Hawaiian Bahá'í community. George Augur had long been interested in Japan. At his Hawaiian home, he even had a Japanese garden behind the house. At some point after he had made a short visit to Japan, he wrote to 'Abdu'l-Bahá saying that he 'would like to go to make an indefinite stay' in that country.[1] 'Abdu'l-Bahá replied on 21 November 1913 and George received a life-changing Tablet. The Tablet read:

> O thou dear son!
> From thy letter the fragrance of the rose-garden of significance was inhaled, that praise be to God, thou art assisted by the Divine Confirmations, hast found the way to the Kingdom of God and thy heart and soul are quickened. Arise thou to perform the blessed intention that thou art holding and travel to Japan and lay there the foundation of the Cause of God, that is, summon the people to the Kingdom of God. Japan has great capacity, but there must needs be a teacher who will speak by the confirmations of the Holy Spirit. I hope that thou wilt become assisted in this.[2]

George's desire was to obey the Master, but one of his friends in Honolulu tried to convince him that going to Japan at that time was a mistake. George picked up the *Hidden Words*, opened the book and the first words he saw were, 'O My Servant! Free thyself from the worldly bond, and escape from the prison of self. Appreciate the value of time for thou shalt never see it again, nor shalt thou find a like opportunity'. Those words left no doubt in his mind. On 21 May 1914, George left Honolulu for Japan, and Mrs Augur went to visit their son in California.[3]

An interest in Japan

Just before George received his Tablet from 'Abdu'l-Bahá, Agnes began to seek her own direction. At some time previously, a Japanese woman named Ume Tsuda had visited Honolulu on a lecture tour. Agnes described her as a 'wonderfully alert and enthusiastic little lady, from the night I heard her speak I was captivated with interest in Japan'.

> Then I began to search for books about the country, taking notes on its history, religions, and culture. Little did I dream that it was the guidance of God which was preparing me for future work in that country. During those days an inspiration came to me that I would go to Japan, but it did not occur to me that it would be to teach the Cause of God. Afterwards circumstances were such that the way did not open for me to go, and I wondered why the inspiration had come, and spoke of it to a friend. She said, 'It means you are going but it is not yet the time.'[4]

Then one day, possibly near the beginning of 1912, Agnes's father wrote, 'Agnes is to go to Japan and I have put the money in the bank for her when the right time comes.' It was a surprising statement by him, but Agnes wrote, 'Although the spiritual veil was not lifted from his eyes, he was often inspired to guide me.' A year or so later, on 22 February 1913, William De Witt passed away, followed six weeks later by his wife, Abigail. Their passing opened a new phase in Agnes's life and she began to look for what path she should take:

> I had read words of 'Abdu'l-Bahá spoken in England in which He said, 'I have a lamp in my hand searching through the lands and seas to find souls who can become heralds of the Cause. Day and night I am engaged in this work.' The words rang in my ears and I supplicated that His lamp might find me. One morning the Master seemed very near and a joy filled my heart with the inspiration that I was to go to my beloved spiritual mother, May Maxwell in Montreal. I felt a Tablet was coming to me and later that day it was received. The Master did not write, though, that I was to go to Montreal, but the inner guidance had come . . .
>
> May Maxwell had once written me that some day I would come

to her home. At the time, during the life of my parents, it had not seemed possible, but now the way opened, and in October, 1913, I left Honolulu. In the Maxwell home, which had been blessed by the presence of the Master, I spent a month. May was then the mother of a little girl whom 'Abdu'l-Bahá called His child. One day while there I read His words in which He said the believers should learn Esperanto. From that moment there was ignited in my heart the desire to obey His request.[5]

That inspiration, obedience and her involvement with Esperanto would have far-reaching consequences in Japan.

In the same month that Agnes left Honolulu for Montreal, 'Abdu'l-Bahá wrote her a Tablet that she did not receive until January 1914. By that time, Agnes was in Brooklyn, New York, staying with one of her father's cousins. The Tablet set her feet on a new and entirely different path from the one she had been walking:

O thou dear daughter!

Thy letter was received. It became the cause of infinite rejoicing for it expressed eloquently thy faith and thy turning thy face toward the Kingdom of God. This light of guidance which is ignited in the lamp of thy heart must become more brilliant day by day and shed its light to all parts. Therefore, if thou travelest toward Japan unquestionably Divine confirmations shall descend upon thee.[6]

The journey to Italy

This new path clearly would lead her to Japan, but the getting there was the first problem. The doors began to open and Agnes wrote, 'My father's youngest sister [Lottie] was married to an Italian, living in Italy, and they had invited me to come and stay with them.' Since that was going 'towards Japan', Agnes headed toward Italy.[7] She went to New York and boarded a steamer. A group of Bahá'ís came to the dock to see her off:

Among the friends who came to the steamer to see me off was dear little Mrs. Rufus Powell, from Brooklyn. She brought me an Esperanto student book, which she had covered with linen on which she had embroidered a green star. The precious little book which traveled with me '*toward Japan*' gave me the foundation of the Esperanto language. Others among the New York and Brooklyn Bahá'ís brought me remembrances, and in my stateroom I found flowers. The love of the friends remained with me as I sailed away. While many of the passengers on the steamer read guide books, I found my joy in reading 'Abdu'l-Bahá's words, which were a spiritual guide book. To a dear sister in Brooklyn I wrote: 'Cunard R.M.S. 'Ivernia', May 19, 1914. When the steamer sailed out, I lost sight of you dear friends, but after all it did not matter for your love was with me and I felt it . . . On Sunday I was feeling that ten days had gone by and I had apparently accomplished nothing when after dinner the young lady who sits next to me asked me what my religion was. She was tremendously interested and I gave her everything in one dose as we sat under the stars on deck. She is a wonderful soul and was able to grasp all I gave her, only she says she has no faith . . . We have stopped at Madeira and Gibraltar and on the shores of Madeira I said the Greatest Name. We have in Honolulu two Portuguese ladies [Laura Marques and Elinor Freitas[8]] who are interested in the Cause, and their parents came from this Island and were of those who left and helped to form a colony in Jacksonville, Ill. in order to obtain religious freedom. A number of times on this voyage have passengers called out to look at a rainbow, and then the deep realization of the meaning of the rainbow has come to me, that it stands as the sign of the One Who is here now in flesh and blood!'[9]

Upon arriving in Genoa on the steamer, Agnes found a note from her Aunt Lottie slipped under her stateroom door. Agnes wrote, 'My Aunt met me the morning of May 21, at Genoa, and my Uncle came later and together we came to Milan. The first church we entered in Genoa, such a restful feeling came over me as I said the Greatest Name. I spoke of the uplift I felt to my Aunt and she said, "It is because so many prayers are said in these churches one feels the atmosphere . . ."'[10]

After lunch in Genoa, the trio boarded the train at 2:30 pm, reaching Milan four hours later. Agnes remarked that 'Aunt Lottie's house is lovely, so full of beautiful things and in such taste . . .' She noted that she had 'a dear little room and the use of the beautiful writing desk in the living room . . .'[11]

After a few days in bed with a cold, Agnes played the tourist, going shopping with her Aunt and visiting places such as the Castillo Castle, listening to the symphony and going to the Poldi Pezzoli Museum.

All was not idyllic, however. Agnes wrote to her sister, Mary, on 10 June that they had planned to go out on Lake Como, but they could not get there because

> there has been a disturbance here yesterday & late night, caused by the socialist party. No cars are running as there is a general strike. I believe it is all over Italy as a demonstration of disapproval of the government. A few days ago some soldiers, who had been provoked, shot at some anarchists & one young man was killed near here . . . Uncle Guido says the socialists would like an excuse to stir up a revolution. Aunt Lottie & I were out yesterday morning walking & took a carriage home, but we did not see any disturbance. Sat night though, there was a tremendous row near here & I could hear the smashing of windows etc. & later a troop of soldiers marched by & all was quiet. From my window on a side street, I can see many ladies out alone, so it can't be very serious.[12]

This was just a precursor of the war Agnes was about to be caught up in.

Agnes did not stay long in Milan because her Aunt and Uncle were booked to sail to Hawaii. She wrote, 'I have no plans as yet but God will surely guide me. I can trust Him, can I not?' Her Aunt knew someone in Switzerland and suggested that she go there but Agnes noted that she would have to go somewhere where she could live cheaply. She noted that she had corresponded with Alma Knobloch in Germany, so decided to go there.[13]

Agnes and her Aunt and Uncle all left Milan on 1 July. Agnes wrote to her brother, Arthur, that 'I am going to travel with Lizy Amport, the Swiss girl who lives with Aunt Lottie as far as Lucerne where we will stop over, then I am going on to Germany, probably to Leipsig & will know when I hear from Germany in a few days . . . Germany is less expensive than Italy to live in.'[14]

On 2 July, Agnes wrote to Mary saying that there had been a change of plan, but she was very unclear what the new plan was to be, except that she would go to Germany. She stayed in a pension in Locarno Monti, Switzerland, at the north end of Lake Maggiore.[15] Several weeks later, on 28 July, Agnes was in Ascona, a town adjacent to Locarno. Her letter began with the possibility of spending a week at a cabin in the mountains, all the interesting people she was meeting and what the weather was like. How she came to be in Ascona, she explained to Pauline Hannen:

> I have been wonderfully guided and cared for by the Hand of God. I wrote you from Locarno where I was waiting to meet Mme Forni. One day the telephone rang to tell me Mme Forni was at Ascona, the next village and wanted me to come to lunch. Strange to say she was at the very place my Aunt had wanted me to go to at first, as Frau Hofmann, the manager, was a friend of my Aunt and she spoke to me in the telephone saying she was my Aunt's good friend and my Aunt had written her of me. I cannot tell you how good it sounded to me, for I had come to the point where I longed for a loving heart and the sight of a Bahá'í. Though it was pouring it did not take long to go to the funicular railway and down Locarno Monti, then by automobile stage four miles to Ascona, and then a climb up another mountain to Monti Verita. There on entering the dining room the first thing I saw was *The Star of the West*, on the table. It seems it had long been Mme Forni's wish to make this place a Bahá'í center for Switzerland and they had first ordered the magazine. I had to return to Locarno that night but the next day I went again and had a wonderful time with Mme Forni and Frau Hofmann. They joined me in saying the Greatest Name 95 times for God's blessing on that mountain (may it indeed become a mountain for Truth!) . . . Mme Forni is Polish-German, but married to an Italian. She has had a wonderful life and marvelous experience in healing the sick. The next day I moved to Monti Verita and Mme Forni left for her mountain home the following day, expecting to return to take me there in a week, but it was not in God's Plan.[16]

War breaks out in Europe

World War I started on 28 July while Agnes was in Monte Verità and suddenly, she had to change plans again. But she had a big problem with her baggage, which consisted of a trunk. She wrote, 'My trunk was sent on ahead of me by slow freight to Stuttgart & ought to be there in the station. On Aug 1st I mailed the key & receipt to a lady living in Stuttgart, asking her to keep the trunk for me. I have heard nothing. A week ago a girl here wrote in German for me & then the Consul telegraphed but no answer.'[17]

Agnes needed money to travel and walked a long way to the bank, but because she could not remember the name of the proprietor of her pension, they would not give her the funds. She said:

> I was caught. And all communication was cut off, and I only had enough money to pay my board, but not my railway fare to go to Geneva. And they said the train to go [to Geneva] will go the last time that Sunday, as the soldiers – they needed to use the trains. And so I had to get very brave, because I was very timid, and ask to borrow the money. And there was a professor of the Geneva University who loaned me the money. They were going, and I went, and got to Geneva.[18]

When Agnes arrived in Geneva, the mysterious Hand of God was at play. Agnes wrote:

> Through prayer I was led to come to Geneva with some French people and have been wonderfully cared for. I came to see the American Consul and he has been my best friend, but I was not able to cash my money until after I received this Tablet.:

>> O thou my dear daughter!
>> Thy letter was received. It imparted great happiness. Praise be to God that that dear daughter is sacrificing herself in the Path of Bahá'u'lláh and enduring every difficulty.
>> It is now more advisable for thee to depart directly to Japan and while there be engaged in the diffusion of the Fragrances of God. From there thou mayest return to India and from India to the Holy Land.
>> Today the greatest of all divine bestowals is teaching the Cause of God, for it is fraught with confirmations. Every teacher is confirmed and is favored at the divine Threshold. In the estimation of the Ideal King, the army which is in front of the battlefield is encircled with the glances of His

mercifulness, and in the sight of the Divine Farmer, the sower of the seed is accepted and favored. I hope that thou mayest be like a realm conquering army and a farmer, therefore thy voyage to Japan is preferred to everything else. Still thou art perfectly free.[19]

Agnes received the Tablet on 22 August. She was unable to accept the invitation to go on pilgrimage until 1937.

In a letter written on 6 September, Agnes described the miracle that happened next:

> My trunk was in Stuttgart where it had gone before me from Milan. I was ready, though, to go to Japan without it, as 'Abdu'l-Bahá wrote, *'thy voyage to Japan is preferred to everything.'* Everyone here said it was impossible for me to get my trunk, but I knew there was a spiritual power they did not count on. I supplicated 'Abdu'l-Bahá, if it were His will I might get it, and in a few days I had it. It was a wonderful proof of the power of the Center of the Covenant. Consul Keene telegraphed for me and it came. I felt I had to fall on my knees and thank God, it was truly wonderful. Then all my money affairs are arranged and I can go easily to Japan. When 'Abdu'l-Bahá wishes us to do anything and we are ready, the means are also ready.
>
> Now I am only waiting for the steamer. I hope to sail September 19, from Marseilles . . . You may know I am eager to do His bidding. You see dear, as I have felt and once dreamed, as I told you, it is not the time for me to go to 'Abdu'l-Bahá, and I have found the fact that I have not seen Him an aid to my teaching. That is not necessary. It is only faith which counts. I thank God for His wonderful love and mercy to me that I am permitted to so go forth, and dear, never forget that you share in everything with me.[20]

Agnes was told that hers was the only piece of baggage that came through. She had not been too worried because 'Abdu'l-Bahá had used the word 'favored, that "every teacher was favoured". He mentioned it twice. Then the communication opened with London, and I was able to get my money from London. And then, it had accumulated, and I had money enough to go to Japan.'[21]

In spite of Agnes's success, everything was chaos around her. Many others were also having great difficulties with lost luggage and the great problem of getting money. Through the aid of the American Consul, she was able to have her money draft cashed: 'Today I got all my money cashed. In all I have about $1600 in the cashing hut. I am thankful to have money. The consulate people are certainly kind in every way. They have been simply deluged with people from morning til night & even Sunday. People come here by the hundreds to get trains to Paris etc. to get away.' [22]

While in Geneva, Agnes went to the Universal Esperanto Association where she met a Russian Esperantist. The woman told her about a blind Russian young man in Japan, Vasily Eroshenko, who was also an Esperantist, and asked her to look him up. Agnes wrote, 'This was the opening which brought great blessings into my life through friendship with the blind. The Russian lady took me to her home where I gave the Message. She said she would tell of it in city and town. She translated part of the Honolulu Unity Calendar into Esperanto and gave it to me to take to her blind friend in Tokyo.' [23] This was the beginning of a long association with the Esperantists.

In Geneva, Agnes found that the P&O steamship company had a ship going directly to Yokohama from Marseilles on 19 September. It would stop at Port Said; Colombo, Sri Lanka; Singapore; Hong Kong and Kobe before reaching Yokohama. But another problem suddenly blocked her path!

I couldn't get passage! There was a German cruiser in the Mediterranean Ocean torpedoing steamers, and so all the steamers had stopped going through. But the Japanese, only the Japanese steamer went through. And this steamer was filled in London before it left.

And so I sent a cable to the head office in London, but with no result. And then I wrote to the American Consul in Marseilles, where the steamer would stop, and he wrote back, 'There's no passage before November.' And then, as a last resort, I wrote a personal letter to the agent in Marseilles, and I said, if he could get me on the steamer, I would accept anything. Then I didn't know anything further to do. And I was praying a prayer of the Bab's: 'Is there any remover of difficulty save God?' But, that was my last resort. There was nothing more that I knew that I could do.

And there was a knock at my door. And I was handed a telegram.

And it was from this agent. And he said if I would telegraph and come immediately, he'd get me on the steamer. Then they told me that I could not take a trunk, and that the trains were being used for the French soldiers who were wounded that were being taken to southern France. Sometimes the passengers were being left at places where there was no food, and all these things – which were true!

But, the American Consul said, 'You try. You speak French. You go and try!' So, I did. And I checked my trunk! And I went through to Marseilles! At the stations where we stopped, I saw the soldiers and the nurses. And then I went to get a visa from the American Consul. And I told him I had come, and I brought my trunk, and I was going to sail the next day. And he said, 'You can never get your trunk! You can never get a trunk through!' I went to the hotel, and it was already there in the hotel.

Then I went to see the agent about my passage. I told him I would accept anything if he got me on the steamer. Well, he said there was a German lady six months before who had bought her passage, but France and Germany were at war. And he said, 'I will give you her place, and if she comes, I can have her arrested.' So, the next time I was in Germany, I told the Bahá'ís that it was one of their countrymen who helped me go to Japan. [24]

Only Agnes and a French lady, Mme Casulli, boarded the steamer, the *Miyazaki Maru*, and they both shared the unfortunate German's state-room. Agnes said that 'It wasn't an elegant steamer, but there wasn't a better room on the steamer, although I'd been willing to go steerage. And, not only that, she [Mme Casulli] became a Bahá'í – it was God's plan – on the voyage. And she wrote to 'Abdu'l-Bahá. And we were always happy.'[25]

Agnes did not immediately tell Mme Casulli about the Faith, but waited until they reached Port Said. The ship stopped briefly at Port Said and Agnes wanted to meet Ahmad Yazdi, but she felt she needed to give Mme Casulli some explanation about why she would leave the ship. She decided to mention the Bahá'í Faith to her, though she expected she would have no interest. Agnes did not expect what happened next:

On the steamer was a Greek young man who was often with us, as he spoke French . . . He had been obliged to leave Belgium, where he had been in business, and was returning to his home in Port Said. As we three were together on the deck I told Mme Casulli that I was a Bahá'í and asked if she knew of the Faith. She replied 'no,' but the young Greek immediately became aflame to know of the Cause. I gave him some pamphlets . . . As he knew Mirza Yazdi, whom he said was a very good man, he accompanied me ashore to his store . . .

One evening as I sat with Mme Casulli, I saw she was looking at my Baha'i ring stone. I told her it was a Bahá'í stone and she replied that she had thought so. Then I began to tell her of 'Abdu'l-Bahá. She listened and said it was the message she was waiting to hear. God assisted me to speak in French, which she said became almost perfect as I told her the Message. From that time we were united by a new spiritual bond. She told me that as she was French, people generally spoke with her of material things, but she said that I was different and did not speak of clothes . . .

One evening Mme Casulli left me to write. When she returned she asked me if I knew to Whom she had been writing. Then she showed me the beginning and the ending of her letter . . . it began, 'To Thou Prophet Whom I seek,' and ended, 'I hope to attain the highest and say I am a Bahá'í.' At Hong Kong dear Mme Casulli left me . . . Before we parted, as I was writing to 'Abdu'l-Bahá, I asked her if she wished to add anything. She replied, only that she might have a Tablet from Him, and that when her husband's contract would be up in Hong Kong, that she might return to her country and teach the Cause of God. From Japan I wrote to the friends: 'I have had a letter from my French friend, Mme Casulli, in Hong Kong. She writes me: "I translated with much pleasure the Tablet that you sent me with your last letter and I wish to receive one for myself, for I am certain that 'Abdu'l-Bahá is with me.""[26]

When the ship reached Aden, where the Red Sea meets the Indian Ocean, the captain was ordered to stop because the German cruiser *Emden* was attacking ships in the area. They stayed in Aden for five days and Agnes was thrilled to 'go ashore in Arabia and touch for the first time holy ground where a Prophet of God had lived. Unaware of the reality of Muhammad, most of the passengers were not interested and I was the only lady to go ashore twice.'[27]

On 4 October, Agnes wrote to Mary from Aden: 'It is my first sight of the real native life, where I saw, I suppose, a hundred camels used in all sorts of manners, to ride, to draw water carts & even a kind of carriage. I also saw the little Egyptian donkeys. There are three races of people here, the Arabs, Bedoins, & Ethiopians who interested me much.'[28] Agnes mentioned that she had been 'enjoying the swimming tank' every day.

When the captain received permission to sail, they proceeded without lights until they reached Hong Kong. When they arrived there, they learned that the *Emden* had captured five other ships in the area.[29]

After a voyage of five weeks, Agnes arrived in her first Japanese port, Kobe.

7

THE JAPANESE ADVENTURE

1914–1917

Arrival in Japan

As the steamer approached Kobe, one of Japan's principal port cities, in November 1914, Agnes sent a 'supplication to 'Abdu'l-Bahá for His guidance, putting all my trust and care in Him'. She wrote the supplication in a letter, but never mailed it, sending it through prayer instead, 'but He heard my prayer'. She wrote:

> I have not been out seeking people, but they have all seemed to be placed in my path in the most wonderful ways. Oh, the whole world is simply hungering for this Message of Truth and Love and there is joy unspeakable for all those who will arise and go forth into the 'front of the battlefield.' The first day, as we landed in Kobe, the way opened to give the Message to a shipmate, and as we traveled on the train to Kyoto, the *Star of the West* was being read by my companions. My good friends, Mr. [Philip] and Mrs. Dodge, had written to me to stop in Kyoto and see a young lady who had once been in Honolulu. I little thought I was going to give her the Message, but so it was. And then again on the train coming from Kyoto to Tokyo I met a young Arab who devoured the Message in the few hours we were together.[1]

Upon her arrival in Kobe, she found letters from Mrs Dodge and Mrs Suguki (whom she had known in Honolulu as Miss Lane before her marriage) awaiting her. Mrs Dodge suggested that she go to Kyoto by train to meet Lillian Nicholson, who had taught school in Hawaii. So, Agnes changed her steamer ticket for a train ticket. An American man, Mr Scott, and his daughter, who had been travelling on her steamer, invited Agnes to join their party for the train ride to Kyoto.

Agnes spent her first day in Japan exploring Kobe by rickshaw and taking a trolley to the nearby city of Osaka. The next day, she took the train to Kyoto, which had been the Imperial Japanese capital for almost a thousand years, until the Imperial court moved to Tokyo in 1869. Agnes went to the Daibutsu Hotel where Lillian Nicholson lived. Lillian saw Agnes enter the hotel:

> I do have a beautiful memory and a perfectly clear picture of a lovely glowing faced, young, blond lady as she entered our hotel dining room in Kyoto, Japan with two men who seemed so happily absorbed in what she was saying. We all turned and watched you as you entered. Really you were beautiful and a light seemed to shine right through you, more like a shining spirit. Later I had the pleasure of meeting you in one of the other rooms. I was attracted to a little ring on your finger (later I learned that it was a Bahá'í ring) and used that as an excuse to talk to you as I was keenly interested to know what it was that gave you such a radiating spirit. You happily and graciously then told me of what the ring stood for and something of the Baha'i religion and what it had done for you, something of the wonderful change that it had made in your life.[2]

Agnes was delighted to meet Lillian, a young American woman, since she had not been able to talk with one since leaving New York, except for one in Geneva. Lillian had been teaching in Kyoto for three years and the two young ladies found much in common to talk about. Agnes also received her first mail for many weeks, including a letter from Corinne True containing newspaper clippings with an article about the Bahá'í Faith written by Isabel Fraser.

Agnes left on the express train for Tokyo on Friday 6 November. She shared a compartment with an English couple and a 'dark-skinned' young man. Agnes greatly wanted to share the Faith with her companions. Finally, she showed the couple a paper and asked:

> 'Have you seen this?' They looked at it and then returned it to me unaware of its reality. My attention was then attracted to the young man who was looking intently at the paper. Then he asked me if he might see it. Soon after the English couple left the train. The young man then told me that as soon as I spoke to the couple, he had a

great desire to know what it was I had. He said he did not wish to be bold, but the light he saw in my face was like that of a young girl at her first party. We spent several hours together before he left the train at Yokohama. He told me that he was an Arab, and a Muhammadan from Shanghai. I told him of the Bahá'í Faith and before we parted that night, I had given him my book of the *Hidden Words* and *Prayers*. He said for the first time in many years he would read a prayer from the book that night.[3]

Agnes arrived at the station in Tokyo at 9 p.m. and was met by her Hawaiian compatriot George Augur and a few others. She was taken to the home of Mr Sakurai, where she was to stay. Mr Sakurai had also hosted Aurelia Bethlen in 1910 and George Augur, when he first arrived.

The next day, Agnes went to Yokohama to see about getting her luggage, which had arrived on the steamer. She found that travelling in Japan was fairly easy: 'The maid went with me that morning and bought my tickets, then when I reached Yokohama a rickshaw man was ready to take me to the consulate.' Her American friend, Mr Scott, from the train trip to Kyoto, met her and took her to the consulate where she collected her baggage and seven letters.[4]

Agnes went to the telegraph office on Sunday morning and sent a one-word cable to her sister Mary in California. She cabled simply 'Agnes' which let Mary know that she had safely reached Japan. That single word cost her $6.50.

Beginning the life of a pioneer in Tokyo

Philip and Mrs Dodge held meetings in their home every Sunday, so on 8 November Agnes crossed the road to the Dodges to have dinner and to attend the meeting. She wrote, 'after it was over [I] found myself surrounded by three Japanese men to whom I told the Message of Bahá'u'lláh. I told them where I was living, that I had come to Japan only for the sake of the Bahá'í Cause, and that anyone was welcome to come to see me at any time.'[5]

On Tuesday, Agnes went out with Mrs Dodge to see a lantern procession, then the next night Mr Scott took her for a two-hour rickshaw tour of Tokyo. On Wednesday the 12th, Mr Odaka, Mr Sakurai's brother, took her to Takinogawa Park to see the autumn maple colours.

Unfortunately, when they arrived, they were told that they were ten days too early.[6]

George Augur and Agnes decided to hold Baháʼí meetings every Friday, a practice they and others continued very consistently for many years. At the first Friday meeting, on 14 November, five people attended, including one of the Japanese men who had been present the previous Sunday, and Akinobu Naito, a teacher of English in a Japanese school who was teaching George Japanese. The group read from the Baháʼí writings and said prayers, then George shared part of a Tablet he had received from the Master:

> O thou herald of the Kingdom of God! Thy letter was received. A thousand times bravo to thy high magnanimity and exalted aim! Trusting in God and while turning thy face toward the Kingdom of Abhá, unfurl thou the divine Flag in Tokyo and cry at the top of thy voice: O ye people! The Sun of Reality hath appeared and flooded all the regions with its glorious light; it has upraised the Standard of the Oneness of the world of humanity and summoned all mankind to the refulgent Truth. The cloud of Mercy is pouring, the zephyr of Providence is wafting and the world of humanity is being stirred and moved. The divine Spirit is conferring eternal life, the heavenly lights are illumining the hearts, the table of the sustenance of the Kingdom is spread and adorned with all kinds of foods and victuals. O ye concourse of men! Awake! Awake! Become mindful! Become mindful! Open ye the seeing eye! Unstop the hearing ear! Hark! Hark! The soft notes of the Heavenly Music are streaming down, ravishing the ears of the people of spiritual discernment. Ere long this transcendent Light will wholly enlighten the East and the West! In short, with a resounding voice, with a miraculous power, and with the magnetism of the Love of God, teach thou the Cause of God and rest assured that the Holy Spirit shall confirm thee.[7]

Agnes's first weeks in Tokyo were very busy and full of spiritual excitement. The day of 26 November was triply special. It was the Day of the Covenant, the anniversary of Agnes's declaration as a Baháʼí, and Thanksgiving Day in America. Agnes wrote:

> That day I had a joyful Baháʼí party to which the friends both Japanese

and European were invited. Since that day this room [in the Sakurai house] has been our Bahá'í center, and I have felt it is not for me to say who shall enter it. It is His room and all are His children. This is the front door of the house and my bedroom adjoins, so it is very convenient for me, and nearly every day the Message of the Kingdom is discussed here with someone. 'Abdu'l-Bahá's picture, which Mrs. True gave me in Chicago, has a prominent place in the room. The other day when an American lady, who had heard the Message, came to see me, her eyes filled with tears as she looked upon this picture.

The Message of the Kingdom has certainly been raised in Tokyo! Shortly after my arrival, a Japanese lady reporter, who came to see me, wrote the first article which appeared in the newspaper which is considered the best in Japan and has a very wide circulation.

The lady reporter, Miss Tanaka, had been educated in an English School and spoke English fluently. I told her from my heart of the Cause. She did not take notes. but the article she wrote for the *Asahi,* when translated, I found to be remarkably fine. Was it not a sign of the New Day that in that oriental country, it was a woman whom God chose to write the first article about the Divine Cause![8]

Then George was asked to write an article on the Faith for a theological magazine. This was later printed as a booklet to give away. A Buddhist newspaper also printed a series of articles about the Faith. Another woman Japanese reporter, Ichi Kamichika, visited Agnes and, as she was leaving, asked to borrow her photograph of 'Abdu'l-Bahá. The next day, a story and the photograph appeared in the newspaper. Agnes noted, 'The fact that I am a young lady traveling alone and teaching the Cause seems to impress the Japanese greatly. I have been twice asked for my picture for their papers. I am so happy to think, though, that for the first time, the picture of 'Abdu'l-Bahá has appeared in a paper of this country, and that it should have been a woman who had it printed speaks of the time in which we are living.'[9]

Sometime during the end of 1914, Agnes came into contact with a budding young potter named Bernard Leach and introduced him to the Faith. Two decades later, after becoming well known, he seriously began to explore the Faith, officially becoming a Bahá'í in 1940 through another artist, Mark Tobey.[10]

Agnes was amazed at how accepting the Japanese were of the Message of Bahá'u'lláh. She wrote:

Every Friday new faces appear in the meeting and many hearts have been touched. A young Japanese man who was one of thirty Oriental students to visit 'Abdu'l-Bahá one night in New York, has attended our meeting and told beautifully of his experience, though he is not a Bahá'í, and does not as yet realize who 'Abdu'l-Bahá is. On Christmas day a young man was brought to the meeting who was thirsting for Truth. I felt in my heart he was sent by 'Abdu'l-Bahá and he told me afterwards, he felt he had received a Christmas present.

Shortly after my arrival in Tokyo, a Japanese came to see me. As he did not speak English, I asked my landlord to translate for me. He said he had read in a newspaper of the Bahá'í Revelation and he believed Bahá'u'lláh was Miroku [the 'return' of Buddha] whom the [Japanese] Buddhists were expecting. As I explained the Bahá'í teachings to him, the landlord became interested and remarked that he liked the Bahá'í teaching because there was no quarrelling in it. He referred to the many Christian sects which came to the Orient, but denied the truth of Buddha and did not unite among themselves.[11]

On 29 January 1915, Agnes wrote:

It is such a wonderful life God has permitted me to have here in Japan and how grateful I should be. As Dr. Augur said the other day if we should thank God throughout eternity it would not be too long . . . Every Friday new souls come. My room is consecrated to 'Abdu'l-Bahá and I have asked His blessing in it, so I feel I have nothing to do about who come to the meetings . . . One Friday a rather strange looking man came. That day Dr. Augur did not come. He said he had heard through the Buddhist paper which [was] printed in four editions about the Revelation and at the end gave the name of this house and Friday afternoon to anyone wanting to know more. They did this entirely of their own accord. From this man the next week came a most beautiful soul to me, so we never know when a soul comes to us what will be the outcome. God surely leads me to those who need me and I don't feel that I need seek any out . . . I woke up the other morning with such joy. It was that I was independent of all on this earth. [12]

Vasily Eroshenko

While in Geneva, Agnes had met an Esperantist who asked her to visit Vasily Eroshenko, the 24-year-old blind Russian youth living in Japan. In February 1915, Agnes attended a meeting of the Universal Esperanto Association. When asked to give a talk, she spoke about the Bahá'í Faith. Before leaving, she was given Vasily's address and soon he was going to her apartment twice a week. Though Vasily was blind, he had travelled alone to Japan from Moscow. He quickly became interested in the Faith and had 'taken down in English Braille some of the Bahá'í teachings which I have read to him, and then he has translated them into Esperanto, and they are to be printed in a Japanese Esperanto paper. Now we are translating the *Hidden Words* into Esperanto. Dr. Augur's Bahá'í booklet has already been put into Braille for the blind to read. My Russian friend is studying massage in the School for the Blind here.'[13] Agnes and Vasily quickly developed a deep friendship.

Agnes became very involved with the Esperanto group. Every Wednesday, Vasily would collect her and take her to the meeting. At first, she felt a bit uncomfortable because she was the only woman, but their kindness soon won her over. She was invited to their dinners and other activities. At one meeting, she met a professor from Hiroshima who asked her to come and give them the Message of the Bahá'í Faith. Vasily translated the Arabic *Hidden Words* into Esperanto, as well as eleven principles of the Faith. The Japanese Esperanto publication, *La Orienta Azio*, published a series of articles on the Faith and also translated the Honolulu Bahá'í calendar. Agnes wrote:

> One day I visited the home on the outskirts of Tokyo where the *Orienta Azio* is printed. It is an old grey haired man who does this work in his simple Japanese home, surrounded by a beautiful little garden . . . He said he was sorry he had no chair for me to sit in, but I told him I like sitting on the floor in the Japanese way.' This man did all the work on the publication himself, which was printed and bound in artistic Japanese style. He continued to publish from the Bahá'í Writings until July 1916 [shortly before he died].[14]

Teaching contacts

As Naw-Rúz 1915 approached, Agnes told those coming to the Friday classes to come on 21 March, the Bahá'í New Year. She wanted to make it a happy day, but did not do much planning. On the morning of the 21st, she was completely surprised when:

> an elderly professor in the School of Science came bringing in his own hands a beautiful potted plant. This was a great surprise for I had only met the gentleman a few times at the Esperantist meetings. It seems that my blind Russian friend, Mr. Eroshenko had told him of the day. In the afternoon came others, some bringing gifts which I shall always deeply treasure. It seems strange that all the remembrances I received on that day came from Esperantists, and all the greetings were written in Esperanto. One of the greetings came from a group of Esperantists in another province. I had met their secretary, and as they were having a springtime meeting on this day, they all wrote on a card wishing me greetings as they said they knew it was a day dear to my heart as a Bahá'í.[15]

One of Agnes's students, Kenichi Takao, asked her to go to the Unitarian Church with him. She did so and was introduced to the minister, Rev Uchigasaki:

> When I was introduced to him he said, 'We first had Shintoism. Then we united with Buddhism and later Christianity came in Japan, and we are ready to listen to every new message.' Then he invited me to speak in his pulpit on the Bahá'í Revelation which he would translate into Japanese, and said he would give me part of his time. My heart sank, as I had never spoken in a church and was unprepared, but Mr. Takao said to me, 'God will help you.' During the service he passed me a note on a card on which he had written topics as a guide for my talk. In the note he wrote he would pray 'very strongly' for me. When the minister called on me, with Divine assistance I arose and gave the Message, so that even Mr. Takao was astonished.[16]

Mrs Dodge had introduced Agnes to an American woman in Yokohama who was married to a Japanese man. The woman's daughter was at first attracted to the universality of the Bahá'í teachings, but could not accept Bahá'u'lláh. The American woman happened to mention the Faith to her tailor, Sanzo Misawa, who was a 'spiritually minded man', and introduced him to Agnes and the two began a long friendship. Sanzo was to become a great help to the Cause in the future.[17]

George Augur returned to Honolulu in April, hoping to return in the autumn with Ruth. He left with Agnes happily spreading the Faith in Tokyo. Their efforts had reaped great results. On 19 May, when an English weekly publication featured a photograph of 'Abdu'l-Bahá, Agnes wrote, 'This is the second time 'Abdu'l-Bahá's picture has appeared in the Far East. The first time it was in a Japanese paper, but in both instances it was the work of a woman, which is most interesting from the Bahá'í standpoint . . . This is the ninth Tokyo publication which has printed something concerning the Bahá'í Cause during the last six months. Is not this a proof that "the Ideal King is with those who are in the front ranks of the army".'[18]

On 23 May, Agnes had a celebration for the Declaration of the Báb and invited her friends to come. She printed copies of the photograph of 'Abdu'l-Bahá and each participant was given one. Agnes wrote that 'We had a most happy time together, the friends staying until 7 p.m., which I think was a proof that they were happy. Mr. Eroshenko played on the violin and we even tried to sing some of the Bahá'í songs of Mrs. Waite, and I read from Mrs. Grundy's book.' Vasily had finished his translation of the *Hidden Words* and Agnes gave a copy to a literary writer, Mr Ujaku Akita. The next day, he wrote to Agnes saying, 'Yesterday was very interesting to me. I wish to express my great pleasure to you. That night I spent in reading your translation of the *Hidden Words*. They give me entirely new strength and every word resounds more profound to me than when I read them in the English translation. I feel proud to know that this translation is finished by the patient work of our dear Eroshenko.' Ujaku wrote many articles about the Bahá'í Faith for literary magazines.[19]

Ujaku kept a journal during Agnes's first months in Japan. On 21 April 1915, he wrote: 'Visited Miss Alexander. Dr. Auger's lecture. I visited Aoyama at noon met with friends and went to meet Miss Alexander at the Mr. Sakurais in Kudanzaka at 7 pm. There were also Indian. I met Mrs. Kate. Eroshenko played the violin (Russian folk song). It was a very interesting party so far. Miss Alexander was wearing beautiful ball gowns with blond hair.'[20]

Kikutaro Fukuta: The first Japanese Bahá'í

One day, a Japanese teacher called Mr Naito attended one of the Bahá'í meetings. He then told his class that 'there was a lady in Tokyo who was teaching a new religion, and if any of them wished to meet her, he would introduce them'. Four came with him to meet Agnes. One of them, Kikutaro Fukuta, told her that 'when his teacher mentioned a new religion, it was a great day in his life for he immediately felt it was the truth'. Another student 'copied the entire book, *Ten Days in the Light of Akka* [by Julia M. Grundy] writing in a beautiful fine script in a notebook. When it was completed he had it bound and brought it to me to write on the fly leaf. It was just nineteen pages. I wrote a prayer that all his family might become illumined by the Light of the New Day.' The student later wrote to Agnes saying, 'I can only see God through spirit and Truth which comes out of the lines of that religious book.'[21]

Kikutaro Fukuta, or Fukuta San, was a very shy young lad and Agnes wrote about his encounter with the Faith:

One day a young student visited me who was very shy, but by the look in his eyes I knew his heart was touched. He told me that I was the first person he had ever talked with in English outside of his school, that a few years ago his father failed and he had to be apprenticed. He found the life of an apprentice very hard, but someone told him to try and read the Bible. This he did and found some comfort, but many of the old teachings he could not accept. Now someone is giving him his education. I will copy the note he sent me after his visit as I know it will touch the hearts of my sisters. 'Dear Miss Alexander, I thank you very much for your kindness in offering me your spiritual hospitality and material ones, but my English is too poor to express to you my deep thankfulness. I am now living alone in a lodging and pray every morning and night. Whenever it may be, wherever it may be, when I feel loneliness, I pray in heart and voice. Weak as my power is yet I will do my best for Bahá'ism. I have found truth in the words of 'Abdu'l-Bahá and I believe that it must be the Manifestation of God. . .' This boy learned some of the simpler of the Bahá'í prayers . . . We are all one in the work of the Kingdom and I am only an instrument, while those who given me their love have also a part in the work . . .

Fukuta San, as we called him, came regularly to the Friday meetings. He was the first one to come and the last to leave. Every week he would borrow a book from my Bahá'í lending library and then return it the following week and take another to read. When I remarked that he never asked questions, he replied that he found the answers to all his questions in the books he read. Out of the Empire of Japan, God chose this poor boy whom He endowed with the great gift of recognizing His Messenger. Soon I saw the light of the Kingdom in his eyes and invited him to come to see me on a Sunday.[22]

On 25 June, 18-year-old Fukuta San wrote his letter to 'Abdu'l-Bahá, declaring his belief in Bahá'u'lláh. Encouraged by Agnes, he wrote it in Japanese because of his limited English. The young lad translated it as best he could into English for Agnes:

O my Master 'Abdu'l-Bahá! How great mercy and benevolence that Thou hast descended upon us through an apostle Alexander! Though I am a base and poor youth in this world, I am being awakened and bathed in the ocean of Thy mercy, so happy that I pity the king and the prince who are wandering about in the dream of temporal variance. Accept, O Master, my deep thankfulness from the bottom of my heart. I am very sorry when I think of our fellowmen who take no thought about real happiness and do not rely upon the warm hand of Thy love. O my Lord! Water me forever with the fountain of mercy, and I will never refuse Thy command whatsoever it may be, and excuse me of my sins, and allow me to awake them.[23]

Martha Root in Japan

On Friday 21 July 1915, Agnes's 40th birthday, Martha Root arrived in Yokohama. Agnes had been expecting her, so she sent a letter to the Thomas Cook travel office to be given to her. The letter asked Martha to come to Tokyo. Agnes was excited because Martha was the first Bahá'í woman she had met since she left New York, with the exception of Mme Casulli, who had become a Bahá'í on the voyage to Japan. Agnes had gone to the beach that day and returned to find Martha in her room. Kikutaro Fukuta wrote to Agnes, saying, 'I like her (Miss Root) very much. She told me she was poor when young and I was greatly encouraged to know poverty is not a hindrance.'[24]

That afternoon was Agnes's normal Bahá'í meeting day and six of her students came and met Martha. They arranged for another meeting on the following Sunday and 14 people came. During that meeting, a group photograph was taken, the first Bahá'í photo taken in Japan.[25] Ujaku Akita noted that he went to one meeting with Kikutaro Fukuta and 45 others, saying that Martha 'was talking eagerly about Bahaism'.[26] On Sunday morning, Miss Tanaka, the woman journalist who had published the first photo of 'Abdu'l-Bahá in Japan, came and interviewed Martha, then printed a long article about Martha being a Bahá'í and her travels around the world for the Faith. Martha, being a journalist herself, took advantage of her occupation to interview Premier Okuma Shigenobu and to gather information on the upcoming coronation of Emperor Yoshihito and Empress Sadako. Her notable journalistic coup was being shown the clothing that would be worn at the coronation which, combined with her description of them and of the ceremonies that would occur, was published in America.[27]

At one point, Agnes and Martha went with Fukuta San to his very humble abode in a poor part of the city. As they entered, he said:

> 'Let us pray,' and handed me the *Hidden Words*. As we turned to leave, facing us on his blackboard were written these words. 'These days are swiftly passing and once gone can never return. O people awake! O people awake! Awake! Awake!' He read from the *Hidden Words* and Miss Root was greatly impressed with the way he read, and the wonderful part is how he comprehends the words of Bahá'u'lláh . . . The morning after Miss Root and I had visited his humble room, a card came to me from him, and this is what he wrote: 'Dear friends, I have never had more solemn pleasure than that of yesterday evening. Thank God! Yours, K. Fukuta.'[28]

At some point during Martha's brief visit, she and Agnes went to Karuizawa, a small town below Mt Asama, one of Japan's most active volcanoes. They went there to meet a friend of Roy Wilhelm's and stayed in the Mampei Hotel, but were only able to stay for two days because of Martha's schedule.[29]

Martha left Japan for Hawaii on 31 July. After her departure, Agnes wrote: 'I have not told the friends how I am missing my sister, Miss Root, since I returned to Tokyo. She left me on the 31st of July and Aug. 2 I went to the shore. She left a bright spot behind her and certainly sowed seeds for the Cause.'[30]

Two days after Martha left, Agnes spent three weeks at the coast reading and relaxing. On 20 August, she wrote that 'I have been by the sea shore for three weeks. There I could write and read and had the privilege of receiving many beautiful letters from my Japanese boy friends . . .' Fukuta San wrote to her that:

I am teaching my friends, but when I told them about Bahai at first they were surprised and asked, 'What, new religion in this country? Renewed? It is the same. How is the founder, has he done a miracle as Christ did?' . . . I pity them whatever they may say I should awaken them. A few friends listened to my remarks and, as they wished to know of this Cause . . . I am very happy even though I am opposed by my friends. <u>Nothing can steal away my spiritual happiness.</u>[31]

During Martha's visit, Agnes wrote to Mrs Dugdale Dunn in England, emphasizing her optimism and happiness in the face of the war then overwhelming Europe:

Baha-ollah prophesied of this war, but said after it would come the 'great peace'. We can see how the world is truly 'asleep' as the prophesies say it will be. Indeed, the Bahai belief is absolutely satisfying and joy giving, but to find it one must turn to God alone & put aside all preconceived ideas . . . I may stay for sometime enough in Japan.[32]

George and Ruth Augur arrive

George Augur returned to Japan accompanied by his wife, Ruth, on 12 October 1915. George had felt a strong urge to return and Ruth had agreed. When they arrived, they found a letter from 'Abdu'l-Bahá's secretary dated 8 August awaiting them. The letter, which had been sent to Honolulu and then forwarded to Tokyo, read:

Your beautiful petition, redolent with the spirit of humility and devotion and diffusing the Fragrances of love and affection was read this morning to the Beloved of our hearts as He was walking to and fro in the parlor of the Pilgrim Home. His face beamed with heavenly smile as He heard your name and the signs of satisfaction and pleasure appeared from His Godlike Countenance. As I read your simple and direct words He listened to them attentively thus grasping your sincerity and faithfulness in this glorious Cause and your zeal and enthusiasm to teach those who are yet uninformed with these heavenly principles. Then breaking His silence He said: 'Write to Dr. Augur to return to Japan as soon as the first opportunity offers itself to him. Great blessings will descend upon the soul who teaches the Cause in that country. Its people are endowed with great capability . . . The seed of this quality must be first planted in the ground of their hearts, but the Japanese are already endowed with this quality. Should five or six of them be thoroughly grounded in the teachings of this Cause and attracted with its fire, great results will be forthcoming.'[33]

So connected was George with the Master, that he had acted on the Master's suggestion before receiving the letter. The Japanese Bahá'í community now consisted of four, Agnes, George, Ruth and Fukuta San.

The coronation and a Hiroshima visit

Agnes was invited by a newspaper writer, Miss Kaichika, to go to Kyoto for the coronation of the Emperor in November. To attend, Agnes had to get a permit from the American Embassy and even then, she was restricted from attending the coronation itself. But the event was still fascinating:

Only nobles and embassy people could attend the ceremonies connected with the coronation. The nearest other people could get to it was to see the procession, when the Emperor passed to the palace and again when he left for Tokyo, when the priests carrying the case which contained the sacred treasures, accompanied the procession . . . it was most impressive, being in a large crowd of Japanese, opposite the palace where the electric lights and decorations were brilliant. Some time before the procession appeared, the Japanese people seated themselves on mats on the ground, and there was a dead silence only broken by an occasional whisper. As I was a foreigner, I was allowed to sit on a stool . . . when the Emperor passed . . .[34]

While waiting at the palace, Agnes met Miss Macadam, who was related to Jessie Turner, Agnes's co-author for the Hawaiian fruit cookbook. Agnes later joined her and her companions for a visit to the island of Miyagima. She wrote that her trip 'on the Inland Sea . . . was beyond my expectation and Miyagima was <u>heavenly</u>. We only spent a day and night there.'[35]

Returning from Miyagima, Agnes went to Hiroshima at the invitation of the Esperantists in Tokyo. On 9 December, she spoke to 60 students and teachers at the Normal School. She was worried before the talk because usually religion was a forbidden topic in Japan's public schools. She tried to think of what she could say, but 'when I stood before the eager faces of the students, it was by inspiration I spoke. After the hour was over, my Esperanto friend, Mr. Takahashi, came up to me and said, "You said you were not a lecturer, but you spoke eloquently like a trained lecturer."' Agnes passed around a copy of the newspaper from Palo Alto, California, in which the full issue had been given over to reporting 'Abdu'l-Bahá's visit and talks when He was there in 1912.[36]

Agnes wrote of her amazement at the teaching opportunities that she was given:

I am staying here in a Methodist Mission School, but I know that it is by the Will of God that I am here, for I did not seek it for myself. There are no foreigners here, with the exception of two teachers in the Normal School, except the missionaries, and no place for a foreigner to stay, so I went alone to a Japanese Inn. It was rather difficult and unpleasant for me being alone, but I kept saying to myself the words of 'Abdu'l-Bahá to me, '*the Ideal King is with those who are in the front ranks of the battlefield,*' and most truly are these words true. The next morning Mr. Takahashi came and took me out, and I told him I should like to visit a kindergarten which has become famous through the book *The Lady of the Decoration* by Frances

Little. The moment I met the kindergartener [teacher Miss Fulton], I felt I must give her the Message. We were asked to stay to lunch, and then, when they found where I was staying alone, they asked me to come and occupy their guest chamber. I felt a difference between the kindergartener and the others, I mean in a broad sense, and it seems she is not a missionary, only paid to teach the training school. She is from Teacher's College, New York. She has become very much interested in Esperanto and has asked me to talk to her training girls about it. The Esperantists invited her with me the other evening to a dinner they had, and we had a lovely time. One of the Japanese papers here has written a very good summary of my talk in the Normal School. It made me very happy to have one of the students (Mr. Maedo) come to see me and tell me that all the students had said I had been an inspiration to them. Could I ask anything more in the world![37]

Miss Fulton had been in Japan for 28 years.

One group of women decided they wanted to learn Esperanto, telling Agnes, 'You inspired us.' It was the first group of Japanese women to study the language. Agnes noted that 'I am so happy my visit here is not in vain, but <u>nothing</u> is in vain when we follow Divine guidance.'[38]

Agnes enjoyed Hiroshima. Everyday there, she went for walks or on rickshaw rides around the area. She wrote, 'It is especially lovely being on the Inland Sea and surrounded by mountains.'[39]

Back in Tokyo

Agnes left Hiroshima the day after Christmas and returned to Kyoto, intending to stay and teach the Faith there. But try as she might, she couldn't find a place to live that wasn't expensive. Finally, she gave up and returned to Tokyo, writing that:

I am back in Tokyo again, though why I am here I cannot say, only that it must be God's will . . . I was looking for the right place to stay, but found nothing when suddenly a great inspiration came to me to return to Tokyo, and the overwhelming feeling of joy which came to me is beyond anything I have felt in my life before. It has seemed to me that something very wonderful must be happening in the Bahá'í world.[40]

Arriving in Tokyo, Agnes was met by Vasily, Fukuta San, Kenichi Takao and Miss Tanaka. While Agnes had been gone, the Augurs had continued the Friday Bahá'í meetings. Pioneering in Japan had proved a challenge for George Augur. Financially, it was a struggle and his heart problems were not helped by the stress of living in a huge city like Tokyo. Ruth, on the other hand, delighted in being there. She told Agnes that 'sometimes in her little room she feels as though she would burst with joy'. In February, the Augurs moved to a tiny house near the coast in a town called Zushi, about 90 minutes from Tokyo by train. Why they went, Agnes didn't know, but George indicated that they felt guided to go there. They invited her to visit them anytime she wished, even though the house was so small that there was no guest bedroom.[41]

Agnes hosted the next Friday Bahá'í meeting alone, but had 15 people attend. She was commonly asked how many Japanese had become Bahá'ís and always answered that she was 'sowing seeds' and not trying to make converts. Of these meetings, Agnes wrote:

> Our weekly Friday Bahá'í meeting has just closed. Every week new souls come and hear the Message. One of those who came today said he had heard of the Bahá'í once before, through a journalist lady who spoke in the YMCA. I told him it was our Martha Root, and then read from a letter received this week from her, so we never know when the seed will spring up. There is a rich vineyard to work in here in Japan and many, many workers might be laboring in it. I do not seek the people out but they continually come to me. Four university students who cannot come on Friday afternoon, are coming on their only free afternoon, that is Saturday. As I am to be in Yokohama at an Esperanto meeting this Saturday, they came instead last night. Such earnest, nice young men and so eager to learn the Truth.[42]

The importance of Esperanto

Fukuta San put some Bahá'í books in the local library and soon thereafter a young Japanese man showed up at his door with one of the books in his hand, eager to know more. Then the photo of 'Abdu'l-Bahá was published again, this time in a magazine called the *New Tide*, along with an article on the Bahá'í Faith. It included the 12 Bahá'í principles written in both Japanese and Esperanto. The author was Ujaku Akita, and it was his third article on the Faith. Akita learned of Esperanto from Vasily and said that 'when he found Mr. Eroshenko who was blind doing three different things, he resolved that he would study Esperanto for three hours every day, and very soon after, to Mr. Eroshenko's astonishment, he began to write in Esperanto' in his articles.[43]

Esperanto had become one of Agnes's primary teaching tools. At an Esperanto meeting in Yokohama, Agnes spoke on the language using quotations from the words of 'Abdu'l-Bahá that Vasily had translated for her. She was the only woman and the only foreigner, other than Vasily, at the meeting. Vasily gave his own talk on 'Universal Love' from 'Abdu'l-Bahá's words in *Paris Talks*. Later, Agnes was invited to another Esperanto meeting, this one in Tokyo, on the' Universal Principles' of Bahá'u'lláh. Her talk was made with quotations from 'Abdu'l-Bahá and Bahá'u'lláh translated into Esperanto. The publication *Japana Esperantisto* printed some of the *Hidden Words* in one issue. A Brooklyn Bahá'í even sent Agnes a contribution toward the printing of the *Hidden Words*. The Esperantists were sowing Bahá'í seeds in Japan.

Agnes received a long letter from an English Esperantist dated 21 March 1916, who wrote that he had come across a translation of some of Bahá'u'lláh's writing by Vasily and Agnes. The man was Dr John Esslemont, who had become a Bahá'í a little over a year before and then began studying Esperanto. He wrote that:

> I first heard of the Bahai Movement in Dec. 1914 from a Quaker lady. From the first it appealed to me more strongly than anything else had ever done . . . Bahaism seemed to me to sum up what was good and true . . . and to be a glorious revelation of which . . . other teachings were but broken and partial reflections . . . Six or seven months ago I took up the study of Esperanto and find that very attractive and inspiring. I am therefore delighted, as you may imagine, to hear of the good progress both the Bahai and the Esperanto Movements are making in Japan . . .
>
> At the feast of Narooz held in London yesterday, I spoke about Esperanto and told the friends about your letters . . . I hope that before long we shall have good Esperanto translations of all the most important works of Baha'o'llah and Abdul-Baha. Then, surely, Bahais all over the world will hasten to learn Esperanto and all will

be able to worship God and communicate with each other in one language . . .[44]

Esslemont would later write the immortal book, *Bahá'u'lláh and the New Era* with the encouragement and guidance of both 'Abdu'l-Bahá and Shoghi Effendi.

The Japanese Bahá'í community celebrated Naw-Rúz on 21 March. In addition to being a Bahá'í celebration, the day was also a special Japanese holiday. At the meeting, Agnes noted that there were four nationalities represented: Japanese, Russian, Indian and American. One of the group corrected her saying, '"No there are five nationalities." This puzzled me, then he explained that he meant that 'Abdu'l-Baha was present.'[45]

In an April 1916 letter to her brother, Arthur, Agnes described the Japanese school system:

In Japan the school year ends in March and begins anew in April. I think it an excellent idea. The students have their examinations while they are fresh before it becomes hot. They say the Japanese students only study for examinations. There is great competition and everything depends on examinations. A student who has just taken an examination to the Higher Commercial school here, told me there were 2,200 applicants while only 110 would be admitted. With the students in Tokyo it seems to be all study and no play.[46]

A Japanese contribution for the Mashriqu'l-Adhkár in Chicago

Agnes was very interested in the Mashriqu'l-Adhkár that was being built in Chicago. In a letter to the Bahá'í friends, she described what she had been inspired to do and the reaction of the community:

A few weeks ago it came to me very strongly that Japan should have a share in the building of the Mashriqu'l-Adhkár. I told my thoughts to the students and said that though I knew not one of them had a cent more than they needed in getting their education, yet through God all things were possible, and if in our hearts we desired to help the way would open for us. Shortly after this Fukuta San came to me and said that he liked the idea of giving to the

Ma<u>sh</u>riqu'l-A<u>dh</u>kár and that he had one dollar which he had saved from text books which he wished to give to the fund. This touched me deeply, for as you know, Fukuta San has nothing of his own, but receives a small monthly allowance for his schooling. The second to offer a contribution was Mr. Eroshenko. Last spring he gave a talk on Russian music with musical illustrations. He had hoped to make some money from this to help himself, but after the expenses were paid, there was neither profit nor loss. Last week he went to another city and gave the same lecture in Japanese, hoping to make a financial success this time, but he returned with but 50 cents profit, and he told me that he wished to give this to the Ma<u>sh</u>riqu'l-A<u>dh</u>kár fund. So this is the beginning of the first contribution which will come from the land of Japan . . .

Last night at a large public meeting for the propaganda of Esperanto, Mr. Eroshenko spoke. He took for his subject, 'Nur estas Tempo por Semi sed ne por Rikolti'. These are the words of 'Abdu'l-Bahá, 'Now is the time to sow but not the time to reap.' He told about the Ma<u>sh</u>riqu'l-A<u>dh</u>kár, that at this very time in Chicago the Convention for building the Temple was being held, that the Temple was to be for all nations and religions, that many of the nations had contributed to the fund and that it was hoped Japan also would have a part in this.[47]

The Japanese daily, *Nichi Nichi,* published an article she gave them about the Temple.

Daiun Inouye, a Buddhist priest

In the spring of 1916, Agnes received a letter from an English Bahá'í, Dorothy Hodgson, telling her that she and some French friends were travelling to Japan and would be in Kobe. A friend in Japan suggested that Agnes take them to a Buddhist festival near Kobe. To Agnes, 'It was the Hand of God' because it inspired her to do so, although she was not aware of the reason for it. When they arrived at the festival, only a single person there could speak English, a young Buddhist priest named Daiun Inouye. Daiun accompanied them to Mt. Rokko, the high point in the mountains north of Kobe from which they had a very good view of the city. Agnes gave Daiun the only Bahá'í publication she had in Japanese, a pamphlet written by George Augur. When Daiun read it, his face lit up and he exclaimed, 'This is what I believe!'[48]

After returning to Tokyo, Agnes and Daiun corresponded and she sent him various writings by 'Abdu'l-Bahá. He then translated those of the Master's talks that were about peace and began publishing them in a Buddhist paper called *Chugai Nippo*. He wrote to Agnes that he 'would like to come out boldly for the Bahá'í Cause', but he was also worried, writing, 'Though it would be glorious for my religious life as a child of truth, yet I fear for my family's distress.'[49] Though Daiun did not officially become a Bahá'í for another 22 years, he became a very important part of the Bahá'í community because of his translation work, including Esslemont's *Bahá'u'lláh and the New Era*. That story will come later in this book.

Vasily leaves Japan

Vasily left Japan to go to Siam (Thailand) in the summer of 1916. Agnes gave him a copy of *Some Answered Questions*, which she had read to him, and he was very enthusiastic about having it. His journey to Siam apparently was quite difficult, with Agnes writing that he 'passed through some trying experiences on his way, but was assisted by the Unseen Hand'. In Siam, he met Russian Jews and often visited two particular families. He told two girls in the families about the Bahá'í Faith. In a letter to Agnes, he wrote, 'I told them of the Bahá'í. They listened with great interest. One of them excitedly and wholly unexpectedly asked me, "Tell me is Christ on this earth?" I replied, "Bahá'ís say that he is." "But you personally, do you believe?" I felt that she wished Christ might be here, but I replied, "I study the question." Now she is reading *Some Answered Questions*.'[50]

Vasily had many dreams in which 'Abdu'l-Bahá guided him, but he was never able to make the final decision to accept Bahá'u'lláh, 'Although he had love for the Bahá'í teachings, he did not experience the great joy which comes through acknowledging and turning to the Center of the Manifest Light.' In the end, Vasily, who greatly promoted the Faith in Japan and was of immense help to Agnes in her efforts to spread the Faith, became a Communist and 'lost the inspiration he received through the Bahá'í teachings'.[51]

At one point, a group of Agnes's friends from another city came to

Tokyo, but 'did not, however, strengthen the Cause of God'. Agnes did not expand on this except to quote a portion of a Tablet of 'Abdu'l-Bahá addressed to the Honolulu Bahá'ís and sent to her by Dorothy Hodgson:

> If ever anyone desires secretly to shake their faith in the Covenant and Testament, they must remain firm and know of a certainly that that person has evil intentions. They must listen to the words of whomsoever calls the people to the Covenant, and they must know that if anyone desires to shake their faith, that he is a stranger to Bahá'u'lláh, because such a person thinks of sowing seeds of division in the Cause of God, aiming to scatter the Bahá'í unity so that meanwhile he may propagate his own selfish desires.[52]

Tokujiro Torii

Agnes had a busy summer in 1916. In August, she went to Matsushima, about 200 miles (322 km) north of Tokyo, for 19 days. During her stay, a lady in the next room had become ill and Agnes felt impelled to visit her with a photo of 'Abdu'l-Bahá. When Agnes showed the woman the photo, she exclaimed, 'It is 'Abdu'l-Bahá!' Her father and husband were both Persian and her husband a Muslim. The woman had been brought up as a Catholic and did not see eye to eye with her husband on religious matters. After Agnes explained some aspects of the Bahá'í Faith, the woman immediately wrote to her husband to tell him about it. Then, an Englishman who lived on the western side of Japan, wrote to her and described a strange experience he had had:

> [The] Englishman, who was a teacher, heard of the Bahá'í Cause through reading the weekly publication *Far East,* which had published several articles about the Bahá'í Faith. He wrote to me and asked some questions which I was happy to answer. In his home on Sunday mornings he held a service. One day in July, 1916, a letter came to me from the first Japanese to whom I had earnestly talked of the Bahá'í Cause when I was a young Bahá'í in Green Acre, Maine, in the summer of 1901. He was then studying at a Theological school in Cambridge, Massachusetts. Afterwards I corresponded with him for a while, until it became clear his mind was closed to

the Light of the New Day. [The Englishman] wrote: 'I wonder if you ever remember a little Japanese whom you met at Green Acre, Maine, about a dozen years ago. After the service this morning, Mr [the Japanese friend], mentioned how interesting were the teachings of Bahá and this at once reminded me of you, so I told him I used to hear the teaching of that great prophet through a lady in America, whose name is Miss Agnes Alexander. Then he produced your letter to my surprise and my delight.'[53]

While in Matsushima, Agnes received a letter from Tokujiro Torii. This young man, 23 years old and blind, had been a student at the Government School for the Blind and had been introduced to both Esperanto and the Bahá'í Faith by Vasily. Tokujiro graduated from the school in the spring of 1916, married a woman named Ito from his village of Ejiri, in Shizuoka province, between Tokyo and Nagoya, and began teaching in a small school for the blind. Before he left for Siam, Vasily asked Agnes to go to Ejiri and help Tokujiro with Esperanto. Agnes at this point could read and write Esperanto Braille and she began corresponding with him in that language. Vasily had given Tokujiro some information about the Bahá'í Faith and, since Tokujiro edited a journal for the blind, he asked Agnes to help him write an article about the Faith for the journal because 'he felt the Bahá'í Cause would give light to the spirit of the blind people'. He asked Agnes to 'please guide me'.[54]

In his letter, Tokujiro asked if Agnes could visit him the last week in August, because a Mr Nakamura, a blind teacher who had lived in England for two years and who spoke English, would be there and could translate. Ejiri was halfway between Tokyo and Nagoya, so Agnes returned to Tokyo where, she wrote, it was

> exceedingly hot and I became ill. It seemed as though I could not be of help to anyone and even dear Mrs. Augur said she thought 'Abdu'l-Bahá would not want me to go. Perhaps it was God's purpose to empty me of everything that He might use me. When the morning came to go, putting some Bahá'í literature in my suitcase, I went to the train. After a ride of five hours, Mr. and Mrs. Torii and Mr. Nakamura met me at Ejiri and guided me to a Japanese Inn. As Ejiri was a town where no foreigners lived, it was the only place for me to stay. We had a visit and then they left me. Throughout that night

there was geisha music and noise in the Inn and I spent a sleepless night. In the morning when the dear friends came I read them from the book *Ten Days in the Light of Akka* and other Bahá'í writings. Mr. Nakamura was then teaching in a Christian school for the blind in Tokyo, and was the editor of the only religious journal for the blind in Japan. He asked me if I would write about the Bahá'í Revelation for the blind women of Japan. He said I might be unlimited in the length of my article as nothing had yet been done for the blind women, whom he said had double darkness, that is, of spirit and body. He was devoting his time to try and better the condition of the blind in his land.[55]

Agnes spent several days with Tokujiro reading the Bahá'í Writings and explaining what they meant. One day, he suddenly told her that he wanted to write to 'Abdu'l-Bahá about accepting the Faith, but wanted to wait for inspiration. After Agnes left, Tokujiro and his wife walked through the fields until a 'great light and happiness' came to him. On 7 September, Agnes received his letter, all written in Esperanto Braille. In an article in *The Bahá'í World*, Tokujiro wrote about the experience:

That radiant morning is not forgotten! It was on a day in August, 1916, that I found the eternal Light which I had sought and sought with a longing heart for a long time. At that time I was living in a town by the seashore where the beautiful Mount Fuji could be seen on the horizon. There came a messenger of the Kingdom of Abhá and lifted up the veil of my soul. She taught me this simple truth that, 'Possess a pure, kindly and radiant heart, that thine may be a sovereignty, heavenly, ancient, imperishable and everlasting.' She brought new light into my heart, a new thought into my mind and a new ideal into my life. Every word she spoke to me was wonderful and luminous. It dispelled the darkness from my soul, brought fragrances to my heart like the breeze from the green fields, and made my inner sight keener and fresher than ever. This messenger who made me see the Sun of Reality was indeed Miss Agnes B. Alexander, my beloved spiritual mother from Tokyo. Since that bright morning of my spirit, everything in the world has changed for me; the world into a beautiful garden; strangers into brothers and sisters; sorrows into joy; despairs into hopes and even evil into good. Everything stood in its beauty and perfection in the hands of the creator. I can never, never forget that blessed day . . .'[56]

Tokujiro had become blind at the age of three. He learned English by listening at an English class. Since his wife could not read English, she would spell out the words to him. Back in Tokyo, Agnes wrote the article Mr Nakamura wanted for the blind Japanese women and he translated it into Japanese Braille. The article was printed in both Japanese and Braille. Several blind women wrote to Agnes about the solace they found in the Bahá'í Writings.[57]

Money to publish these materials came from Harry Randall. Much later, when Agnes wrote to Harry's daughter Bahiyyih Ford, Agnes noted that 'I met your father the second time in Greenacre in 1918. When I was in Japan, he was a great help and it was through him that literature was published in Japanese in 1916 and 1917 . . . Blessed his soul! He sent me in all $200, which was used in that way.'[58]

Back in Tokyo

In September 1916, Agnes visited the Japan Women's College with a letter of introduction to President Jinzo Naruse. He had met 'Abdu'l-Bahá in London in 1912 and when Agnes mentioned the Faith to him, he invited her to speak in the College's chapel. On 23 September, Agnes spoke about the Bahá'í teachings and especially those concerning women. A teacher who had been educated in America translated for her. Afterwards, President Naruse showed her a book he had, titled *The Reconciliation of Race and Religions* by Prof. T. K. Cheyne of Oxford. The President was spiritually attracted to the Faith, and died not long after Agnes's visit.[59]

After being in Japan for almost two years, Agnes finally moved into a Japanese house of her own on 1 October. In addition to being much more comfortable for her, when Fukuta San's financial help for school was stopped he was able to move into the house as well. On the first Friday in her new home, she held her usual Bahá'í meeting which was attended by three students from Waseda University and Ujaku Akita.[60]

Kenzo Torikai, a Japanese Bahá'í from Seattle, Washington, was in Japan on his first visit in 12 years. He was the first Japanese to return to Japan after finding the Faith elsewhere. Agnes gathered her group and had a photograph taken with Kenzo. It included George Augur, Ujaku, Kenzo, Fukuta San and Agnes. Kenzo was in Japan until November and spent most of his time with his relatives in the western area. Though religious teaching was forbidden in schools, he was still able to present the basic Bahá'í principles in many schools in his home province. [61]

On 10 November, the Bahá'í meeting at Agnes's house was conducted by Fukuta San in Japanese and, with Ujaku and some of the students, they organized a group to begin translating Bahá'í literature into Japanese. Later in November, Agnes twice went to Ejiri to visit Tokujiro Torii and his wife. Afterwards, she wrote: 'From being with him and his wife, my heart was filled with great love and peace and it is still with me.' Twelve from her group in Tokyo celebrated the Day of the Covenant on 26 November. [62]

At some point during her time in Tokyo, a Japanese minister of the Unitarian Church asked Agnes to come and give the Bahá'í message. She noted that it was the only church to do so. [63]

Ichi Kamichika: A woman imprisoned

Agnes had met Ichi Kamichika in the spring of 1915. Ichi was the woman reporter who first published 'Abdu'l-Bahá's photograph in a Japanese newspaper. She came to a few Bahá'í meetings and met Martha Root when she visited Japan. In the autumn of 1916, Ichi was imprisoned for unknown reasons, and she and Agnes began corresponding. In a letter written on 24 November, Ichi wrote:

> Much obliged I am for your kind letter as well as for your love which does not change even for my horrible condition. Thanks to sympathy of all the friends, I am passing my prison days well and comfortably, please do not worry yourself imagining I am miserable and distressed . . . I am so grateful for your friendship shown these days and for what I owe you I am intending to do my best even in here. [64]

Agnes sent Ichi the booklet *From the Greatest Prisoner to His Prison Friends* by Soraya (Isabel) Fraser-Chamberlain. The book, published in 1916, is about 'Abdu'l-Bahá's imprisonment in 'Akká. In spite of hearing that she would only be allowed a few minutes through a small opening,

Agnes went to the prison with hopes of seeing Ichi. When she met the officer in charge and gave him her card he immediately recognized her, saying, 'I know you, I have read your letters to Miss Kamichika and every word of the booklet *From the Greatest Prisoner to His Prison Friends* which you sent to her. You may see her at any time.' Agnes was taken to an office room and was able to speak openly with Ichi in the presence of an officer. Agnes was at that time writing an article about the Bahá'í teachings on women, which she gave to Ichi, hoping that she could translate it. In a letter to Agnes, Ichi wrote:

> . . . today I had a happy chance to talk to the head officer of this prison and asked for the permission to do your translation and was allowed. I feel so happy, because you helped me in so many ways but I did nothing to please you, but now I can do it even though that is a small work and you really mean, not for yourself, but for me. Freedom and comforts of life seem so precious when one thinks of them in a prison. But I also know very well that this place was the best place for me. Prison will make me very meditative and thoughtful and will work a great deal for my growth. [65]

The translated article was titled *A Message of Love to the Women of Japan*; it became the second publication of the Bahá'í teachings in Japan and was distributed among Japanese women.

Two Tablets from the Master

Tokujiro Torii and his wife visited Agnes during the New Year holidays. He had completed his translation of the *Hidden Words* into Braille and three blind men sat with him reading his *Kasitaj Vortoj* (Hidden Words in Esperanto) with their fingers. This Braille version of the *Hidden Words* had been given to the blind Esperantists of the world, and in January 1917, Tokujiro received a letter from a blind Danish Esperantist saying that she was 'greatly interested' in the *Hidden Words* and requesting more copies. Tokujiro said that 'he felt the blind people can understand the spirit better than the sighted. When more Bahá'í literature is translated into Esperanto, then it can be printed in Braille for the blind, and in this way the blind people all over the world can be reached with the Message . . . One reason Mr. Torii says the blind can unite easier than the sighted is because they all have the same writing, that is Braille.'[66]

On 7 February 1917, Agnes received the first of two Tablets from 'Abdu'l-Bahá that year. It had been sent on 27 October 1916:

O thou heavenly daughter!

Thy letter through Mr. Hannen was received from Japan; likewise the letters of Mr. Fukuta. The contents of both letters imparted exceeding joy, for each word was an eloquent tongue explaining the wonders of the Love of God and elucidating the story of the attraction of the heart with the breaths of the holy spirit.

Praise be to God, that thou hast become assisted to promulgate the word of God in Japan. Ere long this circle in Japan will be enlarged, obtaining heavenly blessings.

God says in the glorious Koran: 'A seed, growing out of it seven ears and every ear containing one hundred kernels, and God is able to double this for whomsoever He willeth.' This verse means this: Whenever the Word of Truth is proclaimed, it is like unto a seed, which sown in a pure soil brings forth seven ears and every ear produces one hundred kernels and God says again that for whomsoever he desireth, he will double this number, that is: He will make the seven hundred kernels fourteen hundred.

Now I hope that thy call in Japan may be like unto that seed, so that it may obtain heavenly blessing and benediction and the souls be educated and taught the oneness and singleness of God, the truthfulness of the prophets and the usefulness of the Divine Teachings.[67]

After the first Tablet arrived, Agnes was overjoyed: 'I cannot tell you of the wonderful peace and joy that has overflowed in my heart ever since. This is the first time since receiving word from 'Abdu'l-Bahá to come to Japan, that any message from Him has reached here, and Fukuta San is blessed by being the first Japanese in his own land to receive words, "from that Pen whose greatness, glory and splendour will shine down the ages".'[68]

Ten days later, on 17 February, Agnes received a second Tablet. It had been written three days after the first:

O thou daughter of the kingdom!

Thy letter dated July 15, 1916, was received. Its contents indicated that thou hast organized a meeting in Japan. Consider thou what a great favor God hast bestowed that such spiritual meetings are being held in Tokyo and such heavenly gifts are being distributed.

God says in the Koran: 'The example of the people of faith is like unto a field which obtains freshness and verdancy from the rain descending from the clouds, attaining to full fruition and finding the blessings of the Kingdom! There is no doubt that day by day it will grow and develop and in the end the ears of the sheaves will be laden with God's benediction, bringing forth one hundred fold.'

Now, ye are the fields of the plain of Reality and are under the protection of the educative rays of the Sun of Truth. At every moment ye obtain a new vitality from the rain of divine bestowals and ere long ye will produce full grown seeds which are blessed by the care and attention of the Divine Farmer. There is no doubt that such will be the end.

Convey on my behalf the utmost longing and greeting to the friends residing in Tokyo as well as the recently arrived travellers and say to them: All the individuals of humanity are farmers. Every soul sows a certain kind of seed, but at the season of the harvest there will be gathered no result, except the seeds which are sown by the believers of God. That alone will obtain heavenly blessings. Reflect that His Holiness Christ and His Holiness Mohammed scattered such holy seeds that the fruits of which are being gathered until now; but all the other farmers were finally doomed to regret and disappointment.

Upon ye be greeting and praise.[69]

Agnes's seed sowing in Japanese society had been primarily through students, Esperanto and the blind. In a letter to the *Star of the West*, she noted that there were three blind people at her recent Friday Bahá'í meeting and Tokujiro was energetically working for the Faith.

Agnes had tried to publicize the Faith in every way she could, including sending letters to various publications. One, the English language *Japan Advertiser*, had printed many letters she had sent, so:

One day I felt the urge to take something I had written for the Bahá'í Anniversary Day, May twenty-third, of the history of the Cause, to the editor of the *Japan Advertiser*. By nature I was extremely timid, and I often told the friends it was a proof of the power in the Bahá'í Cause that I come alone to Japan and live and stand alone. Because of an experience I had once had, it took courage for me to go to see the editor. This undoubtedly was a test to make me braver. As I ascended the stairs to the office I repeated the Greatest Name. To my great surprise when I met the editor he arose from his chair and taking my hand said, 'I know you.' Afterwards I realized he must have sympathized with the letters I had sent to the paper with my card. Without any hesitation he accepted my article and we had a friendly talk about spiritual things. In obeying His guidance I witnessed His confirmations! [70]

On 22 February 1917, Agnes wrote to her brother Arthur, describing some of her activities and her home:

I have been going to Yokohama every week lately. It means a day each time, in order to get some sewing done. I always go to my friend Miss Tartar's to lunch & she helps me . . . It has been quite cold the last two days but I have learnt to dress warmly and so keep comfortable in my house. The rug from home is a comfort and quite suited to a house where one does not wear shoes. I certainly enjoy this house . . . One can open the sides of the house and live in a lanai if one wishes. If the sun shines at noon, I often have lunch in the open sunshine though in the morning it is about 30°. I enjoy the quietness and having all the room I want, as I have four rooms for my own use besides numberless cupboards. [71]

Though George Augur lived two hours away from Agnes, he still came to her house every Friday for the Bahá'í meetings. She greatly appreciated his presence because he was 'a great help, as his knowledge of the Teachings is so great. In answer to almost any question, he can quote the exact words of 'Abdu'l-Bahá or Bahá'u'lláh.' [72]

Agnes celebrated her third Naw-Rúz in Japan on 21 March. A dozen young men participated and afterwards Agnes wrote, 'Now that the young men are established in the Cause, the "other wing" must be developed before the bird can fly. Until this is done, farther progress cannot be great in this land.' [73]

Yuri Mochizuki: The first Japanese woman to accept the Faith

During this time, Agnes began corresponding with a young Japanese woman, an orphan, who had read a magazine article about the Faith by Ujaku Akita and was 'hungering for the Water of Life'. Since the woman did not know English, Fukuta San translated the letters back and forth and Agnes sent her some of the things that had been translated into Japanese, including *A Message of Love to the Women of Japan*. One day, the young woman sent Agnes a letter describing how alone she was and she was striving to care for herself by writing and asking if she could come and live with her, noting 'that she was willing to do any humble work in order to live a noble life'. Agnes immediately told her to come, prompting one of her friends to exclaim, 'You do not know her.' Agnes responded, 'She is God's child.' So, on a July day, Yuri Mochizuki, 'a pretty girl of about sixteen years' arrived at her door. Since Yuri spoke no English, Agnes greeted her by 'putting my arms around her we conversed in the language of love'.[74]

Yuri quickly began to study English and deepened her interest in the Faith until she accepted Bahá'u'lláh and on 26 July 1917, Yuri wrote the first letter from a Japanese woman to the Master:

To the Holy Servant of God!

O the Inexhaustible Fountain of Love and Mercy! O the Teacher who gives new life and strength to the weak lambs in the world! I feel very happy and honored having been born in a secluded village in a corner of the Orient, Japan, to be able to write a letter to the Divine Teacher. May you be the Light which illumines and consoles the troubles of my heart for ever and ever! I pray you that I may be filled with your teachings so thoroughly that even a little motion of my poor flesh and spirit will constantly praise your name.

My thought is your teaching; my beauty is your teaching; my courage is your teaching and my love is your teaching.

Miss Alexander, who came here and worked for the first time in this Cause, is now going back to her country. We little Japanese Bahá'ís feel ourselves just like stray sheep that have lost their shepherd who fondled them so tenderly, but we accept it without any complaint at all if it is His Will. When we are left alone we must work in the teaching of God, praying for His help, so that He may give us great strength. Even here in Japan there are many who are thirsting, and we will let them know of you, so that they can be refreshed and regain their lives from the Sweet Fountain of the Truth.

I am studying under the care of our Bahá'í mother, Miss Alexander, having your Name and picture upon my writing desk, whose merciful eyes are watching over me, and I can gain from them always life and strength.

Oh my Teacher! Let me cry in thanks, you are my whole life![75]

Unexpectedly Agnes had received an urgent cable to return to Honolulu. Since Yuri was living with her and she had to give up her house, Tokujiro Torii and his wife, Ito, said that they would take Yuri in. Tokujiro and his wife were moving to Tokyo and Agnes and George Augur arranged to pay the rent for a house for them and Yuri so that the Friday Bahá'í meetings could continue. Agnes also promised to provide funds so that Yuri could go to school.[76]

Agnes left from Yokohama on 27 July 1917. Tokujiro Torii and Ito rode the train for five hours to see her off. Yuri was also there at the dock and then went to Ejiri to stay with the Toriis until they completed their move to Tokyo. Ito Torii brought one of the first copies of the Braille book done by her husband, *Seek and It Shall Be Given You,* for Agnes to take with her.[77] She left behind three strong Bahá'ís and many people attracted to the Faith.

In the December issue of *Everywoman* magazine, Agnes wrote about her experiences of teaching the Faith of Bahá'u'lláh in Japan:

The young people of Japan, like those of other lands, are searching for some new truth suited to this age and time. The religion of their parents has become superstition, which no longer touches their hearts. They, perhaps more than any other people, are free from prejudices, having had in their country Shintoism, Buddhism and Christianity. But the Christianity which does not conform with science has no hold on them, as science has come fresh and new to them, and they wish to prove everything through its lights. Through the revelation of Bahaollah they learn that science and religion must accord, and this is acceptable to them.

It was my privilege to meet in Japan these eager young souls and to tell them of the Message of Unity which is found in the Bahai teachings. Among those who are awakened in that land to the call of the New Spirit, is a young blind man. Deprived of physical sight, this young man has clearer insight into the spiritual realm, and his great desire is to help the blind people of his own land, who are suffering in double darkness of spirit and body. This young man has translated from the English into Japanese braille, the teachings of Abdul Baha and Bahaollah, and these are published and circulated among the blind of Japan, and they are finding light and joy through these life-giving teachings.

This young blind man, whose name is Tokujiro Torii, says that since he has found the light, 'every prejudice in my heart is forgotten. Truly, there is no country, no nation, no race in my heart, everything is equal in the presence of the Almighty, indeed, "the heart is the real country."' In a message to the friends in America, he has sent the following words:

'Dear friends, we hope you will consider what is coming out of the empire which most of you regard as the warlike nation in the Orient – the new spirit of us, the spirit of new Japan to come, is in reality being filled with new, fresh ideas of faith, love and peace; although the government of Japan may seem inclined to militarism, yet, you must not overlook the fact that to say the least, there is an unquenchable fire for peace at the bottom of your young men's hearts. Our free spirit is not fettered by material civilization. We are as yet small in numbers but are firmly convinced that God is the helper of the weaker. O friends, would you not love Japan newly appearing, at whose heart, though unseen now, is streaming the pure spirit of Bahai? Truly, the Bahai spirit is the spirit of this age. Truly the Lord is showering boundless mercy upon us, the Japanese, too. We wish you to understand our sincere hope and final desire.'

Mr. Torii is also working to spread Esperanto, which is a branch on the tree of brotherhood, among the blind of Japan. Among the sightless there are many Esperantists, and it was my pleasure often to meet with them and to feel the touch of their spirit of brotherhood.[78]

For the next two years, until Agnes returned to Japan, the Toriis kept up the Friday Bahá'í meetings.

8

TWO YEARS IN AMERICA

1917–1919

As early as January 1917, the feeling had begun to grow in Agnes that she should visit her sister Mary in California. Then in February, Agnes had gotten a feeling that she should return to Hawaii for a visit as well, and she went so far as to pack a bag in readiness. From that point, she waited for guidance. On 16 July, one of her brothers sent her an urgent cable and she quickly made the arrangements. She was on a ship and headed for Honolulu on 27 July. It was a bittersweet departure. She wrote, 'I had perfect assurance that it was God's will that I should come, and it was really best for the Japanese Bahais, for now they must depend upon themselves more.'[1]

Agnes arrived in Honolulu on 21 August and was interviewed by the *Hawaii Advertiser*. She said that she was surprised at how clean Honolulu looked and she gave credit to a group of women called the Outdoor Circle. The article said that Agnes had returned from a nearly four-year trip around the world, describing her adventures through Europe as war befell that continent, her ship's hide and seek with the German cruiser *Emden* and her two years in Japan.[2] The Hawaiian Mission Children's Society reported that Agnes had 'returned from Japan full of enthusiasm regarding the "signs of the times".'[3]

When Agnes reconnected with the Honolulu Bahá'í community, she noted that 'the Cause does not make an active showing at this time'.[4] Agnes did not waste any time and quickly submitted two articles to *The Friend*, which styled itself the 'Oldest Newspaper West of the Rockies'. The first article, published in the October 1917 issue under the title of 'The New Education – A Universal Language', described the necessity of a common language and promoted Esperanto.[5] The second article was published in the January 1918 issue, 'Dawning of the New Age', was about how the rebirth of religion was at hand.[6]

Agnes never does explain about the 'urgent' cable from her brother and does not even say which brother sent it. Nothing in her letters gives any hints of any particular problems within the family either in Hawaii or in America. In any case, she spent less than a month in Hawaii and left Honolulu on 13 September, arriving in San Francisco on the 25th.

California

Agnes spent the next several months in California, probably spending time with her sister Mary and brother Willie, who both lived in the San Francisco area. The only correspondence we have about her family activities during this time is a December letter to her brother Arthur, who still lived in Honolulu, about the family home, Maluhia. Apparently, the people renting the house were leaving and Arthur wanted to sell it. Agnes wrote to say that as a last resort, the house could be sold, but 'I want, as you know, to keep the back part of the yard for I will not always live in a trunk and there is the spot I would like to have a house among the trees planted by papa and mama and as papa said he believed we could get an entrance to Wilder Ave. by exchanging with the Thomas' a piece for the back yard and a street entrance . . .'[7]

Agnes noted that the family in California were going to have a quiet Christmas and forgo the giving of gifts. She wrote that 'Annie is home for the holiday and brought about a dozen turkeys with her for Xmas dinner. Aunt Annie and Uncle Charley [Dickey] go by this steamer as they expect to sell their Nuuanu house.'[8]

On the last day of the year, Agnes wrote a remembrance of Lua Getsinger to commemorate her passing a year and a half previously:

To the One Who 'loved her Lord.'

She has ascended to the Throne of Majesty and Power and her life has become a 'crown of roses'. In His Path she shed her precious blood and attained unto the station of martyrdom. From the highest horizon she shines as a brilliant star, radiating brightness and giving divine utterance to her weak sisters of the world. She has become a glorified saint in His Presence.

In the mortal life she endured all trials, even unto death. Sick, hungry and alone she spread the Fragrances of God without money or price.

Through His Divine Favor she was chosen to become the spiritual mother of a nation, the first martyr in His service to yield up her life for America. Eight years before the passing of her spirit, she wrote and sealed letters to her four most beloved sisters, to be opened after her death, offering her chance of heaven as a ransom for their sakes, that if she should be released from mortal life first, and ascend unto the Presence of Baha'u'llah, she would ask of her Lord to close to her forever the gates of heaven and send her into the depths of hell, a ransom for them, that they might attain unto His greatest blessings, while she would forever dwell in the depths of darkness.

Oh America! Oh America! Where are the Baha'is? Do we know and love our Lord? We who refused the Bounty, she whom the Lord of the world sent forth as a 'guide' unto us. She the pure and spotless in His sight!

His precious Gift will never be known. It is forever sealed from our eyes. Oh, how can we His children of America, who have received from His Boundless Favor, how can we atone for this our loss? Will He, our Beloved accept from us the sacrifice of our lives at His Threshold, that His Gift to us may become revealed? If we cease to dispute and join in one glorious unity, playing on One instrument the melodies of the Kingdom, will He, our Lord, accept this of us and forgive our most terrible sin and short sightedness? Will He in His Great Compassion and love blot out our transgression?

Oh my Lord, oh my Lord accept at Thy Throne of Majesty this Thy maid servant, that she may spread Thy Truth to the women of other lands in the name and love of the sanctified soul, Lua Getsinger.

Dec. 31, 1917 Piedmont, California.[9]

Agnes reconnected with Ella Cooper and Louise Bosch, two of her closest friends and correspondents. She had last seen Louise at Green Acre in 1901, on her return from that life-changing trip to Italy. Agnes wrote, 'The love which was ignited between us in Green Acre in 1901, was renewed and I was privileged to spend many days in spiritual refreshment in their home in Geyserville.' Louise was also very interested in

Japan and before Agnes left Japan, had begun corresponding with one of Agnes's Japanese students, T. Tachibana. In March 1918, Agnes sent out a plea to the Bahá'ís about T. Tachibana and Japan's first female Bahá'í, Yuri:

> May I ask the especial prayers of the friends for a young Japanese who is eagerly seeking true religion, T. Tachibana. When he heard of my departure from Japan he wrote a beseeching letter ending, 'Oh how I long for the jewel which you will send me before my tiny but bright little light goes out.' In his last letter he writes, 'My elder sister, please pray for me and assist me to touch the Holy Spirit in which you are being guided.' The letter ends, 'From your poor, thirsting for true religion and feeling loneliness friend.' . . . When it is His Time I expect to return to Japan and with the little sister Yuri Mochizuki, to work especially for the women, for without the two wings, the bird cannot fly. Some of the friends already know of this sister whom God guided to me before I left Japan. At that time she could not speak or understand a word of English, but her heart was touched by the New Spirit which is pervading the world. In the little Bahá'í home in Tokyo, the flower of her soul has blossomed forth, and through His Divine aid, she can now write a beautiful English letter, and if God so wills, she may become the spiritual mother to the women of Japan. She is an orphan in the world, but 'Abdu'l-Bahá has consoled her heart and brought her peace.[10]

In late 1917, Ella Cooper and Agnes sent a record of 'Abdu'l-Bahá's voice to the Japanese Bahá'ís. It arrived, but not in one piece. On 9 January 1918, Tokujiro Torii wrote that:

> The voice record of 'Abdu'l-Bahá has just arrived today and a thousand thanks to you and Mrs. Cooper, but, alas, dear sister, it has been broken into just two pieces! O what a sorrow to my heart! I will try to have it mended, but I don't know that it can be done. By this matter, however, I have been taught a good lesson that it is a great error for a man to try to seek the spiritual among the material. We can't find the Eternal in the transitory. Indeed, I have realized myself that I can, I must hear His Voice with my spiritual ears, not my physical ears; and I must see Him with my spiritual eyes, not

material sight . . . But please give my utmost thanks to Mrs. Cooper who sent it to me so kindly.[11]

Agnes spent quite a bit of time at the Geyserville Bahá'í School near Geyserville, California. Interestingly, Geyserville is just a short distance north of the Azalea Camp near Healdsburg where Agnes had spent five weeks during the summer of 1896. Agnes noted, 'I have spent the fast here at Geyserville. It is my fourth visit here. Some day this place should be a beautiful garden of God for the pure seeds have been sown here, but it is not an easy field where the village minister holds the people from turning to the Truth.'[12]

The National Bahá'í Convention

For the first time in her Bahá'í life, Agnes had the opportunity of attending the National Bahá'í Convention in Chicago. She travelled with Ella Cooper and arrived on Monday, 21 April 1918, several days before the Convention officially started. Agnes wrote:

The next day in the afternoon we went to Mrs. True's to a meeting. In the mean time Martha Root and a beautiful believer from Boston had arrived, and in the evening we went together to a dinner of a society called the 'Human Welfare Society'. We were the guests of the brother from Boston, Mr. Richard Mayer and he was invited to speak and gave the Message. From that moment the days were filled, and the believers began arriving. Mr. Mayer had a parlor for the use of the believers here in the Auditorium Hotel which is used by the believers for the meetings, and the majority of the believers stay here. On Wednesday May Maxwell arrived from Montreal. She did not know that I was here at the time and went to another hotel, but during the days of the convention, I had the great privilege of sharing my room here with her during the day, and at night she returned to sleep in her hotel. Our meeting was a glorious happily one. I found my little mother of Paris just where I had always felt she should be, in the light in the convention, spreading fragrance and harmony among all. She was like a bird flitting from one to another during all those days. And the great power and strength which was given to her, showed that Abdul Baha is indeed her healer.[13]

Agnes had not initially planned to go, noting that her 'coming to Chicago was very sudden', but that she had been guided by God in answer to her prayers for Him to show her where to go, 'I was guided here, I knew that the spiritual corner stone of the Mashrak El Azkar would be laid, for it had been shown me, that I was to be present at that time, but that time would not have come, if the believers here in Chicago had not arisen and obeyed the Voice of God.'[14]

What Agnes was referring to was an outbreak of Covenant-breaking. A group of Chicago Bahá'ís associated with Luella Kirchner began a reading room, initially with the Master's approval, where the Bahá'ís could read and discuss the Bahá'í Writings. But in 1917, the group declared that the elected Chicago House of Spirituality was invalid and elected their own Chicago Bahá'í Assembly. Then they began following the writings of Mr W.W. Harmon who claimed that 'through[his] interpretation of Baha'o'llah's Word . . . the Bahais would receive divine illumination'. At this time, 'Abdu'l-Bahá was completely out of contact with the rest of the world due to the World War and Mason Remey had managed to establish a Commission of Investigation into Covenant-breaking.[15] So, the Bahá'í community was in turmoil. Agnes wrote to the Bahá'ís in Japan:

> Without the spiritual corner stone being first laid, the material one could never be laid, and the reason it was never laid before, was because of the division in the Cause of God here in this center. The believers were struggling to do away with this difference, but in vain. At last a committee was formed to investigate, and through the study of the Holy Words of Abdul Baha and Baha-ollah, to find what was the root of the trouble. In their investigation, they found that some of the people who called themselves by the name Bahai and held meetings, were in truth not following the explicit commands of Abdul Baha and Baha-ollah. This is violating the Covenant of God, and Abdul Baha says that when we discover such violation, to use His Words which were in a Tablet to Mr. Remey:– 'As soon as they see the least trace of violation of the Covenant, they must hold aloof from the violators.'
>
> When the believers, through reading and studying the Holy Words prayfully, discovered that many who called themselves Bahais were disobeying the commands of the Center of the Covenant of

God, they immediately did as commanded and cut themselves from such violators, – ceased to associate with them or permit them to come to their meetings. Thus the believers have attained a great spiritual fragrance through obedience the Center of God's Covenant. Before this time, the believers in America had not understood perfectly this command and therefore were not able to protect the Cause of God from those who in truth were enemies of His Cause.[16]

Agnes, as she always did, saw the positive side of the situation – the increased unity and the attainment of 'a great spiritual fragrance through obedience to the Center of God's Covenant', writing that:

Abdul Baha says that each prophet of God has had an opponent. As the prophet manifests attributes of God, so the opponent shows the opposite qualities . . . when the Light of God shines in the world, it makes a shadow, and the greater the Light of the Sun, the greater the shadow it will cast, but this is a proof that the sun is shining . . . The very fact of a shadow must make us rejoice, because through it the Truth of God is proven to be shining and existing. But in order to protect the Cause of God, we have to simply obey explicitly Abdul Baha in everything that He tells us.[17]

Unfortunately, because there was no communication with 'Abdu'l-Bahá, the concept of the 'least trace of violation of the Covenant' resulted in many people being suspected and/or accused of violation. When communication with 'Abdu'l-Bahá was re-established in the autumn of 1918, the Master did confirm that Luella Kirchner had broken the Covenant,[18] but did not include most of the others who were thought to be violators.

The Convention began on Saturday evening, 26 April, with a banquet on the top floor of the hotel and Agnes was asked to speak about the Bahá'í activities in Japan. She was quite nervous about speaking, but 'Abdul Baha heard my prayer and assisted me, and in front of me was the shining face of my spiritual mother. I was indeed relieved and happy when it was over'.[19] Agnes described the Convention:

Mr. Lunt spoke most beautifully of the Mashrak el Azkar and my little mother spoke with the fragrance of God. She was indeed like an empty reed on which the Divine breezes were playing. She said today there is only One speaker in the World, so we do not come together but to investigate Reality. She said the greatest principle of Baha-ollah is the principle of the Most Great Peace. Today the world is in the phase of nationalism . . . In reality nationalism is being destroyed on the battle field that internationalism may be born. They are fighting to bring peace, but not the peace of Baha-ollah . . . Not until the people of the world hear This Voice can their problems be solved. The sun shines on a heap of rubbish and causes a stench, but the sun is not the cause. The sun brings all forth, so the Sun of Truth is today bringing all forth. When light and darkness meet and the world turns to the light, then the great change comes. The world today has the greatest opportunity of the ages – to know the Manifestation of God while He is in their midst. Love is the law . . .

Mr. Randall spoke the next morning with great feeling of the story of the great storm on the water when the disciples were with Christ. Dr. D'Evelyn spoke of statesmanship as harmonizing with the spiritual ages in which one lives.

In a meeting held at Mrs. True's to discuss the position and duties of the Bahais regarding peace, May Maxwell spoke with power, and the following are a few thoughts from what she said. – Are we to be silent when the Voice of God is speaking? If we are the living among the dead humanity of the world, is it not our loyalty to help them on the spiritual plane and not only on the material plane. The world can take care of the material but there are only a very few to awaken them to the Center of the Covenant. Is there nothing for us to do?

Dr. Bagdadi spoke and gave the following thoughts. – We believe that love is the creator of peace. If a man and his wife are in love, there is peace, but if not, there is war. The foundation of Baha-ollah cannot be shaken, even if the rulers do not accept it. We are commanded to pray for the government. We must obey and serve the government. Our one duty is to awaken the people and tell the nations that the reason we have war is because the nations did not heed the principles of Baha-ollah. All are heedless.

. . . One morning Mr. Randall spoke in the parlor of the Greatest Name. He spoke of the names meaning qualities, and said that in holding the Greatest Name, we should think of unity, – the weaving together of the Divine qualities. The Greatest Name is the name of the Covenant. It is the circle by which we approach God. God has given us a name which bands us together. It is the One power by which the children are banded together.

It was a joy to meet Mr. Vail from Urbana and the group of believers from there. Mr. Vail's face is radiant with the light of the Kingdom. I am going to Urbana from here, to meet the friends there and it will be a great joy . . .

In regard to the writings of Baha-ollah and Abdul Baha concerning peace, it was decided to make a compilation and a committee was appointed for the work. The culmination of the convention was a unanimous vote to send the compilation on peace when it is finished to all the rulers of the world as far as it will be possible.[20]

The travels of Agnes

Agnes was beginning to get a bit of a reputation from her pioneering in Japan and her writing of articles for *Star of the West* and the Bahá'ís in various centres were eager to hear about her experiences. In June, Joseph Hannen wrote, saying, 'Through Martha Root, I learn that you are now visiting her, and so I take this opportunity of renewing the invitation previously extended, for you to spend some time in Washington.'[21] Then the Esperanto Association of North America invited her to come to their Congress at Green Acre and speak about the Esperantists of Japan. Agnes later wrote, 'This gave me a wonderful opportunity, not only in making a better understanding between the Esperantists of the two countries, but in bringing to their attention the Bahá'í teachings and words of 'Abdu'l-Bahá concerning a universal language.'[22] She apparently spent much of the summer at Green Acre.

Agnes spent several weeks in Toronto in June 1919, staying with Dr Albert Durrant Watson, at the request of May Maxwell, to deepen him in the Faith. Dr Watson was a well-known intellectual and poet who had been attracted to the Faith about three years earlier.[23]

Agnes spent most of the autumn and winter months with her sister Mary in Montclair, New Jersey. Mary was preparing to go to France as part of the war relief effort.[24]

In March 1919, while Agnes was still in Montclair with her sister, she received another Tablet from 'Abdu'l-Bahá:

O thou daughter of the Kingdom!

Although thy letter has not yet been received, yet we do answer it. Praise be to God, that in Japan thou hast been assisted in the accomplishment of a distinguished service. Thou hast raised the Call of the Divine Kingdom and hast led the people to an illumined world and a heavenly Cause. Thou hast become the cause of enlightenment and the wisher for the education of human souls. For those regions are in sheer need of Divine Teachings and are endowed with sufficient capacity. Those souls must be emancipated from the obscurity of blind imitations and be illumined by the light of heavenly instructions. Whosoever arises for such a work, divine confirmations shall assist him and the power of the Kingdom shall be made manifest.

Effort must be exerted that the East and West may be reconciled, that the darkness of bigotry may vanish, that the unity of mankind may be made manifest and that East and West, like unto two longing souls may embrace each other in the utmost of love, for all are the sheep of God, and God is the Real Shepherd and is kind to everyone.

In accordance with the wish of the attracted maid servant of God to the love of God, Mrs. Maxwell, go thou to Canada and stay there for a time and then hasten back to Japan, for in Japan you will be assisted and exalted.

Some letters are enclosed for the friends in Japan. Forward them.[25]

Agnes had her marching orders, together with Tablets to deliver to Tokujiro Torii and Yuri Mochizuki.

Shortly after she received this Tablet, a note from one of the Master's secretaries told her to be at the Bahá'í Convention because 'a great happiness' would await her there. With her direction laid out before her, Agnes went to Montreal in late March and remained with May Maxwell until the Eleventh Annual Bahá'í Convention, which was held at the McAlpin Hotel in New York from 26 to 30 April.[26]

The 'great happiness' followed the unveiling of the Tablets of the Divine Plan, 'Abdu'l-Bahá's plan to spread the Bahá'í Faith across the globe and into every village, town and city. In the Tablet dated 11 April 1916, the Master had placed Agnes's example before the eyes of the world in each of two paragraphs:

Consider ye, that Miss Agnes Alexander, the daughter of the Kingdom, the beloved maidservant of the Blessed Perfection, traveled alone to the Hawaiian Islands, to the Island of Honolulu, and now she is gaining spiritual victories in Japan! Reflect ye how this daughter was confirmed in the Hawaiian Islands. She became the cause of the guidance of people . . .

At this time, in the Hawaiian Islands, through the efforts of Miss Alexander, a number of souls have reached the shore of the sea of faith! Consider ye, what happiness, what joy is this! I declare by the Lord of Hosts that had this respected daughter founded an empire, that empire would not have been so great! For this sovereignty is eternal sovereignty and this glory is everlasting glory.[27]

Only two other people were mentioned by 'Abdu'l-Bahá in those historic Tablets – May Maxwell and Alma Knobloch. Such an exclusive group was for women only. Upon learning of this high honour, Agnes, with utmost humility, wrote that 'I was fully aware that the honor the Master had bestowed, was not for myself, but to the glory of my blessed grandparents and my parents for their noble lives of service to mankind.'[28]

Following the Convention, Agnes travelled to Toronto, where she met May Maxwell, and the two of them proceeded to Montreal. Agnes spent ten days in May's company 'sharing in the Bahá'í work there'. Agnes stayed in Montreal until 10 June, when she travelled to Chicago, where she was met by Lillian James and Albert Vail, who took her to the Temple site for prayers. Agnes spent but a single day in Chicago and on 9 June departed for Piedmont, California, a suburb of Oakland, where she arrived on the 13th.[29] Two weeks later, on 30 June, she sailed from San Francisco for Honolulu.

Agnes left America not knowing whether to stay in Honolulu for a while or not. When she felt guided to stay, she remained there for over a month. Her stay was confirmed by a Tablet she received from 'Abdu'l-Bahá after she arrived in Japan that read: 'Remain for some days in Honolulu and then immediately hasten to Japan.'[30]

On 8 August 1919, Agnes boarded the steamer *Korea* for Japan.[31]

9

RETURN TO JAPAN

1919–1921

The power of prayer

Agnes sailed from Honolulu for Japan on 9 August 1919. She noted that it was the 12th time she had boarded a steamer without knowing any of the other passengers. After leaving the port, Agnes went on deck to supplicate God's guidance that she would be led to ready souls. Soon, a young woman walked up to her and they chatted for a while. The next morning, Agnes was given a letter from Ella Cooper in San Francisco that told her about a young Frenchwoman, Mme Charlotte Conte, who was supposed to be on the same ship. Charlotte was heading for Vladivostok to be married. Agnes's prayer was answered because Charlotte was the woman Agnes had spoken to the day before. Charlotte had met a Bahá'í at Niagara Falls and there had first learned about the Faith. In California, Charlotte was directed to Ella Cooper who had furthered her Bahá'í education. And now, Charlotte was hearing about the Faith from Agnes.[1]

Agnes's prayer to find ready souls worked repeatedly. Charlotte introduced Agnes to two other passengers, Dr and Mrs Shastri. Mrs Shastri had heard about the Faith in Omaha, Nebraska, and had been given some Bahá'í literature, which she still carried with her. She eagerly read the book that Agnes carried. Then one day, Agnes was reading *Some Answered Questions* in a steamer chair on the deck. Leaving the deck for a few moments, she returned to find the book missing. Charlotte said, 'If it is a Bahá'í book, it will not be lost.' The deck steward, having found it apparently abandoned, had put the book in the social hall, and there it was discovered by a woman from Chicago, Mrs Ernst, who found Agnes's name in it and went and found her. Agnes wrote, 'How wonderful was the guidance of God! She was eager to read the book and kept it during the remainder of the voyage. Early each morning she went to the upper deck and read for an hour.' Mrs Ernst lived among the Arabs in Tunis and her wish was to share the Faith with them.[2]

Agnes was also able to speak with other passengers, one of whom was a Filipino doctor. He took some Bahá'í literature. She also re-met Bryan Yamashita, to whom she had been introduced in Honolulu. He had been to a Bahá'í meeting in Washington DC and later introduced her to a Japanese banker from Yokohama. She met Bryan several years later in Tokyo when he surprised her by pulling out of his pocket a Bahá'í booklet she had given him on the ship.[3]

Where to live?

Agnes arrived in Yokohama on 19 August and began looking for a place to live. Initially, she had to stay at the Station Hotel, 'where day and night the trains of the Empire came and went and I see and hear them from my window'. She noted:

> I knew, though, that it did not matter where I was as long as I was under His guidance. The Bahá'í children, Mr. Torii, Mr. Fukuta and Yuri Mochizuki came there to see me. My work, I felt, was to first strengthen them, so that through them the Divine torch would blaze in Japan. Yuri San had just graduated from the Girls' High School, and was writing for a Japanese newspaper, the *Yomiuri*. She wrote a beautiful article about the Cause and my return to Japan, which was published in the paper. Mr. Torii brought a blind young man, Tomonaga Noto to see me. He had told him of the Bahá'í Message, and his heart was touched by the love of the Master. He was a poor young man who lost his sight when seven years old, and his home life had not been happy. Soon after he wrote a supplication to the Master.[4]

Sometime after Agnes's return to Japan, Kanichi Yamamoto, the second person to become a Bahá'í in Hawaii, came to Japan from California. His wife had come over previously, but had died and he had come to collect his four oldest boys to take them back to California. Agnes was able to meet him in Tokyo and then was at the dock when he sailed back to Berkeley, California. It was a difficult job for him to care for four young boys, but soon after his return he married his wife's sister.[5]

On 26 August, Agnes went to Yumoto, Ikao, Joshu, in the mountains 75 miles (121 km) north of Tokyo to get out of the heat and noise of the train station area.[6] How long she stayed is not certain, but she was back in the Station Hotel again by early October because it was the only place she could find. 'I am back in Tokyo in a room beside the train tracks', she wrote, 'but it is the only place I can find, so I have to endure the noise. I have never seen a place change as Tokyo has in two years . . . Automobiles have increased as everything else has prospered here in Japan. To get about without an automobile one has to endure the crush . . . or hire a rickshaw at a big price for the long distances of Tokyo.'[7]

By 23 October, Agnes was in Kyoto, where she spent several weeks spreading the Faith. One day she went to the Kyoto Imperial University and met the assistant librarian, Mr Tamigiro Sasaoka, who gladly accepted Bahá'í books for the library and became a friend to the Cause. Tokujiro Torii had given her a letter of introduction to a blind Christian pastor in Osaka, Mr Kumagae, who was also an Esperantist. She visited Mr Kumagae and his wife twice and once attended an Esperanto meeting with him at which they asked her to speak.[8]

While Agnes was in Kyoto, she received notice from Roy Wilhelm in America that Mrs Ida Finch was coming to join her. On the train to meet Ida, Agnes met a Japanese man who worked at the Boston Museum of Art and, of course, told him about the Faith. Agnes did not reach Yokohama in time to meet Ida, but Yuri Mochizuki and some of the other friends met her and identified themselves by holding the symbol of the Greatest Name. They escorted Ida back to Tokyo where she joined Agnes at the Imperial Hotel annex.[9]

Agnes and Ida settled into their new accommodation as best they could:

I am happy and comfortable here and have taken my room for the month. It is awfully expensive but can't be helped at present. Every night nearby there are large Japanese functions and hundreds and thousands of dollars are spent lavishly. Last night there was a wedding party of 150 Japanese at an expense of over $2,000. It seems a pity to have so much show for so little account & when the world is suffering. It is the newly rich Japanese merchants who make the shows.

The people in the hotel are quite a different class from before the war. There is such a mixture of Russians, Germans, etc. and people do not dress as they used to. One can really dress as they please.

On Thanksgiving day I went with Mrs. Finch to the reception at the Embassy and met some friends also the Ambassador and his secretary, Mr Macdonald whom I met in Piedmont once when he was on his way to Japan. The Ambassador gave a splendid Thanksgiving address last Sunday.[10]

The date 26 November was the 19th anniversary of Agnes's declaration of Faith in Bahá'u'lláh and at noon of that day, she received a Tablet from 'Abdu'l-Bahá:

He is God!

O thou daughter of the Kingdom!
Thy letters were received. The travel to Japan was in the utmost necessity. Thou hast undoubtedly met the attracted maidservant of God, Mrs. Maxwell, before sailing to Japan, for that maidservant of God is ablaze with the Fire of the love of God. Whosoever meets her feels from her association the susceptibilities of the Kingdom. Her company uplifts and develops the soul.

Thou didst well to travel to Japan, for the seed thou hast sown needs watering. Capable souls are found in Japan. The Breath of the Merciful is necessary to stir and enliven them and to bestow a spiritual liveliness. A blind soul is there but is in the utmost enkindlement, and likewise a priest lives there who is endowed with great capacity. I hope that thou wilt find the doors flung open and become the cause of the guidance of souls . . .

Convey to the friends of Geyserville the intensity of my love and my spiritual attachment. At dawn I entreat at the Threshold of the All-Knowing God and beg for them the exaltation of the Kingdom.

Remain for some days in Honolulu and then immediately hasten to Japan.

Upon thee be Baha-El-Abha![11]

This was the Tablet that confirmed Agnes's decision to have spent a month in Honolulu before continuing on to Japan.

That afternoon, they held their usual Friday Bahá'í meeting and

Agnes felt the power of the Tablet when a new participant came, Kenjiro Ono. He was a blind young man who had lost his sight at the age of three from fever. His disability did not deter him and he entered the Christian Mission School as the only blind student. He first heard of the Bahá'í Faith in the Torii home.[12] He became a frequent visitor after Agnes found a house, when he came almost daily to hear Agnes and Ida Finch read to him from 'Abdu'l-Bahá's talks, and the book *Ten Days in the Light of Akka,* which he took down in Braille. He soon wrote of his acceptance to the Master. He had a beautiful bass voice and learned to sing many of Louise Waite's songs.[13]

During this time, Agnes returned to the Japan Women's College to meet the new President Aso, who had replaced President Naruse after the latter's death. He asked Agnes to speak to an association that was investigating the difficulties faced by women in Japan on the topic of 'Woman's Problem from the Standpoint of the Bahá'í Revelation'. Following her talk, President Aso asked her to write it down so that it could be translated into Japanese.[14]

Agnes and Ida had to stay in the annex of the Imperial Hotel until they could find a house. Agnes wrote:

> I knew that all was in God's hands and He could open all doors. I had promised Yuri San that when I returned to Tokyo, she could live with me. In December I heard of a little Japanese house, which was soon to be vacated, and went immediately to see it before even the landlord knew the tenants were intending to leave. In this way, through His favor, I was enabled to procure it. Then I sent for the furniture which I had left in Japan.[15]

When on 17 December 1919 Agnes rented the house, she hoped to move in soon, 'but was waiting for the return of some of my household things which had been left behind here in Japan. They were promised but did not come. Saturday was set as the last day for moving and that morning a boy was sent with a note asking if I could only get my bedding I would move. It did not come. I did not wish to buy new and remained at the hotel.'[16]

Ida moved into the new house, but since Agnes didn't have any bedding she returned to the hotel that night, but she 'felt something dark was foreboding'.[17]

A devastating fire

Agnes described what happened next:

On the night of December 28 a strange catastrophy [sic] came to this servant . . . At dinner I felt a darkness and wondered at it as I had always been so happy there, but within an hour or two it all happened, the hotel annex where my room was burned down. Strange it was I was the first of the guests who saw the fire and gave warning to ot[h]ers, but as I was getting my things hurriedly to put them out the window, the lights went out, the manager, who only was thinking of his responsibility for the guests, came into my room and ordered a boy to take me out. The boy obeyed, my things were all left. I was made to understand that they would care for them, but it was all false. My room was on the ground floor and so it only was a matter of stepping out of the window. At the time I was taken there was no danger and everything could have easily been taken out, I was literally held a prisoner and not allowed to return until the building had burned to the ground. That night I could only thank GOD for the Reality in my heart which could not be burned by fire and say, Thy Will be done, teach me LORD. Strange it was that of the things I threw out of my window before being taken, there was only one sheet of Bahai literature and it was a page from a compilation on Violation. The next day all water soaked and covered with ashes I found a compilation I had made on the Covenant and also the book 'Through Warring countries to the Mountain of GOD.' It seemed these could not burn. The latter had some hitherto unpublished pictures of the BELOVED. In a basket a day after, I found a few pieces of HOLY WRITINGS. At times infinite sadness came to me when I thought of HIS HOLY WRITINGS and TABLETS to me which had all burned that night, but I can trust my LORD and I know He is able to give me all I need. He knows all and I can only turn to HIM. Now I must teach without all the HOLY WORDS I had been copying and compiling for so many years. My material loss was very great, but the spiritual is the only one that can be thought of. For several days I longed only to be near HIM for once, that HE might console, but He knows it all and HIS LOVE and Mercy are without limit.

Many beautiful letters came from friends here in Japan, among them from the dear blind brother and the priest whom ABDUL BAHA referred to in my last TABLET which was received on NOV. 26.

'My calamity is My providence', and I pray that it may be so that the CAUSE of GOD may be more quickly spread in Japan, then I will rejoice only. Already it has aided in my spreading the MESSAGE here.[18]

In the Hawaiian Mission Children's Society Annual Report, a note was included saying that 'She occupied the room next to the crossed wires which started the blaze, and gave the alarm. An employee rushed to her room, flung a red blanket around her, dragged her to a window humped her up on his back and slid down a rope, where he deposited her in an automobile to view her belongings go up in smoke. Her loss represented about $1,000 in money but far more than that to her.'[19]

Agnes spoke to the proprietor of the hotel and he said that 'he was afraid the smoke might affect me and so he told the boy to take me out. I didn't know myself what was happening only that everyone was going towards the hotel while I was being taken away.'[20]

Agnes received sympathetic letters from many people around the world, and the local Japanese people mourned her loss as they admired her acceptance of it. Mr S. Saiki, of Kukuoka, Kyushu, wrote her a poem:

I receive your Tablets and felt heartily a Bahai woman's Sacrifice. I sympathise with you so much.

It burns, the fire, like a devil's tongue,
However it cannot devour a faithful woman's belief,
It can smoke Tablets, but not teachings of Love.
Now, in the smoke and fire,
Lo, a woman keeps her love to others
Burning her things in vain and despair
But her notice of danger helped others in safe,
Thus a Bahai woman shines
Nobler and finer than a star on that night.

This is just my feeling expressed in imperfect English. So live in Peace, and God's Blessing upon thee.[21]

Mr Saiki was greatly attracted to the Faith and had written a book in which he mentioned the Faith.[22]

Recovery

A few days later, Agnes wrote that:

> I have been through a strange calamity. My things burned, but not what is in the heart. The above address is the house I rented with Mrs Finch, who came here to serve. I was to have moved in but the necessary things, which a lady had of mine, did not come, & I was caught, but . . . He knows best. I could only say Thy Will be done. The Holy Literature is gone, even His writings to me but . . . our picture of Him and the bit of Persian rug was saved as I had taken it to the little house by hand.[23]

Like many who suffer calamity, Agnes thought about what-if:

> I should have never waited on a person whom I had been warned was not to be depended on to return my things. I should have simply bought some more bedding and come to the house on that fatal Saturday. That morning I sent a messenger boy to Mrs. ___, who had my things, asking if I could get the bedding only I would move that day. Now I have no relationship with the lady, but I was indeed burned before I took the stand. Her reputation is not the best.[24]

Many people heard that Agnes had lost everything and many tried to help:

> This morning I received from Miss Denton a lovely piece of Japanese crepe. I really don't know what to do when I do not need, also Mrs Gordon in Kyoto, a dear English friend, sent me two beautiful warm night dresses and a shawl. I really am not needing any. Another lady sent me one, she said to show her sympathy. Miss

Denton has also sent me some Japanese study books. I had quite a number and lost them all and they are quite expensive now.[25]

In the letter to Arthur, she asked that he send the clothes in 'my wardrobe in the west room. I could fix them for summer. My best summer things all burned in the wardrobe trunk. There is no hurry, though.'[26]

Agnes was living in borrowed clothes when, a few days after the fire, she met a newspaperman, Mr Mathewson. 'I was wearing borrowed shoes until I could find some, also a hat which was given me,' Agnes wrote. 'From that I suppose he made his story. Newspapermen are dangerous, but still he meant well.' Reliving the moment, in a letter to her brother Arthur, she lamented, 'What you wrote is perfectly true. In 5 minutes, if I had been allowed I could have saved everything. My room was small and all my things together. It was only a matter of snapping my trunk together and putting it out the window & all other things could have been taken in no time . . . There is no use talking of these things now.'[27]

Agnes spoke to a lawyer and he talked to the hotel manager. He said only that 'some others who lost by not being notified have brought a suit against the hotel and Mr Hayashi said he could do nothing for me because of this.' Agnes wrote that she had seen Mr Hayashi since and 'his attitude was very different. Instead of appearing kindly, he appeared angry.'[28]

To Ida Finch, the fire was a confirmation of her feelings upon her arrival in Japan, which were quite the opposite of those felt by Agnes. Ida wrote:

There are terrific contending forces here which are using their murky devilishness to uproot the Cause, and this element will have effect just as long as we in any way associate with these opposers. Association is devastating and work is hindered while it continues. I prefer not to mention names . . . but we have this to rely upon, 'as soon as they see a trace of violation', etc.

The fire and its consequences . . . causes us to reach the point of making a stand for the Center of the Covenant and have nothing whatsoever to do with violators...

When I entered this city, before I even spoke to Miss Alexander, or had met her even, I felt darkness and oppression here. Of course in my ignorance I was unaware how to place it or locate it, but I think you should know about the facts, that it exists and that it is active through human agencies. More about it I care not to write, but your connection with the Beloved should inform you.

Do not think there is nothing being done, for the Spirit is giving direct guidance and a more solid foundation is being laid.

Firm souls are not affected. The opposition, however, is not from the Japanese . . .[29]

Agnes appended a note to Ida's letter that said: 'Those of the Japanese who are confirmed in the Covenant clearly comprehend this. The dear blind brother wrote:- "Truth is truth and it will win the last victory."'[30] The person involved was not a Bahá'í, so Ida's understanding of 'violation' was rather inaccurate since only Bahá'ís can break the Covenant they accept upon becoming Bahá'ís, but with all the Covenant-breaking problems America had been going through – Mason Remey's investigation of Luella Kirchner – it is obvious that Ida was very concerned about the concept of violation.

Agnes joined Ida in the little house. They each had their own little room upstairs, while Yuri and a servant lived on the first (ground) floor. Agnes considered the smallness of the house a blessing because it was easier to clean. The house was in a 'crowded district of little shops and little children whose playground was the street'.[31] She wrote, 'We have a very good woman who comes in and does all the work but cooking, and Fujo San [Yuri] helps in the morning so we are quite comfortable . . . I am very happy in the house. It is dear, – new and clean and pretty, though it is small, but down stairs the two rooms can be made into one by removing the sliding doors. That is the advantage of a Japanese house.'[32] Agnes wrote that they 'live simply and Mrs. Finch and I take turns in seeing to the meals as our cook does not know about foreign things. She is a quiet gentle old lady and always pleasant. She cannot read or write which is rather inconvenient for us, but [Yuri] does the interpreting when she is at home.'[33]

Shortly after Agnes, Ida and Yuri had settled into their new home, Roy Wilhelm sent her a booklet of the writings of Bahá'u'lláh and 'Abdu'l-Bahá that he had compiled. Daiun Inouye, the Buddhist priest, and Mr Saiki, who had once been a Christian evangelist, translated the booklet into Japanese.[34]

Agnes had lived in Japan for several years by this time, but her Japanese was still rudimentary. With the new Japanese book Miss Denton gave her, she decided it was time to begin learning the language of the country she lived in.[35]

The Japan Agnes was experiencing at the beginning of 1920 was very different from the one where she had arrived in 1914. She wrote:

Japan is a country of great changes these days. Things are moving, and old Japan will have to pass. The hope of Japan is the students. They are the ones who will move the country. All the student class are not sympathizers of these things. They want to be friends with other nations. I heard a very telling talk by one of the Imperial University professors the other day. He said that if it was known what he was telling us, he would be imprisoned for one year. He told how military Japan makes things go just the way they want, even cablegrams are doctored to suit them. There has been tremendous demonstrations for universal suffrage which ended the other day when the Imperial messenger arrived and the diet was dissolved.[36]

Three schoolgirls

While in America, Agnes had prayed that she and Yuri would be able to guide Japanese women into the Faith. But she noted, 'instead of women it was girls whom God guided to hear the Message of Baha'u'llah'. Yuri was only able to have one free day each week and she chose Friday, the weekly Bahá'í meeting at Agnes's home. Yuri had graduated from the Girls High School, which was conveniently close to their home, and arranged for Agnes to give a talk to girls from the school which she would translate. The results were surprising. Agnes wrote:

After it one of the girls, Haruko Mori, came to me with great love. She was later blessed with a Tablet from 'Abdu'l-Bahá. Yuri San invited any of the girls who wished to come, to the home on Friday afternoons when we would have meetings. As the girls knew very little English, she translated for them. We had very happy meetings. The girls learned some of Mrs. Waite's songs, as 'Softly His Voice is Calling', 'Great Day of God', 'Tell the Wondrous Story', the 'Benediction', and also some of the Bahá'í prayers.[37]

Haruko was 17 years old and wrote to 'Abdu'l-Bahá through Sachiro Fujita, the young Japanese man He had taken from Chicago to California back in 1912 and who was at that time in Haifa serving Him there.

Another of the schoolgirls to embrace the Faith through Yuri's efforts was Mikae (Chu) Komatsu:

One day a girl from the Tsuda English School, Miss Mikae Komatsu, came to our Friday meeting. As she entered the room I felt a wave of joy. Yuri San was absent that day, so she took her place and translated for the girls. She was eighteen years old. From that day her soul was quickened by the Divine Revelation. She not only learned the Prayers by heart, but said them three times daily, thus she soon became a flaming torch and brought her school friends to hear the Bahá'í Message. During the summer she poured out her heart in letters to me. On July twenty-sixth, she wrote: 'Dearest Mother, I cannot find any words to thank you for your kindness. O the kindest mother! How glad I am to be with you and to talk about the Greatest Power. You, the most merciful mother guided me to God. I always think of you and thank you for it. I do not doubt that God will assist me in any matter and I am always with God.

'Praise be to God, the Fragrance of the Greatest Rose is scattering all over the world and the gentle Shower from Heaven is fertilizing us. How happy we are! How Joyful! Joyful! Joyful! I feel I am born again.

'I shall be very happy if I can do any service to you. (I believe my service to you is likewise to God.) I will do my best to spread this Blessed Message because, you see, those who do not know His blessings are very unhappy, I think. Please let me do something that will help you. I will willingly do whatever it may be. I feel your home is just like mine. I am always afraid I stay too long and bother you . . . but I am your dearest daughter, as you know, isn't it? Let us always say the Greatest Name...'[38]

Mikae wrote to 'Abdu'l-Bahá and received her Tablet in return:

O thou blessed soul! Thy letter was received. It was not a letter. It was a scent bag of the muskdeer from which the fragrance of the love of God was perceived. After I read it, I turned to the Kingdom of the Merciful and supplicated so that thy soul may become purified; that thy heart may be converted into a brazier of the fire of the love of God; that in every moment thou mayest find the Light of Truth radiating; that thou mayest kindle the lamp of Guidance; that thou mayest seek heavenly joy and happiness, and mayest consecrate thy life to the service of the Heavenly Father. I feel the utmost kindness towards thee, and I pray, through the infinite Bounties for a spiritual dynamic force and a heavenly blessing unto thee. Convey to all the friends my greetings and love. Unto thee be the Glory of Abha! [39]

In August, another schoolgirl, Hide Tanaka, accepted the Faith and wrote to 'Abdu'l-Bahá on the same day, her 18th birthday:

O, the Centre of the Covenant of God!

God has awakened me through Miss Alexander and it seems to me that I know Thy love, Thy power, and Thy spirit.

I left the English Church mission school called Koran Jagakko only five months ago. I was not satisfied with Christianity although I was there for five years. But now I hope awfully to be a Bahai. It is only four weeks since I knew about Thee. I know so little, and want to know so much.

O Father! Make me a flower of the Rose garden, too.

I see Thy picture which Miss Alexander has given me on my desk. Thy wonderful eyes thrill me every time I turn my face toward Thee.

How wonderful it is I can write to Thee this evening, for today is my eighteenth birthday. I shall never forget this wonderful day.

August 8th, 1920

Miss Alexander's child, Hide Tanaka[40]

At the celebration of the Declaration of the Báb, 23 May, all the girls gathered in a park and wrote messages to 'Abdu'l-Bahá who responded with a Tablet to the group:

O ye daughters of the Kingdom! Your congratulation on the Feast has been received. Its perusal imparted joy and happiness. Through the Bounties of the Supreme Lord do I hope that these daughters of the Kingdom will, day by day, progress so that they may, like unto a magnet, attract the Divine confirmations. I am always supplicating for you that ye may attain to the Most Great Bestowal and act and behave according to the Teachings of His Holiness Bahá'u'lláh. Upon you be the Glory of Abha![41]

Upon receiving the Tablet, the girls had a photo taken of them with His first Tablet. The Master sent them another Tablet, which they received in March 1921:

To the daughters of the Kingdom, Otoe Murakami, Kimiko Hagiwara, Kazu Fukusawa, Haruko Mori, Yuri Takao, Yuri Mochizuki, Japan. Unto them be the Glory of God, the Most Glorious! He is the Most Glorious!

O ye daughters of the Kingdom: The reflection of your forms (photograph) arrived in this Holy Land. Praise be unto God these figures are luminous. From your eyes the light of the love of God is emanating. This picture has been taken while ye have been in the utmost of joy and happiness. Praise ye God, that in this age of youth ye have entered the Kingdom of God! Ye have become enlightened. Ye have become celestial, divine and heavenly.

Through the graces of His Holiness, Bahá'u'lláh – May my life be sacrificed for His friends, I cherish the hope that ye will day by day progress more and more in the Kingdom of God; that each one of you will shine like unto a brilliant star from the horizon of the Supreme Guidance, thus proving to be the cause of guidance unto others, giving sight unto their eyes, hearing power unto their ears and quickening unto their hearts. Upon you be the Glory of Abhá![42]

Because of the young people coming into the Faith, Agnes wrote an article for the *Magazine of the Children of the Kingdom* in June 1920. In it, she wrote about how the first Japanese Bahá'ís were all young people:

Dearest Juniors:

Would you like to know something about your Bahai brothers and sisters in far away Japan?

They are almost all young people, for the older people of this country are not awakened from the winter sleep. The young are wide awake and searching as if in the dark for a light to guide them.

The first one who found Abdul Baha was a poor young student. He came to the Bahai meeting where students gathered on Friday afternoons to be taught of the Teachings of Abdul Baha, and as soon as he heard of our Beloved Master, his heart was rejoiced and his eyes brightened. Later he wrote in his native tongue a beautiful letter to Abdul Baha. His name is Mr. K. Fukuta. He now works in a store where he has become the trusted clerk and keeps the keys to the stores and money. At present he is ill, but let us pray for his recovery, that he may arise in the Master's service . . .

The first young sister in Japan to receive the Bahai Message in her heart, was Fuyo [Yuri] Mochizuki. In the little country place where she was living, she read a newspaper article telling of Abdul Baha. Then she wrote asking that the Water of Life might be given to her thirsty heart. At that time she did not know a word of English, but now, after two years of study, she can read and write, and is beginning to interpret from English the Teachings. She is writing for a daily newspaper and thus is enabled to spread the Teachings. She also was blest with a Tablet from Abdul Baha in which He wrote: 'Rest thou assured, therefore, that thou are always within sight and art encompassed with tender cares.'[43]

In August, Hide Tanaka gave Agnes $1 for a subscription to *The Children of the Kingdom*. Agnes was delighted because Hide was 'the first Japanese girl . . . to subscribe to the magazine'. *Children of the Kingdom* was a magazine for children and junior youth put together by Ella Robarts between 1919 and 1924 and published in Boston.[44]

Agnes was very taken with Chu Komatsu, describing her again as 'a torch of the Kingdom'. Agnes asked her to write something for the *Children of the Kingdom* magazine and she did so. The story ended up being more about her becoming a Bahá'í than about the Faith itself, which bothered her, but Agnes told her that 'it would help to make the unity between the children of different countries'.[45] Chu's story for the magazine told about how she had embraced the Faith like a

> young bud which grows larger and larger through the gentle showers from the sky. I have grown and grown in the Kingdom of God, being fertilized by the Heavenly shower . . .

They [the other schoolgirls] respect Mrs. Finch as their Bahai grandmother and Miss Alexander as their mother. We are very happy in the care of Mrs. Finch and Miss Alexander.

We had a little Baha'i feast on the 1st of August at the Bahai home. We sat on the 'tatami' [floor mats made from rice straw] in two rows before the picture of Abdul Baha, and we had a feast talking with each other about the Blessed One. Even though there assembled only nine girls, we were very happy with our grandmother and mother. We translated a Tablet from Abdul Baha into Japanese and asked Miss Alexander for a talk. Our mother, Miss Alexander, told us a beautiful story about Abdul Baha's family and so on, and she said that we were all one . . .[46]

Agnes and Yuri began each morning by reading from the *Hidden Words*, after which Yuri would translate that day's Hidden Word into Japanese. When the Fast came, Yuri kept it along with Agnes and Ida, 'the first Japanese Bahá'í to observe it in Japan'.[47]

Karuizawa

In mid-August 1920, Agnes went to Karuizawa, a resort town with hot springs about 60 miles (97 km) northwest of Tokyo situated below the symmetrical cone of 8,425-foot high Mt. Asama (2,568 m). Being at an altitude of about 3,300 feet (1,000 m), Karuizawa was much cooler than the coastal cities and was where many missionaries had their summer homes. As she rode the train to the town, Martha Root was her inspiration. She stayed at the Mampei Hotel and amazingly was given the same room that she and Martha Root had been given in 1915. On that visit, the two women had stayed for only a single night, but this time Agnes was determined to spend two weeks.[48] The Japan Women's University had its summer campus in Karuizawa and she quickly connected with the schoolgirls there:

At the Woman's University summer home in Karuizawa is a great pine tree where the girls go at dawn every morning and sit in quiet meditation. Their former president, Mr. Naruse, who passed to the beyond last year, had met Abdul Baha in London and he had the spirit of the Teachings. The tree is on the top of a hill and there the girls were told of Abdul Baha this summer. It was my privilege to tell them about another pine tree, that of Green Acre of which this one reminded me so deeply. It seemed like a twin tree in the East and some day I feel many, many will be worshiping in the Greatest Name under this tree. The girls took a photo with Abdul Baha's picture in the center with some of the Bahai books scattered about, so a pure seed was planted under this pine tree and in the future it may produce many harvests.[49]

Kenjiro Ono, one of the five blind Bahá'ís, was in Karuizawa that summer attending a summer school. Agnes met him each morning early in the garden and read the *Seven Valleys* to him for an hour before he went to school. One Sunday, 21-year-old Kenjiro went to both Japanese and foreign churches asking to speak after the services were over. In those that accepted his offer, he gave them the Message of Bahá'u'lláh.[50] About the blind, Agnes wrote: 'It is very wonderful at this time that the spiritual Light is rapidly spreading among the blind. One of these friends is both blind and deaf, but through His Great Love and Mercy, she has been visited by Abdul Baha. She wrote that He came to her while she was sleeping and brought great Joy, love and peace to her, that she felt His hands and face and that the blessing remained after He had left her.'[51]

Connecting with China

Agnes returned to Tokyo in September and one day read a newspaper story about a group of Chinese newspapermen from Canton who were visiting Japan. Immediately, she felt 'a burning desire . . . in my heart to tell them of the Bahá'í Message before they returned to China':

When Yuri Mochizuki . . . came home from the newspaper office where she worked, I asked her if she had heard of the visitors. She replied that they had visited the newspaper office but she did not know where they were staying. The next morning, as I knew of no other way to find them, I turned to the Beloved and supplicated His assistance. While in prayer the name of a Japanese friend, a clerk in the Imperial hotel, came to me. I went right to the hotel and asked him if he could tell me where to find the visitors. To my surprise he replied that he had not heard of them, then suddenly he said, 'Call up the Chinese Legation and ask them.' As I did not succeed in telephoning, I decided to go to the Legation myself. At the Legation entrance I met the gatekeeper and told him my errand. He escorted me to the office and I procured the name of the Inn where the group was staying, but learned they were away for the day, and would remain only two days longer in Tokyo. The gate-keeper, who was of Chinese-Japanese parentage, and spoke English fluently, seemed delighted when I told him of the Baha'i Cause and gave him some booklets. Indeed, it was the wonderful guidance of the Master which led me to the Legation, and the contact I made there opened the way later for me to meet a secretary who became very friendly to the Cause, and was one of those who spoke at the memorial meeting for the Beloved Master.

The next morning, with Yuri San's help, I telephoned to the Inn and asked to speak with someone of the group who understood English. To the one who came to the telephone I gave my name and address and asked him to come and see me. Later in the morning he arrived. He looked very uninterested, but as soon as he heard of the Bahá'í teachings, his whole expression began to change, until when he left his face was radiant. Mrs. Finch had a supply of Bahá'í books to sell, and he procured all available books to take with him to Canton, where he was an editor of the *Canton Times*, a leading newspaper of China. The following morning he returned accompanied by a friend, Mr. S. J. Paul Pao, of Shanghai, whom he had told of the Bahá'í teachings. Mr. Pao was delighted to hear of the Cause and over and over again repeated, 'Wonderful teachings! Wonderful teachings!'

I gave the Canton editor a photograph of 'Abdu'l-Bahá and asked him if he would publish an article in his paper when he returned to Canton. To my great delight, after his return, he sent us a copy of the *Canton Times* in which the photograph of 'Abdu'l-Bahá appeared on the front page with translations of Words of Bahá'u'lláh and 'Abdu'l-Bahá. The translations continued to be published in twenty-five editions of the paper, which he sent to us. As the *Canton Times* was widely circulated in China, the knowledge of the Bahá'í Cause was spread far and wide throughout the country. A proof of this came later when I had occasion to visit the Chinese Legation and inquired if the Minister had heard of the Cause, and was told he had read of it in the *Canton Times*. At another time I asked a Chinese student if he would send something to be published in the newspaper in the northern province of China where his home was. He told me afterwards that he received a reply that they had already read of the Bahá'í teachings in the *Canton Times*.[52]

Star of the East

The impetus for the next big Bahá'í advance came between 4 and 14 October 1920, when the 8th World Sunday School Convention met in Tokyo. Over a thousand foreigners together with many Japanese Christians attended the grand Convention. The presence of so many people led to a surprising new publication, *Star of the East*. Agnes wrote:

> What happened was that a little Japanese Bahai magazine suddenly came into existence, and my child Yuri Mochizuki is the editor. You know in my last Tablet Abdul Baha mentioned her in these words,
> 'Extend my great kindness and praise to the maid servant of God Fuyo (Yuri) Mochizuki, so that she may with a divine power, a heavenly purpose and Godly motive, start her writing and that the Breathings of the Holy Spirit may help her pen'.
> The little magazine was thought of and in one week it was in existence. Surely this was a great matter when it was the work of a young girl and a blind young man! And also all that it contains is her work and that of two blind young men, Mr Torii and Mr Ono![53]

During the time of the Convention, Agnes had one day found Yuri and Kenjiro talking intently. When she asked what they were discussing, the pair told her that they were planning to publish a Japanese Bahá'í magazine. Within a week, the *Star of the East* was published. Kenjiro wrote, 'Now it seems that the reign of Grace is coming upon this land. The beautiful dawn of Light has reached us and the waves of the light from the *Star of the West* have attained the East and our little magazine has been born.' The first issue appeared on 19 October. Publication continued every month for two years. It wasn't long before this new publication came to the attention of 'Abdu'l-Bahá. Yuri received a letter from Fujita in which he wrote, 'The copies of the *Star of the East* were received and presented to the Master. He was very pleased with your work.'[54]

Agnes described Yuri and Kenjiro's brainchild:

On the cover is the number nine, in the star copied from the *Star of the West*, and below this are the words of Bahá'u'lláh in both Esperanto and Japanese, '*Ye are all the fruits of one tree and the leaves of one branch.*' Then on the first page, one of the *Hidden Words* from the Persian in Esperanto, (Dr. Esslemont's translation) and also in Japanese is printed. The week after the first number was published, six Tablets came to Japan, and since then they have continued to come, so each new Tablet is translated into Japanese and sent out by this means. Already a number of persons have been attracted to the Cause through this little messenger, who had never before heard of the Bahá'í Teachings. [55]

Agnes described how they put the newsletter together, saying, 'I get all the translations and Yuri San writes the rest, but the translations and the ones to ask to do them come only through His guidance. Then also I give Yuri San the news items from the Bahai world which will be of interest to the Japanese.'[56]

'In short, it has a long description, but I mention it briefly'

On the day that the first issue of *Star of the East* came out, three Tablets arrived from 'Abdu'l-Bahá for Haruko Mori, Kenjiro Ono and Yuri Mochizuki. To Haruko, He wrote:

O thou beloved maid servant of God! Praise be unto God, that through the guidance of Miss Alexander thou couldst hear the Call of God. Then strive as far as thou art able to spread the Divine Teachings, so that thou mayest become distinguished with this great Bestowal among the women of the world. Unto thee be the Glory of Abha![57]

Kenjiro's Tablet read:

O thou who art a favored servant at the Threshold of the Most High! Thy letter was received. Verily, verily hast thou suffered much in thy life time. Do not thou be grieved because of the loss of thy sight. Praise be unto God, that thy insight is keen. Do not thou lament over thy poverty, for the Treasury of the Kingdom is thine. Do not thou worry that thou couldst not study in the material schools, because thou hast received lessons in the Verses of the Oneness (of God) in the Divine University. Offer thou thanks to God that thou couldst finally attain to Truth. Then be thou firm and steadfast so that the doors of the Most Great Bestowal may be opened unto thy face. The greatest of all questions is steadfastness and firmness. Every tree which is firmly rooted grows. Unto thee be the Glory of Abha![58]

And to Yuri, 'Abdu'l-Bahá wrote:

O thou beloved maid servant of God! Do thou observe the divine Bounty! We are in Haifa and thou in Tokyo, nevertheless how (our) hearts have become related to one another! This is through the power of the Kingdom which has made the East and West embrace each other. I feel the utmost kindness towards thee. If thou art able to write the story of Qurratu'l-'Ayn as a drama, thou are permitted to write it. Unto thee be the Glory of Abhá![59]

Yuri received another Tablet the next February, acknowledging her efforts with *Star of the East* and giving her a special Tablet for inclusion in it:

O thou art a new grown tree on the meadow of Truth! Thy letter dated October 14, 1920, has been received. As it was indicative of the susceptibility of thy conscience, it became the cause of joy.

Japan is like unto a farm whose soil is untouched. Such a soil as this has great capacity. One seed produces a hundred-fold. Now, praise be unto God, ye have found such a farm. Ye must develop the lands; ye must free them from thorns and weeds; ye should scatter the seeds of the love of God thereupon, and irrigate them with the rain of the knowledge of God. Rest ye assured that heavenly blessing will be bestowed!

It is my hope that in that farm ye will become divine farmers. The enlightened people of Japan are tired and disgusted with the superannuated and putrefied blind imitations. They are assured that these blind imitations are pure superstitions without any truth. Therefore they have the capacity to hear the Call of God. The land is untouched. We will have to see what the divine farmers will do!

At present thou hast started a journal. It is my hope that this journal will shine as the Star of the East. In the journal write thus:

When the horizon of the East was covered with immense darkness; when dark clouds were predominate, and when all the heavenly stars were concealed to the eye, His Holiness Bahá'u'lláh, like unto the sun shone forth from the horizon of the East, and with radiating splendor He illumined the Orient.

The Light of the Sun of Reality consisted of heavenly teachings which were spread in the Orient, because there the obscurities of blind imitations of religious, sectarian, racial, political, economic and home prejudices were in ascendancy. The darkness of these prejudices had dominated the Oriental world to such a degree that it had blinded all the eyes and deafened all the ears. There prevailed quarrel and strife, warfare and bloodshed.

In short, it has a long description, but I mention it briefly. When the Sun of Truth shone forth with all might and energy, these obscure and dark clouds dispersed and the splendid Day presented to the eye an aspect with such freshness and beauty that the wise became astonished; the sick were cured; the blind received sight; the deaf obtained hearing; the dumb proved eloquent, and the dead quickened. A heavenly table was spread in the Orient. The divine teachings like unto an unshakable edifice were instituted.

The first principle of Bahá'u'lláh is independent investigation of truth, that is, all the nations of the world have to investigate after truth independently and turn their eyes from the moribund imitations of the past ages entirely. Truth is one when it is independently investigated, it does not accept division. Therefore the independent investigation of truth will lead to the oneness of the world of humanity.

Another one of these teachings, is the oneness of the world of humanity. All mankind are the trees of the divine garden and the Gardener of this orchard is the Most High, the All-Sustainer. The hand of His Favor hath planted these trees, irrigated them from the cloud of Mercy and reared them with the energy of the Sun of Truth.

Then there remains no doubt that this heavenly Farmer (Gardener) is kind to all these plants. This truth cannot be denied. It is shining like unto the sun. This is the divine policy and unquestionably it is greater than the human policy. We must follow the divine policy.

The point is this that some people are sick; some are immature and ignorant, and some without any knowledge of their beginning and of their end. The sick should be cured; the immature should be brought to maturity, and the ignorant should be taught to become wise and not that enmity should be exercised towards them.

Similarly describe fully in that journal the other teachings which thou are acquainted with, one by one, a detailed description: For example, that religion must be the cause of concord; that it should agree with science and reason; that it must be a factor of progress to the world of humanity, that it should be free from blind imitations. Another example is that all prejudices are destructive to the foundation of the world of humanity.

Other examples are: The equality of men and women; the universalization of knowledge (education); the creation of one universal language; justice and righteousness; economic facilities among mankind; the need of the world of humanity of the breaths of the Holy Spirit; the establishment of universal peace; the institution of the Supreme Court of Arbitration; the freedom and equality of all mankind; the brotherhood of the world of humanity, and other teachings like these which are mentioned in the Tablets of God. Describe all these teachings fully in the most eloquent and sweetest terms expressive of the most charming realities and insert them in the journal.

It is my hope that thou together with Miss Alexander will be confirmed to accomplish this service. Miss Alexander is the herald of Truth in Japan. Rest assured she will be confirmed and assisted. Unto you be the Glory of Abhá![60]

Tablets also arrived in February for Kenjiro Ono and Tokujiro Torii. Kenjiro's read:

O thou heavenly person! Praise be unto God that having rent asunder the veils and having seen the rays of the Sun of Truth, thou didst turn thine attention to the Center of the Covenant. Rest thou assured that thou wilt be confirmed to give sight to the blind and hearing power to the deaf, and even thou wilt give life to the dead! Unto thee be the Glory of Abhá![61]

Tokujiro wanted to travel and spread the Faith and the Master's Tablet spoke to that:

> To the one who longs to enter the Kingdom of God, Mr. Torii –
> May his soul be enraptured!
>
> O thou who hast turned thy attention to the Kingdom of God!
> Thy letter arrived and imparted joy. Thou hast been longing to
> spread the Light (the Teachings) in those regions. My wish is also
> that the Musk of the love of God should be diffused in that land,
> and that Miss Alexander and Mrs. Finch may conjointly strive so
> that the rays of the Sun of Reality may be projected all over that
> country.
>
> Whenever the means of travel is secured, thou art permitted to
> come. I am supplicating God to strengthen thee and make thee
> grow like unto a lily in the Garden of the Kingdom.
>
> O faithful friend! The inhabitants of that region are bright and
> noble-minded. Through the great distance, however, the musky
> Breeze has not yet reached their nostrils. They know not of the rise
> of the Sun of Truth upon the horizon of Persia. If you who are there
> be self-sacrificing and become enkindled with the love of God, and
> like unto stars shine from the horizon of Truth, that country will
> before long be turned into a paradise of comfort. Japan will become
> illumined, and like unto a meadow and a rose-garden will invigor-
> ate the hearts of every assembly. Do ye strive as hard as possible in
> order to be attracted to the Beauty of the Beloved of the World, and
> through the fire of His love inflame that kingdom.[62]

It was an amazing time for the group of Japanese youth. In addition to
the youth, Mr Saiki also received a Tablet that read:

> O thou who art seeking the Truth! Thy letter has been received.
> Thou hast taken much pain in inventing the new Japanese writing.
> Thou hast rendered a service to the world of humanity. May God
> reward thee!
>
> Today, however, there exist many kinds of writing. That which is
> most necessary and is assisted by divine confirmations is the propa-
> gation of the heavenly Call. It is this which energizes the world of
> existence. It is this which bestoweth life unto the dead souls, which

refresheth the dried tree and ornamenteth it with leaves, blossoms and fruits. Concentrate all thine energy in this that thou mayest make heavenly progress, that thou mayest attain to the sight of the Sun of Reality, that thou mayest become the cause that the dead body of Japan may attain to heavenly life, may be endowed with solar illumination and like unto the moon and star it may shine forth!

This is important! Convey on my behalf the warmest Abha greeting to all the friends one by one. Unto thee be the Glory of Abha![63]

Agnes was slowly trying to learn Japanese, studying it a little each day. She noted that she knew enough of the language to 'keep house and travel, yet it is quite a different thing to attempt polite conversation which is most complicated. It is not like English where we use but one vocabulary for everyone and everything. Here one must know many different expressions for the same thing.'[64]

On Christmas Day, 1920, Agnes and Ida invited a large number of children from their neighbourhood. They had to take out the furniture and remove the sliding doors to make room for all of them[65]

In January 1921, a series of articles in the newspaper resulted in over 50 inquiries about the Faith, many from the country outside of Tokyo. 'Abdu'l-Bahá's picture had appeared five times, three times in Tokyo papers, once in a paper in the far west of Honshu and once in Hokkaido. An illustration of the Bahá'í House of Worship in Chicago was printed in a Tokyo newspaper the previous October for the first time.[66]

In March, Agnes received a letter from Mason Remey who had just visited 'Abdu'l-Bahá at Tiberias in the Holy Land. Mason wrote:

After greeting us He asked what I had heard about the Bahai work in Japan. I told Him as much as I could remember of the news contained in your recent report which had reached me, and then He spoke very beautifully of your service to the Cause. He told me that I should write to you and convey to you His love and spiritual salutation, then He said:– 'Miss Alexander has gone to that part of the world (Japan) with great spiritual power and she had been confirmed by the angels of the Kingdom.' Then He went on to explain the meaning of 'angels of the Kingdom', that they were not the Supernatural beings imagined by some people, but that they signified the spiritual forces and powers of the Kingdom of God.[67]

By July, Agnes was living quietly in her house, unworried about what to do next. She wrote that she was 'trusting only to His guidance in all things. He never fails and so I am safe. I have not a plan, but I know each day He will guide and show the way. I must keep our little "Star" shining, and this is the greatest work I can do at present.'[68]

In August, Tokujiro Torii spent a few days in Tokyo and, of course, he and Agnes renewed their bond. She hadn't seen him for a year and a half, though they did correspond constantly. Tokujiro was a teacher in a school for blind children in the 'far west of Japan'. One night while he was in Tokyo, Agnes hosted Tokujiro and three other blind Japanese for supper. All of them were involved with the *Garden of Light*, a Braille magazine for blind children. Agnes noted, 'They are all wonderfully united and that is the secret of their success with the little magazine for the blind children.'[69]

IO

KOREA, CHINA AND JAPAN'S GREAT EARTHQUAKE

1921–1923

In the spring of 1920, Agnes had suddenly been inspired by Korea. As she had done years before with Japan, she read everything she could find about the country. A Korean friend helped her and she realized that without her knowledge of Japanese, it would have been very difficult to go alone. As experience would soon show her, the Koreans were quite a different people. That winter, Agnes met a young Korean, Mr Oh Sang Sun, and told him about 'Abdu'l-Bahá and the Glad Tidings. Oh Sang Sun returned to Korea with a Japanese friend, Mr Yanagi. Both Oh Sang Sun and Mr Yanagi subscribed to *Star of the East*.[1]

In May, Agnes received a letter from Mr E. Kim, a Korean Esperantist. He had been teaching the Faith in Korea by writing letters in Esperanto to others conversant in the language and now wanted to write to 'Abdu'l-Bahá. Agnes's reaction was 'Oh, how ripe the fields are, just waiting for the sowers!' Her desire to visit Korea to directly teach the Faith was rekindled.[2]

Suddenly, during the summer of 1921, Agnes was inspired with the idea that it was the time then to actually go to Korea. In a Tablet to Fanny Knobloch, when she was pioneering to South Africa, 'Abdu'l-Bahá had written that:

It may be that the government of those regions will check thee. Thou shouldst say: 'I am a Bahá'í and am a friend with all religions and nations. I consider all to be of one race and count them as my relatives. I have divine love and not racial and sectarian love. According to the palpable written command of Bahá'u'lláh I do not pronounce a word pertaining to politics, because we are forbidden to interfere in political affairs. We are concerned with affairs which are heavenly.

We are servants unto the world of morality. We consider that religious, racial, political and national prejudices are destructive to the world of humanity. We believe that the whole of the surface of the earth constitutes one home and all mankind form one family.'[3]

To get permission to visit Korea, Agnes contacted a Japanese minister, Viscount Shibusawa, who questioned her for an hour and a half. When she showed him the quotation from 'Abdu'l-Bahá, Agnes was surprised at his reaction:

Viscount Shibusawa was delighted with these words, especially that the Bahá'ís did not interfere in political affairs. To my great surprise, raising his hands he announced with a smile that he would himself give me introductions to the Governor of Korea, and others with whom he was personally acquainted. Then he expressed his admiration that I had come alone to Japan, and had stood alone and taken nothing from anyone. I felt overwhelmed for little had I dreamed of receiving introductions from him. The All-Pervading Power of God was manifest! A few days later a messenger brought me three letters of introduction from Viscount Shibusawa written with his own hand in beautiful Japanese style on long scrolls. One was to the Governor of Korea, another to the head of the Daiichi Bank of Seoul and a third to the head of the same Bank in Pusan.[4]

Mr Yanagi visited Agnes the day before she left and gave her his card to show to Mr Yamagata, the editor of the only English paper in Korea, the *Seoul Press*. He advised her to confer with him and follow his advice.[5]

Agnes took a train from Tokyo to Shimonoseki on the southwestern most tip of Honshu Island, and then boarded a steamer for Fusan (Pusan), Korea. From the seaport, she took another train to Seoul, arriving on 19 August. The differences between Japan and Korea were obvious from the train:

Though I have seen Koreans both in Hawaii and Japan, yet it is quite different to see them here. The day's journey on the train from Fusan to Seoul was most interesting to me. Korea is quite different from Japan, and the people have held to their old ways, probably since the time of Christ. It is apparent they are not commercial people. Their dress, though, from the first appealed to me, and really the Japanese dress has lost charm. The weather was very hot when I arrived and the Korean modestly clothed from head to foot in the pure white linen robes was attractive. They wear pure white here unless children and then they color the skirt or jacket in one of the bright Korean colors which is most attractive.

Too, I like the modest way the women wear their hair parted exactly in the middle and brushed shiney down with a pug on the neck. The little girls are the quaintest. Their hair is done in the same way but [with] a braid with long ribbon streamers down the back. Then their overskirts come to the ground with quaint Korean slippers. One has to see them though, to understand. There is some-thing attractive in the young men.[6]

Agnes stayed in what she called 'the best Hotel I have been in, in many ways, in the Far East', the Chosen Hotel. It was built on the grounds of the 'wonderful' Temple of Heaven, cost $4 per day (with a 5% discount if rented for a week) and was full of tourists, business people, mis-sionaries and others, including John D. Rockefeller (which she spelled 'Rockfellow').[7] Agnes felt as if she was 'going to her family', instead of to a strange land where she knew no one, with one exception. On enter-ing Korea she was 'thrilled with interest and realized that it was a virgin country' she was 'entering where no spiritual violation had yet come, and where the soil was fresh and pure and ready for the divine seeds'.[8]

In the afternoon of her first day in Seoul, a young deaf man, Mr Kurita, who had been introduced to the Faith by Tokujiro Torii, came to see her. Deaf since birth, he 'was so skilled in lip reading that I was not aware of his deafness until he asked if we might change our seats to a lighter place as he was reading my lips. Then I remembered that Mr. Torii had written me of him, that he was an eager Christian, but was attracted to the Bahá'í teachings, and was the first one among the deaf in Japan to be interested in the Cause.'[9] During her stay Mr Kurita did whatever he could to help Agnes. When she tried to thank him for his help, he said that he did it for the sake of 'Abdu'l-Bahá.[10]

The next day, Agnes went see the Governor, taking with her the letter of introduction from Viscount Shibusawa. The Governor was away, so:

I was presented to the Governor General, Viscount Saito, a distinguished man. After a short conversation in which I presented him with a Japanese Bahá'í booklet, his secretary and two others from the Foreign Relations Department of the government interviewed me. None of these men had ever heard of the Bahá'í Cause. To each one I gave a copy of the Japanese Bahá'í booklet and explained the Bahá'í teaching that one must respect the government of the country where he resides, and therefore I desired to do everything in harmony with the government. Two hours were spent at the government offices that memorable morning. During the time the Chief of Police was communicated with and told of me, and that I should be given freedom to teach in Korea. The power of Bahá'u'lláh was truly manifested! With a light heart free from care I returned to the hotel. Mr. Kurita came again that afternoon with some friends and together we called on the Director of the YMCA, Mr. Hara, to whom I had been given an introduction at the government offices.[11]

Agnes then went to visit the First Bank with one of her letters of introduction. The head of the bank dropped everything and spent an hour with her talking about 'spiritual things'. He invited her to return and also invited her to his home for dinner.[12]

The English-language daily newspaper carried a note about her arrival and the purpose of her visit, so she visited its office the next morning. Later in the day, she returned to her hotel and found a reporter waiting for her with an introduction to Viscount Saito's English secretary and asking her to come to the newspaper office for an interview. At the interview, Agnes was asked for her picture to put with the newspaper story. Instead, she offered them a photo of 'Abdu'l-Bahá. Ultimately, she said they 'compromised, asking her to have her picture taken holding His photo, but as she said she could not do this, His Picture was copied, but in the end a picture was taken in the garden as a souvenir, so they said. This picture was used though, and placed together with Abdul Baha's in the newspaper the next day.'[13]

Agnes really wanted to find her friend Oh Sang Sun, but was having no success. Finally, she turned to 'Abdu'l-Bahá. Soon afterwards, while driving with Mr Kurita and some of his friends, suddenly there was Oh Sang Sun walking along the street. He went back to the hotel with her, introducing her to many people on the way. For the rest of her stay in

Korea, Oh Sang Sun was her constant companion and opened many doors for her.[14]

The next day, with Oh Sang Sun, she visited the leading Korean newspaper, a meeting that resulted in the image of the Chicago Temple and a photo of the Master appearing in a Korean newspaper. In the afternoon, an official from the Governor General's office, who had spent a dozen years in America, came to learn about the Bahá'í Faith.

As people in Seoul heard about Agnes and her activities, they began almost queuing up to meet her. On 22 August, a man named Mr Datte from the religious section of the government came to the hotel to see her. They had much in common because he had lived in Hawaii for 20 years and knew her family. He had worked in a store on Main Street in Honolulu connected to one of the plantations. Now he worked for the government, and Agnes described him as 'really a kind, gentle man, and I feel a real friend'.[15] In the afternoon, her deaf friend Mr Kurita gave a party for her with 14 people, including Japanese ladies and young men as well as a missionary and his wife.[16]

Agnes went to a reception given by the International Friendship Association the next day. There were many officials and 'leading men' of Seoul, plus three ladies. Agnes noted that 'This was the first time Japanese ladies had been invited, but as this servant was the only lady, they invited them for her company.' The group asked Agnes to speak on the Bahá'í Revelation and the next day, both the Korean and English newspapers printed notices of the meeting.[17]

At the end of the first week in Seoul, Agnes had met and spoken with the Governor, the newspapermen and several others in high positions. Then on 2 September, on one day's notice, Agnes gave her first public talk in Seoul. She had wanted to meet the Korean youth and was told about the Chundokyo, a society of young people that included 'Confusianists, Taotists and Buddhists and today Christians'. Oh Sang Sun introduced her to one of the group's leaders and a meeting was set for the next night. Oh Sang Sun took Agnes to the meeting and served as her interpreter:

Mr. O. first spoke as an introduction. Though I do not know what he said, yet he seemed filled with great fervor. This servant trusted only Abdul Baha to guide her words and spoke simply, Mr. O. translating into Korean. The one point emphasized was the Center,

Abdul Baha, to whom all could turn for comfort. The friend from the religious section of the government I had asked to come, and he brought word to me from one of the heads of the foreign relations department that he was very glad I was going to speak and sorry he had been too busy to see more of me . . .

So Abdul Baha made the way so easy, and this servant felt perfect freedom in speaking. Afterwards one of the leaders of the society came in great joy, saying the Teachings were what he believed. Mr. D[atte], the Japanese friend from the government, talked in Japanese with him, and it seemed as if a great unity was being made. He gave his card which showed he belonged to the officials of the government, but he explained that he had known my family in Hawaii and as I was alone, he was helping me . . . Mr. D. said he thought there were 1,500 present. It seemed a large number but Mr. O. thought about 900. I do not believe that anywhere has the Bahai message been given for the first time publicly in a new country to so great an audience.[18]

On 5 September, Agnes met Mr Roh, a young Korean who had met 'Abdu'l-Bahá in the Holy Land. She had been told about him by Anna Kunz, who had met him when she visited 'Abdu'l-Bahá in 1921. Anna had told Agnes to look Mr Roh up if she went to Korea. Agnes tried, but was unable to find him until Oh Sang Sun managed to locate him. Initially, Mr Roh was out of town, but he returned on 5 September and both he and Oh Sang Sun coincidentally arrived at the Chosen Hotel at almost the same time:

All that day the Invisible forces had been guiding that these two friends should together in unity arrange a booklet for their people, and the contents of that booklet had been given to this servant, which was the words of Abdul Baha with a short introduction. Sitting by the side of the Temple of Heaven these wonderful inspirations came, it seemed they were fulfilled in the meeting in the evening. This servant realized the great capacity of the friend, Mr. R. It seems he has been permitted to have the best that education could give, after six years study in Japan he spent six more years in the United States, graduating from Columbia college and also a Theological seminary, then he spent a year at Oxford University.

On returning home he visited the Holy Land, expecting to go to Haifa to see Abdul Baha, but unexpectedly at the Sea of Galilee, he found Abdul Baha occupying the room next to his! There he had several interviews. When he told Abdul Baha what his work was to be, Abdul Baha told him to teach only the words of Christ from the four gospels. Mr. R. is connected with a mission, teaching in a Christian college, also a theological school and preaching. He is in sympathy with us though not yet aware of the Great Center. He feels the need of this day, and though he cannot work openly, he is one in heart. The next day unexpectedly to us both, we had another meeting.[19]

The First Bank invited Agnes to address them on 6 September. About 50 employees of the bank gathered after work. She spoke in English, which not everyone understood, but she felt that seeds had been planted. Afterwards, the banker took Agnes to his home where a 'wonderful Japanese feast' was served to the nine people present. The banker had purposely chosen to have nine people because it was the Bahá'í number.[20]

The 8th of September was the day of the Bahá'í Feast of 'Izzat, so Agnes and Oh Sang Sun invited their friends to the Korean YMCA for the event. Eleven came and asked many questions about 'Abdu'l-Bahá as to His station, His daily life and the history of His life. At the end, cards were passed around for each to write something to send to the Master. They wrote: 'The message of Truth which shines all 'round the universe', 'Various streams running into the same ocean', 'Just now I found the brilliant light of Bahai', 'The universal supreme mountain of Truth', and 'Oh freedom! Oh Bahai!'[21]

The next evening, the young Korean men from the YMCA gave Agnes a 'feast'. She described it as 'a heavenly feast and again those present wrote their names to be sent to 'Abdu'l-Bahá and a photograph was taken'.[22]

On another day, Agnes went with Oh Sang Sun to a Buddhist school where he taught. He again introduced Agnes and translated what she said. Agnes began by showing them a photo of 'Abdu'l-Bahá. At first, she wrote that 'some of the faces of the students, perhaps one or two, looked a trifle amused, but they grew more and more earnest. This servant lingered afterwards. The inspiration came to [send] a greeting to

Abdul Baha from that spot, and so a few who also had lingered wrote in Korean while Mr. O. and another teacher who knew English wrote in English.'[23]

On 17 September, Agnes met with those interested at the Korean YMCA. Oh Sang Sun gave an introduction and then Agnes talked about unity to the nine present. The next day was Agnes's last day in Seoul and she delivered 19 bunches of flowers to the poor patients at the Severance Hospital. Agnes left the next day, 19 September, the same day that in 1914 had seen her departing Marseilles for Japan; this was also the day she had left Honolulu for America in 1917. [24]

Back in Tokyo

Agnes received her next Tablet from the Master shortly after her return from Korea:

> O thou who wanderest in the divine Path! In the path of God thou didst leave behind thy familiar country and traveled to those distant regions, so that thou mayest spread the Teachings of God and give the people the Glad Tidings of the Kingdom of God. Be assured that confirmations will reach thee and thou wilt become assisted in accomplishing a great service to the world of humanity. A thousand tidings reach thee! Thy brother, Ono San, also will be confirmed and with the utmost joy and happiness he will come back. Unto thee be the Glory of Abhá! [25]

This Tablet answered one of Agnes's unspoken prayers: 'When the Tablet reached me, I was overcome with gratitude and thankfulness to the Beloved Master Who had heard the unwritten prayer of my heart and answered it in His great Mercy. The prayer was for the blind brother, Ono San.' Interestingly, Ono San had been corresponding with a Black American Bahá'í in New York, Roy Williams, and Roy had received a Tablet from 'Abdu'l-Bahá written on the same date as the one Agnes had received. Agnes had been ill, and in Roy's Tablet the Master wrote: 'I supplicate to the Kingdom of Abhá and implore for Miss Agnes Alexander exalted spirituality and great comfort.'[26]

Back in her house, Agnes was having an apparently novel experience: living without any servants:

Since my return I have been alone here without a servant. I knew when I returned that my servant could not come immediately back as she is with her daughter in law who has a baby and other little children to be cared for . . . I have gotten along wonderfully. It is a new experience, but I have proved that I can do it. Of course it takes time, especially when I have company, but I find a pleasure in the service and in the evening when I have been alone, I have gone to bed tired. It will be three weeks on the 12th, since my return, but it has gone so quickly. It has rained most of the time. That makes the house workless, as there is no dust. As Yuri San will probably not come back, I am thinking of getting a girl from Miss Tsuda's school, one whom I like very much, but I have not yet spoken of it and so do not know. I would like also to make a change in a servant. They are as hard to get here perhaps as at home. I would have to pay more though, if I had one who knew something. My old lady only asked $20 a month, but she was very poor as a servant, though a good old soul . . .[27]

At some point, Agnes's brother Arthur sent her a diploma, possibly belonging to their father. When she showed it to a Japanese friend, 'he became delighted and said, "You have a treasure". That is because the Emperor Meiji has signed his name in his own hand, and then it was during the Hawaiian monarchy, which now is past. This young man said it was the first time he had seen the original writing of the Emperor Meiji, as it is hard to get now. The Emperor Meiji is almost . . . worshipped by the Japanese.'[28]

In November, Yuri Mochizuki, the first female Japanese Bahá'í and editor of the *Star of the East*, left Japan and sailed for France. Of this amazing young woman, Agnes wrote: 'For a year she had faithfully edited, proofread, and sent out the *Star of the East* on the nineteenth day of each month. Through this little medium, the Word of God was scattered throughout Japan.' Her place as editor of the *Star* was taken up by Kenji Fukuda. Kenji was

a man with a family quite different from all who had come under the divine guidance in Japan. For thirty years he had been studying religions, and for three years was a Christian minister. He heard of me through the Esperanto secretary in Tokyo, and came to ask me some questions about the Bahá'í teachings. I answered all his questions and then he said it was very wonderful, that all that I said was exactly what he was thinking. I replied that he was a Bahá'í before he ever heard of Bahá'u'lláh. He became illumined and joyful in finding the Cause and offered to edit the *Star of the East* with Miss Mikae Komatsu's assistance, which was continued for another year.[29]

The Passing of 'Abdu'l-Bahá

The Bahá'ís in Japan received a cablegram on 28 November from the Greatest Holy Leaf that read: 'His Holiness 'Abdu'l- Bahá has ascended the Abhá Kingdom.' It was followed a short while later by another: 'May His spirit assist us in serving His Covenant and being united more than ever in promulgating His Cause. 'Abdu'l-Bahá's family.'[30] Agnes quickly shared the message with the other Japanese Bahá'ís and also with the newspapers in Japan, Korea and China, including a booklet about the Bahá'í teachings. She wrote:

> These were published in both Japanese and English newspapers giving great prominence to the Cause. An editor of an English paper in China, who had never heard of 'Abdu'l-Bahá, began his story in a humorous vein of his wonderment on reading the cablegram, as to who 'Abdu'l-Bahá was? Then after he read the Bahá'í literature which was enclosed he continued at length a splendid article with quotations from the Teachings. In the Beloved Master's passing a great power was released in those Far Eastern countries. [31]

Agnes never had the chance to meet the Master in person, but wrote that she

> did not feel the sorrow at the time, which others who had met Him experienced, for He seemed to be still as near to me as ever. This perhaps was God's mercy and recompense to me because I had not had the privilege of meeting Him. My first thought on receiving the cablegram was that we would never again receive Tablets from Him. Then I began to collect the precious Tablets He had revealed to the Japanese living in Japan.[32]

Tokujiro Torii wrote to Agnes: "Abdu'l-Bahá passed away, but His eternal living spirit is always with us and puts us to greater and closer unity. The Day of God has passed, but the Star of Truth is shining more brilliantly in the firmament of the hearts of humanity.' The Bahá'ís in Tokyo held a commemoration for 'Abdu'l-Bahá on 4 December in the house that Agnes and Ida Finch shared. Agnes placed notices in both English and Japanese newspapers and sent out 95 invitations.[33]

There were 36 people who gathered to remember the Master, including six women. Mr Sanzo Misawa took the train from Kobe, a 12-hour journey, in order to attend the gathering. All the furniture had been removed and cushions placed on the floor to accommodate everyone. Eleven people spoke, including two of Agnes's 'girls', Haruko Mori and Otoe Murakami. Others who came were Kenji Fukuda, Mr Ho (Korean), Mr H. L. Yang (Secretary of the Chinese Legation), and Clara Smith. Agnes noted, 'It was very wonderful to consider the power which 'Abdu'l-Bahá gave the girls, Otoe Murakami and Haruko Mori, to speak among so many men in that oriental country where women were only beginning to meet with men, and their speeches touched the hearts, for they knew their Lord and His love surrounded them.' Some of those who were not Bahá'ís also spoke, but 'all hearts were inspired by His love and it was a blessed gathering'.[34]

The year 1921 ended with a big Christmas party. Again, all the furniture was removed – and stored in places such as the bathroom – and 77 children plus eight adults packed in. Agnes noted that they were able to have so many people because 'children do not take up much room on the matted floor'. Agnes and Ida gave the children oranges, candy and cakes and everyone enjoyed the pretty little Christmas tree.[35]

The Guardian's first letter to Japan

The new year began with the Feast of Sultán. Agnes sent out special delivery cards and five girls came. The girls didn't know English, so it was difficult for Agnes to explain anything to them because her Japanese was still very weak. The girls were contacts of Yuri Mochizuki.[36]

Shoghi Effendi sent his first letter to Japan on 26 January:

My well-beloved brethren and sisters in 'Abdu'l-Bahá:
    Despondent and sorrowful, though I be in these darksome days,

yet whenever I call to mind the hopes our departed Master so confidently reposed in the friends in that Far Eastern land, hope revives within me and drives away the gloom of His bereavement. As His attendant and secretary for well nigh two years after the termination of the Great War, I recall so vividly the radiant joy that transfigured His Face whenever I opened before Him your supplications as well as those of Miss Agnes Alexander. What promises He gave us all regarding the future of the Cause in that Land at the close of almost every supplication I read to Him! Let me state, straightway, the most emphatic, the most inspiring of them all. These are His very words, that still keep ringing in my ears: – 'Japan will turn ablaze! Japan is endowed with a most remarkable capacity for the spread of the Cause of God! Japan, with (another country whose name He stated but bade us conceal it for the present) will take the lead in the spiritual reawakening of peoples and nations that the world shall soon witness!' On another occasion, – how vividly I recall it! – as He reclined on His chair, with eyes closed with bodily fatigue, He waved His hand and uttered vigorously and cheerfully these words in the presence of His friends: – 'Here we are seated calm, quiet and inactive, but the Hand of the Unseen is ever active and triumphant in lands, even as distant as Japan!'

My dear and steadfast friends! Now if ever is the time for you and for us to show, by our unity, service, steadfastness and courage, the spirit that the Master has throughout His lifetime so laboriously, so persistently kindled in our hearts. Now is the time for us to prove ourselves worthy of His love for us, His trust in us and His hopes for us. Japan, He said will turn ablaze. Let us not, in any way, whatsoever, retard the realization of His promise. Nay, let us hasten, through our service, cooperation and efforts the advent of this glorious Day.

The bereaved Ladies of the Holy Household, receive with comfort and refreshing gladness any news that may come to them from that wonderful and distant land. They all know what the Master has graciously spoken about the future of the Cause in that land. They all expect from it a rapid transformation, a spiritual transformation even more sudden and startling than its material progress and advancement, for the Power of God can achieve wonders still greater than those the brilliant minds of the Japanese can achieve. This they firmly believe, for more than once, the Master has spoken of the spiritual potentialities hidden in the nature of these capable people. They all await with eagerness the joyful tidings that your letters to them shall bear in future.

We all wish so much to know more about you, about your little rising Bahá'í community, your number, your meetings, your activities, your difficulties, your plans, your distribution all over Japan and the neighboring islands. We shall all pray for you most fervently and in a special manner at all the Three Hallowed Shrines and beseech the Master, under whose Wings we are all, to guide you, to sustain you in your work for Him.

I shall never fail to send you all the news I receive from different parts of the Bahá'í world that you may know of the efforts and triumphs our brethren, the loved ones of 'Abdu'l-Bahá, are achieving and will achieve after Him.

Persia, the leading nation in the Bahá'í world, to-day, will, I am confident, through its centre, Tihran, communicate with you all, that the East and West, even as our Beloved One has so much wished it, may become even as one.

The letter our dear sister, Miss Agnes Alexander, had written to Mr. Fujita, gave us such a joy and was read at the sorrowful gathering of His friends, in the very room He used to receive His friends and meet them every night.

Ever awaiting your joyful news,

I am, your devoted brother in His love and service,

Shoghi[37]

The doll project

The idea of contributing to the Temple Fund for the construction of the Chicago House of Worship was on Agnes's mind and was pushed along by letters from Victoria Bedikian, a tireless letter writer. The Japanese Bahá'ís didn't have money to contribute, but in March 1922, Agnes came up with the idea of sending dolls from Japan, Korea and China which could be sold for the Fund.[38] Agnes bought the dolls and the girls made kimonos for them. They also began collecting other Japanese things that could also be sold to the American Bahá'ís. In June, she wrote to Victoria about how the project was progressing:

Yesterday I did up a box of little dolls! Oh, Victoria how I want them to reach your hands! Eleven little dolls fitted into the box! These are the small ones which are more easily sent. I also have three other packages to send to you. One is Japanese prints, one writing paper and another some small paper parasols that the children might like for the dolls. I am now waiting to hear if a lady who is going to America will carry these with her as far as San Francisco, where they could be mailed. The postage here is so dear . . . I feel as though these little dolls were like living beings to carry a loving message to the friends in America . . . Around each doll is a label with a number and on another paper enclosed I will give suggestions as to the prices which might be put on them . . . The dolls are all dressed in the best of cloth, though they are not all the most expensive dolls . . . The satin bag enclosed with the dolls is made from a piece from Kyoto, the old city, and is considered quite rare. The prints are not expensive except two which I have marked . . . There are some pictures from Japanese magazines which my servant girl gave me, and some prints from Miss Wilkinson who is living with me. The little silk handkerchief came from the girl who sews for me, – a poor girl . . . It was my servant girl who gave the first doll. Isn't it the poor who do the first work![39]

The doll project expanded. Agnes noted that Yuri Takao, a 16-year-old girl, dressed one doll and Mikae Komatsu brought Japanese cards to send.[40] Mrs Kanae Takeshita, 'a lovely Japanese lady who heard of the Cause from Mrs. Finch', interested her friends and 'many beautiful dolls were dressed and contributed, resulting in a great doll family which continued to grow for more than a year'. Agnes wrote:

We have been dressing Japanese dolls to send to America and sell for the Temple. Now the doll family has increased and through His confirmation reached more than a hundred. Mr. Torii interested his wife and sister in the work and they sent us some beautifully dressed dolls. A student who attended the meetings was leaving to go to California and enter the University there, and offered to take with him a suitcase of dolls. We packed six of the largest and nicest of the dolls and sent them by him to be delivered to Mrs. Kathryn Frankland in Berkeley. The smaller dolls were sent to Victoria Bedikian in Montclair, New Jersey, and some to others.[41]

In addition to the doll project, proclamation of the Faith continued in Japan. On the day of the Declaration of the Báb, three Tokyo newspapers printed articles about the anniversary of the Faith. Ujaku Akita published three articles about the Cause in a Japanese magazine called *New Tide* which also reproduced the picture of 'Abdu'l-Bahá.[42]

China to the forefront

In 1917, Ahmad Sohrab, in his diary, quoted 'Abdu'l-Bahá as saying: 'China, China, China, China-ward the Cause of Baha'o'llah must march! Where is that holy, sanctified Bahai to become the teacher of China?'[43] This quotation may have inspired both Martha Root and Agnes to turn their eyes toward China. Agnes's second encounter with the Chinese, after the newspapermen in 1920, came in April 1922 when she had the chance to teach Esperanto to 16 Chinese students. In addition to learning Esperanto, they also learned about the Bahá'í Faith.[44]

Agnes was commonly inspired to do things and go places. On Sunday morning of 23 April, she had 'a wonderful inspiration' of visiting Hawaii for about three months and it filled her with joy. Then on 19 May, while groups of Chinese students were visiting Tokyo, she had another inspiration that she would go to Pekin (Agnes uses 'Pekin' and 'Peiping' interchangeably in both her letters and her *History of the Bahá'í Faith in Japan*. Today it is called Beijing). She noted, 'Now I know these are truths, but when they will be fulfilled I do not know. It may be very long and I do not know to which place I will go first. Now China has become a new and wonderful country to me. I feel that I would go only to Pekin on a visit from here.'[45]

In May, five groups of Chinese students came to Japan from different parts of China. On the 18th, a group of 19 young Chinese women from the Peiping Women's Teachers College appeared in a photo in the Tokyo newspaper. Agnes wrote, 'In my eagerness to meet the girls and tell them of the Bahá'í Cause, I went to the newspaper office and asked if I might attend the dinner, and received an invitation . . . After the dinner I met two of the Chinese girls and arranged to call on them.' Agnes was particularly attracted to one of the girls, Chien Yung Ho:

> She said that the Chinese Women's Association of Peiping wished to give all people a chance to live, and especially the lowest class, that

all mankind should be allowed happiness without the limitation of sex, race or country. She said they had lost interest in politicians and were developing their interest in world ideas; that they wished to do their utmost for the happiness of the whole population without respect to religion or race, and that their future aim was to establish correspondence with the women of the world.[46]

The next morning, Agnes was again inspired that she would go to China. She then did just what she had done when she had been inspired about going to Japan and Korea: she looked up every book she could find on China. The girls stayed in Tokyo for two weeks and Agnes visited them several times. Agnes saw the group off at the train station and wrote that 'Miss Chien . . . put her arms around me and said, "You are my teacher." She invited me, when I would come to China, to visit the school where she was going to teach and tell the pupils about the Bahá'í Teachings. A year and a half passed and this was fulfilled when Martha Root and I traveled together in China in 1923.' After they left, she corresponded with Chien Yung Ho, who wrote:

> Traveling to Japan gave us the good luck to meet you, who accepted us with your very warm heart. . . Our school-mates recently have a conference called, 'Female Freedom Extending Conference.' The purpose of it was to discuss and settle things regarding education, constitution, economics, labor, etc., with respect to females. The meeting will be held weekly and famous people are invited to give lectures and magazines are to be published . . . Besides this conference, a Women's Suffrage Conference has been established by the Peiping girls . . . I would appreciate it very much if you let me have 'Abdu'l-Bahá's writings . . . All of us are remembering you and desiring to hear from you at all times.[47]

Agnes also met a group of 34 Higher Normal School students from Wuchang, another group of Higher School students from Peiping and yet another group of 50 Higher Normal School students from Chengtu in Szechuan province. Mr H. C. Waung brought four of the Chengtu group to Agnes's home and 'gave me the opportunity to tell them of the glorious Message of Bahá'u'lláh'. The group told her that:

they had traveled for a month to reach Tokyo. The first twelve days were through rough country in sedan chairs, then by river steamers until Shanghai was reached, where they embarked for Japan. One of the students said that the people of their province were ready now to do anything which would be for the good of the people. He said: 'All countries are now searching education. In our educational work we have two problems. The first is financial. We have not enough money and this is due to the government. The other problem is that many of the old school people hesitate in adopting new ideas and because of the isolation of Szechuan province, education is difficult.'[48]

One of the students from the Chengtu group, Kai Tai Chen, wrote an article for Agnes about the changes happening in China based on the teachings of 'Abdu'l-Bahá, which she published in the *Star of the West*.[49]

The last group of Chinese students Agnes met was from the Higher Normal School in Canton. Out of this group of 22 students, Agnes connected with one. Mr Waung told Shik Fan Fong about Bahá'u'lláh and His message and he immediately became infatuated with it. Mr Waung brought him to visit Agnes on a day when the rest of the group were on an excursion. After returning to Canton, Shik Fan Fong wrote to Agnes:

Therefore the principles of 'Abdu'l-Bahá will be surely welcomed with heart and soul in Canton. So far as I have returned to Canton many of my friends have come to see me and asked me what I had gotten from Japan. I always named out firstly you, the universal teacher, and Bahá'u'lláh, the beloved Master. In fact, you are the most figurative feature in my record of this journey. I have tried to convey His Message of Truth to my friends whenever and wherever I have met with them and they have been heartedly welcomed. After I have studied all the pamphlets and paper you gave me, I shall translate some of them into Chinese. . .[50]

New Bahá'ís and visitors

One day, a Keio University student named Susumu Aibara came to see Agnes. He was the first Esperantist at the university. He heard about the

American Esperantist and went to her house one day to invite her to a meeting of the University's Esperanto group. At that point, he knew nothing of the Bahá'í Faith. Agnes 'felt a great inspiration' and immediately began telling him about it. Susumu quickly accepted the Faith and spread it through the University.[51]

Another student, Keiji Sawada, who attended the Government School for the Blind in Tokyo, also began to visit Agnes. His material eyesight was failing, but his spiritual eyes saw very clearly and he was able to introduce the Faith in his school. He brought many of his fellow students to talk with Agnes.[52]

Agnes also met Tomojiro Hamada, a country boy from Tokushima on Shikoku Island who made his living selling honey. Agnes said 'he had a spiritual light'. After returning to Tokushima from Tokyo, he wrote to her saying, 'Now I have no friend of spirit because I am so little. Tokushima is very old. It is like the night. I hope soon will be the sunshine on this city.'[53]

In October, Agnes's cousin Samuel Baldwin came from Maui with his wife Kathrine and two of her friends. They invited Agnes to go with them to Kyoto and Miyanoshita, which is in the foothills of the mountains north of Tokyo. During this visit, Kathrine asked Agnes to talk about the Faith and from that point, Kathrine became a 'firm and ardent Bahá'í' and an enthusiastic teacher of the Faith in Hawaii'.

At Christmas 1922, Agnes and Ida again had their children's Christmas party. Over 90 children came, filling every possible space in the little house.[54]

Martha Root returns

Martha Root returned for her second visit to Japan on 10 April 1923. 'Abdu'l-Bahá had told her to 'travel . . . to the different parts of the globe and roar like unto a lion',[55] and according to Agnes, she was like a 'swift flying bird under the guidance of Shoghi Effendi, she passed through the countries singing the melodies of the Kingdom'.[56]

Martha was met by Agnes and Ida on the dock in Yokohama and stayed with them for ten days. Agnes had a full schedule set up for her. She arrived in Tokyo at 6 p.m. and her first talk was an hour later to 200 students at the Japanese English School and that was followed by the Government School for the blind, Keio University, where the students and faculty had a tea party with her after the talk. Susumu Aibara, whom Agnes had first met a year previously, arranged for the university talk followed by another tea party. Susumu afterwards wrote a letter to Agnes and Martha addressed to the 'Peace fighters'. Then there were talks at the Tsuda English School, the English Speaking Society, the Japanese Women's Peace Society and the Esperanto Societies of Tokyo and Yokohama. Agnes wrote:

> Because of Martha's selflessness and devotion, her presence brought confirmations wherever she went. In my home we had a gathering for her and twenty-one were present. Another afternoon we entertained some Burmese young men and told them of the Bahá'í cause. In my guest book Martha wrote: 'I have spent two weeks in Heaven with my precious sister, Agnes. Ya Bahá El-Abhá!'[57]

The Japanese police, however, suspected that Martha had Communist sympathies and followed her around for a week. At an Esperantist meeting, Martha mentioned that the Faith was spreading in Russia and a 'conservative' Japanese newspaper story reported that the Bahá'í teachings were 'a doctrine practically the same as communism'. A wire service picked up the story and the *Pittsburgh Post*, in the city Martha had begun her own journalistic career, passed the story along with embellishments under the title, 'Pittsburgh Girl Trailed by Tokio Police as "Red"':

> The police today visited the Tokio home of Miss Agnes Alexander, a relative of the famous family of missionaries and traders in Hawaii, who is entertaining Miss Root. They questioned the servants at great length . . .
>
> Miss Alexander has been suspected since entertaining the Russian poet Eroshenko, who was deported from Japan a year ago as the result of a charge of Soviet conspiracy in connection with the Bahai movement.
>
> Miss Root . . . today appealed to the United States Embassy for protection. She had no intention of offending Japanese officials, she declared, and hopes to succeed in explaining to them why Bahaism does not menace Japan politically or religiously.[58]

Other Japanese were very taken with Martha's message. One, Count Okuma, whom Martha had met at Waseda University in 1915, later met Agnes and said that Martha had given him a book on the Faith and that he was quite taken with the teachings. To Agnes he said, 'I am glad you have come to my country to spread these noble principles.'[59]

Both Agnes and Ida accompanied Martha to Kyoto, where they met the Esperantists and with people from the headquarters of the Oomoto religion, which had once spread across the country, but was later disbanded by the government. From Kyoto, the three women continued to Osaka, from where Martha sailed for China.

Agnes was back in Kyoto later in the summer and told a young Esperantist, Y. Yasuda, about the Faith. On her way back to Tokyo, she stopped in Nagoya where the Esperantists were holding a conference. She wrote:

> During a few days spent in that city, the Cause was made known through newspaper articles, two of which carried my picture. One of those who became attracted to the Cause, was a Japanese Christian minister, Mr. N. Nagano, who was carrying on a social work among young men. He wrote me after my return to Tokyo: 'I was very happy that I happened to meet you in Nagoya, and to hear personally from you about your Message, of which I had some knowledge through some pamphlets. Thanks for your kindness to send several kinds of pamphlets. They will be distributed among those who have some interest with the great teaching of Brotherhood . . . I know many friends here, mostly among young men, who have interest, more or less, with religion in the broad sense. They are not Christian, but seeking after something spiritual. I am thinking that if you stay here and try to spread your Message, it would be very effective. I myself would be able to help your work with full energy, as I have much interest with your Message . . .' Another young man, Hiroshi Yamada, an ardent Esperantist, became a real friend to the Cause.[60]

The eager, lovable students of Japan were helping to usher in the day when the New World Order of Bahá'u'lláh would be established. In most of the higher schools of Japan young ardent Esperantists were to be found who were promoting the Bahá'í principle of a universal auxiliary language. The students in the schools formed groups and taught their fellow students. Through the wonderful means of Esperanto, the Bahá'í Message became known in the important centers of Japan, where it met with keen response and no prejudice.[61]

Agnes's sister, Mary Alexander, was the first of their family to visit Agnes in Japan. Mary was returning from France and stopped off for a while. Agnes met her in Kobe and took her back to Tokyo. In spite of the many letters Agnes had sent to Mary about what she was doing, Agnes wrote, 'The veil was not lifted from her eyes, but her spirit towards the Bahá'ís was always loving and tolerant. She was a devoted Christian and satisfied in her faith.'[62] Agnes took Mary to the mountains of Yumoto for 16 days, from 8 to 24 August. After that, Agnes returned to her little house in Tokyo and Mary went to do some hiking on and around Mt Fuji.[63]

On 10 May, Shoghi Effendi himself wrote to the Japanese Bahá'ís and Agnes, noting Martha's visit:

The beloved of the Lord and the handmaids of the Merciful in Japan: Susumu Aibara, E. Tanakamuru, Y.S. Lo, K.C. Ling, N. Yawata, H.C. Waung, M. Hataya, E. Noguchi, F. Takahashi, Ida Finch, K. Sawada, Kenjiro Ono, Tokujiro Torii, Agnes Alexander, Yoshio Ishigura

Dearest brethren and sisters in Bahá'u'lláh:
The most welcome letter of our dearly beloved Bahá'í sister, Miss Agnes Alexander, imparting the glad news of the progress of her glorious services in Japan has rejoiced my heart, and has served to strengthen my hope and confidence in the future glories of that far-eastern land.
The Ladies of the Holy Household are highly gratified and comforted to learn of your untiring labours in His Vineyard, of the success that has attended your efforts, of the perseverance and ardour with which you conduct your teaching work in those distant regions of the earth. 'Abdu'l-Bahá is with you always, and your success is assured!
May the visit of our beloved sister, Miss Martha Root, to your shores stimulate widespread interest in the Cause throughout Japan, China and the Pacific Islands, and consolidate the foundation of

the Edifice of the Cause in those far-eastern regions. I shall ever pray at the Three Holy Thresholds that the seeds now scattered bear abundant fruit and the promises of our beloved Master be speedily fulfilled . . .

It is my earnest hope that the friends in Japan will from now on write me frequent and detailed letters, setting forth the account of their various spiritual activities, and giving me the plans for their future services to the Cause of Bahá'u'lláh.

Our devoted brother, Mr. Fujita, is well and happy in the Holy Land, and together with the Ladies of the Household and myself is engaged in the service of the various pilgrims that visit in these days this sacred Spot. He is faithfully and actively carrying on the work which he has started so whole-heartedly during the Master's last years on earth.

I trust that the letters addressed to you by the newly-constituted Spiritual Assembly in Haifa have contributed their share in informing you more fully of the onward and irresistible march of the Movement throughout the world.

Awaiting your joyful letters,

I am your brother and fellow-worker, Shoghi[64]

The Great Earthquake

On the morning of Sunday 1 September 1923, Agnes sent a cable to the 11th Esperanto Congress of Japan being held in Okayama, 'saying that I was praying for their illumination, that all those present in the congress might find the star of Reality and through it the words of Abdul Baha might [inspire the] assemblage.' Ida had returned from Peiping on 28 August and she and Agnes were relaxing in their little house.[65] At noon, a massive earthquake lasting for several minutes slammed across Tokyo. Agnes wrote:

suddenly a violent tremor shook the house and continued to grow in violence. We fled to the little street. In that moment when the earth trembled and the roofs of the houses fell, one realized the powerlessness of man and God's power over all. As soon as the first great tremor subsided, I rushed into the house and procured my hand bag in which I carried the Prayer for protection revealed by

'Abdu'l-Bahá . . . When the earth began again to tremble, I read the Prayer aloud. Three times this occurred, and each time quiet came after the reading . . . It is God's mercy to us that we could seek the protection of the Greatest Name and did not know of the terrible tragedies which were taking place in the city, two-thirds of which was destroyed by fire, and thousands lost their lives, while several millions were left homeless. The front of the little home was thrown out, and the plaster walls crumbled, but His love and protection was there.[66]

In a letter she hastily wrote that afternoon, Agnes said:

We here in Tokyo have gone through a severe earth quake. We know there have been fires in different parts of the city but do not know of anything yet serious. . . My sister and I have felt this month would be the time we would go to Peking [Peiping], etc. but His plan that He carried out, and as yet it is not all clear [what will happen]. Slight earth quakes are continuing. We do not have running water or gas, telephones or electric cars, but of course this will be remedied before long, God willing. The Imperial Theatre has burned I hear.[67]

Ida also described the powerful event:

We were together when the great catastrophe came to beautiful Japan, talking together when, without the slightest warning the house began to shake most violently. Miss Alexander escaped to the street, but it seemed impossible for me, so after it was over I joined her in the street, unharmed. We read the prayer of protection and remained on the street most of the afternoon for the quaking and shaking continued at intervals all day and for many days after. The house, as well as all other houses, was damaged and must be repaired that it may be an adequate shelter. I jumped into the little front garden and while repeating the Greatest Name saw the earth open around me and the house-front falling toward me . . .

The newspapers have not exaggerated. Quite a million people, in Tokyo alone, are homeless, while we were preserved to serve Him better . . .[68]

The earthquake, later known as the Great Kanto earthquake, strongly affected the Tokyo and Yokohama area and was measured at 7.9 on the Richter scale. Over 140,000 people were killed, more than half of all brick buildings in the cities were destroyed and a tenth of all supposedly reinforced buildings collapsed. The quake sent a tsunami up to 39.5 feet high across the Sagami Gulf where it destroyed the town of Atami.[69]

Obviously, everything was confusion with fires breaking out all over the cities and no means of communication still functioning. Agnes wrote, 'From the moment of the earthquake, everything stopped; there was no running water and the fires could not be put out; the trains and tramways, the gas, electric lights and telephones all ceased operating.'[70] She also wrote:

> The day of the fire and Sunday [2 Sept.], the next day, Mrs Finch and I stayed closely here because always we were threatened with fire and we had to be ready to escape any moment. For two days and nights we did not take our clothes off. Day and night shakes continued but not severe as the first, but severe enough to make us flee for protection to the open street, for things fell from all sides during the great quake and we did not know when it might happen again . . .[71]

Besides being greatly worried about the other Bahá'ís and her friends, Agnes had no idea of what had happened to her sister, Mary. While Agnes worried about Mary, Mary was experiencing the force of the earthquake in a completely different environment:

> I was in suspense without any news whatever of Agnes for fourteen days after the earthquake . . .
>
> Agnes and I left Lake Yumoto August 21st. I . . . decided to go up to Hakone to try to see Fuji by moonlight and to get a breath of mountain air . . .
>
> Then suddenly came the word to meet the two girls from Shanghai at Gotemba . . . for the walking trip around Fuji . . . We were standing in front of the hut just ready for the ascent when the earthquake came. It was terrific. One cannot describe the way the whole mountain shook and heaved, or the sickening sense of helplessness one felt. Everything seemed to give way. The stones built against the hut all tumbled, the ground cracked in front of it and we all

scattered trying to find safety, not able to go where we tried to, running and falling down as one does in a bad dream. Two of us went toward the cleared space of a former avalanche but rocks were flying and spinning down it. Finally, no one could stand, and we all sat on the ground where we happened to be. There must have been a lull when the guides called and beckoned to us all to come to the left of the hut, where a large clump of law shrubs, like stunted guava trees, would check the rocks in their descent. We stood there each holding on to the trunk of one of the shrubs, while it seemed as the mountain would shake itself to pieces. I fully believed our end had come . . . we would be either swallowed up in a crevice or caught in an eruption. There were cracked places everywhere. I can still see the top of Fuji swaying. While we stood there, the Japanese mother praying aloud, the guides from the sixth station rushed down telling us to run! big boulders were coming!

The clouds again obscured the view. The wind had dropped, and there was a stifling stillness when we began the descent of seven miles past landslides, fallen trees and rocks, with the trail entirely torn up in places. Thinking Fuji had been the center of action, we talked about how worried Agnes would be, knowing me to be on it.

As I was gesturing in conversation with the young Japanese lady, our excited guide turned back and expostulated, 'Don't walk with your hands! Walk with your feet and walk fast!'. . .

We heard terrible reports about Yokohama and Tokyo. Yotsuga was named as a part of Tokyo where the fire was raging, and you can imagine my anguish thinking of Agnes. The railroads were down between Yokohama [and] Gotemba and one between Gotemba and Kobe. Three cars had been overturned on the track at Gotemba.[72]

Mary was able to send a letter to Agnes by a businessman, but heard nothing in return. Not until 14 September did she encounter a lady from Tokyo who had seen Agnes, reporting her 'as calm and well and her house safe!!'[73]

During these tragic times, Agnes spent her time

helping to care for the homeless children, and cheering the hearts of the friends. She writes of how, for four days 'after the great quake and fire masses of humanity passed along the broad roadway near (her) home, coming, coming, coming from the burning district below, where they had been driven out by the fire.' When she went through the streets she 'was dazed'. It was too overwhelming to be comprehended. Along the roadway there was scarcely anything to be found to eat. Everything had suddenly come to a standstill. But with tremendous energy the government took hold and food was brought in from the outer provinces.[74]

Of those first few days, Agnes wrote:

> It was not until Tuesday Sept. 3rd I went out as I did not want to leave Mrs. Finch . . . but a neighbor, Mr. Suzuki of the Asahi newspaper advised me to go to the American Embassy and a good student acted as my guide and helper. Really I could not have gone alone for the way was so changed by the fire and I only knew Tokyo by the tram lines and with the great earth quake they ceased as everything else did, for there was no more water running, electricity, gas, etc. Many trams were burned up, for they all stopped . . . and nothing could be brought in therefore we have no bread or flour etc
> . . .
>   I found the American Embassy in ruins, nothing left but four stone pillars. At the Imperial Hotel which did not burn, the Embassy is keeping office and there I went for information concerning Mary.[75]

On 8 September, one of Agnes's neighbours came saying that 'we must all flee as the fire was drawing near but after all it was found not to be necessary'. Agnes found out that 'Two thirds of the city was burned out, that is the great business part and the two most thickly populated districts, that of Henje and Fukagawa . . . Nearly the whole population of these two districts were consumed by fire.'[76]

On the 10th, Ida was evacuated by the US Government and put on a steamer for Seattle, free of charge. Agnes noted that 'we are well provided for, but the conditions of Tokyo are dreadful. Think of a million people homeless and many many without money. The figures I quote from a Japanese editor of a leading paper. Of course no one can say exactly. Two days ago I was told 47,000 bodies had been removed, but it is said in one place there were 20,000 killed by the fire.'[77]

When Ida left, Agnes invited a Japanese woman and her son, whose home had been destroyed by the fire, to stay in the home with her. With all the destruction and death, Agnes said that 'All the Bahá'ís of Tokyo were protected.'[78] She wrote about

how beautifully some of the Japanese Bahá'í friends were protected. Miss Murakami escaped with two young friends, dodged the fire here and there, until in the evening she left her home in the suburbs. Mr. Tanaka, with his little boy of nine years, had started out to travel and spread the Bahá'í teachings, but was caught on the way by the earthquake. On his return home he found his house in ashes. But his bank book had been preserved. So his money was saved. Our Bahá'í brother, Mr. Torii, was attending an Esperanto Congress in Okayama when the earthquake occurred. He tells of how many times the Bahá'í teachings were referred to at that Congress.

The Japanese Bahá'í friends have decided to make their center at present in Kobe, where Mr. Misawa has offered his store as a center. Miss Alexander writes of the beautiful services of the priest [Daiun Inouye] whom 'Abdu'l-Bahá loved.[79]

On 25 September, Agnes was surprised when Mary suddenly walked into her house. It had taken many days for her to get permission to enter Tokyo.[80] Mary and Agnes went to see some of the 700 children who had been separated from their parents. Mary wrote, 'The largest death toll in one place was at the park in the Hongo section of factories where the police drove the people into a park for safety from the fire – 32,000 of them, who were not burned but smothered to death, or suffocated [to death] by the heat. Then there were the 2,000 women locked in the Yoshiwara [Tokyo's red-light district] who burned to death.'[81]

Bahá'ís around the world responded to the disaster by contributing funds to help with the refugees, Agnes wrote:

Through Roy Wilhelm, two hundred dollars ($200) was sent to me from the beloved Bahá'ís of New York, to be used to help earthquake sufferers. With the money, Mr. Misawa of Kobe who had a tailor shop, had garments made for the refugees who flocked to Kobe from Tokyo and Yokohama. Another blessed contribution of forty-five Egyptian pounds came from Haifa. In a letter from the Spiritual

Assembly of Haifa, November, 1923, is the following: 'One of the friends, Ali Effendi of Jaffa, invited all the friends of Haifa and Akka, to a reception on Mount Carmel. In the meeting he humbly stepped forward and addressed beloved Shoghi Effendi and stated that he believed that all such general gatherings should yield some material result, and that as he had heard that the Guardian of the Cause wished that some contribution be sent to the suffering ones in Japan, he contributed ten Egyptian pounds. Other friends present took part in the subscription, as well as members of the Family. A sum of forty-five Egyptian pounds was contributed and will be sent to Japan forthwith.'[82]

A letter written on behalf of the Guardian proclaimed Agnes's survival a miracle and also promised financial help:

Your letter to our very dear Shoghi Effendi was most encouraging and created in him new hopes for the spread of 'Abdu'l-Bahá's great and noble message after this painful calamity in Japan. It was indeed a miracle that amid a city all shaken to pieces and turned to ashes by the wild flames, the Lord should have kept you so safe and unscathed. We can never doubt that this as a direct proof of the mighty Task which the Lord has wanted you to take up and fulfil in that far away East. Shoghi Effendi has always looked forward with great expectations at the progress of the Cause in Japan to which he attaches very great importance.

The Japanese are really progressive people and such vital teachings which comprise the principles of the Bahá'í religion are sure to seize their attention and arouse a deep interest in them. Your presence in Japan was always a means of comfort to Shoghi Effendi's heart because he fully realized the zeal and ardour with which you had taken up your work there and although Japan might now miss you, he is sure that wherever you are you will strive to your utmost in spreading far and near this message of Peace to humanity. Furthermore he hopes that you will not give up altogether your interest in that promising country, but as long as you are away you will keep your tender plants all fresh and green with stimulating messages to them. . .

You would, I am sure, be very interested in the contributions of

Agnes Alexander dressed in a Japanese kimono, probably taken in 1915, soon after her arrival in Japan

Agnes Alexander with Vasily Eroshenko in Tokyo in 1915. Vasily was a blind Russian youth who taught her Braille in English and Esperanto, thus opening many doors

Group in Japan, 1915. Left to right, back row: Ito Torii, Agnes Alexander, Tokujiro Torii, 5 unknowns; front row: Kikutaro Fukuta, the first Japanese to embrace the Cause in Japan, Martha Root, unknown, Ujaku Akita, 2 unknowns

Tokujiro and Ito Torii with Agnes Alexander in 1916. Mr Torii said there came to him one day 'a messenger of the Kingdom of Abhá and lifted up the veil of my soul . . . Every word she spoke to me was wonderful and luminous. It dispelled the darkness from my soul, brought fragrances to my heart like the breeze from the green fields, and made my inner sight keener and fresher than ever.' (Bahá'í World, *vol. IV, p. 490)*

Group in Tokyo, 1916:
'At the top left is Kikutaro
Fukuta, first Japanese living
in Japan to declare his Faith.
Next is Miss Alexander
then Mr Ishida. Bottom
row: Yoshio Tanaka, who
became a Bahá'í, Masaru
Mizutani, Dr [George]
Augur, Yuzuru Kawai, then
the famous writer Ujaku
Akita and Mr Morishita.
Ishida and Kawai were
Waseda University students
who were friends of Akita.
All attended Bahá'í meetings
held by Miss Alexander and
Dr Augur.' (Sims, Traces
that Remain)

Victoria Bedikian (left) and Agnes Alexander outside an art supply store in Montclair, New Jersey, April 1919

In 1920, these girls in Agnes Alexander's Bahá'í class wrote a message to 'Abdu'l-Bahá, who responded calling them 'daughters of the Kingdom'. A photographer took this picture of the girls with their Tablet placed on the table. Far right: Yuri Mochizuki; far left: Otoe Murakami; standing right Haruko Mori. The other three girls are Kimiko Hagiwara, Kazu Fukusawa and Yuri Takao

*Shortly before Christmas 1920,
Agnes invited the children of the
shopkeepers on the street where
she lived to a party. Fifty-eight
children attended; the blind Bahá'ís
Tomonaga Noto and Kenjiro Ono
sang for the children, and Yuri
Mochizuki told them Bahá'í stories.
Ida Finch and Agnes are at the top,
left corner; Mr Noto (with glasses) is
near them. At the top, second right
from the tree is Yuri Mochizuki;
next to her is Kenkichi Futakami,
and Mrs Futakami in the right
corner. Behind her, almost obscured,
is Mr Ono*

*Agnes Alexander in Berkeley,
California, in the 1920s*

In 1921 Agnes was the first to take the Faith to Korea. This photograph was taken at the Chosen Hotel in Seoul at the request of Mr Kurita (to right) a young Christian Japanese who was teaching the Korean mute and was of great assistance to Agnes during her visit. He had been born deaf but could do lip reading in English. Agnes wrote that he was so skillful that she was not aware of his deafness. The two other young men in the photo were friends of his. (Sims, Traces that Remain*)*

Agnes Alexander, Martha Root and Ida Finch in Japan; photograph taken in April 1923 at the home of one of the early Bahá'ís, Mrs Kanae Takeshita, during Martha Root's second visit to Japan. Top: Ida Finch, Agnes Alexander and Kenkichi Futakami; below: Martha Root and Mrs Takeshita

Agnes Alexander and Martha Root attending an Esperanto gathering in Peking (Beijing), China in 1923

Ito Torii, Agnes Alexander and Tokujiro Torii, about 1923 in Japan

Children of the Great Earthquake of 1923 with Agnes Alexander. On 1 September 1923, this earthquake with a magnitude of 7.9 struck the Tokyo-Yokohama metropolitan area. 'The death toll . . . was estimated to have exceeded 140,000. More than half of the brick buildings and one-tenth of the reinforced concrete structures in the region collapsed. Many hundreds of thousands of houses were either shaken down or burned in the ensuing fire touched off by the quake.' (Encyclopaedia Britannica)

the friends and also the members of the Holy Household, including our dear Shoghi Effendi, for the relief of the poverty-stricken Japanese. They shall be communicated by the Spiritual Assembly of Haifa under whose auspices it has been. It is with a deep sense of sisterly affection that they have contributed this sum.[83]

Agnes received letters from many other Bahá'ís proclaiming their happiness that she was safe. Some of these included the Greatest Holy Leaf, Fujita, Yuri Mochizuki, Roy Wilhelm, Rufus Powell (New York), Albert Vail, Louis Gregory, Jeanne Bolles, Mariam Haney, Ziaoullah Asgarzadeh (London) and Victoria Bedikian.[84]

China

The fire set Agnes on a new path, one that took her away from Japan for the next four years. She wrote:

> During the time of the calamity there, when it was thought the fire would reach my house, in my heart I gave up everything: then when it was spared I said to Mrs. Finch, who was with me, 'This house is not for me any longer.' And so it was, for on Oct. 12th, I left it for good, selling my household things . . . Then I felt the freedom to go forth wherever He willed . . . We stopped two days in Kobe, Japan, three in Seoul, Korea, and then on to Peking where I joined Martha Root in the work of the Cause.[85]

Agnes now began to prepare to go to China. First, she had to rent her house during her absence and this proved to be easier than she expected:

> My house is rented and all furniture sold today. The wonderful thing is that I will receive 100 yen more then I asked for the furniture, but He wills it to be so. Now it will be easy for me to go to China, and all the money is at hand . . . An English gentleman, who was very anxious for the house, offered me yen 100 extra if I would give him the first chance . . . Conditions are somewhat better here now, but still terrible crowds on the cars and continual moving of belongings, etc. It will take months to regain order, and years to become again settled.[86]

On 12 October, Agnes and her sister Mary left Tokyo for China. They took the steamer from Yokohama and spent two days in Kobe on the way. From Kobe, they sailed to Korea and made a three-day visit to Seoul. On her first visit two years previously, nine young Korean men had accepted the Faith and written to 'Abdu'l-Bahá. This time, Agnes was able to see Oh Sang Sun and Mr Roh and spoke at a Buddhist college.[87] In addition, she arranged for the translation and publication in Korean of a little Bahá'í book in the series 'Number Nine'. She was also able to establish a Bahá'í Centre where the Bahá'ís and others could meet.[88]

Before Mary Alexander and Agnes reached Beijing, Martha had called on the President of Tsing Hua University, Dr Yun-Siang Tsao and his wife. Dr Tsao had studied at Yale and Harvard and then worked in London as a secretary at the Chinese Embassy. Mrs Tsao, Swedish by birth and a naturalized American citizen, had married Dr Tsao in London and was a 'truth seeker and a member of the Theosophical Society'. Martha arranged for Agnes to speak on the Bahá'í Faith at the University in an auditorium to all of the students. After a Chinese luncheon with the Tsaos, Agnes met with those students who wanted to learn more. The four students who came were quite diverse. 'One had been brought up as a Muhammadan, another as a Christian and a third had no religion' and they all had different questions. By the time the Beijing visit was over, Dr Tsao had become a Bahá'í and supported the Faith in public talks and in his writing. He translated *Bahá'u'lláh and the New Era*, *The Wisdom of 'Abdu'l-Bahá (Paris Talks)* and many pamphlets into Chinese.[89]

While in Beijing, Agnes met Lieut. K. Tsing, whom she had met once before when he passed through Tokyo. The Lieutenant was in charge of an aviation training school and invited Agnes and Martha to speak about the Faith there. Tsing began the meeting with an earnest talk and then translated for the two women.

One day, Martha met Mr P. W. Chen and he asked if she knew Paul Pao. Agnes had met Pao when he was the editor of the *Canton Times* and had visited Tokyo in 1920. After meeting Agnes, Pao had published a long series of articles about the Faith in his newspaper and Agnes was delighted to be able to reconnect with him when she found he was living in Beijing. Pao now worked at General Feng's school for the children of army officers. Through him, Martha and Agnes were able to share the Faith with the children. On 4 November, Pao helped them arrange the first Bahá'í feast in Beijing, which was attended by Pao, Chen and five others. From the beginning, Chen greatly assisted Martha and Agnes in their efforts, helping them speak at meetings and introducing them to people. One of those people was Mr Deng Chieh-Ming, who became an enthusiastic follower of the Faith. He translated some of the Bahá'í books brought to Shanghai by Pao, parts of which had been published by the *Canton Times*.[90]

After almost five weeks in Beijing, they began a slow journey to Shanghai. Agnes wrote that teachers she had met in Tokyo lived in two of the cities they would pass through, and an Esperantist with whom she was corresponding lived in a third, so they had ready opportunities to talk about the Faith. They had hundreds of Chinese Bahá'í booklets that had been translated by C.W. Waung in Tokyo and these were distributed in all the schools they visited.[91]

Agnes, Martha and Mary left Beijing on 25 November in the company of Deng Chieh-Ming, who went with them as far as Tientsin (now called Tianjin), their first stop. Agnes wrote, 'It happened to be a Chinese train which had a special compartment for women. When the Chinese women in the compartment saw us entering they were frightened. Then the kind friend, Mr. Deng, who had accompanied us, explained to them who we were and that we were friends, which put them at ease.' The following day, Mary continued the journey to Tsinan (now Jinan) alone, while Martha and Agnes gave two talks in Tientsin and left on a midnight train.[92] Their next stop was at Ginanfu (called Chin-ch'eng in Garis's book on Martha Root), where an Esperanto student, Daniel Yu, arranged for them to speak at the Shangtung Christian College, which he attended. Daniel translated for them.

Mary found the train ride by herself, and as the only foreigner on the train, rather gloomy, writing, 'There were armed soldiers on our train and at every station,' and 'The whole of China seems to be a graveyard with graves on the farms.' When they all met in Tsinan (now Jinan), Mary wrote:

Tsinanfu, altho the capital of the province, except for the German-looking modern buildings, is a squalid place and I shall remember it as a city of squeaking wheelbarrows, that filled the streets with dust. The Institute, a large Museum, showing the history of progress in various ways, where in one room a religious service is held every hour for whoever may chance to come, is most unique . . . Agnes and Miss Root spoke here as elsewhere.[93]

The following day, Martha and Mary went mountain-climbing, while Agnes went on ahead to the station nearest Chufoo (now Yentai), the birthplace of Confucius. Martha and Mary arrived at two in the morning in bitter cold, and they all overnighted there. The next morning, they travelled to Chufoo itself, a trip described by Mary:

Agnes and Martha sat on the floor of the only vehicle available for the twelve mile trip, a queer springless little cart with an emigrant-like rounded blue top, drawn by a tiny donkey. I walked to keep warm. The long way lay over a flat plain. Being without a guide, we passed by the cemetery containing Confucius grave without knowing it. In the late afternoon, we reached the interesting gates of the walled town. The people crowding the streets seem of the poorest . . . When at last we came to the great Confucian Temple, the most beautiful in China, the sight of its wonderfully carved white marble columns was worth all the discomfort of the journey. In the middle of the temple is a large statue of Confucius, and on either side of it are statues of his disciples. One of the courts contained the remains of a tree that Confucius had planted himself, the cistern where he had drawn water, etc. Agnes and Martha spoke in a Normal School of young men.

We were sent for later to have tea with the direct descendant of Confucius, the head of the clan, and his mother, who live in the temple grounds. At the gates of the temple this time we were greeted with a bugle salute. The petite mother walked out from her door rather unsteadily on her bound feet to meet us. She wore thickly padded waist trousers of blue brocaded silk, and above her forehead, over her snapping bright eyes, a black satin band with a large green jade in the middle, holding her hair in place. Beside her stood the sturdy little son of five . . . As we sipped clear tea in small round bowls on silver saucers and ate sweet meats, she told us through an interpreter, that she intended to have her son study in all the different countries. When we left at twilight, . . . we bought a candle and a paper lantern for the dark, almost interminable trip back to the station hotel. There the Chinese had prepared an elaborate dinner

for us that we partook of at nine o'clock, taking the train again after
midnight.[94]

It was a cold trip and the train was not heated. At one point, Mary
thought that there was an emergency when she saw a missionary doctor
'running at full speed the length of the corridor'. It turned out that she
was just cold and was trying to warm up.[95]

Their next stop was Tsuchowfu (also called Shuchowfu). Mary (who
was continuing her journey) commented 'they missed a bandit experience of ten days before when the bandits had attacked the place to free
their chief . . . They had been overcome and the heads of thirteen of
their number hung on the city gates'. When Agnes and Martha arrived
at what they thought was the city, they discovered that they had not
really arrived:

Martha and I dropped off the train at Tsuchowfu, where Miss Chien
Yung Ho, whom I met in Tokyo from the Peiping Teacher's College,
had become principal of a school. She had invited us to stop there and
tell her pupils of the Baha'i Cause. We had expected to let her know
when we would arrive. As it happened we did not know in time, and
our message reached her only after we had arrived. It was very early
on a cold morning that our train reached Tsuchowfu. Just as Martha
and I stepped from the train, two American men were boarding it and
asked where we were going. We found that the Chinese city of Tsuchowfu was distant from the railroad stop. They had come to the train
in rickshaws and told us to take them and go to the house they had
just left where a warm fire was burning. We were certainly protected
and cared for by the Hand of God. The owner of the house where we
were taken was an American who was in the Standard Oil business
and was accustomed to taking in guests. When we told him of the
school we wished to visit, he offered to go with us to the Chinese city,
several miles distant, and inquire at the American Mission hospital
where to find it. The school was near the hospital, and within an hour
after our unexpected arrival, we were telling the Glad Tidings to the
pupils in that far away school. Then Miss Chien and other teachers
arranged a gathering for us in the afternoon and we remained with
them until evening, when we returned to the home of our kind host,
and left early the next morning on our way to Nanking.[96]

When the women arrived at Nanking (now called Nanjing), Mr T.Z. Wu, whom Agnes had met in Tokyo, was teaching in a middle school. Through him, they were able to speak to his students and at other schools in the city, with the English teachers as interpreters.[97]

Mary described the last stop before Shanghai, Soochow, to which she travelled a day before Agnes and Martha. Soochow is now called Suhou. Mary wrote:

Soochow with its narrow streets and canals, is uniquely Chinese and fascinating, such ancient and unchanged walls, one pagoda of sixteen hundred years, old gates and bridges, and stone worn with the tread of generations of a thousand years, and too it is famous for its beautiful silk. It thrilled me to pass down the narrow streets overhung with gay blue and yellow and pink pennants emblazoned with great Chinese characters, often of silk. I enjoyed the queer sensation of being where everything was utterly foreign, where I could not even make myself understood. It was awkward, however, when on alighting at a few fascinating shops of embroidered silk, I had to give up trying to make any purchases . . . At first I relished the way my rickshaw man let out peculiar yells and squeals and quarreled with others to clear the way, but after riding several miles, this turbulent babel, so different from the courteous, quiet of Japan wore on my nerves. The tall pagoda with the unusual Chinese ornamentation on the courtyard gates and wall, and the first really fine statuary that I had seen in the temples of China, delighted me beyond measure . . .

We had a pleasant call from Mrs. Wilkinson in the evening. She gave us the addresses of shops to buy silk . . . Martha arrived the next day . . . That afternoon we visited some enchanting characteristically Chinese gardens, with little lakes, islands, and hills, winding pergolas, tea houses, gay with trees still in autumn coloring. We also visited some temples [with] mellowed orange colored walls . . . Riding after dark with Agnes in a rickshaw ahead of me, under the gorgeous pennants hung across the narrow streets in the Chinese lantern lighted shopping section, amid deafening noise . . .

The last day Agnes and I took a rickshaw a very long way out through the poorest, dirtiest part of the town to the lovely old leaning pagoda . . .[98]

On the train to Shanghai, Agnes, Martha and Mary were taken under the care of Mr Evans, a missionary at Hangchow College. Mary noted that 'Shanghai is so foreign [to the rest of China] that Agnes said she felt as though she were in America again'. A French lady from Marseilles living in Shanghai invited the women for dinner. The next day, Mary went to cash a cheque at the Oriental Bank. When asked for a reference, she gave the name of a Mr Raven, whom she had known 20 years before in Honolulu as a university volunteer to the Cuban war. She had heard was then living in Shanghai. To her great surprise, moments later Mr Raven himself appeared! He was the president of the bank and one of the richest men in China. He quickly whisked the women off to his home, where they stayed for the next two weeks. Mary wrote, 'Our efforts to leave them by themselves for Christmas proved a joke, since they invited fifteen guests to the Xmas dinner . . . The community Christmas tree, and pageant, and singing out of doors one evening before Xmas was something to remember. We certainly were charmed with the delightful American colony there. We were dined, tiffened, and teaed.' [99]

Martha and Agnes spread the teachings of the Faith as they did in every city. From Shanghai, Martha continued her Chinese travels, while Agnes and Mary departed for Honolulu on the 27th. Their steamer made brief stops in both Kobe and Yokohama before crossing the Pacific to Hawaii. Agnes's plans were not settled as she sailed away from Japan:

We have bought our tickets through to California, so I will have the privilege of meeting the friends there before returning to this wonderful Far Orient. We may stay many months in Hawaii, as we are allowed on our tickets to stay a year if we wish.

Martha will remain here for six weeks more 'probably' and then go to Canton, etc. Now we can only tell you that we are very happy and that His assistance has always come to us whenever we have needed it. The experience we have had in this trip from Peking has taught us how to travel in China, and we can assure the friends it is not difficult. The English language is spoken here more than in Japan. It was the Bounty of God that Martha Root and I could travel and speak together, for together we felt His confirmations and Power. My sister, although not a Bahá'í in name, yet has a most beautiful spirit. She went with us as a tourist to see the country, but we all helped each other. [100]

Early the next year, Agnes received a letter written on behalf of Shoghi Effendi, which included a personal note at the end in the Guardian's own hand:

My dear Bahá'í sister,

Your letter to Shoghi Effendi was very gladly received and he was most delighted to hear of your activities in the wonderful country of China. There is such a wide field for service and we only need active and whole-hearted teachers to spread far and wide the Message of Bahá'u'lláh.

Your letter was translated into Persian and the contents with all the encouraging news was shared with the resident friends here in Haifa. The faces glowed up when they heard of the great many cities with all their quaint names wherein you had had the great privilege of proclaiming the emancipation of this Movement and the declaration of the life-imparting principles for which the Cause stood for. I suppose in those far-away lands the only mention of the Movement would be a startling novelty to the people.

It is very unfortunate that you are forced to leave for the time being your work in that country and Japan but Shoghi Effendi earnestly hopes that you will soon return and take up your blessed task again.

The members of the Family join me in extending to you our heartfelt greetings and earnest prayers for your success.

In his own hand, Shoghi Effendi wrote:

My dear and esteemed Bahá'í sister,

Your glorious services in those remote regions of the earth are never to be forgotten. I ever pray on your behalf and wish you to remember the sacred interests of the Cause in far-away Japan as you are that radiant herald who has raised the Call of Salvation in its very heart and to whom it owes a great debt of gratitude. Fujita is with us happy, active, and extremely helpful. His presence is such a help and support to me in my work. I never, never forget you.

Shoghi[101]

At the end of the year, Agnes summarized the excitement of the previous few months in a letter to the friends:

> So many beautiful letters have reached me since coming to China from you all that I wanted immediately to write and express my gratitude to you, but because of the constant work of the Cause it never was possible, even though, several times I had put the paper in my typewriter ready to write.
>
> I deeply appreciated all your love for the servants of God who went through the calamity in Japan . . . for on Oct. 12th, I left it for good, selling my household things to the one who took it from me, and gave away other things, storing, etc. Then I felt the freedom to go forth wherever He willed. My sister accompanied me. We stopped two days in Kobe, Japan, three in Seoul, Korea, and then on to Peking where I joined Martha Root in the work of the Cause.
>
> Nearly five weeks were spent in Peking. The doors opened in wonderful ways and we were enabled to give the Message to thousands of students in the schools. On Nov. 25th, we left Peking, stopping at six places enroute to Shanghai and speaking in the schools in these places. Those were never to be forgotten moments. The places we stopped at were Tientsin, Tsinan, Chufu, Shuchowfu, Nanking, and Soochow. Chufu was the home of Confucius and there we felt wonderful inspiration, as though we met His spirit. Yesterday Martha and I spoke here for the first time in Shanghai.
>
> My sister and I leave on Dec. 27th for Honolulu. We will only be in Japan the two days when the steamer stops at Kobe and Yokohama, but in the future it is my hope to return there and visit all the dear friends, then on to Korea for a long time, and then CHINA. We have bought our tickets through to California, so I will have the privilege of meeting the friends there before returning to this wonderful Far Orient. We may stay many months in Hawaii, as we are allowed on our ticket to stay a year if we wish.[102]

Agnes did return to both Korea and China, but only for a few weeks each. And though she expected to stay in Hawaii for 'many months', that visit would last for three years.

BACK IN HAWAII

1924–1927

Maui, Hawaii and Kauai

Agnes wasted no time on relaxation in Hawaii. In February 1924, she went to Maui with Kathrine Baldwin. Kathrine had, the previous year, been instrumental in bringing the first person of Hawaiian ancestry into the Faith, Mary Fantom. Mary became a staunch and devoted Bahá'í who served for many years on Maui's first Local Spiritual Assembly and began the first Bahá'í children's classes on the island. Both Kathrine and Mary lived in Sprecklesville, a beach community just off the end of the modern Maui airport. Through Kathrine's efforts, Agnes was able to speak to a number of groups. She returned to Maui in April and spent two weeks with Sila Smith, a Bahá'í who lived at Makawao. Agnes attended meetings and participated in a children's class and a Feast.[1]

Also in February, the Governor of Hawaii, Wallace Farrington, and his wife hosted a reception for the crews of three Japanese training ships that visited Honolulu. Agnes attended and, when approaching a group of midshipmen, asked if any of them knew Esperanto. One answered her in that language. The sailor said that 'he had often read in the Japanese papers of the Bahá'í Cause' and knew Agnes's name.[2]

In May, Agnes went to the west side of Hawaii for two weeks to visit the only Bahá'í there, Leona Thompson. Leona had learned of the Faith when visiting in Washington DC and Agnes had met her on her return to Hawaii in February 1924. Leona and her husband, Judge J. Wesley Thompson, lived in Kealakekua, south of Kona. The Judge never became a Bahá'í, but was very sympathetic to the Faith and was able to get Agnes an invitation to speak at the Christian Mission Church of Kona at the Sunday morning service. A young Japanese man there, Soeno Inouye, heard her talk with 'wrapt attention and delight'.

Soeno was a reporter for the *Honolulu Advertiser* newspaper, and afterwards wrote two 'enthusiastic' articles about the Faith that appeared in the paper in May and June. His first article, titled 'Baha'i "Revelation" in Kona Captivates both Haole and Oriental and Esperanto Is Advocated', read:

> That even this staid district is keeping pace with the changing world – not only in material things but also the higher concern of the spirit – is happily evidenced by the wide interest aroused hereabout over the Baha'i 'Revelation', perhaps the most ethereal of all religious teachings. Its utopian doctrines are now captivating both the haole residents and the younger Orientals, and its swift appeal is largely due to the local expounder, Miss Alexander, a widely-traveled lady possessed of radiant eloquence and much charm. She addressed the audiences at the high school, the Christian church, and the Buddhist temple – which certainly testifies to the amiable and all-embracing character of her message. By her long residence in Japan and by her friendly contact with the native population there, Miss Alexander has acquired an intimate knowledge of Japanese people, their homeland customs and their modes of thought. And in addressing the transplanted Japanese here she is adroitly utilizing this insight. Besides, Miss Alexander's vivid reminiscences of the Tokyo earthquakes enthrall even those listeners too young or too simple to comprehend her iridescent gospel. Forty years ago the only religion preached here was a dogmatic brand of Christianity, suitable to the native minds of the day. Later on, Buddhism and rational Christianity arrived, and now comes this highly sophisticated Baha'iism. All proves that Kona is truly progressive, even in her spiritual yearnings . . .[3]

These articles resulted in a positive editorial in the *Honolulu Advertiser*. The *Honolulu Star-Bulletin* also published an account of Agnes's talks, so her message went far beyond the small town of Kona.

Agnes and Leona then went to Hilo, where Agnes was invited to share her message with a group of high school students, at a Buddhist temple, and to a group of Japanese youth at a Christian Church. The local newspaper, the Hilo *Tribune Herald*, published articles on each of her talks. Leona later implemented a plan for students to write essays on peace with prizes donated by the women's clubs of the island. Dr David Starr Jordan, who had met 'Abdu'l-Bahá at Stanford in 1912, was so impressed with the resulting essays that he wrote her a congratulatory letter. Unfortunately, Leona died in Washington DC in 1925.[4]

In July, Agnes went to the island of Kauai to visit a cousin at Eleele, on the south coast. Her cousin was the manager of the McBride Sugar Plantation and his wife held afternoon parties, which Agnes attended in hope of finding invitations to speak on the Faith. Praying earnestly for divine assistance, she wrote:

> That afternoon a lady sitting at a table with me suddenly said, 'I wish we might have something worthwhile and have Miss Alexander tell us of the Baha'i Cause.' It seemed at that moment light burst forth. I joyously asked the lady where she had heard of the Cause. She replied that on a steamer coming from San Francisco she had heard Mr. C. M. Remey speak of it. The next day I asked my cousin if we might invite some ladies to his home, that I might tell them of the Cause. With his consent, his wife, who was in sympathy with me, invited by telephone about twenty ladies to come the following afternoon. A lady of the Quaker faith who had heard 'Abdu'l-Baha when He spoke at Stanford University, was visiting in Eleele and I asked her to come and tell of her meeting with 'Abdu'l-Baha. With but one exception all the guests came, although they had only a day's notice of the gathering.
>
> In its July 15th edition, the Garden Island weekly, published in Lihue, mentioned the gathering under the heading, 'Baha'iism Explained by Miss Alexander', The Honolulu Advertiser also, in a special news item from its Eleele correspondent, carried a notice of the gathering. Thus through divine assistance the first seed of the Baha'i Message was sown on that island.[5]

Shoghi Effendi wrote to Agnes through his secretary, John Esslemont, in December 1924. John had arrived just two weeks before at the invitation of Shoghi Effendi. The Guardian was buried with work and at this time was in bed ill. Most of the letter was about why John had ended up in Haifa and the Guardian's illness:

> As Shoghi Effendi is overwhelmed with work and has, moreover,

been in bed for a few days with a sore throat, he has asked me to answer your loving and prayerful letter of October 31st . . . Shoghi Effendi's indisposition, I am glad to say, is not serious, and we hope in the course of the next few days to have him amongst us once more with his energies fully restored . . .

Shoghi Effendi has been made very happy lately by good news of the progress of the Cause in many places, particularly in Germany and Australia. In Germany there are now some twenty centres and several of these have their own Spiritual Assemblies.

In his personal note at the end, the Guardian wrote:

My spiritual sister:
The letter signed by yourself and the Honolulu friends stirred my soul and refreshed my mind. I pray for you all and wish you the highest success in all your noble endeavours. I am looking forward to seeing you establish various powerful Bahá'í centres in those remote islands of the world. The power of God is working with irresistible potency through you all. Persevere. Persevere to the end and your work will surely be crowned with magnificent success. I will never forget you.[6]

Orcella Rexford, Orol Platt and Valera Allen

In January 1925, Orcella Rexford and her husband Dr Gayne Gregory, Alaskan Bahá'ís travel-teaching their way to Haifa for pilgrimage, were in Honolulu and gave a public talk. Through the talk and the subsequent classes conducted by Mamie Seto, several people came into the Faith. Agnes probably met the couple, though her letters and writing do not mention that she did so.[7]

In February, Orol Platt and her husband passed through Honolulu on their way from Los Angeles to Japan. Orol was an early American Bahá'í who brought the mother of actress Carole Lombard[8] into the Faith. A group of the Honolulu Bahá'ís met them at the dock when their steamer arrived. Since their next stop was Kobe, Agnes wrote to Sanzo Misawa. When the Platts arrived in Kobe, Sanzo was there to meet them. Afterwards, Orol wrote to Agnes:

Since leaving Honolulu you have been in my mind so lovingly am sure you have received my thoughts . . . We traveled on to Osaka – finally landing at Kobe – here came great joy – soon awaiting orders to land when a knock came at the door and our Brother Mr. Misawa introduced himself. He had received Miss Alexander's post card and hastened to the ship . . . Then I asked particularly to see the Buddhist priest [Daiun Inouye] after receiving Miss A's letter. Mr. Misawa took us to his temple where we visited about half an hour, and then we all went to the Oriental Hotel for luncheon. I had quite a visit with the priest – and I had brought with me on the ship, *Baha'i Scriptures.* In the morning I had taken it with me to Mr. Misawa's shop for him to look through it, but when we visited the Temple and found our Buddhist priest brother with many Bahá'í books, I presented the *Baha'i Scriptures* I had with me to him to read, as he said he enjoyed reading Bahá'í literature . . . The Buddhist priest said he would write me, and it is a great privilege and bounty to water, even if only a drop, the pure seeds planted in the hearts of these glorious souls by our sister Agnes Alexander.[9]

In the spring of 1925, Agnes bought a small house on Terrace Drive in Manoa Valley of Honolulu. This allowed her to entertain friends and gave her a base from which to teach the Faith.[10] It gave the Bahá'í community several places for activities. In addition to her house, Kathrine Baldwin hosted Bahá'í study meetings on Wednesday evenings, and Friday afternoon meetings were held in the Augur home. Mamie and Anthony Seto, who became Bahá'ís in Honolulu in 1919, also held meetings in their home. Mamie (O'Connor) was Irish American and Anthony was the first Hawaiian Bahá'í of Chinese descent. Anthony was an attorney and had been admitted to the Supreme Court of Hawaii. Later, he was also a Trustee for the Honolulu National Spiritual Assembly and involved in purchasing land around the Shrine of the Báb in the name of the Palestine Branch of the National Spiritual Assembly of the Bahá'ís of the United States and Canada.[11] Mamie later served on the National Spiritual Assembly of the United States.

From 1 to 15 July, the Institute of Pacific Relations was held in Honolulu. Representatives came from Australia, Canada, China, the United States, Japan, Korea, the Philippines and New Zealand as well as Hawaii. It was an unofficial meeting about the affairs of the Pacific.

'Its aims', Agnes wrote, 'were to get at the issues confronting the Pacific peoples, constructively by a free interchange of thought.'[12] It was an obvious opportunity for the Bahá'ís.

In January 1926, the Pan-Pacific Union held a meeting and luncheon in Honolulu. Agnes wrote that 'there was a very representative audience of over three hundred, composed of persons from all races and creeds'. The meeting was in honour of Chief Abbot Sonyu Otani, supreme head of the Shinshu sect, 'the greatest and most progressive denomination of Buddhism in Japan'. Agnes noted, 'The spirit of oneness so fundamental a teaching in the Bahá'í Cause is reaching all receptive hearts the world over, and it is very gratifying to see how the note of universalism and harmonious cooperation was apparent in all the speeches at this luncheon.'[13]

On 21 February, Agnes was back on Kauai where she was invited to speak at a meeting held in the Lihue Memorial Parish House. The programme was a series of talks about 'present day religions' and Agnes spoke about the Bahá'í Faith. She wrote:

> With divine assistance the night of the meeting, I was enabled to explain the Baha'i teachings to an attentive audience. The next morning I was again invited to speak to a group of Hawaiian ministers who had gathered for a conference in Lihue. This was an especially happy occasion, as my grandfather [William Patterson] Alexander was once stationed as a missionary on Kauai, where he preached on Sundays at Koolau, under the shade of a kukui grove, to an audience of about four hundred natives. As my grandfather's name was known among the ministers, they received me most kindly.[14]

A newspaper later published an article entitled 'What is the Baha'i Movement?', which Agnes had prepared from addresses given by 'Abdu'l-Bahá.

Agnes went to California in the autumn of 1926 and remained until 20 March 1927.[15] We have no information about what she did while there.

In February 1927, Valera Fisher and Emma Maxwell arrived in Honolulu to serve in the Wesley Home for girls. Valera was a Bahá'í, but Emma was not when she arrived. Valera was very impressed with Agnes when she met her:

> Being a new Baha'i there was no greater thrill for me than to be in

the presence of those who had been in the Faith during the days of
the Master. So when I met Agnes I was immediately attracted to her
and she was the essence of kindness to me.

On my days off she would often invite me to her home in Maura
Valley or we would spend a weekend at her cabin up on Mount
Tantalus. It was truly a heavenly experience to listen to her stories
about the early believers – beloved May Maxwell; the first English
Baha'i, Thomas Breakwell, who was so precious to Abdul-Baha . . .
and others. She shared copies of the Tablets from Abdul-Baha to
many of these beautiful souls, and we would discuss for hours the
spiritual implication of these messages. She told stories about those
in Japan who had come into the Faith. She spoke of the joys and
spiritual victories to be won in the countries of the world. She
encouraged me to join the ranks of the pioneers and I knew in my
heart I could never feel entirely happy until I had attained this goal.

Of all of her wonderful attributes in my opinion, her most outstanding attribute was her absolute obedience to the Will of God.
She believed implicitly that she would be guided unerringly if she
turned her heart and mind to Baha'u'llah in prayer. I was reminded
of the Words of Baha'u'llah in the Seven Valleys – 'a servant is drawn
unto Me in prayer until I answer him; and when I have answered
him, I become the ear wherewith he heareth . . .'

Sometimes her guidance would come with the arrival of unexpected Tablets from Abdul-Baha and in later years letters from the
beloved Guardian. Or she would receive a strong conviction of what
she must do. For instance she became firmly convinced when the
time came for her to return to Japan.[16]

Valera later married John Allen and the couple pioneered to Africa
during the Ten Year Crusade, becoming Knights of Bahá'u'lláh.

Emma became a Bahá'í during her year in Honolulu. When asked
by Agnes to write about her time there, she wrote:

I don't think there is anything of value I could add. I received a
GREAT deal from all of the friends of Honolulu and it will always
be dear to me because there I received or ABSORBED the 'spirit'
of the Faith surrounded by various races and cultures of the 'Cross-
Roads of the Pacific'. The many visits up Manoa Valley to your

home and that of Mrs. Sweezey's where the classes were held are like precious jewels in my book of memory. The homes of the Seto's and the Rowland's were oases of hospitality long to be remembered. Dearest Utie's (Miss Muther) face shines like a star of guidance in my memory. She possessed true reverence and spirit of humility equalled by few.[17]

Agnes was in Berkeley, California in March and gave a talk to Japanese students at a YMCA luncheon. That was followed by a presentation to a large group of Japanese at the Buddhist Temple there.[18]

Planning another return to Japan

In May, Agnes received a letter from Shoghi Effendi:

> My dear co-worker: I long to hear of your determination to return to Japan and pick up the thread of your unsparing efforts and activities for the promotion of the Cause of God. I feel that your destiny lies in that faroff and promising country where your noble and pioneer services future generations will befittingly glorify and thankfully remember. May the Beloved remove every obstacle from your path and enable you to resume your active work in that land. Shoghi[19]

It was her first intimation that he wanted her to return to Japan for a third time – and the Guardian continued to emphasize returning to Japan over the next several letters. Agnes replied the next month that she would go, and on 22 August received the Guardian's response. He promised her divine assistance from the Supreme Concourse:

> My dear Bahá'í Sister,
>   Our dear Guardian has instructed me to acknowledge the receipt of your welcomed letter dated June 3, 1927. He is delighted to hear of your intended visit to Japan where he hopes and prays you will receive your full share of confirmations from the Abha Kingdom.
>   He cherishes great hopes for your future contributions to the progress of the Cause in that far away and promising country. He wishes you to write to him frequently of the progress of your activities and of those whom you will interest in the Teachings of

Bahá'u'lláh.

He would specially request you to prolong your stay in Japan as the soil is exceedingly fertile and the workers are so few in number. The hosts of the Supreme Concourse will surely aid you and assist you in your endeavor to spread the Faith which the world needs so vitally today.

In his own hand, the Guardian added both a warning of the difficulties she would face, but also the rewards she would receive:

Dear and precious sister: Do not feel disheartened if you meet at first with trials and obstacles in His Path. I will pray for their removal and will supplicate for you Divine Guidance and strength. Your reward is indeed great and glorious in the world to come for all your endeavors and exemplary services to the sacred Threshold. Shoghi.[20]

With the Guardian's letter, Agnes set her sights on the return to Japan, choosing the date of 10 January 1928 for her departure from Hawaii. The first two times she had gone to Japan had been very different from each other and, with Shoghi Effendi's note, she wrote that 'Knowing the conditions existing in Japan, I was fully aware that my path would not be easy, but with His assurance and the glorious words of the Guardian I could leave all in God's hands.'[21]

Her next letter from Shoghi Effendi gave her a strong push:

Dear Bahá'í sister,

I am instructed by our dear Guardian Shoghi Effendi to acknowledge the receipt of your letter dated August 24, 1927, and to express his sadness and regret at the unhappy situation now in Japan. He feels strongly that you should make every effort to return to that spot, and through personal contact and prayerful effort achieve harmony and understanding among the friends. Meanwhile you should through correspondence, put the friends in Japan on their guard less they should accept from anyone however lofty his position anything contrary to the teachings. You should encourage them to study the teachings, to associate with one another intimately and to study the motive of every soul.

Our Guardian will pray that your efforts may be successful and that you will be enabled to resume soon your pressing work in Japan.

Assuring you of our Guardian's earnest prayers for the removal of every obstacle from your path.

In his personal note at the end of the letter, Shoghi Effendi strongly encouraged her return to Japan:

My dear and precious co-worker:

I cannot exaggerate the importance, nay the urgent necessity of your return to Japan. Your place there is vacant, and the opportunities are varied and brilliant. The few friends there have to be nursed and assisted to renew their activity and consolidate their work. I will pray that you will be guided by our dear Master who loved you so dearly and wanted you so keenly to train and guide the rising generation in Japan into the light of this Divine Revelation.

Your true brother, Shoghi[22]

With that powerful incentive to propel her, Agnes prepared to return to Japan.

The Guardian was not alone in raising the call of Japan. During the summer of 1927, the Institute of Pacific Relations held their second Conference in Honolulu. Agnes met the Japanese, Korean and Chinese delegates. Dr Shiroshi Nasu of the Tokyo Imperial University was one of the Japanese delegates. He had heard about the Bahá'í Faith from Roy Wilhelm in New Jersey and had the bounty of receiving a letter from the Guardian. When he returned to Japan, he wrote back to Agnes: 'As our steamer nears Yokohama, Fuji San is in sight. This is the symbol of our welcome to you! Come to Japan!'[23]

Hawaiian activities

In September, while planning her return to Japan, Agnes started a Sunday morning children's class, meeting 'under a spreading monkey-pod tree' near the Bahá'í cottage on Nuuanu Street. The cottage was given by Kathrine Baldwin for use as a Bahá'í Centre. The eight children sat on a 'great stone' under the tree and learned prayers and verses and listened to stories about Bahá'u'lláh and 'Abdu'l-Bahá.[24] When Agnes departed for Japan, Mamie Seto took over the class.

George and Ruth Augur, who had returned from Japan in 1919, had moved back into their Honolulu home. In July, due to increasing age and poor health, they moved to an apartment on Waikiki Beach. On 9 September, George suffered a stroke and passed away five days later.[25] A letter from Shoghi Effendi read: 'He was deeply grieved to hear of the death of Dr. Augur. He prays that in seeking eternal rest, his soul may soar to heavenly kingdoms and attain an everlasting bounty. Surely he is now where he would much love to be. Please convey to his family Shoghi Effendi's deepest sympathy and regret.' In the *Bahá'í World* (1928–1930), the Guardian named George as one of the 19 Disciples of 'Abdu'l-Bahá.[26]

Since the passing of 'Abdu'l-Bahá in 1921, Agnes had been collecting His Tablets to the Japanese in Japan with the hope of someday publishing them. She wrote to the Guardian about the project and received his strong support:

My dear Bahá'í sister,

Our dear Guardian wishes me to thank you for your letters of September fifth and ninth sent together.

He has been very much interested in your project to publish with the collaboration of Mr. Horace Holley the Master's Tablets to the friends in Japan. He hopes that when finally accomplished it will succeed to direct the attention of the friends in general as to the great importance of spreading the Movement in that mighty and growing country. Perhaps the suitable preface which Mr. Holley has suggested will also be a means of encouraging the reader as to the prospects of Bahá'í labours and services in Japan.

We have always realized the wide field Japan presents, but what a pity that few have been able to do much and many circles and classes of people have not yet been convinced of the growing necessity and importance of the Message.

I think it would be a good idea to publish together with the Tablets . . . in which He praises and shows the importance of Bahá'í work in Japan. It is of course for you and Mr. Holley to see if such a plan is practicable.

With loving greetings from all the members of the family.

In his personal note to her, Shoghi Effendi wrote:

My dear and precious co-worker:

Though immersed in an ocean of activities and cares, I find always the time to think of you and express to you in writing my sentiments of love and appreciation of all you are doing for our beloved Cause. I trust the way to Japan may open soon, and that you may resume in that important field, the work so dear to your heart.

Your true brother, Shoghi[27]

Return to Japan

On 28 November, Agnes received her fifth letter from the Guardian since the previous May. In the letter, Shoghi Effendi reiterated his grief at the passing of George Augur, then spoke to her impending departure for Japan:

Our Guardian is delighted at the prospects of an early departure for Japan. That you have now fixed the date and will be soon in the active field of service, will be to him always a source of genuine pleasure. Your success will ever be his fondest hope and desire and he would be always glad to hear from you directly when there. May your sustained efforts be richly blessed.

With much love from the members of the family.

In his personal addendum, Shoghi Effendi wrote:

My dear and precious sister: I am glad that the date of your voyage to Japan is at last settled and I hope and trust that you will be enabled to consolidate the great work you have initiated in Japan. My prayers will accompany you wherever you go, and I ask you to assure the loved ones in Japan of my continued prayers for their progress and spiritual advancement. Shoghi.[28]

On 30 December Shoghi Effendi sent her yet another letter about her trip to Japan. It arrived on 19 February 1928, after her arrival in Japan, and gave her the challenge of establishing the first Japanese Local Spiritual Assembly:

My dear Bahá'í sister,

I am instructed by our Guardian to thank you for the card of November twenty-sixth, saying that you had already booked your passage for Japan.

This bit of news has filled Shoghi Effendi's heart with pleasure and with hope. He sees with one eye the immense field and the promising results which modern Japan presents, and with the other, the absence of sufficient and capable workers. That is why he welcomes your resumption of activity and travel in Japan with genuine pleasure and hopefulness and awaits your good news most patiently. With you are his prayers, his high hopes and his fondest good wishes.

It would he thinks be splendid if you could establish permanent centers there and perhaps in Tokyo bring enough friends into the Cause as to form the first all-Japanese Spiritual Assembly in the world, and to put them in touch with Assemblies throughout the world.

In his own hand, the Guardian wrote:

What a relief to learn that you are at last on your way to Japan where I trust and pray you may witness the growth of the Cause so dear to our hearts. I will pray that your efforts may meet with the fullest success and that you may be enabled to establish a powerful centre in the heart of that promising country. Shoghi.[29]

12

JAPAN AND CHINA

1928–1933

Before Agnes departed from Honolulu on 10 January 1928, she went to visit Governor Wallace Farrington, a long-time friend of her family and whom she called 'a man of high principles'. For her journey, he gave her a letter of introduction bearing the Seal of the Territory of Hawaii and which mentioned the Bahá'í Faith. He also commended her to all government officials she might meet in Japan.[1]

Agnes's departure from Honolulu was not as smooth as she had hoped: she left the key to her trunk at home. Luckily, the steamer had a key on the ship which fitted it. Agnes was the only first class passenger to board in Honolulu and there were 30 other first class passengers already on board. Only three were women: a Japanese lady, the wife of a missionary to China and one other she did not meet. The sea voyage was normal, meaning that there were smooth days and rough days. Agnes wrote:

> We have had one rough day, but as today is smooth, I am taking advantage to write, for it may not be so long. I sit at a table with a missionary & his wife going to China, an Arch Bishop, the ship's doctor, a Japanese. My state room is large & the Japanese stewardess pleasant . . . The one Japanese lady has been around the world – She has a girl's school in Nagasaki. She is traveling alone which is quite unusual for her race – I find her very pleasant and friendly. I have also talked with a Japanese who has been three years in Geneva at the League of Nations . . .
>
> The last days on the steamer were rough and I could not write more . . .[2]

Agnes was able to share the message of Bahá'u'lláh with the American wife of a Filipino man and the young Japanese who had first learned of the Faith from Martha Root in Geneva.

When Agnes landed in Japan, Susumu Aibara, who worked in the Tokyo Branch of the League of Nations, met her at the dock and whisked her and her baggage through Customs. Agnes found a message awaiting her from Miss Guppy, an American friend living in Tokyo, telling her to go straight to the Sakurai house, where there was a room ready for her. Agnes had stayed there for a while in November 1914 the first time she came to Japan. It was in that small room that the first Bahá'í meetings had been held.[3]

Japan had changed each time Agnes returned. When she had left after the earthquake in 1923, both Tokyo and Yokohama were mostly destroyed. But now she returned to find that massive reconstruction had taken place; they were being built up again into modern cities. She noted that 'Tokyo & Yokohama are new cities with all new buildings – In Tokyo one can get a taxi for 1 yen to any place in the city – Rickshaws seem scarce now. It would seem quite out of the question for me to have my auto here.'[4] It was 'one great upheaval all the time'.[5]

Agnes was well used to driving a car, but she was not prepared to drive in Tokyo:

> This is not the place for a lady to drive an auto. The streets are bad & there are many bicycles & disorder. One can hire an auto within the city for 1 yen fixed price, so it is very convenient. There are 2 men to manage the taxi. One drives, & the other jumps out to inquire the way. The street cars are usually jammed & one has to hold on to a strap. I have fallen naturally into the ways of Tokyo. It is not the Tokyo, though, which I knew before the earthquake. There still is much dust which seems to have remained from earthquake times. One day I went out to the house where I lived in Yotsuya and met some of the kind neighbors whose shops I patronized formerly. They all looked prosperous.[6]

With all the chaos on Tokyo's streets, Agnes wrote that in a normal month, 16 or 17 were killed on the roads and more than a thousand injured. 'The people seem not to fear the autos, and the autos are so reckless . . . I have learnt to shut my eyes at times when it looks dangerous.'[7]

There were great material changes, but some things had not changed:

One thing which is nice is that they are friendly and honest. After four years absence I was struck right away with the Japanese friendliness and politeness. It is a quiet, comfortable feeling one has among them. The faithful, polite 'red caps' delivered my small baggage from the taxis to the train and I had no trouble transferring everything. Miss Guppy has a nice Japanese house a few doors away & I am taking two meals with her as they only serve breakfast here. Sakurai's is the same place as ever and one has to put up with things. The room is 75 yen a month with breakfast. I regret I did not bring along with me the rug for I surely need it here. There is nothing but an oil cloth on the floor of this room. I found it very cold with a jet gas for heat but yesterday got an oil stove, then it snowed last night & is not so cold now . . .[8]

Soon after Agnes settled into her room, Yuri Mochizuki, the first woman to accept the Faith in Japan and who had lived with Agnes, came to see her.

On 6 February, a cold and snowy day, Agnes went in the afternoon to visit Fanny McVeagh, the American Ambassador's wife. When Agnes had arrived in Japan on this trip, the Ambassador, Charles McVeagh, had invited her to visit. When she did, she tried to present him with a booklet on the Faith. To her great surprise, he said that he already knew about the Faith. Charles had met 'Abdu'l-Bahá in Dublin, New Hampshire in the summer of 1912. During that meeting, 'Abdu'l-Bahá had appeared to be exceptionally tired, and Charles, whose brother was the US Secretary of the Treasury at that time, asked Him a question. The Master sat forward on the couch and 'sent thundering forth with this mighty Spirit which seems to come at His bidding, and told of how people throughout the ages have worshipped the <u>Dawning Points</u> instead of the Sun which rises in different places and which is the <u>Reality</u>.'[9] No one realized at that time the effect His talk had on Charles, the future Ambassador to Japan. The Ambassador proved to be very helpful in opening doors for Agnes. She told her brother, 'I have found Mr McVeagh a fine friend.'[10]

Agnes's new address was 'c/o Sakurai, 31 Nichome Fujimicho, Kudan, Tokyo'. She explained the meaning of the address in a letter to friends:

'Ni' is two, and 'Chome' is block. 'Fuji' is the sacred mountain. 'Mi' is to see, and 'Cho' is street, so it means the street where one can see Mt. Fuji. 'Ku' is nine, and 'dan' is steps. It is above the nine steps, and here it was that I came when I first arrived in Tokyo, and where the first meetings were held and the first student wrote to 'Abdu'l-Bahá. That was in November, 1914, though it was the following spring when Mr. Fukuta, the young student saw the Light of this Day. I had never expected to be back here again, but as it was His guidance, it must be His bounty.[11]

Kathrine Baldwin, her cousin's wife, came to visit and had a room next to Agnes's at Sakurai's.

On 5 February, Agnes went with a Japanese girl into the countryside to visit Yuri Mochizuki.[12] Yuri was translating a booklet called *What is the Bahá'í Movement?* into Japanese and Agnes hoped to publish 2,000 copies.[13]

Agnes was asked to speak at the Pan-Pacific Union luncheon about the Bahá'í Faith on 24 February. The invitation came about because the Director of the Union in Honolulu, who was 'kindly disposed towards the Bahá'ís', gave her a letter of introduction to the Union in Tokyo. Taking a leaf from Martha Root's methodology, Agnes wrote out her talk before-hand, trying to keep it as close as possible to the words of 'Abdu'l-Bahá. Having the written copy came in handy, because after the talk she was able to give it to reporters from two English-language newspapers. Both printed it in their editions the next day. Agnes noted that the 'luncheons here are quite formal and are presided over by a Viscount. In introducing me he said that he did not know what the Bahá'í Movement was, but afterwards spoke very kindly and said he also believed in the principle of the oneness of religions at their foundations, and then, turning to me he added that he hoped the Movement would have success here.'[14]

One of those involved with the Pan-Pacific Union was Dr R. Masu-jima. He was an international lawyer she had met at a Pan-Pacific Food Conference in Honolulu meeting in 1924. His Bahá'í-like talk at that meeting had attracted her attention, so she met him and was invited to a garden party on 21 March. Agnes wrote:

On March twenty-first, there was held a Garden Party here given by Dr. Masujima in his garden. He is the Chairman of the Good

Relations Club of Tokyo, which is one of the Pan-Pacific clubs started by Alexander Hume Ford, the Director in Honolulu. Dr. Masujima is a friend of the Baháʼís. He likes the Teachings which he heard from Mrs. Cook (Mrs. Inez Greven) and her sister in New York. He also knows Mountfort Mills. March twenty-first is a national holiday here. It may be called 'the day of ancestor worship', and in Japanese is 'O Higan'. Dr. Masujima did not know it was the Baháʼí New Year day when he invited me to his party on that day. It was a most beautiful day and there were gathered about one hundred persons, Esperantists, Baháʼí friends and others. Dr. Inazo Nitobe, who was one of the secretaries at the League of Nations for eight years, was the speaker of the afternoon. His talk was truly along the Baháʼí lines and was inspired. He told how international congresses had come into vogue since the year 1840, and how they have increased steadily in numbers ever since then . . . He told me that in Geneva he had met some of the Baháʼís, Lady Bloomfield, Mountfort Mills, Mrs. White. He is a Quaker and his wife an American, and they stand for better understanding between the nations. Last year Dr. Masujima had a party in his garden and gave a talk on the Baháʼí Teachings, which was afterwards published here. I am told by a Japanese friend that it was very good indeed. So we can see how seeds sown in the West often bear fruit in the East.[15]

Though Dr Masujima remained a staunch friend of the Faith, he did not become a Baháʼí.

One day, Agnes met two European women travelling to China. These were the Englishwoman Miss Pye and the Frenchwoman Mrs Drevet. Agnes noticed that Miss Pye was wearing a beautiful Baháʼí ring and asked about it. Miss Pye said that she was not a Baháʼí, but had been given the ring by Jane Whyte, an early Scottish Baháʼí who had hosted ʻAbduʼl-Bahá in her home. Agnes was particularly interested in this because Jane's son, Sir Frederick Whyte, had led the English delegation at the Institute of Pacific Relations conference in Honolulu the previous summer.[16] Sir Frederick had also been instrumental in ensuring that the British army prioritized the safety of ʻAbduʼl-Bahá when they drove the Ottoman army out of Palestine during the First World War.[17]

Easter Sunday and Buddha's birthday coincided on 8 April and Agnes took advantage of the day to present the Faith to the Blind School.[18]

Agnes received her first letter of the year from the Guardian in April, an encouraging one about pioneering:

Our Guardian has received with extreme pleasure your letter of February nineteenth from Tokyo.

He is so glad to know that you are finally there and actively busy in a work to which he pays the very greatest importance. Being pioneer work it is bound to be slow, but he hopes that it will soon pass beyond the pioneer stage and that Baha'i Assemblies and groups composed of full fledged and confirmed Bahá'ís will replace your isolated individuals with which you now communicate.

You have with you to help you, our Guardian's prayers, his good wishes and his eager expectations, and coupled with your sustained endeavours, they will surely produce the greatest results.

He wishes me also to extend to you the happy greetings of the Bahá'í New Year. He prays that it may be all throughout the world, a year of incessant activity, of sober stock-taking and of gloriously achieved results. Forging our way ever-onwards the next one must find us a good deal ahead.

The Guardian's personal note read:

My dear co-worker:

Please assure the dear friends in Tokyo of my brotherly affection, and sincere and continued prayers for the success of their efforts in the service of our beloved Cause. May the Beloved aid you to assist them and guide them in their task, and strengthen you in your efforts to consolidate the work that has been started in that land. Your well-wisher, Shoghi[19]

A problem with Communism

Agnes wrote to the Guardian on 23 April and received another in the long series of letters from him, this one encouraging her to publish more articles about the Faith in Japanese periodicals:

I am instructed by our Guardian to thank you for your letter of April 23rd with your news-letter enclosed.

He was very pleased to receive the encouraging news that it contained and to learn that an article had already appeared on the subject of the Cause in the press. Perhaps you will make an effort that similar articles may appear in others so as to attract the attention of the reading and thinking public. Of course your ultimate goal, Shoghi Effendi is sure, is nothing less than the establishment of a capable, devoted and progressive Bahá'í center there, and that he wishes me to assure you of his unfailing prayers and of his readiness to help and cooperate with you.

It is sad that the police may have doubted the ultimate aim of the Bahá'í Faith, but you will surely remove that apprehension and you can then have absolute liberty.

The family all wish me to extend their love and heartfelt good wishes to a devoted and trusted pioneer of the Bahá'í Faith in Japan. They wish you success from the bottom of their hearts . . .

P.S. The published Tablets on Japan make impressive and encouraging reading.

Shoghi Effendi's personal note said:

My dear and valued Bahá'í Sister:

I wish to assure you in person of my eagerness to hear from you regularly, frequently and in detail, of my continued prayers for you, and of my sense of pride and satisfaction in view of your devoted and pioneer services in that promising country. Though trials, tests, anxieties and cares beset your path, yet you should never falter in your faith and hope that eventually, through you and those who after you will tread your path, the sovereignty of Bahá'u'lláh will be firmly established in that land and your heart's desire will in the end be fulfilled.

Your true and affectionate brother, Shoghi[20]

The problem Agnes was having with the police was not clear at this time, but a few months later the reason became apparent:

In the fall of 1928, I suddenly discovered that the young women's Esperanto group which I had been attending each month was held in the home of Communists. Because of conditions existing in Japan at that time, Communism had spread, especially among the youth and many students were imprisoned. I was myself watched by the police, as well as those who came to see me, although I was striving to eliminate the cause of Communism by the power of Bahá'u'lláh's Teachings. The beloved Guardian was aware of these conditions and continually sent me his reassuring messages. I had loved the Japanese friend at whose home the women's Esperanto group met, for I realized her potential qualities. When I discovered that she and her husband were Communists, I had a visit with her and explained the Bahá'í Teachings, and with sincerity she told me of her life experience. She had been educated in a Christian school and had studied theology, but had turned from religion because she saw the falsity in many things she was taught. Then I invited the young women who met at her home to my room at New Year's time when they were free from work, and served them tea and explained the Bahá'í Teachings to them. A loving spirit was present and some questions were asked. Through His bounty, divine seeds were surely sown. After that day I did not meet again with the group and later a letter came from the Guardian with his instructions.

There was at that time in Japan a religion called Oomoto, which had rapidly spread throughout the country. The head of the religion was regarded by the followers as a Manifestation of God. They used Esperanto in their propaganda. In their publications they had taken some of the Bahá'í principles and teachings and published them as their own.[21]

When she discovered these problems, she immediately wrote to the Guardian. His reply came in January 1929:

He has been very surprised to learn that the Oomoto religion of Japan has published a statement to the effect that the Bahá'í Revelation is a branch of their religion. Our Guardian would urge you to publish an emphatic contradiction and to show it by the translation of some of the writings.

As regards the gentleman who has been studying the Cause for his university thesis, Shoghi Effendi would advise you that if the translations he has made of the Bahá'í writings are confined to the teaching of the Cause, and are correctly and faithfully rendered, you should make an effort to have them published so as to create interest among the intellectual classes. It is such a pity that the youth are animated with communistic ideas instead of thinking of ideas more constructive, but it is always necessary to keep away from communistic organizations lest the Cause be confused as a movement for the same purpose.

That your task is exasperatingly slow and difficult and that it needs endless perseverance, Shoghi Effendi knows only too well, but he sincerely hopes and prays that you will eventually succeed to build a Bahá'í pioneer's everlasting foundation in those mighty islands.[22]

Communism was a very touchy subject in Japan at that time. Writing some years later to 'Marion', Agnes noted that up to half of the students at one of the Tokyo universities identified as Communist and that hundreds had been jailed. The police were suppressing the roundups from the news and 'Newspapers cannot afford to publish anything unless it is permitted.'[23]

Opportunities and the Guardian's encouragement

The All Japanese Religious Conference was held in Tokyo from 5 to 8 June 1928 with 1,500 delegates from Buddhist, Christian, Shinto and other backgrounds, including the Bahá'ís. Only three foreigners were allowed to speak and one of those was Agnes:

Through His power I was invited to be a member of the Conference and to speak a few words the evening of the 'get together' banquet . . . It . . . was a great sight to see the fifteen hundred delegates of that assembly. The night of the banquet there were fifteen speakers. Without the language one could sense the wonderful spirit of the meeting. When my turn came, the director, who himself interpreted for me, asked me to speak two minutes. As I arose the audience did not know where to look, for I had been sitting at one end of the room, and the director had come over to be near to me. He then said, 'Koko', meaning 'here', and all eyes turned and Bahá'u'lláh guided the words which were spoken. His name was mentioned and His words, 'Ye are all the leaves of one tree . . .' and the words of 'Abdu'l-Bahá, 'Religions are many but the reality of religion is one. The days are many but the sun is one . . .' There was a great response shown to His words . . . The next day the members of the Conference were invited to visit the Imperial Gardens of Shinjuku, which are only opened on rare occasions. When I went to the Conference Hall, on the steps I met the German minister who had spoken in Japanese the night before. His first words to me were of the great impression the words (which had been put into my mouth) had made the night before. From the Conference hall the members walked to the gardens, about a mile distant. It seemed like a pilgrimage, the members walking in files of twos and threes. During the walk I was enabled to speak of the Bahá'í Revelation to the German minister and to a Canadian missionary who interpreted for the only other English speaking person that night. The missionary had been in Japan twenty-three years, and he also spoke to me of the impressiveness of the (His) words of the night before. It was all together a wonderful demonstration of His power and I thanked my Lord for all His goodness and assistance to this servant. Every word spoken at the Conference is recorded, so His great words go down in the history of this first independent all-religions conference in Japan. In the past the government has tried once or twice to have such a conference, but this one came from the people themselves and was entirely independent.[24]

The conference sent messages to religious associations around the world, including one to Shoghi Effendi. His reply 'expressed keen interest in the work of the Association and the assurance of his hope for its success'.[25]

At her home, Agnes was finally able to expand her living space: 'I now have a sitting room here of my own and pray that His love will be felt here. It is the very room where in 1915, I entertained Martha Root on her first journey around the world, and where many happy Bahá'í meetings were held in the past when I lived in Japan the first time. This is my third visit to Japan and each time it has only been through His direction that I have come here to work.'[26]

In July 1928, Agnes rented a small cottage on Lake Nojiri, in the mountains northeast of Tokyo not far from the Sea of Japan. American missionaries had built summer cabins on the lake to escape the heat of the lowland cities. Agnes wrote that her cottage had a living room and kitchenette and that she had a small girl staying with her. Lake Nojiri was a nice quiet area and Agnes planned to study Japanese while there and had acquired a 'Japanese lady teacher'. Agnes noted: 'This is a most beautiful lake situation. There are 90 houses in the foreign settlement.'[27]

On Christmas Day 1928, Agnes received another letter from the Guardian, written on 14 November. Her collection of his letters was becoming quite impressive. This letter again addressed being a pioneer:

> Dear spiritual sister,
>   . . . It always gives him great pleasure to hear of the progress of the Cause in distant lands and he prays for those who are undertaking the task with great zeal and unfailing sacrifice. The activities of such devoted souls will surely leave everlasting traces on the history of man. The pioneer work is always the most difficult and entails the greatest sacrifice. Be thankful to God for having chosen you to undertake such a task. The Master always looked to the Eastern countries as a ready field of service and promised a great harvest to the one who would first sow the seed.
>   Shoghi Effendi wishes me to assure you of his prayers that your task may soon bear its fruits and enable you to establish important centers in those lands.

At the end, the Shoghi Effendi added:

> My dear and precious co-worker:
>   Your letter has served to reveal once again the undying spirit of devotion that animates you in the service of the Cause. My prayers will be offered again for you at His holy Shrine that you may be assisted to establish permanently a Bahá'í Spiritual Assembly in that land, and help that centre to get in close and constant touch with Assemblies both in the East and the West. Your true brother, Shoghi[28]

On 30 January 1929, reflecting on all that had happened, Agnes wrote, 'This year has been different from any in my life but now with the coming of a New Year I feel inspiration and hope and know that His work will be done and He will assist and confirm, so that although there is nothing apparent to show outwardly, yet His spirit is working. As yet there are no local Baha'i assemblies here.'[29]

Mr Masujima suggested that a selection of Bahá'í books be given to the Emperor Shōwa, better known as Hirohito, who began his reign in December 1926. Agnes had asked the Guardian about the books to be presented and he had replied: 'I will leave the matter entirely to your discretion. Being on the spot, you can best judge as to what and how it should be done.'[30] On 22 May, seven specially bound Baháʼí books, sent in the name of 'Baháʼí ladies of America', were given to the Emperor, accompanied by a note from Shoghi Effendi that read: 'May the perusal of Baháʼí literature enable Your Imperial Majesty to appreciate the sublimity and penetrative power of Baháʼu'lláh's Revelation and inspire you on this auspicious occasion to arise for its worldwide recognition and triumph.'[31]

Another letter to Agnes written on behalf of the Guardian arrived at about this time. It read:

> Your perseverance and constancy in the service of the Cause in Japan, your effort to sow the seed among the educated and enlightened people and at the same time to carry the comforting and inspiring teachings of the Faith to the poor and blind, all these are the cause of deep satisfaction and pleasure to the heart of the Guardian, and he wishes you success from the bottom of his heart.
>
> He wants me to assure you of his affection and prayers for your pioneer work in that great Baháʼí outpost, and of his pleasure always in sharing your good and happy news.

At the end, Shoghi Effendi wrote: 'With the assurance of my keen appreciation of your devoted and constant efforts and of my fervent and continued prayers in your behalf at the holy Shrines, Your true brother, Shoghi.'[32]

The ascent of Mt. Fuji

During the summer of 1929, Agnes decided to make the ascent of 12,389-foot Mt. Fuji (3,776 metres), Japan's holy mountain:

> Starting from Tokyo in the early morning, I met many people on the station platform whence travelers begin the first stage of the journey. They were clad in white robes with mushroom-shaped straw head-coverings, and carried long wooden staffs. Bells were

attached to their belts which tinkled as they moved about. These were the pilgrims who for three days before starting on their pilgrimage prepare themselves, abstaining from eating meat, and in the morning, before reciting prayers, clean themselves by throwing buckets of water over their bodies.

From the foot of Mount Fuji, five routes lead to the summit. By one of these the first four miles [6 km] can now be spanned by automobile. From there the mountain is divided into nine stations before the summit is reached. Ascending the mountain, the pilgrims have their garments and staffs stamped at each of the stations with the mark of the station, and at death are buried in these garments which bear the stamps of their pilgrimages.

The road up the mountain to the fifth station lay through shaded woods perfumed with fragrant wild flowers. On reaching here, night had fallen, and I remained with a guide who carried my luggage, at one of the Rest Houses which now are found at every station. After the midnight hour had passed, the moon came up and soon were heard voices of pilgrims passing up the trail. In rhythmic unison they repeated the words, 'Roku kon Shojo.' Although at the time I was not aware of the true significance of these words, yet their repetition conveyed a suggestion of strength.

Under the light of the moon I followed with the pilgrims up the slippery ashy trail, until at the seventh station the moon slowly disappeared as the dawn came. Here with many pilgrims we stood silent while the wonderful change took place in nature. To the pilgrims, the sunrise is the supreme moment, to meet which they ascend the mountain. It is the time for prayer and worship. All stood in reverence with heads bared while from under the clouds the glorious sun rose illuminating the mountain side and revealing the five lakes picturesquely set at its foot. Looking down the mountain, as far as the eye could see, there was a continuous white-robed procession ascending the winding trail, for not only the pilgrims, but almost all others who climbed were dressed in white.

Again we started up the trail meeting many kind and friendly pilgrims, among whom were some who were weak and were being helped along by the strong, and again and again were the words repeated . . . At the eighth station there is a Post Office where mail can be posted to all parts of the world, stamped from this lofty mountain. From here the climb became more tedious, but at last the reward – attainment to the summit.

Returning to the world below, there came the realization of inner attainment gained through the effort made in the ascent of the sacred mountain. The words which had so often been repeated on the mountain side, I found to mean the purification of the six roots of evil – the eye, ear, tongue, nose, heart and body. By purifying these, evil thoughts are driven away and the heart becomes pure . . . To the pilgrims these words are a potent prayer.[33]

Continuing efforts

As 1929 came to its end, Agnes wrote, 'Tokyo is beginning to be gay on the streets for the New Year. To me the stores are always attractive. Today I have been to the English Speaking Society at Waseda University where I go every Monday noon. I enjoy meeting the students, but today will be the last time for this year.' During the New Year time, Agnes and Miss Guppy spent a day at Atami, a hot spring on the Mt. Fuji side of Sagami Bay.[34]

In January 1930, Agnes wrote, 'Conditions are very different here from former times, but I am only here because it is our Guardian's wish, – it is not of my will, but His.'[35] Later in the month, Shoghi Effendi's next letter arrived, hoping

that you will leave a wonderful group of Bahá'ís in that land. Once they come to appreciate the futility of mere material progress and come to desire a spiritual impetus they will see that the source of all inspiration in this day is Bahá'u'lláh and His teachings.[36]

Later in the month, Agnes began to have a question about her house in Honolulu. It was difficult being a long-distance landlord. The house had been rented, but that lease had expired on 9 January. Since rent payments had been received regularly, she hadn't worried about it and assumed that the lease would be renewed, but she asked her brother, Arthur, to look into the matter. She wanted to either renew the lease or to rent to someone else. The previous agreement was that the renter would keep the place in repair. For this there was no agent's fee and the rent was a low $85 a month.[37]

The problem began to drag out and Agnes was increasingly upset. She had written a new lease agreement with a higher rent, but did not hear back from the renter until late July. Apparently, he was still sending in the $85 and claiming that he was spending the rest on upkeep of the house, but without any proof. By October, the renter had paid no rent for three months. Agnes wrote to Arthur that 'someone needed to go after him' because he 'has no legal right on the house'.[38] Apparently, the matter was resolved somehow.

Agnes's next letter from the Guardian, written on 31 December 1929, arrived on 20 February 1930, in which he praised her for her continuous correspondence and about her staying in Japan:

My dear Miss Alexander,
. . . Your uninterrupted communications telling of consistent and sustained endeavours in serving and promoting the Bahá'í Cause in Japan are gladly welcomed by Shoghi Effendi, and in the midst of his great and absorbing work it brings him much cheer of heart to know that the banner is kept aloft across oceans and seas, and that even under the most trying circumstances you have kept up your quiet and devoted work. It is in view of this that he thinks you might prolong your stay in Japan if is convenient to you.
Of course things seem rather upset there and you must be patient and live and work on faith – in fact it is above all patience and faith that all pioneer work requires.

Shoghi Effendi's personal note read: 'With the assurance of my continued and loving prayers for your success and happiness in the conduct of your arduous and meritorious task, Your true brother, Shoghi.'[39]

At some point, the Bahá'ís in Tokyo were strengthened by two new members: Rev. Sempo Ito, a Christian minister, and Mrs Antoinette Naganuma. Sempo 'became a devoted member of our Bahá'í group and greatly assisted us in the spread of the Cause'. Antoinette was married to a Japanese man and her sister was a Bahá'í. She was familiar with the Faith, but until she fell ill she had not contacted the Bahá'ís. At that point, she asked Agnes to fill in for her at the English conversation group at the YMCA, where she introduced them to the teachings of the Faith. Apparently, these contacts helped Antoinette to embrace the Faith.[40]

During the summer, Agnes was invited to the annual Japanese

Esperanto Congress in Kanazawa at the north end of Honshu Island and described the experience:

> As the train passed through the station for Nojiri, I decided to stop off there for two nights and there saw the Shaw family and the beautiful lake again after two years. I stayed the two nights with Tokyo friends who have a summer home in the village there . . .
>
> A good deal of my six days trip was spent on the trains but I had two nights at Kanazawa and enjoyed the kindness of the Esperantists there and then made another stop off returning by another way where I had been invited by an Esperantist. It gave me an opportunity of getting nearer to some of the people and I enjoyed my stay in the artistic rooms of Japanese inns at the last two places. I had so much attention that I thought I would not care to go to foreign hotels again. The trip was very hot except at Nojiri where the air is from the mountains.[41]

Martha Root returns

Martha Root, who had been in Persia, planned to visit Japan in the autumn of 1930. In preparation, Agnes wrote to Shoghi Effendi about joining Martha in China. His secretary's reply, on 16 January 1930, was that 'Shoghi Effendi wishes me to acknowledge the receipt of your letter dated December 19th 1929, stating your intention to join Martha in China. Shoghi Effendi wishes you to consider it with Martha and see if by your stay in Japan or in your temporary going to China you will best help the advance of the Cause.'[42]

In a second letter, Agnes wrote to the Guardian about Martha's visit and asked about his health. The reply, written on his behalf on 16 March, said:

> My dear Miss Alexander,
>
> I am directed by the Guardian to express his grateful thanks for your kind letter of February eighteenth, enquiring with such earnest solicitude after his health.
>
> Happily he is quite well now and can again devote his entire time to the work he loves best. It is about two months that he had been unwell, but he is now fully recovered.

It is always a pleasure to Shoghi Effendi to know that despite all difficulties and single-handed, you are keeping the torch aflame in Japan and making good of every opportunity. Martha is now in Persia and it would be a splendid idea for you to meet her in China. Of course I am unable to say in how long a time she would be there, but she will surely answer your letter on the subject.

The family are all well and send much love. Shoghi Effendi trusts someday he will have the pleasure of welcoming such a devoted and earnest pioneer as yourself, in Haifa.

Shoghi Effendi's note at the end read: 'With the assurance of my loving and continued prayers for you, and my deep appreciation of your solicitude for my good health, I am your true brother, Shoghi.'[43]

Agnes left for Shanghai in late September 1930 even though Martha did not know for sure that she was coming.[44] Martha was still in Hong Kong when Agnes reached Shanghai, so Agnes spent the ten days before her arrival visiting Dr and Mrs Yun-Siang Tsao, who had moved there from Beijing, the Bahá'í family of Mr Husayn Ouskouli, which consisted of his mother-in-law, his oldest daughter, Ridvaniyyih, and her husband, Suleiman and Mrs Suleimani, his two younger daughters, Ruhania and Jalalia, and son, Qudrat, and the Persian brother, Mr Hossein Touty. Mr Ouskouli had pioneered to Shanghai in 1915 from Ashqabat followed by the Suleimanis in about 1923. In 1954, the Suleimanis pioneered to Taiwan, the first Bahá'ís to do so.[45]

When Martha arrived, she was non-stop action. Agnes wrote:

. . . she began her vigorous work, especially with the newspapers, in which she succeeded in getting many Bahá'í articles published. I shall never forget the historic moment when Dr. Tsao voluntarily offered to translate Esslemont's book into Chinese. Martha was so touched that her eyes filled with tears of joy. From that time Dr. Tsao devoted his only leisure time to this work, which was done at night after busy days. In referring to it he wrote: 'After studying the Bahá'í Faith and the reviving effect it produces over the heart and mind of man, I came to the conclusion that the only way to regenerate China is to introduce the Bahá'í teachings to China, and therefore I began to translate the Bahá'í books into Chinese, so that the Chinese nation may be benefited too by this heavenly

Manifestation. That is why every day after leaving my office, though very tired, I go home and start working on the translations of the Bahá'í teachings, and usually I forget that I am tired.'[46]

Agnes wrote to her brother, 'I got a room fixed up nicely for her [Martha] and she is pleased with it at the back of the house where it is quiet. Her roommate from Shanghai was Carrick Buck the lawyer from Honolulu who I met on the steamer when I went to meet Miss Root. Miss Root will stay here until December 30th and will be with me at Christmas time.'[47]

From China, Martha went back to Japan with Agnes. On her first trip to Japan, Martha had lost her luggage. During the second, she was suspected of being a Communist and followed by the police. On this third visit, the problem was her unappreciated insistence on presenting the Faith to the Imperial Household. On 9 November, Martha received a cable from the Guardian in which he offered his good wishes to the Emperor. With that as a spark, Martha set about to pass on those wishes, much to Agnes's 'distress and embarrassment', since no one just asked to meet the Emperor. It took a month, but Martha's stubborn determination overcame rejections by the American Ambassador and the US Foreign Office, and the ignoring of letters of introduction by Baron Sakatani, a member of the House of Peers. Finally, she turned to R. Masujima and the doors magically opened. On 9 December, Martha, R. Masujima and another went to the Offices of the Imperial Household in the Imperial Garden. Finally inside, Martha presented the Guardian's message, as well as some of the Bahá'í Writings, a prayer rug from Iran, an irreplaceable painting by 'Alí-Muḥammad Varqá, and a red ringstone that 'Abdu'l-Bahá had given to Siyyid Muṣṭafá Rúmí of Burma, who had made the sarcophagus for the remains of the Báb. Martha considered this to be her crowning achievement.[48]

During the rest of her visit to Japan, Martha gave many talks, but the high point was when she spoke over the Tokyo radio station JOAK on 'The Progress of the Bahá'í Movement in the Five Continents'. She read her talk and it was translated into Japanese. The next day, it was published in the *Japan Times*. Though Martha refused payment, the newspaper gave her a beautiful bolt of rainbow-coloured silk. She was also able to get much Bahá'í publicity in the newspapers.[49]

California connections

Early 1931 was a surprising time with a California connection. On 10 January, Agnes and Sempo Ito gave a talk about the Bahá'í Faith at the Buddhist temple of Rev. J. Mori, who also spoke. Since Sempo had been a Christian minister before becoming a Bahá'í, the three speakers came from Buddhist, Christian and Bahá'í backgrounds.[50] Sempo translated a talk given by 'Abdu'l-Bahá in California for the audience. Antoinette Naganuma also spoke 'from her heart' about her marriage to a Japanese and the consequent difficulties between race and religion, saying that the Bahá'í Faith eliminated both of those problems.[51]

Then in May, Agnes participated in a Religious Conference in Tokyo. She spoke about the Revelation of Bahá'u'lláh and quoted what 'Abdu'l-Bahá had said to the Japanese in Oakland, California. A Japanese lady, Michi Kawai, who had graduated from Bryn Mawr College, translated her talk into Japanese. After her talk, Japanese minister Rev. Kodaira approached Agnes and told her that he had been the translator for one of the Master's talks to the Japanese in Oakland in 1912. After the talk, 'Abdu'l-Bahá had invited him for breakfast in San Francisco. Rev. Kodaira said that 'it was a time of great inspiration'. Rev. Kodaira was going to England that summer and wanted to stop in Palestine to visit the Shrine of 'Abdu'l-Bahá. After the conference, the Japanese newspaper *Osaka Mainichi* published Agnes's talk in two issues of their English edition.[52]

Later in the month, the Tokyo Bahá'ís held a celebration of the Declaration of the Báb and one of those who participated was an American clergyman who had hosted 'Abdu'l-Bahá in Oakland in 1912. The clergyman was returning to America and planned to stop in Haifa and visit the Master's tomb.[53]

Keith Ransom-Kehler visits Japan

Keith Ransom-Kehler came to Japan on 25 June 1931, near the beginning of a two-year lecture tour, during which she also advised Bahá'í communities on the Bahá'í Administrative Order, including in Hawaii, Japan, China, Australia, New Zealand, Java, Singapore, Burma, India and Iran.

Initially, Keith was only supposed to stay in Japan for two weeks, but Agnes really wanted her to stay longer:

Although I had only known of our dear sister Keith through the *Baha'i News Letters* and her writings in the *Star of the West*, yet when the cable came from dear Ella Cooper that she was on her way to Japan, a great love and inspiration sprang up in my heart. Even before the cable arrived I had felt a special happiness. Then on the morning before the cable came, a thrill of joy, and the thought that our Guardian was sending some happy message filled my heart. Shortly after the cable that Keith was on her way was handed me. Five days before her arrival, a second cable from Honolulu stated that she would remain 'two weeks' in Japan. This at first saddened my heart, but when I knew if it were His Will, all was for the best, and before she arrived a two weeks program had been filled. It was a happy meeting when she arrived in Yokohama on June twenty-fifth. We felt a peace and joy in being together and Keith said she felt a happiness here. I longed that she might remain longer, as there was so much we could do together, but as her plans had been submitted to Shoghi Effendi, she did not feel she could change them without his knowledge and consent, so two days after her arrival I cabled him asking if it were permissible for her to remain longer. We decided that if no word came in answer, then she would keep to her original plan. The day before she was to leave, when we felt satisfied that we were striving to do His Will only, the following cable was received, 'Whole heartedly approve Keith extend stay love Shoghi.'[54]

So, Agnes had Keith for six full weeks in Japan and she did not let the time go to waste. Keith was kept busy day and night:

All that it meant to Japan to have Keith with me to strengthen and encourage the friends, can never be told in words. Her first public talk the day after her arrival on 25 June was at the Pan-Pacific luncheon. As the speeches there are taken down by a stenographer, I was delighted the next morning to see the most inspiring of her words, under the heading, 'The Bahá'í Movement,' in the *Japan Advertiser*, the leading English newspaper of Japan, which is American owned. This was a great confirmation and showed how when we are in love and unity, the Holy Spirit speaks through us and attracts people to our Cause. That evening we had a gathering of the Friends in my room to meet Keith. The next day, the twenty-seventh, we attended a tea party where I knew her presence would attract to our Cause. In the evening we had a Chinese dinner with some of the directors of the Chinese YMCA after which she spoke to a group of the Chinese students of which there are several thousand in Tokyo. On Sunday, the twenty-eighth, a group met in my room. Keith spoke with our dear brother, Rev. Sempo Ito, translating. Among the group were two Korean students whom Mr. Ito had brought. He told us afterwards that they said they found a 'very good feeling' in the gathering.

At 8 o'clock, the next morning, Keith spoke at the chapel exercises of the Japan Women's University, one of the teachers, a graduate of Vassar College translating. The founder of this university, the late President Naruse, met 'Abdu'l-Bahá when in London in 1912. 'Abdu'l-Bahá urged him to return to Japan and spread the Bahá'í teachings, and in 1916, he invited me to speak in the chapel to the whole school on the Baha'i Movement. So in this university the seed has been sown and the future will show the results. In the evening Keith spoke to a group of students from the Commercial University who had arranged a tea party for us. Keith was delighted with meeting this group of the rising generation of Japan and of having opportunity of talking with them and answering their questions.

The next afternoon, we were invited to the beautiful garden of Dr. Masujima, who shows kindness to the Bahá'í friends. He was away en route to England, but we met in his law library law students from Keio University who gather there every Tuesday to study and have Japanese supper together. Martha and I had both spoken here at different times, so it was good to have Keith reinforce the efforts which had been made. As we were leaving the library, the student who had arranged for our coming accompanied us and asked if we would have our photograph taken with him, to which we gladly consented.

After attending a tea party the next day, we were guests of the YMCA English Speaking Club for supper where Keith spoke. This club has heard the Bahá'í Teachings many times, but as the members are constantly changing, it is almost always a new group. Martha, on her three visits to Japan has each time spoken there and I have spoken a number of times of the Bahá'í Movement, so again Keith reinforced the work. We returned to the club at their request on several Wednesday evenings when they met, and each time Keith spoke. Many seeds were sown and some of the members came to my room to hear more of the Cause.[55]

Agnes noted that after the initial planned two weeks, things just kept happening: 'Without making previous plans, each day was filled and it was very important that Keith had opportunity to speak more of the Bahá'í Administration, of which she is so well qualified to speak.'[56]

During July, Miss Fung-Ling Liu, who was returning to China after studying in America, stopped over for a night to visit Agnes and Keith in Tokyo. Martha Root had suggested to her that she do so. Coincidentally, Liu arrived on the day of a Bahá'í meeting in Agnes's home. Liu's brother had become a Bahá'í at Cornell University and this meeting advanced her knowledge of the Faith. Meeting Liu led to Keith being invited to stay at her brother's home in Canton on her way to Australia.[57]

Keith told the Guardian, 'The contacts which Agnes Alexander made for me in the Universities and the student groups were most rewarding; Friday night Bahá'í meetings were well attended by inquiring students, many nationalities being represented. Agnes felt that the most important of all was the several meetings held for the confirmed Bahá'ís and those about to declare themselves, to study and grasp the import and modus vivendi of Administration.'[58]

Agnes went with Keith when she sailed from Yokohama to Kobe and then the two took the train to Kyoto, where they visited Tokujiro Torii. Keith was very impressed with the Toriis, saying that 'I have never known such kindness.' Tokujiro, being blind, had a bronze relief copy of a picture of 'Abdu'l-Bahá with the Greatest Name carved in wood beneath it. Keith was very touched by seeing 'These spiritual treasures' being 'touched by the fingers of the materially blind' Tokujiro. The next day, Tokujiro and his son, Akira, joined Agnes and Keith on the train and they all went and visited Daiun Inouye before Keith sailed away.[59]

Keith was in India when she was called by the Guardian to the Holy Land, where he gave her the amazingly daunting task of going to Iran as the representative of the Guardian and of the National Spiritual Assembly of the United States and Canada in an attempt to remove the ban on Bahá'í literature being brought into and distributed in Iran. Keith's efforts with the government failed, but she spent the next year travelling extensively through Iran. In October 1932, exhausted from her constant and sacrificial efforts, she contracted smallpox and died in Isfahan. Shoghi Effendi called her the 'first and distinguished martyr' from America and named her a Hand of the Cause of God.[60]

After Keith's departure, Agnes wrote:

From the first day in Japan Keith loved the people and their art. After she left me, in her first letter she wrote that she was planning to return and be with me again, and in her last letter to me written shortly before her passing in Persia she wrote: 'I still like Japan better than any country that I have visited and I often think with love and longing of the precious friends there. Please assure them that I remember each one of them. Give them all my hearty Baha'i love.' I am grateful to God that she came into my life![61]

In July, the Guardian sent Agnes a reassuring letter about persistence in the face of little result:

The high efforts which you have displayed in spreading the Cause in Japan will no doubt produce their fruits. If the results have been relatively meagre, this should not in any way discourage you but it should serve to stimulate your energies and to deepen your faith in the glorious victory foretold by our dear Master. You know how great an interest 'Abdu'l-Bahá had in Japan where he even intended to travel and to deliver the Holy Word. Such a blessing you should always bear in mind in your moments of partial discouragement, when faith and faith alone can sustain and guide us.[62]

Home visits

After Keith's departure in August 1931, Agnes did not return directly to Tokyo, but spent the following 19 days with Tokujiro visiting the homes of some of the former students of the Tokyo Bahá'í group. By this time, the students were dispersed and married. Agnes described these wonderful days:

Probably I am the only foreigner who has visited that village where Mr. Torii's family are engaged in silk manufacture. The whole family could not have been more kind to me and they said it was only balancing what I had done for their son and brother in the past. The night after Keith left, I had spent in Kobe with another Bahá'í sister who, when a school girl in Tokyo became confirmed in the Cause and was often, in those days before the great earthquake of 1923, in my little Japanese home in Tokyo. She is now married and has two lovely boys. She and her husband made me most welcome and asked me always to come and stay in their home and this she said was to repay for what she had received in my home when a school girl. I speak of these things for they came to me so unexpectedly.

This is the time of the year called Obon, when in every family the dead ones are especially remembered. This time and the New Year in January are the two times in the year when workers have holidays. At Mr. Torii's home I had the privilege of taking part as a member of the family in a Buddhist ceremony for the dead ancestors of Mrs. Torii's family. In the village Buddhist temple, with beautiful surroundings, this ceremony was held. All the relatives of the family gathered in the temple where the dear old priest and his assistants chanted sutras, and the members of the family, one by one, paid their respect at the altar. After the ceremony they all visited the family burying ground. It was all a beautiful, sweet atmosphere and the family said they felt it was providential that I was there at that time. One beautiful thing in these ceremonies is that the little children all take part. Another event and fete for the dead was that held in a neighboring town which has an ocean inlet. Here at night beautiful little miniature boats lighted with candles were put in the water, each boat representing someone who had died during the year in the town. Each family also placed a lighted candle fastened to a round hemp mat, in the water. At the same time beautiful fire works were sent up so that the whole scene was one of beauty. The little miniature boats one by one became ignited by the candles on them and disappeared in flames of fire, the symbol of the spirit. This is a very old custom which is carried out every year in this town.

Another thousand years old custom observed is called Tanabata. In front of the house bamboo branches are placed on which paper streamers of all the rainbow colors flutter. These have verses written on the them and are for the stars, as it is believed that on this particular night two stars, male and female lovers meet in the heavens. The Tanabata at Mr. Torii's home was unique in all the world, for on it were written words from Bahá'u'lláh and 'Abdu'l-Bahá, as well as the Greatest Name in both Roman and Persian letters. One of the verses suggested by Mr. Torii was, 'A star has the same radiance whether it shines from the East or from the West. 'Abdu'l-Bahá'.

Leaving Mr. Torii's home, I visited another friend whom I had not met for ten years. He is now the Social Director in one of the Gunze Filature factories and has the spiritual welfare of 700 factory girls under his care. I feel it was a wonderful visit I had in his home where his mother, wife and four children live. Twice I spoke a few words to the factory girls at their time of assembly. In the factory, before the girls retire, a bell sounds and all is quiet. The girls then sit in quiet meditation until another bell sounds. As ten girls live in one room, it gives them an opportunity to commune in quiet. The manager believes that the girls do better work when their hearts are at peace and something is given them to bring spiritual content-ment. This friend felt his interest in our Baha'i teachings renewed and said he was going to begin again his study of the literature. At this place also I was probably the only foreigner who had visited it, and naturally was a great curiosity to the girls.

Now I am here where I came to see after twelve years our Bahá'í brother, Mr. Fukuta. He was the first confirmed Bahá'í when I came to Japan for the first time and had the honor of receiving from the Master the first Tablet sent to a Japanese living in Japan. He is married and has three lovely children and is working in the wholesale rice business. He says he puts the Bahá'í principles in his business and that all his customers know of these. Here I have again received the greatest kindness in this humble home. It is a sorrow to my heart that so many years passed without seeing this spiritual son, but no response had come from my letters to him and I had not known what to think. His address was changed it seems seven years ago, and in all this time he had not received any of my letters. I found that he was still as firm as ever in his faith and now I hope will arise with new impetus to work for the Cause.[63]

In October, Shoghi Effendi sent two more letters to Agnes, the first, on 8 October, mentioning Keith's visit and the second, on 30 October, praising her for her for her visits to the more isolated Japanese Bahá'ís with Tokujiro:

Shoghi Effendi was very pleased to hear that Keith has achieved some success in Japan. The explicit promise of Bahá'u'lláh is that God's spirit will assist all those who, with a sincere and detached heart, arise to spread the teachings. There is no reason for astonishment therefore if the teachers of the Cause find success in their work. May God's spirit continue to sustain them.

Shoghi Effendi wishes to extend a hearty welcome to Mr. Torii to visit the Holy Land whenever circumstances will permit him. Please extend to him as well as to Mr. Inoue Shoghi Effendi's loving greetings.[64]

Shoghi Effendi wishes me to acknowledge the receipt of your letter dated September 2, 1931. He was very glad to hear of the visit you have paid to the home of some of the Japanese friends. In this way you can keep in close touch with them and feed the fire of their enthusiasm for the Cause. It is very important that the friends of a land, especially when very few keep in close touch and if possible visit each other, for in this way more unity of action can be established . . .

Please convey to all the friends in Japan the loving greetings of Shoghi Effendi; he will always remember them in his prayers and ask for them divine guidance and help.[65]

On 22 December, the Guardian sent Agnes her fourth letter of the year, giving her guidance about a proposed trip to Formosa and cautioning her against doing too much:

Concerning your trip to Formosa you could judge best, but Shoghi Effendi feels that the more territory you try to cover the less of actual and lasting work we will succeed to do. It is far better to concentrate upon Japan until some real groups are formed and Spiritual Assemblies instituted. The Cause can never be considered as securely established in a centre until an Assembly is formed for then they can stand on their own feet and carry on the work without any real help from outside. [66]

The first Local Spiritual Assembly in Japan

On 19 March 1932, Agnes wrote in the Baháʼí Record book: 'On the morning of March thirteenth, the guidance came that now was the time to form the first Japanese Assembly of Baháʼís of Tokyo.' Agnes called a meeting for the 15th, to which only four of the Tokyo Baháʼís were able to come. A second meeting was then set for the 18th and Agnes went around and personally visited all the Baháʼís who had not been able to attend the first meeting. There were 11 Baháʼís in the Tokyo community: Rev. Sempo Ito, Mrs Yuri [Mochizuki] Furukawa, Mrs Otoe Murakami, Mrs Kanae Takeshita, Mr Y. Kataoka, Mr Keiji Sawada, Miss Agnes Alexander, Mrs Antoinette Naganuma, Mr Nakanishi, Miss Eito, Mr H. Matsuda. All but Miss Eito and Mr Matsuda were elected.[67]

At the Naw-Rúz celebration, 22 people participated and listened to the recorded voice of ʻAbduʼl-Bahá. Agnes sent a cable to the Guardian that read: 'Naw-Ruz greetings Tokyo Assembly.' His reply the next day was: 'Loving remembrance Shoghi.'[68] In a letter that followed, the Guardian's secretary wrote, 'Shoghi Effendi hopes that this Assembly, which is the first of its kind in that country, will start immediately to take the necessary steps for interesting others and beginning an intensive teaching campaign.'[69]

On 26 March, Agnes informed the friends of the momentous achievement:

> I write to convey to you the glad news of the forming of the Spiritual Assembly of Tokyo, the first Assembly of its kind in the world. It has long been the hope of our Guardian that here in Tokyo enough friends might be brought into the Cause as to form the first Japanese Spiritual Assembly in the world, as a nucleus round which would gather and flourish the future Baháʼí community of Japan. In one of his letters our Guardian wrote: 'My prayer will be offered again for you at His Holy Shrine that you may be assisted to establish permanently a Baháʼí Spiritual Assembly in that land and help that centre to get in close and constant touch with Assemblies both in the East and the West.'
>
> It is now my joyful privilege to write you as the Foreign Secretary of our newly formed Assembly which met last evening for the first time and elected officers. Our Assembly, which was born on the glad

Naw-Rúz day, came into being wholly through the Master's power and guidance . . . At our first Assembly meeting last night it was decided to publish monthly a Japanese Bahá'í magazine beginning in May . . .[70]

Just a month later, at Riḍván 1932, the Bahá'ís gathered together to elect the Local Spiritual Assembly which had been formed on Naw-Rúz. One change was made: H. Matsuda replaced Mr Kataoka, who asked to be relieved.

Visiting Hokkaido

During the summer of 1932, Agnes went to Hokkaido, the northern-most of the main Japanese islands, at the invitation of Tadashi Watanabe, to speak about the Bahá'í Faith at the first Esperanto Congress on the island. Tadashi had learned of the Faith from Ida Finch in America and, when he returned to Japan, he had contacted Agnes. Upon returning to his home in Tomakomai, Hokkaido, he started a monthly paper in which he introduced the Bahá'í teachings. Agnes accepted the invitation. She first went to Onuma where she stayed in a summer boarding house run by an English missionary lady. After several days of rest, Agnes continued by train on 1 August to Muroran, where three young men boarded the train, greeting her in Esperanto and asking if she was Miss Alexander. The four of them had a delightful conversation as they rode to the train to Tomakomai. They were met at the station by Tadashi Watanabe and his wife and,

> two students carrying Esperanto flags welcomed us. A crowd had assembled at the station, among them the Headman, as he is called, of the town, as the local newspaper had announced my arrival. In the evening a welcome meeting was held. I spoke in Esperanto to which Mr. Watanabe translated into Japanese. We sat around a long table, and at my right was the Headman of the town . . . Two Esperanto songs were sung, Espero and Tagigo. The heading on the mimeographed copies of the songs, which were passed around, translated from the Esperanto was, 'Welcome to our Miss Agnes B. Alexander! We will sing, Hope for your future glory, and Dawn for your holy movement.'

... The next morning I left with Mr. Watanabe for Yamabe, the center of the island where the Esperanto Congress was to be held. We traveled all day on trains before reaching the small village where the Oomoto movement had a center. This movement was later disbanded by the government. The Esperanto meetings were held in a school building, and there I spoke of the Bahá'í Teachings and Esperanto. Though the attendance was small, because of the distances to reach the village, yet the seed was sown and those who came were carriers of the Message to their home towns. The evening after the Congress was over, I was asked to speak in the hall of the Oomoto religion on the Bahá'í teachings. The hall was crowded with the country people whose eager earnest faces impressed me. In that far away village God granted me the privilege of planting the seed of the Divine Cause for this Day.

The next day, with Mr. Watanabe and an Esperantist friend, we visited the offices of two newspapers in the town of Asahigawa. From there I went with Mr. Watanabe to his family home in Sapporo, where we spent the night, and in the morning called at the office of the leading newspaper on the island, the *Hokkai Times*. The editor had an article ready to publish about the Congress and added to it something about the Bahá'í teachings and my attendance at the Congress. This I felt was God's great favor, for although the Congress had been held in the center of the Oomoto religion, only the Bahá'í Cause was mentioned. During the day in Sapporo we met a number of Esperantists and returned in the evening to the Watanabe home in Tomakomai. There I spent three nights during which I had the privilege of explaining the Bahá'í teachings more fully to Mr. Watanabe and the young minister. The kindness of Mr. Watanabe to me during our travels and of his wife in their home can never be forgotten.[71]

After the Congress, Agnes returned to Onuma to visit some of the Esperantists she had met. She found Mr Odashina, who phoned a few other Esperantists who were free because it was Saturday:

I suggested that we visit a newspaper and added that I knew God would help us. As the writer was acquainted with the editor of the *Hakodate Shimbun,* he telephoned and arranged for us to meet him. Almost immediately after receiving us the editor proposed that I

should give a public talk in the Town Hall, which he would adver-
tise in his paper, and also publish, and it would be without any
expense to us. It was arranged that I should speak in Esperanto, and
the writer would translate my talk into Japanese. After meeting the
editor we spent a happy afternoon together talking of the Cause. The
two young men from the banks said they had been Christians but
they now had doubts. The other two friends had no definite beliefs.
I returned that evening to Onuma, where I prepared the Esperanto
talk. The subject chosen was, 'Bahá'í the Religion of Religions.' The
next week on my return to Tokyo, I stopped a few days in Hakodate, when the public meeting was held. The night of the meeting, a
flash light photograph was taken of myself and the interpreter, as we
spoke on the platform, which was inserted in the newspaper with an
account of the meeting. The following day the paper published an
article on the history of the Cause with pictures of 'Abdu'l-Bahá and
the Bahá'í Temple of Wilmette.

As I sailed away from the port the day after the meeting, the new
friends were on the wharf waving their hearty farewells. Through
His favor, in every place I visited I had been helped and cared for by
kind friends. Only through the principle of Bahá'u'lláh of a universal language had we been drawn together.[72]

The Guardian was very happy with Tadashi's efforts on Hokkaido.
Shoghi Effendi's secretary wrote on his behalf that: 'He was particularly
glad to learn of Mr. Tadashi Watanabe's recent publication on religion
in which he has written about the Bahá'í teachings and he sincerely
trusts that such an attempt on his part will serve to further the interests
of the Faith and awaken many souls to the sublimity of the teachings
and principles of the Cause.'[73]

On 25 November, the first Persian Bahá'í arrived in Japan on business. The visitor was Mr Hossein Touty. Hossein had pioneered to
Shanghai and Vladivostok and then in 1921 went to the Philippines,
possibly the first Bahá'í to do so. After staying there for five years, he
returned to Shanghai until at least 1938.[74] Agnes wrote, 'Through the
bounty of Bahá'u'lláh, the Tokyo Assembly has a visit from our Persian brother, Mr. H. Touty of Shanghai, who came unexpectedly on
business. He brought us spiritual help and the fragrance of the Master
of whom he told us many beautiful stories of his visit in Akka about

twenty-five years ago, when he spent a month there.' Agnes took Hossein to Kamakura to see a 'great image of Buddha, standing in the open surrounded by verdure'. While there, they bought copies of the three monkeys, the original of which is in Nikko. One monkey has his hands to his eyes, one to his mouth, and one to his ears. The next morning, Agnes wrote that 'on opening the *Hidden Words* the first verse my eyes saw was number 44 of the Persian section: "O Companion of my Throne! Hear no evil, and see no evil; . . . Speak no evil . . ."'[75]

Translation of *Bahá'u'lláh and the New Era* into Japanese

One of Agnes's primary goals from the Guardian had been to translate *Bahá'u'lláh and the New Era* into Japanese. Shoghi Effendi first brought up the task in emphatic fashion in his lengthy handwritten note at the end of a letter in January 1930:

> I would urge you, above everything to arrange for the translation into Japanese of Esslemont's 'Bahá'u'lláh and the New Era'. I feel it of the utmost importance that such a book should be translated and printed at present. The book has already been translated and printed in German, Arabic and Portuguese. Recently it has been translated into Persian, Russian and Esperanto. Why should Japan lag behind? May you be assisted by the Beloved in this task! Shoghi[76]

Two months later, in March, he reiterated his desire for the translation:

> I should like to urge you again to take whatever measure that could possibly be taken to ensure a correct and early translation of Dr. Esslemont's invaluable Book into Japanese. I feel it would be a glorious achievement, and would immensely help promote the Cause in Japan. May the Beloved guide you, sustain you in your manifold efforts and services to our beloved Faith. I will continue to pray for you at Bahá'u'lláh's Shrine from the depths of my heart. Your true and affectionate brother, Shoghi[77]

Agnes had immediately set out to find a translator and in late February, informed the Guardian that Mr Iwahashi, a blind friend, could do the translation if given time. But less than three weeks later, she wrote to say that Sempo Ito, a Universalist Church minister (who would soon become a Bahá'í), had begun the translation. By May, she had formed a committee consisting of Sempo Ito, Susumu Aibara, N. Imaoka and herself to oversee the work.[78]

Shoghi Effendi said that he was 'delighted with the news you gave me regarding the translation of Dr. Esslemont's book into Japanese. I will pray for your guidance and success. I long to hear that it has been accomplished. This would constitute yet another jewel in the crown of your life-long service to the Cause of Bahá'u'lláh.'[79]

Agnes spent a month in Shanghai with Martha Root in October 1930 and inspired by Dr Tsao's translation efforts of *Bahá'u'lláh and the New Era*, 'felt the urgency of seeing about the Japanese translation of Esslemont's book, which was being done in Tokyo',[80] but it proved to be very difficult. By the end of the year, the effort had not progressed as she'd hoped. In a letter to Shoghi Effendi in early February 1931, Agnes wrote that she had found another translator who said it would take two months to finish the translation. But then, by late March, the new translator found other employment and ended his efforts with just a third of the book translated.[81]

By April 1931 an uncorrected draft had been produced[82] but the three translators who had tried to accomplish the task, 'had failed to conform to the beloved Guardian's request to "take every precaution to put it into as good Japanese as possible"'.[83] When the third translator quit, Shoghi Effendi's secretary wrote: 'As regards the translation of Esslemont's book, he was sorry to learn of the sudden departure of the translator, and hence of the impossibility of his completing the work. In view of the importance which he attaches to this translation, however, he would urge you to find some suitable person and arrange for its translation entirely.' The Guardian added in his own hand: 'With the assurance of my continued and fervent prayers for the early completion of the translation of Dr. Esslemont's valuable and unique work, and with my deepest gratitude for your painstaking and devoted endeavours, Your true brother, Shoghi'[84]

In another letter to Agnes dated 13 July 1931, the Guardian said:

In regard to the translation of Dr. Esslemont's 'Bahá'u'lláh and the New Era' in Japanese the Guardian wishes you to do your best to finish this work as soon as possible. There is no need of emphasizing the importance of such a task. The book has already been translated into eight languages and this alone indicates the significance of the work you are going to do. Baháʼí literature in Japanese is rather limited in number and the translation of Dr. Esslemont's book will I hope inaugurate a new era in the religious history of Japan and will be a source of blessings for that land.[85]

After Keith Ransom-Kehler left Japan in August of 1931, Agnes went to Kobe with Tokujiro Torii to consult with Daiun Inouye about completing the translation. Daiun's 16-year-old daughter had died the previous June, and as the group talked, Daiun suddenly said that he would translate the book as a memorial to his daughter.[86]

With Daiun's arising to the task, the translation moved ahead. Shoghi Effendi kept in close contact with Agnes about the translation work, mentioning its importance in 11 consecutive letters between 17 April 1931 and 26 October 1932, when it was finally completed. On 8 October 1931, he sent another letter in which his secretary wrote on his behalf:

> He sincerely hopes that the translation of Dr. Esslemont's book will proceed at a rapid pace, because no real advance can be made in the teaching work without proper literature, and this book is undoubtedly the most comprehensive exposition of the teachings yet written. The language should however be worthy of the theme otherwise it would not make the necessary appeal to the educated classes.

In his own hand, Shoghi Effendi added: 'I am eagerly awaiting the news of the publication in Japanese of that prized book which Dr. Esslemont has so wonderfully laboured to produce. When received it will adorn the newly-restored mansion of Baháʼuʼlláh adjoining His Shrine at Bahji. May the Beloved sustain and bless your magnificent efforts, Your true brother, Shoghi.'[87]

At the end of October 1931, a letter written on behalf of the Guardian said: 'Shoghi Effendi is very eagerly awaiting to see the translation of Dr. Esslemont's book completed and come out in print, for without proper literature the Cause cannot progress very fast.' Shoghi Effendi himself added: 'May the Beloved reinforce your efforts, remove every obstacle from your path and answer your fervent prayers for the consolidation and spread of the Cause in Japan, Your true brother Shoghi'.[88]

In his personal note to a letter written to Agnes on 22 December 1931, Shoghi Effendi wrote that:

> I long to hear of the completion of the translation of Dr. Esslemont's book into Japanese. The Chinese version is now under press in Shanghai. The Persian rendering will be printed this winter in Haifa. We already have seven printed translations and I long to see the Japanese version in printed form. I urge you to hasten the work by every means at your disposal, and to inform me of the approximate printing cost as I am eager to assist financially in its production. May the Beloved enable you to render this great service to His Cause in the not-distant future.
>
> Your true and grateful brother, Shoghi[89]

On 6 January 1932, the Guardian's secretary again referred to Esslemont's book in a letter:

> He was very glad to know that the translation of Dr. Esslemont's book into Japanese is proceeding gradually and may be completed pretty soon. As I have mentioned in my previous letters, Shoghi Effendi attributes great importance to this work, for without it the Cause could not make much headway in Japan. The first thing an interested person asks for is literature and there is no book better than Dr. Esslemont's to satisfy that need and in a clear form give a faithful conception of the Teachings. Please exert all your efforts to have it completed as soon as possible.

Shoghi Effendi's personal note read, 'With the renewed assurance of my continued prayers for your success in completing, speedily and effectively, the translation of Dr. Esslemont's book into Japanese. Your true brother, Shoghi.'[90]

In yet another letter, this one mailed on 25 January 1932, the Guardian's secretary wrote:

> He is very anxiously waiting to hear the glad news of the completion of the Japanese translation of Dr. Esslemont's book. He believes that you should be in constant touch with . . . and encourage him in his task, so that the work may not suffer from unnecessary delay. The

Cause will never be firmly established in Japan and the teaching will not spread much unless you possess proper literature to interest and inform the newcomers and undoubtedly Dr. Esslemont's book is the best available for that purpose.

Shoghi Effendi added, 'Wishing you success in the early completion of the translation of Dr. Esslemont's book into Japanese and assuring you of my continued prayers for your welfare and happiness, Your true brother, Shoghi.'[91]

With all the gracious but insistent pressure from the Guardian, Agnes went to visit Daiun in February. She wrote, 'It was a blessed meeting and we had some happy spiritual visits. While there I occupied the room in the temple which had been his daughter's. We arranged that he would have a helper in the translation work.'[92] The next letter from the Guardian, dated 15 March 1932, showed his anxious impatience with the long effort. His secretary wrote:

It is surely a pity that so many unforeseen circumstances seem to delay the progress of the translation of Dr. Esslemont's book, because upon the completion of that work rests the real start of an effective teaching work in Japan. Anyhow we have to appreciate the great kindness of Mr. Inouye to undertake the task and pray that his handicaps be eliminated. Please extend Shoghi Effendi's greetings and assure him of his deep appreciation for the wonderful service he has offered to render to the progress of the Cause in Japan.[93]

Finally, Daiun completed his translation in April 1932, but then Yuri Mochizuki, who was now the married Yuri Furukawa and was in charge of getting the book printed, felt that the translation was not well suited for the younger generation, so more work yet again delayed the project.[94] The Guardian's next letter about the work was on 30 April and said: 'Shoghi Effendi would like you to keep him in touch with the progress of the translation work of Dr. Esslemont's book. He is very anxious to know how rapidly the task is being achieved, and when it will be ready to go to the printers. He hopes that you are in constant touch with that noble soul who has undertaken to translate it, and are stimulating and encouraging him in his work.'[95] The pressure Agnes felt must have been immense.

In September 1932, Agnes was finally able to tell the Guardian that the work was done. The response was that 'Shoghi Effendi was glad to learn that the translation of Dr. Esslemont's book has been completed. Even though he desires to have the correction properly made he does not wish to have much delay incurred. He likes to see the book come out of the press and ready for circulation as soon as possible.'[96] This letter was sent soon after the passing of the Greatest Holy Leaf. Agnes had sent her condolences and Shoghi Effendi's personal note reflected this:

> I greatly value your words of cheer and loving sympathy. The services you have for so long rendered the sacred Threshold have, I feel certain, brought immense joy and relief to her overburdened heart during the closing days of her earthly life. May her spirit be your guide, your comfort and your help in the great work you are doing for her Father's Cause. The publication of the Japanese version of Esslemont's book will indeed crown your noble efforts in the service of so great and precious a Cause.[97]

On 26 October 1932, the Guardian ordered 100 copies of the finished translation to be sent to him. In December, the first copies of the Japanese translation of John Esslemont's *Bahá'u'lláh and the New Era* came off the presses, and on 12 December, Agnes wrote:

> It was the Temple day meeting and the afternoon when the books, *Bahá'u'lláh and the New Era* were to be delivered from the binders. Mrs. Furukawa and Mr. Matsuda had come especially to help receive the books. We had supper together but not until after ten p.m. were all the 1,000 copies delivered. How thankful we should be to Bahá'u'lláh for this bounty which is at last accomplished and for which Shoghi Effendi has waited so long.[98]

The next letter from the Guardian, dated 15 January 1933, was joyously happy with the news:

> Shoghi Effendi was very glad to receive your letter dated December 13th, 1932, announcing the long-awaited news that the Japanese translation of Dr. Esslemont's book is out from the hands of the printers and ready for circulation. The copies you have sent him he

will place in the different Bahá'í libraries we have here, among them the one in the Mansion of Bahá'u'lláh in Bahjí where the pilgrims will be able to see it and read it if they can.

Please extend the Guardian's deep appreciation and thanks to those who rendered their assistance in this noble work. They will obtain the reward of their labours from the services this book will render to the Cause as well as to the people of their land. He is certain that through it many seeking souls will learn of the truth of the Faith and thereby attain the source of eternal grace and salvation.

The different nations of the world will never attain peace except after recognizing the significance of the teachings and whole-heartedly upholding them, for through those precepts all international problems will be solved and every man secure the spiritual environment in which his soul can evolve and produce its highest fruits.

In His moments of prayer and meditation at the Blessed Shrines the Guardian will think of you as well as of the other friends in Japan and ask for you all divine guidance and help in serving the Faith.

His personal comment at the end of the letter read:

Dear and valued co-worker:
I congratulate you on your splendid achievement. May this newly-published book reinforce your high endeavors and lend an unprecedented impetus to the advancement of the Faith in that land. The books will be placed in the Library of the Mansion, near to the Shrine of Bahá'u'lláh. I urge you to give the book the widest circulation possible, and to mail as soon as possible a few copies to the chief Bahá'í centres in both the East and the West. May the Almighty bless richly your efforts and fulfil your dearest wish, Your true brother, Shoghi[99]

Then came the letter that Shoghi Effendi had waited so long to send. Dated 11 February 1933, it said:

Dear and much-prized co-worker: With feelings of intense delight and gratitude, I have sent, this very afternoon the books you sent me to the library of the Mansion of Bahá'u'lláh at Bahjí. They will be placed by myself side by side with the fourteen printed versions of *The New Era*, and will be a constant reminder of your perseverance, your magnificent efforts, your exemplary devotion to the Cause of God. It is a historic service that you have rendered to the Abhá Threshold. I urge you to send one copy to each of the most important Bahá'í centres in East and West. Its effect, I feel, will be remarkable. Your true brother, Shoghi[100]

Building on that theme, the Guardian responded to her next letter, on 17 April:

Now that you have such a wonderful book translated and published in Japanese, your work of spreading the Cause should be greatly stimulated, because you have first-rate literature to hand to the newcomer and ask him to read it. He can pursue his studies in the privacy of his own room without the need of a teacher or of some person to guide him.

To awaken such deep interest, however, it may be advisable to hold study classes and let the group study the book together and discuss its points as they arise.

Shoghi Effendi's personal note at the bottom said:

The publication of the Japanese version of 'The New Era' marks a landmark in the history of the Faith in that land. May it be a prelude to glorious and unprecedented achievements! Persevere in your historic task, and make every effort to add to the number of the active and avowed supporters of our beloved Faith. Never lose heart. Rest assured and remember that my prayers will continue to be offered on your behalf. Your true and grateful brother, Shoghi. [101]

The Japanese translation of *Bahá'u'lláh and the New Era*, initiated in January 1930, finally sat three years later on the bookshelves in the Mansion of Bahjí alongside the copies of the book in other languages.

A call to Hawaii

By 1933, Agnes had lived in the same house in Tokyo for five years, but it was not a great place and she was not feeling well. On 24 March, she asked the Local Spiritual Assembly whether she should move or not. The Assembly decided that she should, but Agnes could not find any other place.[102] At Riḍván, she received a letter from her brother, Arthur, which said that his wife had just died. She immediately decided to return to Honolulu.

Agnes quickly sorted out her affairs and things. Her library of Bahá'í books, a scroll of the Greatest Name and Juliet Thompson's portrait of 'Abdu'l-Bahá went to Yuri Furukawa, who was elected chairman of the Local Spiritual Assembly at Riḍván.[103] Agnes departed for Honolulu on 30 May 1933 aboard the *Taiyu Maru*.[104]

13

HAWAII AND AMERICA

1933–1935

Agnes was commonly inspired to do something and it was notable that those inspired feelings were also commonly in sync with what the Guardian wanted her to do. On 8 June, Agnes arrived in Honolulu. On that same day, Shoghi Effendi's secretary wrote:

> He was very glad to learn that you have decided to leave for Honolulu as he firmly believes that such a visit will give you a chance to rest and will enable you on your return to Japan, to better serve the Cause. There should always be a limit to self-sacrifice. The Guardian is fully confident that your journey to the Hawaiian Islands will be a great benefit to the friends there and it will stimulate them to pursue with refreshed zeal their Bahá'í activities. Last April we had the pleasure of meeting two of our Honolulu friends, Miss Julia Goldman, whom you have probably met, and Miss Baldwin, the daughter of our devoted Bahá'í sister Mrs. Baldwin. Their visit to Haifa seems to have been very inspiring to them as it is hoped that as a result of their pilgrimage they will redouble their energies in the service of the Cause. Please extend to them, as well as to all our Hawaiian friends, the loving greetings of the Guardian and assure them of his prayers on their behalf. May I also assure you once more of his best wishes. In his moments of meditation and supplication at the Blessed Shrines he will especially remember you and will ask the Lord to bless and enrich your efforts a hundredfold.

Shoghi Effendi added a personal note at the bottom of the letter:

Dear and valued co-worker:

I immensely appreciate your outstanding services in those faraway Islands, and I will pray that you may be assisted to resume in the not distant future your manifold and valued activities in the service of our beloved Faith. Your name will forever remain associated with the rise of the Faith and its establishment in Japan and the record of your incessant and splendid endeavors will shed on its annals a lustre that time can never dim.

Your true and grateful brother,
Shoghi Effendi[1]

Describing her reason for leaving Japan to Ella Rowland, Agnes wrote about needing to be in good health in order to do what God had given her to do:

For some time I have not been well, but of course I do not like to speak of this. I feel that my mission is to be a comfort to those who need it, and also to get refreshed for new and better work in this land, where God has placed me, and so I hope to come back here after the summer in better health to work for our Beloved Lord.

So Ella, dear, the friends will understand my mission, the most important part of which is to be prepared for the work which I shall come back here for. At every turn it seems I find His assurance and guidance which is a great joy.[2]

In July 1933, Agnes was living in her brother Arthur's home when she was surprised by a stranger at the door. He greeted her with 'Alláh-u-Abhá!' The visitor was Mr W. E. M. Grosfeld, who had been a pioneer in Batavia, Java, and with whom she had corresponded at one time when she was in Japan. Mr Grosfeld was on his way to America and, ultimately, to Haifa. He was a Dutch Bahá'í who had found the Faith on a visit to Cairo and immediately accepted it. Agnes quickly organized a luncheon at the Uluniu Women's Club at Waikiki and Mr Grosfeld was able to meet the Honolulu Bahá'ís. She noted, 'Mr. Grosfeld was very happy to meet the believers. As he seemed loath to leave them, two of the friends invited him to stay in their homes, each for a week, if he could arrange to remain for two weeks. He was delighted to stay and we had many happy meetings while he was with us. During that time

the *Star-Bulletin* published an interview with him and his picture.'³
When he finally reached the Holy Land in February 1934, he wrote the
Hawaiian Bahá'ís a letter while staying at Bahjí:

> Our beloved Guardian, Shoghi Effendi, ordered me to write to
> you from the most precious Spot of the World, the Shrine of His
> Holiness Baha'u'llah . . . The Guardian is most interested in that
> beautiful Bahá'í Center in those far islands. Of course he is inter-
> ested in all regarding the Cause and the friends, but he realizes very
> well that your Center is one of the most beautiful. He was anxiously
> waiting for the news I had to tell him from all the Bahá'í Assemblies.
> I spoke about our zealous sister Agnes Alexander and the question
> of Japan. He approves that the work of her teaching in Japan is of
> great importance and thinks that in a short time she will be able to
> return to that country. As I promised, I prayed for you all in the
> Holy Shrines . . . Dear friends, be persuaded that I never forget the
> lovely days I spent in Honolulu. Your great love has touched me
> and I always shall return with my deepest and sincerest feelings of
> devotion. My heart belongs to you, dear Honoluluans. Honolulu is
> a splendid garden with the finest flowers, soft and sweet roses of our
> glorious Bahá'í Cause.⁴

On 7 September 1933, Agnes did a first: she spoke over the radio,
giving a talk on radio station KGMB about Esperanto.⁵

Agnes received her next letter from the Guardian in October. His
secretary wrote:

> It was a real pleasure for the Guardian to read your beautiful message
> dated July 12, 1933, and to share the many news items you gave
> him about the progress of the Cause in Honolulu. He is confident
> that your stay in this inspiring spot will serve to consolidate the
> work that has already been achieved. The friends in Honolulu, who
> as you say, are mostly new believers, will undoubtedly appreciate
> your presence among them, and it is hoped that they will fully avail
> themselves of this opportunity to deepen their knowledge of the
> Teachings and to broaden their vision of the Cause.
>
> In closing please extend Shoghi Effendi's loving greetings to them
> all, and particularly to Mrs. Baldwin and to Miss Barbara Baldwin,

her daughter. With the renewed assurance of his fervent prayers for your advancement and welfare.

Shoghi Effendi's personal note read: 'May the Beloved keep, bless, and protect you and enable you to resume in the not distant future your unforgettable pioneer services in Japan. Your true and grateful brother, Shoghi.' [6]

Maui

In February 1934, Agnes began a six-week visit to Makawao on Maui. Much of her time was with her 88-year-old aunt Em (Baldwin), but she also spent a good deal of time with the Bahá'ís. In a letter she wrote on 4 February, she said:

> The Cause here is advancing with the help of dear Katherine [Kathrine Baldwin]. I have been very happy to take the Friday afternoon meetings since coming, and also a class in the 'Iqan' of Baha'u'llah, the same book we read in Honolulu on Thursday mornings. There is a very lovely spirit among all the friends here. They only lack men. We meet at Mary Fantom's home for the meetings. Katherine has started a Friday morning class to explain the Cause to some of her relatives here. Also she has a Japanese group meeting in the evenings once a week, I believe. Today she is invited to speak of the Cause to a group at a school, so you see how things are advancing here. [7]

Ten days later, Agnes again wrote, saying that 'We have had beautiful meetings here and the way opened for me to meet two of the friends whom I am assured are now fully confirmed and this would make it possible for an Assembly of nine here . . . I feel there is great wisdom in Katherine's being here.' [8]

After the Bahá'í Convention of 1934, Agnes again visited Maui and had 'a heavenly time with the beloved friends who meet regularly twice a week. Everything I can tell them from my notes and otherwise seems to be of the deepest interest to them all. This is a heavenly group made up of so many combined races.' Agnes went on to write: 'During the twenty years since the group was first formed, it has been composed entirely of women from Hawaiian, Japanese, Portuguese, British,

American and Negro parentage. Forgetting their racial and color differences, they are joined together through the Message of Bahá'u'lláh in love and unity.' The Maui Bahá'í community was able to elect its first Local Spiritual Assembly at Riḍván 1935.[9]

In April, Agnes was on the island of Kauai.

North American National Bahá'í Convention

Agnes was elected by the Honolulu Local Spiritual Assembly to be their delegate to the Annual Bahá'í Convention in Wilmette. She sailed to San Francisco aboard the *Lurline*, then visited the Bahá'ís in San Francisco, Berkeley and Oakland. Agnes received a letter on behalf of Shoghi Effendi as she was about to depart from Berkeley for the Convention on 26 May:

> I wish to thank you in the name of the Guardian for your deeply-appreciated messages of February 20th and April 1st, 1934, as well as for the accompanying photographs, all of which testified to the success which has attended your teaching activities in the Hawaiian Islands. Your stay in Honolulu, in particular, seems to have given a new spirit of determination and of service to the friends, and they all surely feel grateful to you for the kind assistance you have extended to them in this respect.
>
> Shoghi Effendi is also grateful to learn that you have been elected as delegate to the coming Bahá'í Convention. He is praying that you may be assisted and guided in all your deliberations and consultations with the other delegates and friends who will attend that important gathering.

Shoghi Effendi added 'May the Beloved cheer your heart, reinforce your high and persistent endeavours, and fulfil your dearest hopes in the service of His Faith, Your true and grateful brother, Shoghi.'[10]

Agnes travelled from San Francisco to Chicago by train with Leroy and Silvia Ioas and George Latimer.[11] The Convention began on 31 May. At an 'open feast' held in the Foundation Hall of the House of Worship during the Convention, Agnes spoke on her experiences. The *Bahá'í News* noted: 'She was one of the most interesting visitors and speakers during the Convention period. It was her first convention in fifteen years.'[12]

Agnes was also able to renew her friendship with May Maxwell after that separation of 15 years. This reunion was momentous enough for Shoghi Effendi to remark upon it:

> Your meeting with Mrs. Maxwell, and your joint efforts to make a deep study of the Master's Will and to better appreciate the position of that document in the administrative system of the Cause will, it is hoped, enable you to thoroughly and befittingly present the subject of the Administration at the Geyserville summer school.
>
> Shoghi Effendi is praying that your presence among the assembled friends and believers in that centre may serve to deepen their insight into the Teachings, and to create among them such a measure of unity and of understanding as to ensure the complete and continued success of this important gathering.[13]

After the Convention, Agnes and May travelled across the country visiting various Bahá'í communities. In Portland, Oregon, they helped bring in a new believer.[14]

Agnes did go to Geyserville as requested by the Guardian, and apparently gave her talk on 'Abdu'l-Bahá's *Will and Testament*. She also renewed another long-standing friendship with Louise and John Bosch. In his next letter to Agnes, the Guardian noted their meeting 'He is pleased to learn of your visit to our devoted Bahá'í friends Mr. and Mrs. Bosch, both of whom have done and are still doing such splendid work for the Cause in Geyserville. Will you kindly convey to them his warmest greetings, and assure them of his continued prayers for their advancement and welfare.'[15]

Looking toward Japan, again

In the same letter in which he mentioned John and Louise Bosch, the Guardian's secretary wrote about Japan:

> Concerning your plan to leave for Japan after your visit to Honolulu, Shoghi Effendi fully approves of your intention to revisit our Japanese friends, and to resume your pioneering work with them. His best wishes for the success of your plans will surely be with you all through this long journey, and it is hoped that as in the past you

will be effectively guided and assisted in attracting and converting new souls to the Faith.

Shoghi Effendi's personal note read, 'May the spirit of Bahá'u'lláh illumine your path, cheer your heart and reinforce your efforts for the continuation and expansion of your historic services and may He protect you, and enable you to achieve your heart's cherished desire, Shoghi.'[16] Agnes arrived back in Honolulu in October.

The Guardian's secretary again wrote on his behalf about her upcoming return to Japan on 1 November 1934:

> The gratifying news of your projected trip to Japan has particularly strengthened his hopes for the future expansion of your labours in that country. He trusts that on your return to that land you will find the friends more eager and ready than ever to carry on the teaching work which ever since your departure to the States seems to have been progressing slowly.
>
> The Guardian will fervently pray for the success of your teaching trip, and he hopes that its results will be such as to encourage you to prolong your stay in Japan until a strong, active and well-united community of believers has been duly established. Your patient, sustained and selfless efforts in this connection, he is convinced, are bound to produce satisfactory and abiding results.

In his personal note, Shoghi Effendi added:

> Dearly beloved co-worker:
>
> I wish to add a few words in person in order to reaffirm my deep sense of gratitude to you for all that you have achieved and for your determination to carry on the work that you have so many years so splendidly initiated. I trust and pray that you may be fully guided and assisted to fulfil your heart's dearest wish. Your true brother, Shoghi[17]

In December, the Honolulu Local Spiritual Assembly appointed Agnes to collect materials for the Hawaiian Archives. She wrote that 'we, each one, of the old Bahais of Honolulu must do our utmost to help our Archives for the future generations which are to come'.[18] This is particularly interesting in light of Shoghi Effendi's request when she went on pilgrimage in 1937 to write the history of the Bahá'í Faith in the Hawaiian Islands.

Also in December, Loulie Mathews and her husband, of Colorado Springs, arrived in Hawaii to travel teach and stayed until February 1935. Initially, Mrs Mathews did not think there was anything for them to do since Honolulu had long had an active Local Spiritual Assembly. Then she had a dream in which 'Abdu'l-Bahá came to her and said:

'You must not rest day or night, there is work to be done . . .' Then He led her to friends in three sections of the city and in parting said, 'Work! Work!' She awoke with a changed consciousness and hurried to offer her services to the Assembly. Then she was guided to find the souls who were waiting. During her stay two weekly meetings were held which she joyfully conducted. One was a series of talks under the auspices of the Honolulu Bahá'ís held in a room in the YWCA, and the other a morning class at the home of Mrs. Katherine Baldwin. She wrote, 'Every Bahá'í meeting became a bright chapter of the Book of Life. No effort was involved. My talents, whatever they may be were not required. My personality was laid aside.'[19]

On 24 April 1935, Agnes wrote: 'Here in Honolulu we have been having glorious meetings ever since my return here last October. Mamie Seto attracted new souls and then Mrs. Mathews who followed her and we have now a glorious Friday morning study class of ladies and four new ladies are before long, I believe, to become members of our Bahá'í community.'[20]

Agnes received another in the series of letters from the Guardian. Sent on 17 April 1935, this one looked forward to her coming work in Japan:

Shoghi Effendi also cherishes bright hopes for your future work in Japan, where, he trusts, you will this time succeed in laying foundations for the establishment of new centers and groups in a not too distant future. He is fervently entreating Bahá'u'lláh to that end, and is confident that through His confirmations and guidance your work will be blessed, enriched and sustained.

His personal note at the end read, 'May the Beloved, whose Cause you have promoted with such unswerving loyalty and devotion, continue to bless your manifold activities, and aid you to consolidate the foundations of His Cause in that promising country. Your true brother, Shoghi.' [21]

14

BACK TO JAPAN

1935–1936

Agnes sailed from Honolulu toward Japan on 9 May 1935. In a letter to her brother Arthur on 16 May, she wrote, 'We have had a smooth voyage so far, except yesterday.' She knew several of the other passengers and shared her dining table with a Dutch couple from Sumatra, a man from Colombia, South America, and one other. In a letter to 'Ella' (unsure whether Cooper or Rowland) on the same date, she wrote, 'I had a wonderful feeling of His confirmations as I sailed . . . and I felt the Guardian very close, so that there could be no sorrow in parting with family and friends.'[1]

She arrived in Yokohama on 21 May and as soon as he received word from her that she was back in Japan, the Guardian wrote through his secretary on 6 July giving her a high goal, but also telling her what she needed to do to accomplish it:

> . . . the news of your safe arrival in Tokyo has greatly rejoiced his heart. He sincerely hopes that this trip to Japan will be quite successful, and that the results achieved will be most encouraging and stimulating to you, and will serve to bring to speedy and successful realization 'Abdu'l-Bahá's deeply cherished hopes concerning the future of the Cause in these far-Eastern countries. The ground, of course, is not yet quite prepared. There is still a tremendous amount of publicity that has to be done before anything solid and enduring can be attained. But the peoples, if not in the large industrial centers, at least in the villages and country, are, as the Master has often remarked, spiritually-minded and eager to absorb a message as sound and as inspiring as that which the Cause offers.
>
> What is most essential at present is to give the Movement the

widest publicity possible, so as to well prepare the ground for future teaching expansion. Nothing short of your perseverance and of the remarkable crusading spirit animating you, and so many of our American brothers and sisters, can insure the eventual and complete attainment of this objective.

The Guardian's personal note said, 'May the Beloved of our hearts, whose Cause you have served and are still serving with such zeal, devotion and constancy, reward you a thousandfold for your ceaseless services, your high endeavors and historic accomplishments for the furtherance of His glorious Faith. Your true brother, Shoghi.'[2]

Bahá'u'lláh and the New Era in Japanese Braille

In March, the Toriis' son, Akira, passed away suddenly at the age of 17. Agnes wrote that 'Abdu'l-Bahá had addressed a Tablet to Tokujiro Torii as 'O thou possessor of a seeing heart!' Akira's name meant 'shining light', and in the Tablet 'Abdu'l-Bahá wrote, 'Convey to thy respected wife my greetings and my message and the same to thy young babe Akira, whose name may be ever blest for it is quite an appropriate one.' Akira was the first second-generation Bahá'í in Japan and was his father's constant guide and companion. The first thing Tokujiro did was to publish a book about his son and then he decided to follow the example of Daiun Inouye. Tokujiro wrote: 'The translator of Esslemont's book, Mr. Daiun Inouye . . . lost his beloved daughter in 1931 and he began to translate Esslemont's book [into Japanese] as a memorial to her . . . On March 14, 1935, he [Akira] unexpectedly left us on this earth and went to heaven. I then began to translate the Esslemont book into Japanese braille in memory of my son . . .'[3]

When he finished the translation into Braille in 1936, he added a note about Agnes in the Preface:

Miss Agnes B. Alexander in 1914 paid her first visit to Japan. Since then she has been working in this country making a center for this movement with purest faith, love and passion for peace. She is really a virtuous lady who never forgets to serve others. Last year she returned to Japan for the fourth time . . . and is devoting herself to the Bahá'í mission. Especially her love toward blind people in

Japan is boundless, which I hope all the readers will note.[4]

Tokujiro's book contained a total of 770 pages in three volumes. The publisher, who like Tokujiro was blind, became very interested in the Bahá'í Faith during the process and 'it made him happy to print it'.

When the Guardian learned of Akira's passing, his secretary wrote on his behalf:

> Regarding Mr. and Mrs. Torii, he is immensely grieved to learn of the passing away of their son Akira, and wishes you, therefore, to convey to them his heartfelt condolences and sympathy for this cruel and unexpected loss they have sustained. Will you also assure them of his prayers for the soul of their departed son, that it may develop and receive its full share of Divine blessings in the next world.
>
> The Guardian has been very much pleased to learn of Mr. Torii's desire to put the Japanese translation of the 'New Era' into Braille for use of his blind friends. He would urge you to encourage him to complete the work as soon as possible, as it may prove of considerable help to the spread of the Teachings throughout Japan.[5]

At the end of the letter, Shoghi Effendi wrote, 'Your past and present services are engraved upon my heart. The Beloved is well-pleased with your constancy, your zeal and exemplary devotion. I am truly proud of the spirit that so powerfully animates you in His service. I will continue to pray for your success from the bottom of my heart. Rest assured and persevere, Your true brother, Shoghi.'[6]

A second letter from the Guardian, dated 19 November, added further praise for both Tokujiro's and her work in getting *Bahá'u'lláh and the New Era* translated into Japanese Braille:

> It gives me pleasure to acknowledge the receipt of your letter to the Guardian dated October 24th . . . conveying . . . the happy news of the publication of the Braille Japanese edition of Dr. Esslemont's book. The three volumes you have been so kind in presenting to him have been duly received and will be placed in the library of the Mansion of Bahá'u'lláh in Bahjí where both the Bahá'í and non-Bahá'í visitors will have the opportunity of seeing the book, and of admiring the splendid achievement you have accomplished for the Cause.

The Guardian wishes me to heartily congratulate you for the success of your efforts in connection with the publication of this new Braille edition of 'Bahá'u'lláh and the New Era' which undoubtedly constitutes a most valuable addition to the literature of the Cause for the blind. He is certain the friends in every land, and particularly the Committee on the Braille Transcription in America, will deeply rejoice at this news, and will receive a fresh encouragement in their teaching efforts.

I wish also to ask you to transmit the Guardian's grateful appreciation and thanks to Mr. Torii for his painstaking labours for the preparation of this new Braille publication on the Cause. He is fervently praying that his services to the Faith in Japan may daily increase in number, effectiveness and power.[7]

Problems and possibilities

Though a Local Spiritual Assembly had been formed in Tokyo in 1928, by 1935 the Bahá'í community was struggling and the Assembly had not been reformed. Agnes wrote to the Guardian about this problem and he, patiently and optimistically, urged her to continue her efforts:

Although no definite Bahá'í group has yet been established in Tokyo, you should not lose heart. Your labours, if sustained, are bound to produce good results. The Guardian feels confident that the seeds you are now so carefully and painstakingly sowing will in due time bear fruit. Patience, perseverance and hard and continued effort are needed in order that your mission may meet with complete success.

In the meantime, Shoghi Effendi will continue praying for you, that the burden of your cares and anxieties may be lightened, and that through Divine assistance and protection you may fully acquit yourself of your heavy and highly-responsible task.

In his personal note, Shoghi Effendi wrote, 'Do not feel discouraged if the work you are doing for His Cause does not bear rich and immediate fruit. The seeds you are so patiently and devotedly sowing will assuredly germinate, and future generations will reap an abundant harvest. The Master is watching over and blessing your historic services. Rest assured.'[8]

Agnes's attitude remained positive in spite of the difficulties. In a letter to Louise Bosch, she wrote, 'times have changed. The old friends have never come together since my return. I have never once, though, felt troubled. If I should be so, then I would not be faithful to God as the Guardian has written "Rest assured".'[9]

Agnes constantly tried to get articles about the Faith into the Japanese newspapers. Ruth Randall Brown, Chairman of the National Publicity Committee in the United States and Canada, in December 1935 wrote to the American Bahá'ís about Agnes's efforts quoting her as saying: '"The Guardian has written me that publicity is the most essential thing here (Japan) now and no foundation teaching can be done until a tremendous lot of it has been accomplished." Already the committee has received two fine examples of publicity from Miss Alexander although she writes the difficulties are great.'[10]

Christmas was always a bit different in Buddhist Japan, but there were enough Christians to make it interesting. On 28 December, Agnes wrote about her Christmas and what was happening in Japan in a letter to her brother Arthur:

> Christmas was a lovely day here, as most of the fall has been, and I have enjoyed the crisp weather when out after two years away from the real winter. In the house it is not always so pleasant, but I have a kind of a charcoal stove which lasts from morning to night and is fairly warm for my two upstairs rooms, where I live now that it is cold, only going down for the bathroom where I have a Japanese tub, which is a joy on cold days to get into. It is heated by gas and is just big enough for me to sit in up to my neck.
>
> Christmas morning I had for breakfast guests Miss Guppy and Mr. Grant. Two others I had asked could not come. The evening before I had dinner with my neighbor Miss Guppy, so we celebrated together. Before Christmas I was present at three Christmas programs. The one which impressed me most was a program from the Tokyo School of Music. They gave Handel's 'Messiah' with over 200 voices and about 50 in the orchestra. It seemed quite wonderful to hear this in a non Christian country . . .
>
> What is most marked this year is the apparent prosperity of the people. The stores have never been so prosperous, nor so brilliant with attractive things. The yen being so low accounts partly for

this as much money is being made in exports, and in Japan articles which were formally imported, are now made here, so that profit goes to this country . . .

It is vacation now in the Schools and also in the Language School where I went twice a week. I may not do much next term there as I have found the reading of the characters trying on my eyes, partly because of the Japanese house and winter time, so that I must use electric light much of the time.[11]

An army mutiny and the seeds of war

In 1931 a Japanese army, led by extremist officers, seized control of Manchuria in defiance of the Japanese government's policies. This began the rise of military influence in Japan. On 26 February 1936, a fate-laden army mutiny struck Japan. A highly nationalistic faction of the Japanese army rose up and attempted to assassinate officers of a rival army faction as well as members of the government. The coup itself failed, but it forced the resignation of the Prime Minister and resulted in the army gaining much more power over the government. Ultimately, this led to the attack on Pearl Harbor five years later.[12] For the general population, news of this event was suppressed. The day after the coup began, Agnes wrote, 'Things were happening here in Tokyo yesterday . . . as yet the full news is not out. I was in my house writing letters until late afternoon when I went out to mail them & to go to a tea . . . I had heard or known nothing until I reached the tea. My servant, of course, knew from the delivery boy, but had not told me.'[13] A few days later, when things had settled down, Agnes again wrote to Arthur about the event:

> I wonder what the world has thought of Japan these days? News has been suppressed here so I presume you would have as much of the truth as we have. Two outstanding men of the country have gone, Viscount Saito and Mr. Takahashi. Men who are respected and honored not only in this country but over the world. The last day before the rebels returned to their barracks, there was no traffic in Tokyo. A regiment of soldiers were all day in the Kudan Park opposite my house but returned by late afternoon when the rebel soldiers in response to the call from the Emperor, returned to their

barracks. That day Miss Guppy, my neighbor, was in and out with news which she got from the Japanese in her house. The radio was the means of spreading the news that day, but when it came time for the news in English which is for five minutes each day, only one sentence was given, that peace was restored. It was a pretty terrific thing which happened when 1400 soldiers went out in the early morning without orders from superiors, only under junior officers. What the world thinks has not yet been allowed to be printed here.[14]

Agnes continued to write to the Guardian and on 11 May, he responded to three of her letters, which always included newspaper clippings and news notes:

> He has deeply enjoyed reading them all, and is truly pleased to learn of the many contacts you have succeeded in forming with distinguished people, and especially with young Japanese students. He sincerely hopes that these will, as a result of continued efforts, be gradually led to embrace the Cause. You should persevere and have full confidence . . .
>
> The Guardian feels also deeply appreciative of Dr. Masajima's kind offer in presenting his library for use by the Bahá'ís. He hopes and fervently prays that this eminent friend of the Cause may become one day a confirmed and devoted believer and that through his services the Faith may rapidly spread throughout Japan.[15]

In August, Agnes complained that the temperature had soared to unheard of heights, reaching 96°F (35.5°C). Agnes didn't slow down for the heat, but kept busy:

> Having my own home and a nice maid makes a great difference and every day there has been something or somebody to see of interest. The last three and a half days of the Student's Conference which was held here of the America-Japan students, I got in as an observer to their discussions and it was very stimulating although the days were dreadfully hot. There were 45 students from 18 universities and colleges in the U.S. and about 159 Japanese students. I met two from the U. of Hawaii, Miss Isabel Hustace and Samuel Amalu. I don't know the latter's ancestry, though I saw that he put the word 'prince'

to his name. He was in the section on religion which I visited and a very bright addition to the group. He told me that Emma Wilcox was his mother. He is a graduate of Punahou School.

I plan to go to the mountains for about a week, up in the Japan Alps where there is a hotel connected with the Imperial Hotel here. I have never been there and the air, they say, is very refreshing.[16]

Samuel Amalu's affectation of the title 'Prince' was part of a property hoax in which he played upon the greed of real estate agents and lawyers in Hawaii. Unfortunately, it landed him in jail.[17]

Visiting Fujita's mother

On 16 December, Agnes received a cable from the Guardian that read: 'Fujita's mother ill urge visit her in Yanai extend assistance.'[18] Sachiro Fujita first saw 'Abdu'l-Bahá from a lamp post in Chicago where he had climbed in order to see over the crowd. At the Master's invitation, the young Japanese accompanied Him to California and back. Fujita had left Japan in 1903 for California and learned about the Faith from Kathryn Frankland in Oakland when he was about 17. He received his first Tablet from the Master in 1905. He was at the University of Michigan in 1912 when 'Abdu'l-Bahá arrived in Chicago, and their meeting changed his life. In 1919, 'Abdu'l-Bahá called him to Haifa, where he remained to serve both the Master and Shoghi Effendi. He and 'Abdu'l-Bahá had a unique relationship, one based on mutual respect and humour.[19]

Agnes was excited to obey the Guardian's request and wrote, 'My heart rejoices for this is God's plan and so it must be a blessing. I have not the address of Fujita's mother but feel I will be assisted in finding it, for through His help nothing is impossible. . .' It was a long journey to reach Yanai, on the coast south of Hiroshima, but as usual, Agnes made the most of it:

The home of Fujita's family is in the far away Yamaguchi Province, the most western province of Japan where I had not yet been. It was an eighteen-hour trip on the train from Tokyo, and I reached there the afternoon of the twenty-fourth of December. A young man met me, and I could easily know that he was our Fujita's brother from his smile. He told me his mother was well again, and soon after leaving my things at an Inn, I went to their little home, partly shop, where they sell Omochi, that is, the New Year rice cakes which are eaten at New Year time in every Japanese family. The mother I found a spirited little lady full of hearty laughter, and one could readily guess where our Fujita inherited his laughter. There were seven in the family; the mother, son, wife and three children, and also a young girl, the daughter of a sister who had died. The children were nice appearing and healthy and spirited. They were the children of a brother who died, but the younger Fujita brother had married their mother so as to be their father. Before going to Yanai, friends said that it was a bad time to go into the country when it was so very cold. Because of country conditions they feared I would suffer, also they thought I would not be able to talk with the mother because of the difference in language of that province. I knew, though, that it was God's plan that I go and it did not matter whatever happened. I took a dictionary with me, but it was not used for we had no trouble at all in understanding each other, and no difficulties occurred. I know this is always true when we arise in His service and respond to His call. Christmas day we had a photograph taken of all the family together to send to our Fujita San in Haifa. The brother said his mother had not wanted to have a photograph taken when Fujita visited them more than two years ago, but when I came from so far, she was happy to have it taken, and it is truly a lovely photograph of this little mother with a sweet countenance. The next afternoon I left, as it was not necessary for me to stay longer. I gave the brother some Japanese Baha'i literature, which he had not seen, and presents for the family.

After leaving Yanai, I stopped in Kobe, where I met three of the former friends. It was four years since I had been there and it was a joy to meet again the dear brother, Mr. Daiun Inouye. He still remained a Buddhist priest. Once he had said, 'The temple is beautiful on the outside, but the spirit of Buddha no longer is there.' Together we visited the friend, Mr. Sanzo Misawa, who had done so much for the friends in Japan, also the dear young woman, Mrs. Mikae (Komatsu) Arakawa and her husband. When I left in the evening to go to Kyoto to the Torii home, Mr. Inouye said to me, 'This has been a very happy day'.[20]

The Guardian encourages steadfastness

Agnes received yet another letter from the Guardian, dated 24 January 1937. She had apparently been worried that her efforts were not advancing the Cause in Japan as quickly as they should and the Guardian assured her that her steadfast efforts were of great value:

> I thank you most sincerely on behalf of the Guardian for your welcome communications . . . and wish to assure you again of his abiding appreciation of the splendid activities in which you are so laboriously and so devotedly engaged for the spread and establishment of the Cause in Japan. Do not feel discouraged at the meagerness of the results you now obtain. The Master's promises regarding the share you are destined to contribute towards the spread of the Faith in the Far East will sooner or later be completely realized. No matter how dark the present may appear, you should feel nevertheless confident that the distant future is immeasurably bright. Strive, therefore, with a joyful, radiant and confident heart to hasten the fulfillment of 'Abdu'l-Baha's glorious promises. Your reward is unimaginably great, and the success that awaits your labours certain.
>
> Regarding your visit to Fujita's mother, the Guardian feels rejoiced and thankful for all the kindness and assistance you have so lovingly extended to her, and would certainly approve of your wish to continue helping her in every way you can. Your spirit of loving kindness, so truly Baha'i, will no doubt deeply touch her, and may draw her very near to the Cause.
>
> With renewed and grateful thanks from the Guardian, and with his loving greetings to the friends in Tokyo, especially to Mr. Torii

In his personal note, Shoghi Effendi wrote, 'With the assurance of my deepfelt and abiding appreciation of your wholehearted and touching response to my request [of visiting Fujita's mother], and wishing you success and happiness from the depths of my heart, Your true and grateful brother, Shoghi.'[21]

Agnes and Martha Root, 24 December 1930. The two dolls were Christmas presents for Agnes from the Japanese. Some 100 of these dolls were made by Japanese Bahá'í children. Agnes then mailed them to Victoria Bedikian and Kathryn Franklyn in the United States to be sold and the proceeds donated for the construction of the Bahá'í House of Worship in Wilmette

Keith Ransom-Kehler, K. Sudo and Agnes in 1931

Buddhist priest J. Mori, Agnes and Reverend Semper Ito at a Buddhist temple in 1931

Naw-Rúz party, 1932, in the garden of Dr Rokuichiro Masujima. Left to right, seated: two unknowns, Kanae Takeshita, Mrs Naganuma with daughter, Dr Masujima, Agnes, unknown, Yuri Mochizuki, unknown; standing: Keiji Sawad, Sempo Ito, Mr Fujisawa, Mr Moriiuchi, Mr Sugimoto, Mr Yamaguchi, Hidehiko Matsuda, Mr Ayabe and Mr Miyamoto

Agnes with teachers and students at the Sakurai Women's School in 1932

*On board the SS Taiyo Maru on the way from Japan to Hawaii in 1933.
Agnes is in the black coat on the right*

*Husayn Ouskouli visited Agnes in Japan in 1935; this photograph was taken on a tour at a
temple. Agnes and Husayn are behind the two women in light-coloured clothes*

Agnes Alexander and May Maxwell in Portland,
Oregon on 3 July 1934

Agnes's home at Kudan Ue, 1936

Agnes with Fujita's mother, December 1936. Hideo Fujita is on the far left. The others are
Fujita's nieces and nephews

15

PILGRIMAGE

1937

Preparations for pilgrimage

Sometime in 1936 Agnes wrote to the Guardian requesting to be allowed to go on pilgrimage. It is not known whether she had earlier received permission, but on 6 October, he cabled to her, 'Advise defer until situation Palestine improves love Shoghi.'[1] Then in November, Agnes received a letter written on behalf of the Guardian giving her permission:

> Regarding your wish to visit the Holy Shrines, he fully approves of it and wishes me to extend to you a most hearty welcome. Since his last telegram to you, advising you to defer your pilgrimage, conditions in the Holy Land have taken a better turn, and the civil disturbances have subsided, although peace has not yet been completely restored. The situation, however, is sufficiently safe to allow visitors to travel in the country.
>
> Hoping this will enable you to undertake your long-cherished pilgrimage to the Holy Shrines, and assuring you again of Shoghi Effendi's appreciation of your labours and of his prayers for your protection, health and guidance.

In his personal note at the bottom of the letter, Shoghi Effendi added 'Dear and valued co-worker: . . . The strike and disturbances in Palestine have at last ceased and the obstacles to your pilgrimage have been removed. I would be so pleased to meet you face to face at this Holy Spot. Your true brother, Shoghi.'[2] The way was open for Agnes to make her first visit to the Bahá'í World Centre.

Then, on 4 January 1937, she received what she initially thought was

261

a disturbing letter from Louise Bosch. Louise related two dreams she had which she thought might involve Yuri Mochizuki:

> In one of the dreams Louise saw a great heap of all kinds of rubbish piled high up. The place seemed to be in Japan. Through a small opening in the pile, to her great astonishment she saw a baby lying in the midst of the rubbish. It looked well and smiling, although the only light it received was through the opening. When I reached Haifa I told the Guardian of the dream. He said briefly that it symbolized the struggling Faith of Bahá'u'lláh in Japan.
>
> After reading Louise's letter, I began to feel that I should not go away and leave the baby under the rubbish heap . . . suddenly I realized that the burden of the baby was not in my hands, but God's, and I could leave all to His care.[3]

Feeling free to go, Agnes booked passage for 20 March. The Japanese Bahá'ís looked upon her pilgrimage as a very important event for Japan. Two of her blind Bahá'í friends, Mr H. Mimura and Mr Kataoka, sent her messages in Braille. Both suspected that she might not return. Mr Mimura wrote:

> You are leaving Japan for the Holy Land. You say you are going for us, all the blind in Japan and not for yourself, so your mission will be noble and sublime. We blind must thank you with all our hearts. You must be very happy about going to see Shoghi Effendi there. I too am very happy to read the book about Bahá'u'lláh. I swear to Him to be a faithful servant of His. When my baby grows up, I will tell her about the Faith of Bahá'u'lláh. You have been so kind to me and all my family. We shall never forget you. Bon Voyage![4]

Mr Kataoka wrote, 'I hope that you will come back again to Japan with good tidings, more love and more light . . . The world is now marching into the unhappiest and saddest direction . . . We should take hands firmly and stand up to bring love and light to the world . . . I wish you a happy travel. Hoping to see you again and craving for your good tidings.' Agnes, too, had a premonition that she was not to return soon. She wrote:

Before leaving Tokyo the guidance came to me that I would not return direct from Palestine to Japan, but would continue the journey to America. I did not speak of this, though, for I wished to wait until I met the beloved Guardian and received from him his directions. I expected to return to Tokyo within a year. How little we can foresee the future!

Consequently, she stored all her furniture and left her Bahá'í library with Dr Masujima.[5]

Many of the Bahá'ís brought presents for her to take to the Holy Land, some for Shoghi Effendi and some for Fujita. When Agnes had first gone to Japan, Mason Remey had given her a 'copy of the Greatest Name which was surrounded by a beautiful design in color of his own workmanship' and this had hung in a place of honour in her home. A year before, however, her house had been broken into and the Greatest Name stolen. Agnes had replaced it with a typical Japanese scroll with a rising sun. She decided to take the scroll and give it to Fujita.[6]

Departure for the Holy Land

Agnes left Tokyo for Kyoto on 16 March. Arriving in that city, she stayed with Miss Denton for two nights and spent another two days with Tokujiro Torii and his family. At Miss Denton's, she unexpectedly met Teresina Rowell, a woman who had previously visited her in Tokyo, and was able to talk with her more about the Faith. The Toriis held a dinner party for Agnes at which Mr Watanabe gave her some incense he hoped she would use in the Shrine of 'Abdu'l-Bahá. Tokujiro also took Agnes to the Buddhist newspaper and she explained that she was on her way to visit the Guardian and the Bahá'í Holy Shrines on behalf of the Japanese friends. A photograph and the story of her pilgrimage appeared in the paper the next day. One point in her story, that she was going on behalf of the Japanese Bahá'ís, proved to be inaccurate – Shoghi Effendi later told her that she was on pilgrimage for herself. Before she left, the editor of the paper brought her two dolls in wooden boxes, one marked for Shoghi Effendi and the other for Fujita.[7]

On the night of 19 March, Agnes took a train from Kyoto to Moji, adjacent to Shimonoseki, the port at the southernmost tip of Honshu.[8]

Daiun Inouye, the Bahá'í Buddhist priest, had asked Agnes to tell him when her train was to pass through Kobe:

> He felt that as I was going on an important pilgrimage, he wanted to see me and say goodby. When the train stopped in Kobe, I heard a voice call, 'Miss Alexander! Miss Alexander!' Then Mr. Inouye hurriedly came into the train and gave me a package containing two beautiful Japanese fans, which he asked me to take to the 'Lord of the Bahá'í Kingdom and his Madam.' There was not time for me to explain that the Guardian was not married as the train stopped only five minutes. We did not know then that the Guardian was going to be married in a few days. While Mr. Inouye was waiting for the train, he wrote on a paper the messages he wished to convey to me and handed me the paper. He wrote: 'We pray God's protection for your safe and sound travel. I shall feel very lonely while you are away from Japan, and will expect you again in Japan in no distant day. Please convey our good wishes to The Lord of the Bahá'í Kingdom in Haifa. The two Japanese fans I offer to the Guardian and his Madam.'⁹

Agnes arrived in Moji at noon on 20 March and promptly boarded the *Kashima Maru*. The steamer was smaller than any she had travelled on for many years. It had been built in 1913, but she noted that 'the passengers & service are pleasant & the food is good'. As the old steamer moved out of the port, Agnes wrote that 'A joyous thrill came to me . . . I saw before me but one land, the Holy Land, and the glorious person of Shoghi Effendi. All the world seemed nothing in comparison to this land & person. What a glorious privilege God has given me that I can go for all the friends in Japan and pray at the Holy Shrines for them all.'¹⁰

The next morning, Naw-Rúz, Agnes spoke to those at the breakfast table of the significance of the day and was then able to talk about the Faith with Mr Kinichiro Yoshida, a young man on his way to the Japanese Embassy in London. They reached Shanghai on the 22nd, where the ship stayed until the next afternoon. Agnes was met at the dock by Bahá'ís Suleiman Suleimani and Husayn Ouskouli and taken to the Suleimani home. Two other Bahá'ís, Hossein Touty and Mrs Chan, came for dinner that night. Because of all the gifts Agnes had been given in Japan, she went out and bought a large leather suitcase for $10. She noted, 'A good many presents have been given me to take to Haifa, the last in Shanghai was a box of tea, so large & heavy that I can hardly lift it, then in Kyoto two boxes of dolls & besides I was carrying a box in a glass case of a beautiful doll which had been a present to me last year.'[11]

The doll in the glass case had come from the students of the Seikei Gakuyen, a boys' private school. The previous November, a teacher from the school had called on Agnes. In June 1930, Agnes had given a talk at an Esperanto meeting arranged by students of the school at which a photograph was taken. This photo was published in the *Star of the West*, *The Bahá'í World* and an Esperanto magazine edited by Dr Hermann Grossmann in Germany. The teacher asked Agnes to speak to an Esperanto meeting on 26 November. This was a particularly important date for Agnes, being both Thanksgiving and the day she had discovered the Bahá'í Faith. In her talk, Agnes

> told of the significance of the day to me in relation to my spiritual life, and also that it was a day on which to be thankful which introduced the Bahá'í teachings. Then I spoke especially of the universal auxiliary language . . . After the meeting was over, I had expected to return to my home, but instead was asked to accompany the students and friends to their hall. There a lovely tea party had been prepared. Several of the pupils and teachers spoke in both Esperanto and Japanese, and a student presented me with a beautiful present, a famous Japanese dancing doll in a square glass case. They wished to show their appreciation of what I had done for their school. A photographer was called and a photograph was taken of the doll being presented to me. When I left Tokyo the following spring to go to Haifa, I carried in my hand the doll in its glass case packed in a box. The first morning in Haifa, when I met the beloved Guardian, I presented it to him and his bride.[12]

Hossein Touty took her back to the steamer in time for its 3 o'clock departure, giving her a box of chocolates to share with her fellow passengers. The next port of call was Hong Kong, which they reached on 24 March. Their stay was brief and they continued towards Singapore. On the way, Agnes met Mrs Rolpa, from Australia, and shared with her a book by Stanwood Cobb entitled *Security for a Failing World*.[13]

Agnes was constantly passing around literature about the Faith and loaning books to the other passengers to read. In Singapore, she gave a booklet on the Bahá'í House of Worship in Wilmette to an Indian man who helped her get a taxi, and on another occasion she loaned *Bahá'u'lláh and the New Era* to a woman who had gone to Vassar College with a Bahá'í. Then she met the wives of two Navy Lieutenants and gave them *Security for a Failing World*. One woman had learned a little about the Faith from an army officer's wife and wanted to know more. She gave another woman on her way to Sumatra a pamphlet by Shoghi Effendi. One day, she met Mr Genyoku Kuwaki, a Japanese scholar, who had heard of the Faith and she was able to have a conversation with him about it. He ended up borrowing *Bahá'í World*, vol. V and *Bahá'u'lláh and the New Era*.[14]

On 2 April, the steamer stopped in Pinang, Malaysia, which she thought was 'beautiful tropical',[15] and then went on to Colombo, Sri Lanka, where she 'took a taxicab with friends from the steamer to a modern Buddhist Temple. I spoke of the Cause to the intelligent taxi driver and gave him a Baha'i booklet and told him I too believed in Buddha.'[16]

On 12 April, the steamer passed near Aden, Yemen, and headed up the Red Sea to the Suez Canal, where Agnes noted that 'A marvelous change has taken place there since I went through in 1914. Everything has developed wonderfully.' Beyond the Suez Canal was Port Said at which Agnes and many other passengers disembarked. They arrived just after midnight on 19 April, and after breakfast in the morning most went to Cairo.[17]

The Bahá'ís in Port Said had been notified of her coming and they were there to meet her with a cable from the Guardian, which said simply 'Welcome'.[18] She wrote:

Before I had had breakfast, two young men came to my cabin door. I recognized one of them immediately as the brother of Mirza Ali Yazdi of Berkeley, California, from his resemblance to his brother, and the other was Jean Aliwafay. The first words Mirza Yazdi said were, 'The Guardian is married and you will never guess to whom.' Without hesitation I immediately guessed, although I had not known that May Maxwell and her daughter had remained in Haifa after the winter. The Bahá'í brothers escorted me to Mirza Yazdi's store, where I met another Bahá'í, Philip Naimi, a Syrian, and later Alu Saad El Din joined us and we went together to the home of Mirza Yazdi for lunch. In the afternoon a meeting was arranged of women to meet me. Nine gathered and one of them translated for me.[19]

Then it was time for the final stage of her month-long journey from Japan to Haifa:

In the late afternoon some of the friends accompanied me by auto to Kantara, the station between Africa and Asia. When I showed my passport at the station before entering the train, it was found that it had expired that very day. It happened there was a Bahá'í in the Customs office who came to my assistance, and it was arranged that I might proceed on my way, but would not be permitted to leave Palestine until my passport was renewed. In the same compartment of the train with me were two English women who were going to Jerusalem to sightsee. As the Bahá'ís who were arranging for my passport kept coming back and forth to the compartment, the ladies became curious and asked me how it was that I had so many Oriental friends. Then I told them that we were Bahá'ís and that I was going to Haifa and gave them a Bahá'í booklet. They showed respect towards all I said and accepted the pamphlet with interest. That night we could not sleep in the small compartment. Before the morning dawned, there was a terrific crash, the lights went out and the train came to a stop. Although all our baggage fell from the racks onto the floor, we were unhurt. The English women thought it was robbers and dynamite. I called in the Greatest Name. It seemed that something which projected from a freight train had crashed into our car smashing in the corridor. We then changed cars and went into another compartment. It was the early hours of the morning and I went into the dining car to get a cup of coffee. There I met an Irish policeman from Jerusalem. When I told him where I was going, he said, 'It is very beautiful there, it is Muhammadan.' The opportunity was then given me to explain to him the reality of the Bahá'í Cause. The accident caused a delay of an hour and a half.[20]

Agnes's pilgrimage

Agnes arrived in Haifa on 20 April 1937, 24 years after 'Abdu'l-Bahá had originally given her permission to come. Shoghi Effendi's brother and Fujita met her at the train station and her Japanese friend took care of her baggage. When she arrived at the Pilgrim House, she was enthusiastically welcomed by May Maxwell. Agnes wrote: 'What a bounty God granted me that after waiting thirty-six years to visit the Holy Land, when at last I reached there my spiritual mother greeted me!' May's primary topic of conversation was her daughter's marriage. She pointed across the street to Shoghi Effendi's rooms on top of the House of the Master and said, 'That is where she is.' Agnes escaped only when she was told that the Guardian would see her in half an hour – she had been without sleep for two days and nights and felt desperately in need of cleaning up, so she hurried away.[21]

Soon, escorted by Fujita, who was carrying the box with the doll in a glass case given her by students in the Seikei School in Japan for the Guardian, Agnes was presented to Shoghi Effendi. Agnes's writings about her pilgrimage vary dramatically. Her pilgrim notes were very business-like and purposeful. The descriptions she included in the *History of the Bahá'í Faith in Japan*, from which most of the following is taken, are clear and enlightening, with some emotion. The letters she wrote to her friends, however, show much more emotion. In the *History*, she wrote:

> The meeting with the Guardian seemed very natural. He spoke of the room we were in, that it was the room in which the Master received His guests, and pointed out the chair in which He sat. The Guardian spoke of the Cause throughout the world and then of Japan and said that the Japanese should establish the Cause in Japan, that the next books to translate into Japanese were the *Hidden Words*, then the *Gleanings*, and afterwards the *Íqán* and *Some Answered Questions*. Then he said I should not return to Japan alone, that I should have help, and that someone might go with me from America. It was a great surprise to me when he said he wanted me to go to Germany, for I had never dreamed of it, but I had hoped I could go to Paris where thirty-six years before I had received the confirmation to go forth and teach His Cause. The Guardian added that I might spend a week or so in Paris and in London.[22]

In a letter to Mary Fantom (Aunty May) in Hawaii, she was much more exuberant:

> At last my dream of the Guardian and Haifa has been realized! What a sublime blessing to meet and converse with our beloved Guardian. He is so young, yet the white hair of age has already begun to show. His burden is so heavy, and yet he has the power to carry ten more of like weight. But, Aunty May, what inspired me was the potent energy of his speech and plans. It is to the believers of action that he looks for help. He wants us to establish the Cause in those countries where there are no believers. This is the day of action, the 'age of transition.' The Guardian does not want adoration as much as concrete success for the New World Order of Baha'u'llah. He said that Miss Jack should be an example to all those teachers who wish to establish the Cause. It takes five years rather than one for sure success.[23]

At this first meeting she

> spoke to the Guardian of the blind and he said that now we are beginning to witness the effect of the Tablets which Abdu'l-Baha wrote to the blind of Japan. He said to tell the blind that the Cause would be the greatest comfort to them and he referred to the words of Helen Keller which are published in the Baha'i World and said they should be quoted. The Bahais now have an international braille transcription committee.
>
> The Guardian said in speaking of Japan that to form a Local Assembly would be the greatest service there and that it didn't matter where it was, in a village or city. He said that he hoped someone from America or Hawaii would go to Japan and help me there. He said that what we require in Japan is the recognition of the Revelation of Baha'u'llah and of His Station.[24]

In the afternoon of that first day, Agnes went to the House of the Master to meet the women of the Holy Family for tea. When dinner was called that night, Sutherland and May Maxwell and Agnes went down to the dining room. Agnes noted that everyone remained standing until Shoghi Effendi and Rúḥíyyih Khánum entered. 'He would say, "Good evening!" to us in his beautiful resonant voice. That first evening he directed me to the seat opposite him at the table, while Mrs. Maxwell sat at his right and his wife at his left. His conversation was inspiring. Addressing Mr. Maxwell, he spoke of the Plan of Bahá'u'lláh, that the Báb had declared and referred to it and 'Abdu'l Bahá had embodied it in a blueprint, as it were, and we were the champion builders to carry out the Plan.'[25]

Shoghi Effendi treated Agnes as an honoured guest. The Guardian asked her to write the history of the Bahá'í Faith in both Japan and the Hawaiian Islands.[26] She also learned that the Guardian spent 80% of his time on correspondence and 80% of his correspondence was from individuals, leaving him little time and energy for the world-wide work of the Cause.[27]

On 21 April, the men went to Bahjí and Agnes joined the women at a little house near the monument to the Greatest Holy Leaf. When they chanted prayers and Tablets, Agnes noticed that the women did not close their eyes or bow their heads, as Christians commonly did. When she asked about it, they said, 'We were listening to the words.'[28]

Agnes very much wanted to record what Shoghi Effendi spoke about in order to share it with others and was relieved when May said that he allowed pilgrims to take notes at the dinner table. But actually doing so proved to be difficult:

> After that every evening before dinner I supplicated the Beloved for His assistance that I might be able to write the words of knowledge which flowed from the Guardian, and only through His help was I enabled to write. I realized afterwards that it was a spiritual matter which depended on one's spiritual condition and not the outward ability to write. When I left Haifa I felt great regret that I had not done better.[29]

The notes she did take, however, became her primary teaching tool during her travel teaching after pilgrimage.

Agnes went alone to the Shrines of the Báb and 'Abdu'l-Bahá on 23 April. When she left, she carried a bouquet of flowers the 'radiant gardener' gave her. Later, Adelaide Sharp arrived from Tehran and they were able to meet 93-year-old Munírih Khánum, 'Abdu'l-Bahá's wife. Agnes said nothing more about that momentous meeting other than it was her 'privilege to sit by her side'.[30]

Agnes had the Japanese scroll she had brought from her home and wanted to give it to the Guardian. At first, she hesitated, knowing that he received many gifts, but:

> The evening after I gave it to him, he spoke of it at the table and said he was going to hang it in the hall in Bahjí. I was deeply touched and said, 'It is a great honor to the nation of Japan!' Another evening when he came to dinner he said he had been to Bahjí that afternoon and had hung the scroll in the hall there, on either side of which he had placed paintings of Dr. Herman Grossmann's, and he asked me when I would meet him to tell him about it. It then became clear to me why the thief had taken the Greatest Name scroll from my home in Tokyo, for otherwise the Japanese scroll would not have hung in Bahjí. At the top of the scroll, the rising sun appeared casting a glow beneath which was the ocean, and between it and in the sky three storks were in flight. Such a scroll would be displayed by the Japanese at times of congratulation, as the New Year season.[31]

On 29 April, Agnes, Zia Khánum (Shoghi Effendi's mother) and Rúḥíyyih Khánum had lunch at Bahjí and spent the afternoon there. In the Shrine, Agnes prayed for her Baháʼí children in Japan. One evening at dinner, Agnes told Shoghi Effendi about the incense that Mr Watanabe wished could be used in the Shrine of ʻAbduʼl-Bahá. She wrote that Shoghi Effendi told her to 'give it to the caretaker of the Shrine, and he would tell him he could burn it in the Shrine, and also that I might burn it in the hall at Bahji when I visited there. I told May Maxwell about the incense and she said: "What a blessing for that blind man!"'[32] When Agnes took the incense to the Shrine of ʻAbduʼl-Bahá, Fujita gathered the violets from the Threshold of the Shrine to send to the friends in Japan.[33]

On Sundays, the men would all go to the Shrine of the Báb and the Guardian would chant the Tablet of Visitation. While they were in the Shrine, the women met in a nearby house by the tomb of the Greatest Holy Leaf. On 2 May, after the women's meeting, Agnes joined the women in the Shrine where the Guardian chanted. Agnes said, 'In his voice there was a power which was different from all others.'[34]

In the middle of this great spiritual event, Agnes had to go to Jerusalem to renew her passport. Shoghi Effendi sent his brother and Adelaide

Sharp with her. He suggested they visit the Church of the Holy Sepulchre, the Mount of Olives and the Mosque of Omar in order to compare them with the Shrines in Haifa and Bahjí. Travelling down by train, they spent two days in Jerusalem. In following the Guardian's instruction, they visited the Jewish, Christian and Muslim holy places:

> On the way to the church of the Holy Sepulcher we passed through the Jaffa Gate to the old city. One felt the utter spiritual darkness of the place and was glad to leave and never return again. On the Mount of Olives we found the trees so very old that they no longer could bear fresh young foliage. These places were in extreme contrast to the spiritual peace and beauty and freshness of the Shrines in Haifa and Bahjí.[35]

On 7 May, Hussein Rabbani took Adelaide and Agnes to 'Akká and Bahjí, where they were to stay overnight. They visited the Bahá'í cemetery outside the walls of 'Akká and then went to the Most Great Prison. Before being allowed to enter, they had to wait for permission, since it was a British prison. Entering the Prison, they went to the room of Bahá'u'lláh, which was in the hospital section. They were unable to see more of 'Akká. From there, they went to the Garden of Riḍván, where the gardener picked mulberries for them. The next stop was Bahjí:

> When we reached Bahji we were each assigned a room for the night. There the surrounding country seemed pervaded with an atmosphere of peace. It reminded me of Makawao, Maui, on the slope of the mountain Haleakala. In the Esslemont room in the Mansion, I saw the Japanese edition of Esslemont's book which had been sent from Tokyo, and also the clippings from Japanese newspapers carefully placed in a drawer. In the hall of the Mansion, I burned the incense which blind Mr. Watanabe had sent by me from Kyoto which Shoghi Effendi had told me I might do. From that blessed place we wrote letters to friends.[36]

It must have been an emotional moment when Agnes saw the fruit of three years hard labour sitting proudly on the shelf in the Mansion. Agnes had her visit to the Shrine of Bahá'u'lláh that evening. Like many other pilgrims, it was a powerful experience:

Last night I entered for the first time the Shrine of the Blessed Perfection and laid my head there, on the sacred threshold, the ultimate aim and hope of all that is on earth. Here one's prayers are answered and one's sorrows laid away. Would that the infinite peace and tranquillity of this sacred spot permeate humanity, but alas, Shoghi Effendi tells us that we have witnessed only the fringe of the darkness to come – may Baha'u'llah save us!

Here last night we laid our heads under the same roof of the Mansion where the Manifestation dwelt for eight years. Here from the marble pillared hall we entered that sacred room, lit, as when He was alive with oil and candles; here we were overwhelmed with the awe and majesty of the greatest Being that ever walked the earth. I was weak and tired after such power. Oh, Aunty May, what divine confirmation! It has enrapted my soul and I am all that I can be through the grace of Him who is Almighty. I pray God to help me to be more worthy of the privileges bestowed upon me and to grow ever nearer to Him and to serve His Cause forever.

We are leaving soon for Haifa. Because of the hostilities of the Arabs we were prevented from going to Akka, so I await that privilege the next time.[37]

Agnes constantly remembered Japan. In the Shrine of Bahá'u'lláh, she and Rúḥíyyih Khánum prayed for the country and the Guardian's wife carried one of the fans Daiun Inouye had sent. Agnes also had a photograph given to her by Ito Torii, and Shoghi Effendi asked if he could keep it in the Mansion because he had few pictures of the Japanese believers.[38]

The notes Agnes took from the Guardian's talks covered wide-ranging topics. In one of her notes, she wrote:

The Cause of God in Haifa is like a kettle boiling all the time! And by this I do not mean the Guardian, he and all of us are enmeshed in something whose power is irresistible. Of course it manifests itself through him, and through his decisions, but the atmosphere is like that. At first I felt like something under pressure but now I am getting so used to it that I am astounded at myself!

Shoghi Effendi says I have no right to call him a mystery! But I can say that at least to me he is a mystery and the result of my observations is that a Guardian is a touchstone applied to us all the time . . . There is no more dangerous maze for people to begin to wander in than the subject of the 'personality' of either the Guardian, or the Master, or even the Manifestation. I do not doubt that Shoghi Effendi has his own personality and temperament, but I believe it is useless to say, 'this is it, or this is not it,' because even his personality, I believe, is used in the grip of his station or the Will of God . . . to test us. In other words, even the personality is shaped to further the interests of the Cause. It's a wonderful subject to think about.

The Guardian is training both my character and my soul. With all the richness of my life, I have outlived it . . . and now here, in the presence of our own so dearly loved and long-beloved Guardian, he is training me with patience, with love, and yet with iron determination, and I have the assurance that he will make of me, if I will let him, what I should and can be. We get from Shoghi Effendi what we let come out! It is something in us that draws it out. It is a spiritual law. Just think, Baha'u'llah knew that hidden language and script all the time, even referred to it, but no one asked Him so He never gave it out.[39]

Shoghi Effendi gave Agnes instructions on a number of subjects. He asked her to visit the Bahá'í centres in Europe, specifically Germany, and America. When she reached Hawaii, he requested that she write the history of the Bahá'í Faith for Hawaii and another history of the Bahá'í Faith in Japan. The Guardian was a little nebulous about Japan, not giving her any firm indication that she should return in the near future. He did tell her, however, when she did return, she should not go alone, but should take someone from America or Hawaii with her:

About returning to Japan, it is not definite when it will be. The Guardian said I should not return alone, that someone from America or Hawaii should go with me and the last afternoon before sailing from Haifa, when I saw him alone, he said that I might choose someone to go there. It is, of course, all in God's Hands, and I can only follow His guidance when it comes.[40]

Travels through Europe

Agnes left Haifa on 12 May. The Guardian's marching orders had been to visit the Bahá'ís in Germany, Paris, and London; and in the United States from the East to the West coast, to attend the three Bahá'í summer schools in America (Green Acre, Louhelen and Geyserville), sharing with all the friends the notes she had written from the Guardian's talks at the dinner table. She spent the next 18 months carrying out his requests.

Agnes sailed on an Italian steamer, reaching Trieste on 17 May 1937. She had received a letter from her Uncle Giulio Ferreri, which confirmed her route as far as Milan, where he lived and where she would plan her next step to Germany. The voyage to Trieste was pleasant and she enjoyed the other passengers, though few spoke much English. She especially enjoyed the musicians on board.[41]

In a later letter to Martha Root, who was visiting Japan during Agnes's absence, she wrote that she had visited six centres in Germany in May, including Stuttgart.[42] On 21 May, Heinrich Himmler announced the '"dissolution" of the "Bahai sect". . . with immediate effect'.[43] The order effectively ended her effort to visit all the German Bahá'í communities. Agnes wrote to the Guardian on 13 June to inform him of this dramatic change. The response written on his behalf was that

> he is indeed most sorry to hear that owing to the unfavourable conditions now prevailing in Germany you have found it necessary to cut short your trip in that country. He would have so much wished that you should visit the North German Bahá'í centres. But he can quite realize that under existing circumstances it would be practically impossible for you to proceed further in your journey, as not only would your activities be closely watched by the authorities, but you would be wholly unable to meet the friends in public. You should nevertheless be happy and thankful for the opportunity you have had of meeting some of the German friends before the present restrictions were imposed.
>
> The Guardian hopes, however, that you may someday again have the pleasure of visiting the believers in Germany, and of sharing with them your many and varied experiences in the Cause.

His personal note read 'May the Beloved vouchsafe to you His richest blessings, and aid you throughout your travels with the hosts of the Abhá Kingdom, and enable you to fulfil, at all times and under all conditions, your dearest and highest wishes, Affectionately, Shoghi.' [44]

From Germany, Agnes went to Paris and then on to London.[45] Records of her activities in those cities, unfortunately, are not available today, but Shoghi Effendi was happy with her efforts. On 16 September, in a letter written on his behalf, the Guardian expressed his pleasure:

> Your letter of the 18th August was most welcome and its contents were read with deepest interest and satisfaction by our beloved Guardian.
>
> He is indeed pleased to know that your trip to France and England has been very successful and that in every Bahá'í centre you visited the friends showed you the utmost kindness and extended to you all the assistance you required. After the sad disappointment and difficulties you experienced in Germany, as a result of the police decree ordering the dissolution of all Bahá'í Assemblies and groups, your contact with the believers outside that country must have surely relieved you somewhat of your sorrow at not having been able to meet the German friends as much and as closely as you would have wished.
>
> It is the Guardian's hope that later on, when conditions in Germany will prove more favourable, you will be able to undertake an extended trip to all the Bahá'í centres throughout that country, and thus give all the friends in that land the benefit of sharing your long and varied experiences in the Cause.

The personal note the Guardian always appended read, 'May the Beloved keep you and bless you and enable you to extend the range and consolidate the basis of your splendid accomplishments, Your true brother, Shoghi.'[46] The Guardian's hope that she would 'someday again have the pleasure of visiting the believers in Germany' came to pass in 1959, when Agnes was able to finish what she had started.

America

When Agnes arrived in New York on 23 July, she planned to carry out the Guardian's request to visit America coast to coast, then return to Hawaii, before ultimately going back to Japan. But it would be a year and a half before she would see Honolulu and 13 years before she would set foot in Japan again.

First, Agnes went to two Louhelen Conferences as requested by the Guardian.[47] On 19 August, she reached Green Acre, Maine, and found 27 letters and many cards awaiting her. It took her a month to catch up on the most urgent correspondence, which she did at Roy Wilhelm's Camp in Maine. In a letter to Elma Adolphson in Hawaii, Agnes laid out the work Shoghi Effendi had given her:

> My days since I left Haifa have all been so very full carrying out the Guardian's requests and now I have yet to visit the Centers in America, as he asked me to do before going to Hawaii. When I reach there he asked me to commence writing the history of the Cause in Hawaii and in the meantime to get all the information here of the data of the many visitors to Honolulu. Then he asked me also to write the history of the Cause in Japan, so you see I have a full program yet before me . . .
>
> . . . In Haifa I had taken notes at the dinner table thinking I would have them for the dear friends in Honolulu and Maui, but I have shared them with all the friends now wherever I have gone and they seem to get much from them, so it seems that this is what the Guardian has given me especially to share.[48]

Agnes spent September bouncing from one place to another. She was in Boston for a couple days, then spent a few days in Worcester and Springfield, Massachusetts, and Ashuelot, New Hampshire, before going to New York for an extended stay. She arrived in New York just in time to hear Marion Holley speak and to meet May and Sutherland Maxwell when they returned from the Holy Land.[49]

Agnes was still in New York in mid-November, but planning to go to Montreal to visit May Maxwell the following week. While in New York, a group of Hawaiian Bahá'ís, including Charles and Julia Goldman and Helen Bishop, found themselves together. Agnes said that 'we were quite a Honolulu party for a few minutes'. The Hawaiians wanted to know when Agnes was returning to the islands, but she still had not a clue. The Guardian's wishes were keeping her very busy:[50]

> Now it seems I will not be going very soon to Honolulu, although I have always been eager to share all I received in Haifa with the dear friends there, and really when I was taking down our dear Guardian's words in Haifa, my thoughts were to get all I could to share with you and the Maui friends, and I prayed for help in doing it. I shall, though, in His time, be more with you and then I will share all.
>
> I am still here in New York and am teaching some friends. One of them is a lady I met years ago in Kona when I was with Mrs. [Leona] Thompson there. Her husband was Japanese, but she is now separated from him and came to be with her parents here in New York. She has a boy in the Mid-Pacific School. She came the first Sunday in January to ask for me at the Bahá'í Center here, and strange it was that I was there. So immediately she began studying, and the next day, through her, I found the other friend whom I had known in Tokyo and who was much touched by the teaching, but I did not know where she was. These two ladies are studying and right here in New York I am now able to work for Japan, for Shoghi Effendi told me in Haifa to concentrate on Japan. He also told me not to dissipate my energies but to concentrate on a few and make them firm Bahá'ís. Now this seems my work right here at present. The friend from Tokyo has her two boys here and her husband joined her three years ago. They have all been to the Sunday meeting in the Center here and also the two ladies come to the wonderful meetings we have on Sunday nights at the Kinney apartment. Then on Tuesday afternoon we have a study class at a friend's apartment who has great love for the Japanese . . .
>
> When I leave here I have many places to visit on the way to Chicago. Now I feel I will surely be there for the Convention . . . Shoghi Effendi told me that when I reached there [Hawaii] to begin my writing, that is, of the history of the Cause there and in Japan. He did not mention the return to Japan, and it seems now farther and farther away to me. He expects me to return <u>sometime</u> and told me when I was leaving Haifa that he wished me to come again with Japanese Bahá'ís, for he wished them to take a part in the

International affairs there when the U[niversal] H[ouse] of Justice will be formed there. It seems to me that cannot be until the 'greatest war', as Shoghi Effendi called it, is over.[51]

The next letter from the Guardian reaffirmed her task of sharing her pilgrimage experiences in the Bahá'í communities across America:

He is rejoiced to know that you have been able to visit so many different Bahá'í centres and groups during the last few months, and that everywhere you have shared with the friends the impressions and experiences you have gathered from your last visit to the Holy Land.

He hopes that in your journey to the Western States, and particularly California, you will also find it possible to extend your stay for some time, and meet as many centres as you can, and thus give the believers the benefit of sharing your manifold and valuable experiences in the Cause. . .

P.S. Regarding your return to Japan, he leaves it to your discretion as to whether you should return immediately or not.

As usual, Shoghi Effendi added his own note: 'Wishing you continued success from the depths of my heart, your true brother, Shoghi.'[52]

Agnes attended the National Convention in Chicago. She spoke about her pilgrimage experiences and about the work being done with the blind in Japan. In addition, she was appointed to the Editorial Committee for the *Bahá'í World*, vol. VII.[53]

From the Convention, Agnes travelled west and south, visiting 19 Bahá'í communities, including Oklahoma City; Phoenix and Glendale, Arizona; Los Angeles, San Francisco and Geyserville, California; and the Louhelen Bahá'í summer schools in Michigan. She didn't move in a particularly direct path. On 5 June, she attended a Feast in Oklahoma City. Sometime later in June, she met with the Bahá'ís in Glendale, Arizona, a suburb of Phoenix, where they had just nine believers. She noted, 'As it was summer, all the meetings in Phoenix and Glendale were held in the evenings out on the lawns and it was very lovely.'[54] One of the Bahá'ís, Maxie Jones, wrote of her visit:

It is quite significant to me that your visit and discussions of the Guardian had seemed so pregnant because soon after you left one day while I was deeply thinking a flash and a picture of the station of the Guardian came to me that he was the mouthpiece of Bahá-u-lláh to humanity today. I had never before seen the need to heed his statements as I do now. And, too, the very significant letters and cablegrams that have since come, I can better understand. How strange, in a way, that we can think we know things, and later wake up to the realization of our blindness. The knowledge of the station of the Guardian is knowledge that cannot be conveyed from one to another by word – but is an understanding of the spirit. I am thankful to Bahá-u-lláh for the Bounty of your visit.[55]

Interestingly, Agnes's talks about the station of the Guardian were directly felt by Maxie, but Harlan Ober got the same impression as stories of Agnes's travels went back to the National Spiritual Assembly. On 5 August, Harlan wrote to Agnes that her talks on the Guardian's station were important:

You have certainly been having a wonderful time in Teaching, and there is no doubt that now that you are in San Francisco, you will be assisted in visiting with the friends . . .

I have a feeling that you have been prepared to bring a very special gift to the friends in the West, as you did in the Eastern part of our country. You have always followed guidance . . .

From the point of view of real knowledge of the station of the Guardian, we all are bereft & are poverty stricken. However in every community there are souls who are searching for reality & for a deeper understanding. The pearls of love & knowledge cannot be disclosed to every believer, except after one has inward guidance, indicating capacity. You are especially equipped for this particular service, and I know that you will be greatly confirmed, because the Guardian's blessing & prayers are surrounding you.[56]

Agnes was in Los Angeles on 30 June and Georgy FitzGerald drove her around and then took her to Geyserville for the two weeks of Bahá'í summer school there.[57]

By the end of July, however, Agnes was back in Louhelen, Michigan, for that Bahá'í summer school. *Bahá'í News* reported that 'An especial favor for the August session was the presence of Miss Agnes Alexander who had recently visited Haifa and had much to tell us of the Guardian's words and wishes. Before she left Haifa the Guardian had instructed her to visit summer schools. Many of the afternoon meetings were devoted to hearing her notes and others to discussing teaching methods.'[58]

About the time of the Louhelen school, Agnes received another letter from the Guardian, which read:

Dear Bahá'í Sister,

Your most welcome messages of April 11 and June 9th addressed to our beloved Guardian have been received, and their contents read by him with profoundest interest and deepest satisfaction.

Your visits to various Bahá'í centres, he is pleased to hear, has been very pleasant and successful, and the friends surely must have all considerably benefited through meeting you and sharing your unforgettable experiences in Haifa. You did certainly well to tell them of the impressions of your visit, as they will no doubt derive the utmost joy and confidence from them, and will receive a renewed inspiration in their services to the Cause.

This letter will find you probably back in California. May I express the Guardian's hope that there too your stay may prove to be as pleasant and beneficial in its results as your travels throughout the Eastern and Central States.

In his never failing personal note at the end, Shoghi Effendi wrote, 'May the Almighty guide you in your steadfast efforts for the spread of the Faith, and give you all the strength you need for the consolidation and extension of your historic services and accomplishments. Your true and grateful brother, Shoghi.'[59]

Harlan Ober again wrote to Agnes in November about the very positive response from the Guardian to her efforts of sharing her experiences in Haifa, with a caveat that there were some people in the country objecting to her use of pilgrim notes:

The letter from the Guardian must make you very happy, and your clear obligation is to share with the friends there unforgettable experiences of your visit. You will find the souls who will treasure this recital, and will be inspired by it.

Just at the moment, some very few persons seem to be leaning over backward in reference to Pilgrim's notes. No doubt the pendulum will swing back again . . . As we know, the Cause has believers in many spiritual states and degrees of understanding. I believe that if we pray we will be led to those who desire and will appreciate any message we have to give. I am praying for you that you may be assisted in raising the Exalted Standard, and in removing the veils from the eyes, so that the shining reality may appear.[60]

Those negative voices, however, proved no test in light of Shoghi Effendi's next letter to her:

Dear Bahá'í Sister,

Your very kind and welcome letter of the 22nd October has duly reached our beloved Guardian, and its contents noted by him with keen interest and deepest satisfaction.

He was particularly gratified to hear of the opportunity you had received of speaking on the Cause over the radio and hopes that such occasions and facilities of teaching and expounding the Faith will be increasingly offered you in the future. You seem to be taking indeed the fullest advantage of your stay in California to help in promoting the cause of teaching there, and now that your return to Japan has been indefinitely postponed, in view of the growing hostilities in the Far East, you will do well to concentrate all your efforts on teaching in America, where the field is both vast and promising.

The Guardian also hopes that as the newly elected member of the Berkeley Assembly you will be able to contribute a notable share towards the efficient functioning, growth and consolidation of that body, and that you will put at the service of this new task you have been called upon to discharge all those qualities which your many years of faithful and uninterrupted stewardship to the Faith have enabled you to acquire.

The Guardian's own note said, 'May the Beloved inspire you to do His will and to extend the range of your beneficent accomplishments and activities in the service of His triumphant Faith, Your true brother, Shoghi.'[61]

After receiving his message, Agnes noted that 'the doors opened for me to speak over many radio stations in the United States in the years 1938 to 1941'.[62]

Agnes had been keeping up with the Japanese Baháʼí community during her travels, and a letter she wrote on 21 November showed her concern and encouragement for Daiun Inouye, the Buddhist priest who had finally given up the priesthood for the Faith and was, consequently, suffering some serious financial challenges. The Guardian's response strongly supported Agnes's advice to Daiun:

Beloved Baháʼí Sister,
   The very kind letter you had written the Guardian dated November 21st, together with the enclosed snapshots representing our dear Japanese friend . . ., have duly reached him, and he was made very happy indeed to hear of . . . determination to disassociate himself from the Buddhist Church, and to henceforth devote most of his time and efforts to the service of the Cause in Japan.
   Much as he regrets to hear of . . . stringent financial conditions, he cannot but fully approve of the very wise and appropriate reply you had given him, in connection with his request for assistance. It would certainly do much harm to the Cause to give such new believers the impression that their services can be secured only in return for financial help, and thus make them believe that the Faith is but a business organization.
   Although, as you have written, . . . is far from having any such low motives, and is a pure and sincere heart, nevertheless it would constitute a very bad example to start defraying all the expenses which he may incur in connection with his teaching work for the Cause.
   He hopes that your reply will not dampen his zeal, but will serve rather to stimulate him to rise to higher heights of devotion and sacrifice in service to our beloved Faith.
   The Guardian will specially pray for him, that he may be strengthened and sustained spiritually, and be led to render distinguished services to the Cause in Japan. He will specially pray that he may be given the full means required for the accomplishment of this high task he had set himself to achieve in service to the Faith and to his fellow countrymen.

Shoghi Effendi concluded the letter with praise for her untiring efforts: 'May the Almighty enable you, while in the States, to render memorable services to the Faith, and contribute an outstanding share to the teaching efforts that are being so strenuously exerted by the believers at the present time, Your true and grateful brother Shoghi.' [63]

Agnes had been elected to the Local Spiritual Assembly of Berkeley, but by December she knew that it was about time to head even further west, to Hawaii. In early December, she wrote, 'As Shoghi Effendi asked me to visit all the centers as far as possible, and particularly in California, it seems that I have now completed the rounds after being in Burlingame last week.' [64] She booked passage to Honolulu with her sister, Mary, for the 16th, noting, 'It has been decided quite suddenly and everything has worked out. I would not go if I didn't feel the inner confirmation. It is the friends there whom I really go to see and share with them my Haifa visit.' [65]

16

HAWAII AND AMERICA

1939–1949

Agnes arrived in Honolulu in late December 1938 and by mid-January 1939 she was working on a biography of Yun-Siang Tsao, the Chinese man who had translated *Baháʼuʼlláh and the New Era*, as well as other Baháʼí books, into Chinese. Horace Holley had asked her to write the story for *The Baháʼí World*. It had not been an easy task. Horace's letter arrived in Japan after Agnes had departed for the Holy Land and she didn't receive it until she was in America. Then she wrote to a lady with whom Mrs Tsao was living, but the woman had left and the letter was returned undelivered. Finally, contact was made with Mrs Tsao and Agnes finished the story.[1]

On 7 February, Agnes received her first letter of the year from the Guardian, written on 3 January. This one confirmed her moving to Honolulu and the diminished possibility of returning to Japan in the near future:

> He has noted your plan to go to Honolulu together with your sister, and trusts you have safely reached there by now, and are engaged in teaching the Cause, and in assisting the friends in their efforts for the extension and consolidation of the Faith in the Islands of Hawaii. Your stay there, he is confident, will bring forth good results, and will be as deeply appreciated by the believers as your sojourn in California.
>
> Now that the prospects of your return to Japan seem to be far remote, in view of the growing hostilities in the Far East, you should endeavour instead to teach in Honolulu, and preferably, if feasible, in those islands of Hawaii which have not yet been opened to the Cause.[2]

Agnes had already begun to take her teaching efforts outside of Honolulu. Wherever she went she also shared her experiences in Haifa and the notes taken of the Guardian's talks at the dinner table in the Pilgrim House.³

The Guardian's next letter to Agnes, dated 22 February 1939, stressed her cooperative teaching work with Kathrine Baldwin. Kathrine had written a letter to the Central Union Church in Honolulu, withdrawing from membership in the church. She wrote to Shoghi Effendi and said that she had told the church that she was withdrawing because there was a New Manifestation, Bahá'u'lláh.⁴ Agnes also wrote to the Guardian and received the following reply:

> Your most kind and welcome message of the 29th January has been received by our beloved Guardian, and he has read its contents with very deep interest and genuine satisfaction.
>
> He is profoundly grateful and happy that you are enjoying your visit to Hawaii, and are finding so many avenues of teaching the Faith. Your services in those far-off islands are certainly most urgently needed, and the friends, and in particular dear Mrs. Baldwin with whom you are in such close collaboration, will no doubt make full use of the opportunity of your stay in their midst to impart a fresh stimulus to the expansion of the teaching work throughout those regions.
>
> The Guardian will ever pray that Divine confirmations may strengthen and sustain you in your noble and indefatigable exertions for the spread of His Cause, and its wider diffusion in that distant land upon which has been conferred the unique and inestimable privilege of being blessed by the mention of our beloved Master. Conscious of such a priceless honour you should indeed redouble your efforts, and leave no stone unturned until you befittingly and successfully accomplish this noble mission you have undertaken to those shores.⁵

In March 1939, following the Guardian's guidance, Agnes wrote, 'I had the joy of visiting the Maui friends. On Naw-Rúz, they all gathered in commemoration of the day at the home of Mrs. Daisy Voss at the Sprecklesville beach where they partook of a luau. From the gathering of love and unity, a message was sent to the beloved Guardian.'⁶

On 3 March, Agnes received a letter from Rúḥíyyih Khánum in which she outlined the highs and lows of the First Seven Year Plan:

> The news from America is so encouraging and makes the Guardian so happy. When the Cause is being so restricted everywhere in the world, almost, it is such a privilege the Americans have of working free and unhampered at such a terribly dark period. I hope we grasp it to the full because we don't know what hardships or restrictions we too may suffer in the future – who knows?
>
> I know wherever you are you are always busy! Indeed, every day, every where there is some way of serving. People are so dead – or at least they look that way to me! It certainly will take an earthquake to awake them. We need not feel too sad for them because after all they have had so many chances, all people, throughout history, of becoming better and more truly human and I guess they threw their chances away.
>
> The Guardian says destiny and free will are subjects that must always be more or less a mystery, but one wonders why and how! Anyway the best way not to mark time wondering is to obey! At least this is my formula. I get so disgusted with my faults and contemplate them – and find myself paralysed and then I realize my only remedy is to just do what Shoghi Effendi tells me to!
>
> This last letter from him to the believers of the West is so marvelous, isn't it? It points out our virtues and our faults in no uncertain terms! I think we certainly need it don't you? And it gives us the charter of so much wonderful work to do. When we realize that these plans the Guardian is now calling upon us to fulfil were laid down over 25 years ago by the Master, it is certainly time we did something about doing our duty 25 years after we were told to!! But of course you and Martha [Root] and the [Hyde and Clara] Dunns and Jackie [Marion Jack] and Leonora [Holsapple Armstrong], all arose long ago! What an example to the younger generation.[7]

The Guardian had announced the Seven Year Plan on 1 May 1936 and it began at Riḍván 1937. Shoghi Effendi wrote, 'Would to God every State within [the] American Republic and every Republic in [the] American continent might ere termination of this glorious century embrace the light of the Faith of Bahá'u'lláh and establish [the] structural basis of His World Order.'[8] The American Bahá'í community had a history of being audacious and achieving wondrous results when the Guardian gave them work to do. But, as Shoghi Effendi told later pilgrims, the American Bahá'ís 'flare up and die down again'.[9] Each year, he had to send them a 'pep talk' to get them going again. The letter Rúḥíyyih Khánum was referring to was sent by the Guardian on 28 January 1939 and bluntly laid out America's responsibilities:

> The period ahead is short, strenuous, fraught with mortal perils for human society, yet pregnant with possibilities of unsurpassed triumphs for the power of Bahá'u'lláh's redemptive Cause. The occasion is propitious for a display, by the American Bahá'í Community, in its corporate capacity, of an effort which in its magnitude, character, and purpose must outshine its past endeavors. Failure to exploit these present, these golden opportunities would blast the hopes which the prosecution of the Plan has thus far aroused, and would signify the loss of the rarest privilege ever conferred by Providence upon the American Bahá'í Community. It is in view of the criticalness of the situation that I was led to place at the disposal of any pioneer willing to dedicate himself to the task of the present hour such modest resources as would facilitate the discharge of so enviable a duty.
>
> The Bahá'í World, increasingly subjected to the rigors of suppression, in both the East and the West, watches with unconcealed astonishment, and derives hope and comfort from the rapid unfoldment of the successive stages of God's Plan for so blest a community. Its eyes are fixed upon this community, eager to behold the manner in which its gallant members will break down, one after another, the barriers that obstruct their progress towards a divinely-appointed goal. On every daring adventurer in the service of the Cause of Bahá'u'lláh the Concourse on high shall descend, 'each bearing aloft a chalice of pure light.' Every one of these adventurers God Himself will sustain and inspire, and will 'cause the pure waters of wisdom and utterance to gush out and flow copiously from his heart.' 'The Kingdom of God,' writes 'Abdu'l-Bahá, 'is possessed of limitless potency. Audacious must be the army of life if the confirming aid of that Kingdom is to be repeatedly vouchsafed unto it . . . Vast is the arena, and the time ripe to spur on the charger within it. Now is the

time to reveal the force of one's strength, the stoutness of one's heart and the might of one's soul.'

Dearly-beloved friends! What better field than the vast virgin territories, so near at hand, and waiting to receive, at this very hour, their full share of the onrushing tide of Bahá'u'lláh's redeeming grace? What theatre more befitting than these long-neglected nine remaining states and provinces in which the true heroism of the intrepid pioneers of His World Order can be displayed? There is no time to lose. There is no room left for vacillation. Multitudes hunger for the Bread of Life. The stage is set. The firm and irrevocable Promise is given. God's own Plan has been set in motion. It is gathering momentum with every passing day. The powers of heaven and earth mysteriously assist in its execution. Such an opportunity is irreplaceable. Let the doubter arise and himself verify the truth of such assertions. To try, to persevere, is to insure ultimate and complete victory.[10]

Agnes was one of those who was doing everything she could to advance the Plan. She wrote to the Guardian at Naw-Rúz and received his reply sent on 22 April. The letter read:

The very cordial message you had written the Guardian on the occasion of the Naw-Rúz feast, dated March 21st, has duly reached him, and he was made inexpressibly happy by its perusal. He wishes me to reciprocate your loving greeting, and to wish you also every happiness and prosperity throughout this year . . .

It was a matter of deep satisfaction to the Guardian to know that you, together with our distinguished and well-beloved sister Mrs. Baldwin, have been elected as Convention delegates by the Honolulu Assembly, and he wishes me indeed to congratulate you both for this evidence of well-deserved praise and confidence shown towards you by the friends.[11]

Shoghi Effendi's personal note in his own hand read, 'Wishing you good health, happiness and continuing success from all my heart, Your true and grateful brother, Shoghi.'

1939 National Convention

Agnes was again elected to be the Honolulu delegate to the National Convention in Wilmette. On 28 March 1939, she noted in a letter that for 'two years I have been constantly moving from place to place, but it is the time to be moving . . . may He guide you all as He will never fail to do if we seek His will and through our beloved Guardian we can today know the Will of Bahá'u'lláh'.[12] On 5 April, she spoke on KGU radio on the topic 'It is a New Bible of Human Power'. Two days later, she sailed from Honolulu.[13]

Addressing the National Convention, Shoghi Effendi cabled his praise for the Americans' efforts during the first two years of the Plan and held Martha Root's teaching efforts as their model. He wrote that the task was 'admittedly laborious, hour laden with fate, privilege incomparable, precious divinely-promised aid unfailing, reward predestined immeasurable. Appeal to all believers, white and Negro alike, to arise and assume rightful responsibilities.' There were also four Bahá'ís from Mexico present and the Guardian specifically mentioned one of them, Pedro Espinosa, as illustrating that Mexico was now in the 'forefront of the southward marching army' of Bahá'u'lláh.[14] With the Guardian's message to spur them on, 81 participants at the Convention arose and volunteered to go forth and teach. Agnes took Shoghi Effendi's messages to heart and after the Convention began to travel around America to both spread the Faith and encourage the Bahá'ís:

This week I made a trip to Milwaukee and spoke there on Sunday twice. First to the Baha'is, reading my Haifa notes, and then in the evening to the public. Afterwards, I was the guest for two days at Downer-Milwaukee College where a very dear friend, Mrs. Ethelwynn Beckwith, who once lived in the Islands, teaches. There I had a very happy talk with the Dean of the College about the Faith. Yesterday I went into Chicago for the first time and spoke at their noon meeting. Anthony Seto came in having arrived from New York. He also spoke and it was a happy occasion.

Mrs. Maxwell is here and I have an inexpensive room by the week and so am staying on, until all my plans are arranged. It is a great bounty to be near to Mrs. Maxwell and have a talk with her each day. Last week I read my Haifa notes to the combined friends of Wilmette and Evanston. So now I am giving those who did not hear last year, the opportunity which Shoghi Effendi has asked me to do, that is, to share with the friends all my experiences, etc.[15]

May and Agnes enjoyed each other's company until 6 June. Two weeks later, Agnes was still in the Chicago area and wrote to May that:

I never thought I should be here so long, but this is the heart of America and the Faith in this land and so it is the most important place to be. I found the work which I wanted to do with colored people in South Chicago and go there every week and sometimes twice. It is a great joy. Then another joy is helping guide in the Temple. From 10 a.m. to 4 p.m. every day there are guides there to take visitors around and sometimes they come in flocks. Yesterday there were 43 persons who came. Before I reached there in the morning a visitor came from Hawaii, a Mr. Hale who said he worked for the Inter-Island [Steram Navigation Company] and was on a three months vacation.

No I don't expect to return at present to the Islands but whatever is best that is only my desire to do. I may not go to Louhelen until the August session, but it is not yet all decided.[16]

Rúḥíyyih Khánum sent Agnes another letter on 13 May in which she encouraged the Bahá'ís to send Shoghi Effendi important news, not trivial things:

His thoughts are so constantly on the progress of the work over there – and I personally feel that the friends, in their fear of over burdening him, get the idea that they must not write at all. In other words real news can never be a burden to him, trivial things, of course, if referred too often to him, are. News of conferences, conventions, new plans, new ways and means. I see his beloved face kindle with interest when he reads such things! And you can imagine how happy that makes me!

The Guardian is an ocean, but the people don't fish in it enough. A very homely simile, but I mean we have no realization of the creative powers of the Guardian, we don't tap the Divine Inspiration ever ready to flow from him into the channels of the work of the

Cause. As I watch him I feel he is more than capable of formulating and guiding plans for <u>every</u> country on earth as well as America. And America is at present, to all intents and purposes the only field free for his plans to evolve in, because almost all other Baha'i countries are either very restricted and stifled at present, or are as yet unripe for big undertakings. So you see I think we should tap the strength of the Guardian into as many departments of our Baha'i life as possible – and to ask is to receive.[17]

Agnes, of course, was doing exactly what Rúḥíyyih <u>Kh</u>ánum was suggesting in her constant stream of new-filled letters.

The passing of Martha Root

Martha Root came to Hawaii from Australia on her way to America on 7 June, while Agnes was in America. It was the last stop for her in the physical world. Agnes later wrote:

In God's plan Honolulu was to become her resting place. Accompanied by the friends Mr. and Mrs. S[tanley] W. Bolton of Sydney, Australia, Martha left the steamer to go to the home of Mrs. Kathrine Baldwin for the day. As she was very ill, she retired to a room to rest. From that hour our precious Martha never left the house. Too ill to continue the voyage, she decided to remain in Honolulu for a week. The week became months before she left her earthly cage. Many plans which had been made for the days she was to be in Honolulu had to be cancelled. Mr. and Mrs. Bolton then spoke in her place over the radio. On August 4, the doctors decided that Martha could not linger long. Every week during her illness the Honolulu Baha'is sent flowers to her, and everything was done for her comfort and happiness. The afternoon of September 28, her spirit took its flight.

After Martha's passing, Katherine Baldwin wrote that she could not understand why Baha'u'llah had permitted her the privilege of having Martha in her home, but friends knew that God placed Martha where she would have loving care and comfort during her last days. Katherine Baldwin offered as her contribution to the memorial to Martha, a plot in a lovely spot in Nuuanu Cemetery, to be known as the Martha Root plot. There, precious Martha was laid to rest. Although she never stepped out after reaching the Baldwin home, she sent two articles to each of the two Honolulu dailies which were published with her picture. At the time of her passing both the newspapers had articles concerning her life and the Advertiser also carried an editorial about her.[18]

Agnes learned about her passing while still in America and in a letter to the Hawaiian friends, wrote a short summary of their friendship:

> Just two days ago I heard of the passing of our precious Martha Root in your midst. Ever since then my thoughts have been of her and with you. She was near and dear to me ever since 1915 when she first came to Japan and we met there. Then in 1918 I spent a month with her in her home with her father. After his death she came to Japan and again was with me in Tokyo, – then again in Peking, and from there we made an historical trip, stopping in seven cities, and meeting and speaking of the Cause everywhere. That was in 1923. In 1930 again I met her in Shanghai first, then she came later and joined me in Tokyo for two months. That was the last time we met. Shoghi Effendi said to me when I left Haifa, 'Keep in touch with Martha', so eternally I pray we may all be in touch and helped by her spirit.[19]

At the beginning of July 1939, Agnes went to Louhelen, Michigan, and stayed in the area until early October. On 8 October she was in Bay City, Michigan, a town with no Bahá'ís. She spoke on the radio twice, using the 'creative word' both times. It was during this time, that Agnes decided she should begin the histories of the Faith in Hawaii and Japan that Shoghi Effendi asked her to write.[20]

The passing of May Maxwell

On 1 March 1940, Agnes's spiritual mother, May Maxwell, passed away at her new pioneering post of Buenos Aires, Argentina. Agnes immediately wrote to Rúḥíyyih Khánum to express her grief and sympathy. Rúḥíyyih Khánum's reply was:

Your letter which just came was a great comfort to me as Mother was your Mother as well as mine and we both adore her! and I know she will be watching over her children here as never before – because now she is free. So often I think of those words of the Master to the effect that 'the bird that is caught in the cage must endure to the end.' We are still caught, but she at last is free and this freedom means so much to one who always suffered in the body as she did all her life.

But it makes such a big gap in life! Mother was Daddy's and my all-in-all. Only the Cause and its Guardian were dearer to us than she – and we received the Cause from her, learned to love it through her example. I am trying to adjust to it, and the indescribable kindness of the Guardian has sustained me as nothing else could. But the loss is very great. Not to have seen her once again is hardest to bear. But I would not have her death otherwise – it was her reward from God at the end of her life that in a great shower of His mercy He should let her become a martyr! Did you know, dearest, that she prayed for this at the Shrine in Bahji?[21]

In her account of May Maxwell's life (see Appendix for the full text), Agnes wrote about her last memories of May:

While in Evanston, during the 1938 Baha'i convention, I gleaned many precious teachings from May. The day before the convention opened, an informal meeting was held to discuss teaching methods. As it was progressing, May entered and was asked to speak. Her words were like light penetrating through clouds. She said Shoghi Effendi had said America needs most, depth, reverence and humility . . .

In the spring of 1939 I spent several weeks with May in Evanston, where we enjoyed, as she expressed it, 'sunlit hours of divine companionship.' In interracial work she had supreme courage. Not only did she adhere to the Master's words regarding the complete union of the colored and the white race, but in her life and actions she lived his behests. One morning I was present when she talked with a friend about the race question. A few of her words that morning I wish to share. She said, 'Consciousness of race is a sign of absence of culture. It is a new world Baha'u'llah has ushered us into.

He has inoculated us with a new virus. The Master never said we must be careful; we must be wise and cautious. He said if we didn't unite, the negro race would rise up. The world is sunk in ignorance. We must not look at what the world thinks. We are sunk in the sea of imagination'. When I said to May afterwards that it had been a wonderful morning, she asked, 'What did I say?' She was a pure channel used in God's hands.[22]

Agnes shared her account with many of the Bahá'ís and received many grateful letters in return. At the memorial service in the Temple in Wilmette, Agnes told about meeting May in Paris in 1901 and in Haifa in 1937.

Writing the history of the Cause in Japan and Hawaii

Agnes knew she would not be going back to Japan for some time, so had asked the Guardian what she should do. A letter written by his secretary on 13 December 1939 said:

Regarding your teaching plans, as your return to Japan seems far remote at present, he would advise that you remain anywhere you wish in the United States and engage in teaching work, and would also approve of your wish to undertake in the meantime writing the history of the Cause in Japan and in the islands of Hawaii, as you are certainly best qualified to write such history, which will no doubt prove of immense interest and value to the friends.

Agnes was also worried about all her books and papers that she had left in Japan. Shoghi Effendi told her that they would probably remain safe, especially since they were in the care of Dr Masujima. The Guardian's personal note said, 'May the Almighty bless your many and incessant activities, guide every step you take, remove every obstacle from your path, and aid you to consolidate the work you have already achieved, Your true brother, Shoghi.'[23] This was her last letter from the Guardian until March 1941.

Agnes explained her thinking about the histories in a letter to the Honolulu Bahá'í community on 16 February 1940:

The first evening at dinner in Haifa, April 20, 1937, he [Shoghi Effendi] asked me to write and then mentioned getting letters from the friends. Later on, April 24th, he said . . : 'Collect as much material as possible before starting writing. Then arrange and systematize them. Either quote or refer to words from the accounts. Quotations from Tablets also.'. . .

While in Michigan I felt the urge to begin writing and wrote of it in a letter to Shoghi Effendi. I was guided to come very suddenly here to Berkeley, not knowing that I should be staying in my sister's home while she was away in Honolulu. So here the way opened for me to be where I could concentrate and write.[24]

She also wrote to Elizabeth Muther, Kathrine Baldwin and May Fantom, asking for letters and stories she could incorporate into the history of Hawaii:

Shoghi Effendi said collect the materials and then either quote or incorporate it. So dear friends I will have to depend on you for much. If all my things were together which are in Honolulu and Japan and also things which I lost in the fire in 1919 in Japan, it would be easy to arrange, but now I have to recollect many things from memory. I am making the beginning now and it can always be added to and improved. I have written two parts which I have called 'Prelude' and 'Awakening' and now as I come to Hawaii, I need much material, so dear sisters will you please write of the Cause on Maui, the beginning, etc. Then Utie will you please write . . . about the time you came into the Cause, the story of it and of how you gave the message to Yamamoto for that is a very important part. I will try and get him to tell me what he can also. Tell the stories of how you came into the Cause, and about the beginnings on Maui, etc. A long story![25]

When Mason Remey heard of her project, he wrote her that he had completed 'the first fifty-one volumes of my Baha'i Reminiscences'. In those volumes were a 'minute account of my visits to Honolulu and also my one and only visit to Japan'.[26]

Agnes was at Geyserville in July 1940, and then was busy in Berkeley a month later writing her Bahá'í history of Japan. She was still writing to her correspondents asking for any letters they might have from her when she was in Japan. To Ella Cooper, she wrote, 'These days I am writing every day on the history of the Cause in Japan. As I have no data with me here, it means thinking back and takes time, but it is what I must do at this time, as I feel the urge, and the Guardian asked me to write it.'[27] Agnes asked Victoria Bedikian for similar help.

Agnes was concurrently working on the Hawaiian Bahá'í history and was delighted when Ella Cooper sent her some letters from Elizabeth Muther, the first Bahá'í to declare in Hawaii. Agnes had already written about how Elizabeth came into the Faith, and had done it by memory, but with the letters, she wrote that 'I feel I can use some of her own words, as Shoghi Effendi said to quote from accounts or use them.'[28]

In November, Agnes spent three weeks with Louise and John Bosch. It was a very special time for her and she wrote to them after her departure, 'How great was His bounty to me that I could have had just those three weeks with you! So much I gained in being with you that it is something which cannot be told in words. It is something in the heart, – spiritual.'[29]

Agnes received her next letter from the Guardian, dated 12 March 1941, while in California:

> He is always happy to receive your news and appreciates your steady and untiring devotion to the good of our beloved Faith. He is sure your trip back to the Pacific coast after the Convention, as well as your visit at Geyserville, was of help to all the friends you contacted, and he hopes you will be able in Honolulu not only to complete your history of the Cause in Japan, but also to lend your active assistance to the Bahá'ís there.
>
> Shoghi Effendi feels the work of the Cause in the Hawaiian Islands is of great importance and hopes you can further its spread there.

Shoghi Effendi added, 'May the Beloved, Whom you adore and serve so devotedly and faithfully, sustain you at all times, reveal to you His will and purpose, and aid you to fulfil His wish in a manner that would redound glory of His Faith.'[30]

Back in Hawaii

Agnes returned to Hawaii on 2 June 1941. Ever prepared to teach the Faith, Agnes met a deaf lady, Hilda Forsgrene, on the steamer who could read lips and taught others the ability. The lady became very interested in the Faith and read two of Agnes's books. Hilda was unable to attend lectures on the Cause because of her deafness, so required a personal contact.[31]

On 12 June, Agnes turned the first earth in a ceremony to begin the construction of a Bahá'í Centre on McCully Street near the Ala Wai Canal in Honolulu. Four months later, the Centre was completed. It was dedicated on 20 October 1941. About 75 people were present and the 'heavenly afternoon closed with a beautiful sunset which nature produced at the entrance of the Ala Wai Canal'.[32]

Then one December morning, the world changed:

When December 26, the fortieth anniversary of the coming of the Baha'i Cause to the Islands of Hawaii drew near, suddenly all things changed. The first crashing of the old order came on December 7, at 7:55 in the morning, when the long predicted conflict in the Pacific Ocean burst forth. Honolulu was taken unawares and bombs caused more than 3,000 deaths among the men in the United States Armed Forces. Shoghi Effendi had said when I was in Haifa in May, 1937, 'The Pacific will become a great storm center in the coming war and there will be great suffering.'[33]

Suddenly, Agnes's adopted country had attacked her native land.

Ten days after the Pearl Harbor disaster, Habib and Bahiriyyih Sabet and their two sons, Iraj and Hormoz, arrived from Iran en route to America. These were the first Persian Bahá'ís to visit Hawaii. Agnes had met the elder Sabets at the National Convention in 1939 in Wilmette. The Bahá'ís had not met together since the Japanese attack because of the city-wide blackout after sunset, but a group did gather at noon on 17 December to greet the visitors. The next morning, the Bahá'ís took the Sabets to Martha Root's grave. Bahiriyyih had travelled with Martha in Iran. The Sabets departed at noon on the steamer for San Francisco.[34]

Shoghi Effendi wrote to Agnes on 14 December with his support during those confusing and troubled times:

His thoughts these last few days have been constantly with the dear friends in Hawaii, and at present he is awaiting a reply from the N.S.A. to his cable inquiring after their safety. He hopes and prays all are well.

In spite of the dark outlook of these days the Guardian feels confident that the believers, so full as they are of love, and confidence in the Plan of God, will surmount every hardship and rise to even nobler heights of service and devotion. The tests and trials of the times will demonstrate the true nature of the people of Bahá, and hold them up as an example to their seeking, disillusioned, followers.

The Guardian is very happy over the work you are accomplishing, and he hopes that, in spite of the difficulty of the times, you will be able to go on teaching, and aiding your fellow-believers, as well as compiling your histories of the Cause in the lands where you have most served it.[35]

Shoghi Effendi personally concluded the letter with: 'May the Almighty protect and sustain you in these days of turmoil and strife, and enable you to promote the best interests of His Faith, reinforce the basis of its institutions, and stimulate the enthusiasm of its supporters, Your true and grateful brother, Shoghi.'

On 26 December 1941, the fortieth anniversary of Agnes's arrival as the first Bahá'í in Honolulu, the Bahá'ís met at the Centre to consummate the incorporation papers of the Bahá'í Faith in the City and County of Honolulu.[36]

Full drafts of the histories are completed

Agnes continued working on her histories of the Faith for both Japan and Hawaii. On 17 March 1942, she wrote to Ella Cooper: 'These days I write and write, and also try to help the dear friends here, as the Guardian asked me not only to finish the writing of the history while here, but also to give active assistance to the Baha'is and so my path is plain and clear and I have no desire, of course, to go any where else.'[37]

By the end of the year, the manuscripts were finally complete in first full drafts. Writing again to Ella, she noted, 'The first writing is finished but it has to be gone over. Also the other history of the years in the Orient are finished in the first writing, in all I have more than 400 pages that of course includes many Tablets, etc.'[38] In 1943, she informed the Guardian of their near completion. His reply, through his secretary, was that 'He was . . . very pleased to hear you have completed the important work of the two histories you were engaged on, and he would like you to send him copies . . . of both, preferably mailed separately so the danger of both being lost will be lessened. You should also file one with the National Bahá'í Archives in the States for safe keeping.' He also mentioned two other topics – church membership and firesides:

> The friends should by all means be encouraged to withdraw from Church membership and be made to realize that, though we as Bahá'ís are ardent believers in Christ, we do not and cannot support Church institutions and doctrines when Christ has come again and brought new laws for the world today and its present needs; to adhere to forms, mostly man-made, and now outmoded and no longer needed, is meaningless. This does not mean they should no longer associate with the Church members; they should cease to be registered members of it.
>
> The Guardian hopes you are able to have fireside classes in your home. This will tax your strength less and is also an excellent method of teaching.

In his own hand, Shoghi Effendi added: 'May the Beloved bless continually your exemplary and tireless efforts in the service of His Faith, and enable you, despite the hardships and trials of these days, to lend a great impetus to the teaching activities of the American believers. Your true and grateful brother, Shoghi.'[39]

It took two more years before Agnes was able to send Shoghi Effendi the completed history of the Faith in Hawaii. While she was still doing the final work on her histories, Rúḥíyyih Khánum wrote to her about what we now know as *God Passes By*:

> My own news is just to report that here we are all rushed as never before. That is why it has taken so long to get my own mail attended to. The work of the Guardian seems to increase daily as the Centenary of the Faith draws near and all the Bahá'ís everywhere seem to be more busy and active than ever before. I just marvel at them. It shows how this Cause is different from all other Causes and moves

by a higher power. The friends in India are just bursting with activity and they seem to be the ones who will take second place next to America . . . if they keep on this way.

All this gladdens the Guardian's over-burdened heart and makes it easier for him to go on carrying his very heavy load of care and work. He is engaged, and has been for over a year, on a wonderful piece of work for the Faith and hopes to get it off to the friends before the Centenary. It will simply thrill you when you read it! But it has been a truly crushing weight for him to carry along with increased amount of purely routine work here. Nothing but the Power of God could keep him going as he does![40]

Shoghi Effendi finally received the finished copy of *Forty Years of the Baha'i Cause in Hawaii* in March 1945. The letter written on his behalf apologized for the lengthy delay in answering it:

Your letters dated August 26th, October 21st, and December 6th, 1944, as well as the one that came with your manuscript, dated January 2nd, have all been received, and the beloved Guardian has instructed me to answer them on his behalf and to thank you for the various enclosures sent in them.

He would have written you before but this last summer he was very tired after his work on 'God Passes By', and the various other labours connected with the Centenary here and elsewhere. Since then he has been gradually attending to much mail that had perforce to wait upon more urgent matters.

It was a great pleasure to receive at last your accounts of the Faith in Hawaii. This is a very interesting and valuable document, and he hopes you will complete the one on the Cause's development in the Orient with which you are so deeply familiar, and to which you have personally contributed so much. He also was pleased to receive the copies of the radio talks which must have done much to bring the Faith before the public.

All your news was good news and rejoiced his heart. He is happy to see that the friends there are so active and that this activity and unity are attracting new souls to the Faith, particularly the youth.

The Guardian's personal comment at the end was: 'May the Beloved bless continually your meritorious efforts in the path of service, guide every step you take, fulfil every desire you cherish for the advancement of His Faith, and enable you to enrich still further the splendid record of your accomplishments for its furtherance and consolidation, Your true and grateful brother, Shoghi.'[41]

Agnes didn't finish her history of the Cause in Japan until early 1946. The Guardian's reply when he finally did receive it showed his appreciation for that and her other efforts:

> He was delighted to see how active you are and to hear that you are regularly giving the teachings over the radio, which is of the utmost importance . . .
>
> Your history of the Cause in the Orient reached him safely, and he was very happy to have this important record. It is a great pity that other old believers, like your dear self, who have pioneered in the early days, have not kept a record of their activities. Such documents will be of great help to historians in the future and an inspiration to younger Bahá'ís.[42]

New directions

The pace of Agnes's teaching work and other services began to slowly increase during the final years of World War II. Sometime during 1943, future Hand of the Cause Abu'l-Qásim Faizi visited Honolulu and he 'had come to know [her] quite well' during his stay. He noted that because of her prescience and spiritual connection with the Guardian, she 'would become excited and elated in the expectation of a letter from Shoghi Effendi'.[43]

Knowing her own impermanence, Agnes sent her collection of letters from the Guardian to the US Archives for safe-keeping in March 1944. The Archives sent her a note saying that they had received 69 letters from her, though Agnes thought she had sent 70.[44] By 1957, Agnes's collection of letters from Shoghi Effendi reached 94.

Another letter from the Guardian came the same month the Archives received the earlier ones, nor did Agnes have to wait long for the next letter, either. Dated 22 July 1944, it came in August and commented on her efforts to make radio broadcasts about the Faith: 'He was very happy to hear that the radio broadcasts on the Bahá'í Faith are continuing and attracting new souls to the meetings. This is a very important activity of the Bahá'ís there, and he is pleased to hear you are helping them so much by writing the scripts.' As in almost all of his letters to her, Shoghi Effendi added his own personal note. This one read: 'May the Beloved bless continually your efforts and graciously assist you to render outstanding services in this, the opening year of the second Bahá'í century. Your true brother, Shoghi.'[45]

Sometime during 1945, Agnes received a letter from Josephine Kruka on stationery from the Hotel Ambos Mundos, Havana, Cuba. Josephine had been a pioneer in Cuba and would go on to pioneer to Norway, whose language she spoke. Evidently, Agnes had had a profound impact on her incentive to arise: 'I think of you often & with deepest of affection. I am eternally indebted to you for you opened the door for greater service . . . I shall always remember most tenderly our meetings at the Convention of 1938 with our beloved May Maxwell.'[46]

Travelling across America in the Second Seven Year Plan

The year 1946 turned out to be a big one for Agnes. The Guardian had given the American Bahá'í community a second Seven Year Plan and Agnes spent the next ten months travelling and doing her best to see its goals met. It started when she went to the National Convention in April. For the first time, she flew from Honolulu instead of sailing on a steamer. She flew to San Francisco on 17 April, then took the train, named the 'Challenger', to Chicago. As usual, she shared the Bahá'í Faith with many of her fellow travellers.[47]

Agnes's teaching work began right after the three-day Convention. During the next eight months, she went to 40 communities from the east coast to the west and from the northern states to the southern. She gave talks and participated in other meetings at almost every stop she made, but the one thing she did everywhere she visited was to meet and talk with as many individual Bahá'ís as she could. Her main concern appeared to be less with proclamation of the Faith than to connect one on one with Bahá'ís in areas where few Bahá'ís lived and to encourage and deepen them. Most of the communities she visited had small or very small Bahá'í communities. She would sometimes spend a whole afternoon with a single believer, at times just talking and at other times studying with them.[48]

May was spent in the vicinity of the Wilmette Temple in Evanston. On 3 May, she went to a youth meeting at Corinne True's home. Two days later, she gave a talk on 'The Age of Conquest' at the House of Worship.[49]

On 29 May, Agnes was in Atlanta, Georgia, from where she wrote to Ella Cooper:

> Here I am 'way down south,' but it surely is through God's guidance and I am happy to be where I am needed.
>
> The Convention, as you will have heard, was the most spiritual and heavenly of all Conventions. I am thankful that I was guided to attend and thus share with the Hawaii friends my notes, as no one else came from there . . .
>
> I shall be here in the south until July probably and then go to Louhelen and New England.[50]

The Guardian's next letter to Agnes was written on 3 June 1946 and commented on her activities, including connecting American soldiers who were Bahá'ís with the Bahá'ís in Japan:

> Your letters of March 15th and May 21st have been received, and although our beloved is always very busy these days he wishes me to write you a line and assure you of how pleased he was to see you were able to attend Convention and be for some time amongst the friends in the States.
>
> He was also very glad to know you have put the soldier Bahá'ís in Korea and Japan in contact with friends in those places, and hopes and prays this will lead to the rebirth of the Cause out there.[51]

A number of Bahá'ís in the military were being sent to Japan at that time and Agnes made sure they knew how to contact the Japanese Bahá'ís.

Agnes was in Charleston, South Carolina on 7 June 1946 and gave a talk on 'The Coming of World Religion'.[52] Two days later, she was in Augusta, Georgia, where she first visited the grave of Zia Bagdadi. Over the next three days, she attended many meetings, then on 16 June continued on to Columbus, Ohio. Her first meeting there was the evening of her arrival at which a dozen people were present, evenly split between black and white. On another evening, she gave the same talk she had given in Charleston.[53]

On 24 June Agnes was travelling again, this time by bus back to Charleston. She remained in the Charleston area for three weeks and stayed with Josie Pinson, with whom Emogene Hoagg had spent her last days. Emogene had become a Bahá'í in 1898 and had been an early Western pilgrim to visit 'Abdu'l-Bahá. After the *Tablets of the Divine Plan* arrived in America, Emogene travelled for six months in Alaska with Marion Jack, criss-crossed America and Europe teaching the Faith and served as Shoghi Effendi's secretary and typing the whole manuscript of *The Dawn-Breakers*. She had passed away in Josie's home just six months earlier[54] and Agnes felt a strong connection with her.[55]

Agnes and Josie had many long conversations together. Agnes examined the main public library and found that it already contained *Bahá'u'lláh and the New Era*, *The Promise of All Ages*, *Some Answered Questions*, and the *Kitáb-i-Íqán*. The library for the Black residents contained *Bahá'u'lláh and the New Era* and *World Order* magazine. Agnes only spoke at one public meeting, at the USO, a charity group who provided services and entertainment for military personnel. This particular meeting was for Black servicemen – segregation was still very much alive in the American South. Agnes noted that none of the 13 hostesses or servicemen had heard of the Faith before except the chairman. Agnes also made short trips to nearby Georgetown and Edisto Island, South Carolina.[56]

On 14 July, Emma Lawrence arrived in Charleston after having driven 400 miles (644 km) from Florida, just to drive Agnes to Greenville, South Carolina. Agnes spent nine days in Greenville, much of it with Emma. Again, Agnes met with as many of the Bahá'ís in the area as she could, spending time with K. Mac Phee, the Bidwells, Dorothy Ford and others. She also visited a blind newspaper seller at the Post Office. At the newspaper office, Agnes was interviewed and photographed and K. Mac Phee arranged to have Shoghi Effendi's *A Pattern for Future Society* broadcast over the radio.[57]

On 25 July Agnes was off again, this time for Atlanta, where she was met by Doris Ebbert. Agnes only spent the 26th in the city and attended a meeting of Black women at a Bahá'í's home and talked with Margaret Ruhe, wife of future House of Justice member David Ruhe, on the phone. Then on the 27th, not being able to get a flight, she boarded a train for Detroit. Agnes noted that she left 'Atlanta on Saturday morning [and] I reached Detroit at 7 a.m. Sunday morning. Then changed to a bus to Port Huron [Michigan] where little Helen [Eggleston?] met me and brought me here, stopping on the way at her grandfather's home.'[58]

28 July was a rest day spent at Twin Lodge Cedarcroft Beach in Port Huron. The next day, Helen and Mary Ann (?) drove her to the Bahá'í summer school at Louhelen, where she stayed for the next nine days. Harlan Ober was one of the primary speakers. Agnes, apparently, was not a speaker at the school.[59]

Agnes left Louhelen with Harlan and Elizabeth Ober for Beverly, Massachusetts on 12 August. On the way to Beverly, they overnighted on the Canadian side of Niagara Falls, then visited Mrs Ketels in Marysville, Ohio. Continuing on the 13th, they stopped at Little Falls, New York to visit Bahá'ís there and spent the night in Utica, New York, arriving in Beverly at 2 a.m. on the 14th. After a day of rest and getting her hair set, they drove on to Green Acre in Maine.[60]

At Green Acre, Agnes shared a room with Beatrice Ashton and Margery McCormick and her sister. During the sessions at the school, Agnes met a young Bahá'í solder, Michael Jamir, who was about to return to Japan, and spent an evening talking with him about Japan and the Bahá'ís there. After 'three heavenly weeks' at Green Acre, Agnes was again on the move.[61]

She was in Beverly again on 6 September, but continued on to Glouster, Ohio, the next day. On the 8th, she celebrated the Feast with Mrs Rogers in Essex, Ohio, and then went on to Boston the following day. In Boston, Agnes wrote in her journal that she 'bought a hat', visited the dentist and had her hair done. On the 15th, she went to Hamilton, Massachusetts, where she spoke in the Bahá'í Centre and talked to a high school history class about Japan.[62]

After a day back in Boston, Agnes resumed her travels, going back to Little Falls and Utica, New York. In Utica, Harry Ford took her out on a drive to see the autumn colours and she attended Mrs Turner's class. Agnes spent two and a half weeks in the area, making side trips with Bahiyyih Ford to visit Frances Stewart in Otter Lake, New York. She also visited Mary Rugge and her husband at their farm.[63]

In a letter she wrote on 25 September, Agnes summed up some of her adventures. She wrote:

I spent two weeks at Louhelen and then drove with Mr. and Mrs. Harlan Ober and Mrs. Obers twin sister to Beverly, Mass. Then the girls drove with me to Green Acre where I remained for three weeks, until the Inn closed, and then returned to Beverly to the lovely Ober home and was there for two more weeks. Now I am here with Bahiyyih Ford, the daughter of Wm. [Harry] Randall and her husband and daughter. It is all His guidance.[64]

Agnes left Little Falls with Bahiyyih on 12 October and drove to Rochester after picking up Frances Stewart in Utica. That evening, Agnes addressed a meeting at the YMCA. The next morning, she had another meeting at the Seneca Hotel. Most of her six days in Rochester were spent visiting the Bahá'ís, including Doris McCandless, Mrs Scepler, Mrs Benedict, Mrs Tinsley and Elizabeth Brooks. She also visited Mary Wilkins, who later followed Mason Remey when he broke the Covenant. She presented her Haifa pilgrim notes at the Lindsey home.[65]

On 19 October Agnes continued her travels by going to Buffalo, New York, where she attended a meeting at the Bahá'í Centre and celebrated the Birth of the Báb. Fred Kappus collected her on the 22nd and drove her to Ruth Thorpe's home in Hamburg, New York. After two days spent mostly with the Thorpes, Agnes went to Jamestown, New York and attended a meeting. On the 31st she drove with Della Emery and 'Dorothy H.' to Cambridge Springs, Pennsylvania, where they had lunch with Lucy Wilson in a hotel where Martha Root had spoken.[66]

Agnes was back on the road on 3 November, this time headed for Cleveland, Ohio, where she spent several days. The day after her arrival, she was at a meeting with 14 participants, three of whom were Japanese and five others Black. On the 7th, Mrs Fisk, a Black Bahá'í, took her to another meeting where eight were present.[67]

From Cleveland, Agnes took the train to Fort Wayne, Indiana, where she spent a week visiting the Bahá'ís. While there, she talked at a meeting at the Bahá'í Centre, attended the celebration of the Birth of Bahá'u'lláh and read her Haifa notes at the Centre on another night. On the 17th she drove to Indianapolis, Indiana for a conference, then returned to Fort Wayne.[68]

South Bend, Indiana was her destination on 19 November. She stayed there until the 23rd, when she headed for Louisville, Kentucky, connecting with Kathryn Frankland. Kathryn was a long-time travel teacher and pioneer who at one time had taken in a young 13-year-old Japanese boy who was looking for work. The boy, who did housework and the washing, was Sachiro Fujita, future companion to 'Abdu'l-Bahá and Shoghi Effendi.[69]

Agnes and Kathryn spent most of her two weeks there doing things together. Agnes gave several talks, celebrated the Day of the Covenant, and was interviewed and photographed at the newspaper. The interview printed in the *Courier-Journal* newspaper read:

> One hundred fourteen years ago, the grandfather of Miss Agnes B. Alexander left his home in Paris, Ky., and sailed on a whaling vessel to the Hawaiian Islands as a missionary.
>
> This spring William Patterson Alexander's granddaughter made the trip from Hawaii to the States in 12 hours by plane. It took her grandfather six months. . .
>
> The Baha'i teacher has traveled around the world twice and has taught in Japan, China, and Korea. She was in Germany in 1937 when the Baha'i faith was forbidden 'because it stands for peace and universal brotherhood.'[70]

Agnes wrote to her brother, Arthur, on 5 December about what she had been doing and what her future plans were:

> Your welcome letter of November 26 reached me here where I have been for twelve days, but leave in the morning for Chicago. I have a room engaged at a hotel in Evanston and shall be there until the 12th when I expect to take the S.P. [Southern Pacific] train for San Diego.
>
> Mary C. has booked us to leave by the 'Matsonia' on January 11, so I am heading westward. I could not stay much longer here without a winter coat . . .
>
> I was thrilled to come for the first time to Kentucky. What brought me here was an old friend, Mrs. Frankland whose home is Berkeley. She got a room for me at this hotel. She herself was here three weeks before she could find even a room. It is the same everywhere, the scarcety of rooms . . .
>
> I was in Cleveland for a few days and spoke with [cousin] Arthur Baldwin over the 'phone. He was leaving and so I did not see him.

He had spent a month in the islands. Also I went with friends to Indianapolis for the day . . .[71]

On 6 December Agnes left Louisville by train for Chicago and Evanston. She attended Race Unity meetings on the 7th and 8th. As everywhere else, each day had its own activity and there was very little time to sit back and rest.[72]

Agnes left Chicago for San Diego on 13 December, arriving two days later. She stayed in the city for five days, meeting with the Bahá'ís before heading for Los Angeles, where she was collected by Bob Buckley and Georgy Fitzgerald and taken to the Biltmore Hotel. While in Los Angeles, she made a trip to Long Beach to have lunch with John Brewer, his wife, mother and son. She left for San Francisco by train on the 24th and immediately went to Berkeley where she stayed until the 11th, when she and her sister, Mary, sailed for Hawaii.[73]

Hawaii and America

Agnes spent about a year in Hawaii before her next travels. After the National Convention in 1947, which Agnes did not attend, Corinne True wrote to Agnes and told her how much she had been missed.[74] The record of what Agnes did during the year is extremely limited, but she did maintain contact with the Japanese Bahá'ís. On 28 June a letter was written to her on behalf of the Guardian by Rúḥíyyih Khánum, that encouraged that contact and gave guidance for them:

> He was very happy indeed to receive the good news of the devotion of the Japanese friends to the Faith, and he feels that the greatest service you can render the Cause is to do everything in your power to encourage and help them. Your letters, the news you give them, and the books you may be able gradually to forward, will teach them and keep them up to date in the development of the Cause and its activities.
>
> He does not feel a so-called 'Bahá'í School' is a wise undertaking for . . .; the great need at present is to teach, and he hopes in your letters you will impress this upon him and the other Bahá'ís there, and assure them of his loving prayers on their behalf.
>
> Your untiring devotion in serving the Cause of God is deeply

appreciated. No doubt the fact that you are free of the Assembly work this year enables you to devote more time to teaching and making new contacts.[75]

The Guardian's ever-present personal note read: 'May the Beloved bless your meritorious efforts, guide your steps in the path of service, and aid you to enrich the record of your imperishable services to His Faith, Your true and grateful brother, Shoghi.'

Agnes was again not a delegate at the National Convention in 1948, but she did attend and afterwards went travel-teaching in the Pacific Northwest between June and October. On 17 June she was in Yakima, Washington. The *Yakima Herald-Republic* reported that 'Miss Agnes Alexander of Honolulu, Hawaii, is the guest this week of Mrs. H. N. Lawrence. Miss Alexander, who is a teacher for the Baha'i faith, came to the states to attend a convention of the sect in Chicago. She will leave the last of the week for Seattle, where she will sail for her home in the islands.'[76] A week later, Agnes was in Marysville, Washington, and was entertained by Frances Smith in her home.[77]

The next record of Agnes's teaching work came from Jamestown, New York, in October 1948. Agnes had previously visited Jamestown in October 1946. A news note reported that 'Miss Agnes Alexander of Honolulu, Hawaii, is the guest of Mr. and Mrs. Ralph Emery . . . She is a Baha'i lecturer and will speak at an open house this evening at the home of Mr. and Mrs. Gregory Wooster.'[78]

Agnes was a delegate to the National Convention in 1949. This time, however, she was not the only one; there were enough Bahá'ís in the islands that First Lt. John Cornell was also a delegate.[79] After the Convention, she travelled to Little Rock, Arkansas, from which she sent a letter to the Bahá'ís of Honolulu:

> Thank you . . . for your letter of June 8. My days have all been so full, that it has been difficult to get letters off, especially as in travelling there are so many necessary ones to be written.
>
> Now I am enclosing some of the papers which I have copied for the friends. Tonight, or rather in the morning at 12:20 a.m., I leave here for Houston, where I will be the guest of dear Roberta's [Wilson] mother. I have already visited nine places, and all has been most wonderful, especially the ten days in Toronto.[80]

On 28 July Agnes was preparing to return to Hawaii. Writing to Ella Cooper, she said:

This morning I decided that I would fly home on Monday the first of August. I am sure this is right and so am busy getting things done . . .

Barbara Davenport writes me that after she joins her husband in Tokyo and they have a house, then arrangements can be made for my joining them there. We can pray for the hastening of the plan as our beloved Guardian has asked me to go as soon as possible.[81]

Agnes received a letter written on behalf of the Guardian, dated 31 May 1949, in which he expresses his hope that she would be enabled to return to Japan:

He thinks it would be excellent if you could return to Japan and meet with your old co-workers there, and assist the new Bahá'ís in their work.

Your long and deep association with this country, which at last has begun to put forth flowers in the Bahá'í world community, would be befittingly crowned by this service, and he hopes the way will open for you to go there as soon as possible.[82]

The *Bahá'í News* reported that Agnes gave a talk at the Baldwin High School in Wailuku, Maui on 19 November 1949, titled 'The Coming of World Religion'. She also gave a deepening on 'Abdu'l-Bahá's Will and Testament in the home of Daisy Voss on the 30th.[83]

17

BACK IN JAPAN, AGAIN:

1950–1957

Rebuilding the Japanese Bahá'í Community

The war had been a huge challenge for the Japanese Bahá'í community and the Bahá'ís had ended up separated and isolated from each other. Agnes had managed to renew her correspondence with some of the Bahá'ís after the conflict, but getting to Japan was not an option for her – it was a militarily restricted country.

However, thousands of other Americans were going to Japan. These were soldiers, the forces occupying the country. In November 1945, Michael Jamir, a medic in the US Army and a Bahá'í, arrived in Japan and began trying to get addresses for the Japanese Bahá'ís. In May 1946, he met Fujita in Yanai. Fujita was working as an interpreter at the train station and his command of English allowed him to share the Faith with the soldiers who passed through. Michael wrote that 'I found him, at 61, youthful and vibrant in his work and enthusiastic in the Bahá'í Faith . . . He brought out his address book. . . and we went over the names of his American Bahá'í friends to see what I could tell him about them and he wishes me to express his loving greetings to them.' After two days together, Michael travelled to Kyoto and was able to meet Tokujiro Torii.[1]

After meeting his first two Japanese Bahá'ís, Michael received 'warm and enthusiastic letters' from Mr Tanaka and Daiun Inouye. Daiun wanted to go to Tokyo to spread the Teachings, but military restrictions prevented this, so he was teaching in Sapporo, Hokkaido.[2]

On 19 June 1948, the Japanese Bahá'ís began their comeback. A group of 11 believers met at the Shinagawa Girl's School in Tokyo and elected an unofficial Local Spiritual Assembly. How this came about was described in an undated document:

During the last war, Baha'i activity came to an almost standstill in Japan. With no literature and communication in regard to the Faith, it is little wonder that activity did not increase. Two years after the clouds of radio-activity faded in Hiroshima, a spiritual spark was ignited in Tokyo . . . the rebirth of the Baha'i Faith in Japan. Mrs. [Masako] Urushi was one day visiting the third brother of the Emperor, Prince Takamatsu, and happened to mention how her daughter's father-in-law, Mr. Inouye, had translated the Book, 'Baha'u'llah and the New Era' and mentioned a few concepts of the Teachings. Mr. [Goro] Horioka who was present at this gathering was much impressed and asked to read this book. He soon realized this was the Truth, the solution to modern man's problems, and sent for Mr. Inouye who was then in Hokkaido to come to Tokyo. Through Mr Horioka's energy and finance, an investigation of the Teachings of Baha'u'llah group was started at Mrs. Urushi's school. During this time, the beloved Guardian in a letter strongly advised Robert Imagire to pioneer to Japan as soon as possible. In the middle of the year of 1947, the first meeting was held at Mrs. Urushi's school. Learning from Miss Agnes Alexander that Lorraine Wright was in Niigata, Mrs. Urushi, Mr. Horioka, and Mr. Inouye made a visit to the Wrights asking if a Baha'i teacher from America could be sent to Tokyo to help them with their activity. Mrs. Wright said she had just received a telephone call from Robert Imagire that he had just arrived in Tokyo.[3]

Agnes returns to Japan

Agnes's great desire was to return to Japan, and on 20 April 1950 in a letter to Doris Ebbert in Atlanta, she exulted: 'At long last I am leaving for Japan! The way is now clear and I leave May 12 reaching there on the 21st. I shall be at an Air Base with Lt. and Mrs J.C. [Jacob and Barbara] Davenport as that is the way I get to go. I am limited to six months, but it may be the time can be extended after I get there.'[4]

When she arrived in Japan, she led an itinerant life the first weeks:

The first week I spent in Tokyo with Robert [Imagire] and Shozo San [Shozo Kadota] who lives with him as Fujita had come from the west of Japan where he lives to meet me at the steamer and stayed with us for a week. Then I was with some Japanese friends for several weeks where many doors opened for me to speak of our Faith. I slept on the tatami (floor) but in the sitting room there were chairs.

Now I am here at an Air Field with the Davenports, as this is the only place I have to stay, and therefore it must be God's plan for me to be here. I have been going over things which came from the storage where my library was, but it was a great sorrow for me to find that my Baha'i books, that is, most all of them were not there. As I had a complete library from the first printing, I had looked forward to making it up to date . . .

This place is an hour by auto from Tokyo, but I have only been able to go there twice. Last Sunday for the July 9 meeting which made me happy.[5]

Agnes stayed with the Davenports for a month and then moved into a room at the Tokyo YWCA while its occupant was away. When that person returned, she wrote to Doris Ebbert:

I did not know where to go, but put my reliance of God (Gl. pp. 200–201). Then this room where I am now at the National YWCA opened for me. So I cannot but feel it is God's plan.

Since coming to Tokyo many doors have opened for me to give the message to people who had not heard of it before, or who knew of it through the Caravan [New History Society – Ahmad Sohrab's Covenant-breaking group]. People are more receptive now here. So I cannot feel that the Guardian would want me to leave. My six months stay will be up the 21st of November and so I ask your earnest prayers that His will only will be done, and that the way will open, if it is His will, for me to stay here longer. My Passport is good for two years.

The Consulate told me that the extension would have to come through Lt. Davenport's request, the way I came, and as yet I have heard nothing from it. So dear, I ask your prayers.[6]

Agnes spent a week in Kyoto with Tokujiro Torii, their first reunion in 13 years. While there, she also spoke three times at a Unitarian Church and 'discussed the teachings with an unorthodox minister, a former governor of a province and a scholar imbued with the ideal of an international university at Mt. Fuji'.[7]

Agnes wrote to Shoghi Effendi on 28 September 1951 that after initially being told that she must leave Japan in June, Lieutenant Lane Skelton assisted her by speaking with the authorities and securing an extension of her stay in that country until February 1952. She joyfully reported that she was no longer a 'dependent' or 'house guest', but was now independent. She also shared her difficulties in finding suitable housing after having moved six times in recent months. [8]

Agnes received her first letter from the Guardian since her arrival, written on 6 October:

> Our beloved Guardian has instructed me to answer your letter dated June 29.
>
> He is so happy to have you at last in Japan, and feels your presence there will be of great help and inspiration to the Japanese friends.
>
> They seem dear and devoted souls, and he rejoices to see that, after all these years, and the long period of patient toil you spent there in the past, the tree of the Faith has struck deep roots, and the fruits are beginning to appear at last.
>
> He feels you, and dear Fujita too, should devote particular attention to deepening the friends in the Covenant, which is the ark of safety for every believer.

As usual, Shoghi Effendi appended a personal note 'May the Almighty sustain, guide and bless you always, give you all the strength you need to enrich the splendid record of your past services in Japan, and enable you to extend continually the range of your meritorious accomplishments, Your true and grateful brother, Shoghi.'[9]

Activities of Ahmad Sohrab's Caravan of the East

On the day before her first visa expired, the Guardian sent Agnes another letter, written by Rúḥíyyih Khánum, approving her continued stay in Japan and the need for her to counter the propaganda of Ahmad Sohrab's Caravan of the East:

> The other day the beloved Guardian cabled Horace Holley to cable you that he approves your staying in Japan. He thought this was a good way of letting the N.S.A. know at the same time his intention
>
> . . .

He feels sure your stay in Japan is of great help to the believers there, as well as of assistance in counteracting the propaganda of Sohrab, and he is happy you will be remaining there longer – as long as possible he hopes.

Please give his love to all the friends there, and to Mr. and Mrs. Davenport, and assure them he deeply appreciates their services, and the fact that they are enabling you to remain longer in Japan.

The Guardian's personal note read 'May the Beloved continually bless your historic and meritorious labours, guide and sustain you always, cheer your heart, and graciously assist you to win still great victories in the days to come, and thereby enrich the long and distinguished record of your services to the Cause of Bahá'u'lláh, Your true and grateful brother, Shoghi.'[10]

Ahmad Sohrab had been 'Abdu'l-Bahá's secretary for many years, but he rejected the Master's Will in relation to Shoghi Effendi. In the late 1920s, Sohrab began developing his own 'religion' called the New History Society.[11] In Japan, this group became known as the Caravan of the East. Those who go against the explicit Writings of Bahá'u'lláh and 'Abdu'l-Bahá, as Sohrab did when he rejected the Will and Testament of 'Abdu'l-Bahá and began attacking Shoghi Effendi, are called Covenant-breakers and one of their primary tactics to turn people away from the Bahá'í Faith was to deviously twist the Bahá'í teachings in subtle ways to make their point of view seem reasonable.

Sohrab's Caravan did create a few problems for Agnes. On 26 November, Agnes gave a talk about the Bahá'í Faith to Crosby Club's Religious Research Meeting, at which almost all of those who attended were members of the Caravan. In a letter discovered by Don Calkins, Agnes was reported to the military authorities after the meeting by a woman who participated. Obviously swayed by members of the Caravan group who filled the meeting, she wrote a very negative letter about Agnes:

I read in the Nippon Times dated 23 November 1950 that the Crosby Club was to hold a religious research meeting in the afternoon of 26 November . . . and Miss Alexander was to be the lecturer.

I attended the meeting without knowing that Miss Alexander is the leader of the Bahai faith in Japan . . .

According to Miss Alexander the very day was the anniversary of Bahai faith and for Miss Alexander herself it was her 50th anniversary of her entrance into the faith. To my embarrassment she received me saying 'You haven't come here by accident. God has sent you to me.' About at 2:00 one of the man participants went out of the room to guide in about five young women and ten young men. He introduced them as leading students of various universities who were interested in the Caravan movement. Then, the lecture started. Miss Alexander told the outline of the Bahai faith, Bahaullah, the founder of the faith, Abdul-Baha, eldest son of Bahaullah, who was appointed by Bahaullah as the center to who all Bahais should turn for instructions and guidance, and that Shoghi Effendi, eldest grandson of Abdul-Baha, was appointed as the guardian of the Bahai faith.

After her lecture the meeting was moved to answers and questions. According to a young man's question I learned that in the United States there are two headquarters of Bahai faith in parallel which Miss Alexander explained as the headquarters in Chicago being orthodox and that in New York, heterodox. She says that the secretary of Abdul-Baha got property through a rich woman and conducted a movement actively and that is the headquarters in New York . . . Since I did not know anything about the Caravan movement, I wanted to learn about it. However, Miss Alexander did not want to talk about it, saying only that that secretary was a wicked man and that the one which had the headquarters in Chicago is the right one. After the meeting was closed I stayed with the Caravan movement members to learn about it further. It appeared that Miss Alexander did not want me to stay and talk with them but wanted to take me out with her. I can't understand why Miss Alexander who follows Bahai faith which proclaims that 'religious truth is not absolute but relative, that Divine Revelation is continuous and progressive . . .' is so narrow-minded as to prevent others from learning the opinion of another side. According to Caravan movement members, the secretary of Abdul-Baha is not a traitor of Bahai faith but he has started the Caravan movement based on Bahai faith.[12]

The Caravan members told the woman that there were 1,000 Caravan members in Tokyo and 10,000 more in other Japanese cities. What the truth was is not certain, but when Sohrab died in 1958, the movement died with him.

Where to live?

Accommodation was a big test during the whole of 1951. Agnes had been able to renew her visa for another six months, but was having great difficulty finding a place to live. In a letter to Doris Ebbert, she wrote that it was because of the Guardian's letters to her that she was able to continue: 'Such joy and power his words give! And too I can fully understand that he is aware of conditions without ever being told. But why should he not be when he is "under unerring guidance" . . . he is "the ark of safety for every believer." . . . I have felt a power greater than ever before.' Agnes also noted that 'It is almost strange how the language comes back to me after so many years of not even thinking of it, but always there is the divine assistance and I learned it for a great purpose.'[13]

By 13 May, Agnes could no longer stay at the YWCA, but as she always did, she put her faith completely in the Will of God:

> I had to give the room to a Y worker who came from Europe. Since then I have moved four times & shall again, but God must have a purpose for all I wish is to serve Him & my heart is here among these people who, as the Master said will 'turn ablaze'. I will be 76 in July, but God gives me strength to work. Darling [Doris Ebbert] if you turn to Japan in the morning & pray for me, that will be a great bounty. The Master said, 'Stand immovable when the whirlwinds of test shall violently blow & the millstone of tread shall turn round.'. . . I have written today to our only Guide on earth, for he alone can guide. How precious to me are his words to me written in his hand on the last two letters I had the great bounty of receiving. Those words are what uphold me continually . . .
>
> I do not know now but whatever God wills I am ready to do. Although my heart is here, it may be that I cannot stay. All we must pray for is His Will to be done![14]

Agnes had to move again in August. She wrote to Ray Wooten, the young former soldier, that 'I must move this week & do not know where it will be, but only with divine help can it be found. The weather has been so hot that I cannot write in my room.'¹⁵ In her regular letter to Doris, started on the same day as Ray's, 26 August, Agnes said:

> I am writing waiting in a bus. This week I must move, but as yet do not know where it will be . . .
>
> Aug 27. Again I am in a bus – Abdul-Baha [said] that tests are for our good and crises brings results. I felt this yesterday in truth. I have not written you that through a Baha'i brother, Lt Lane Skelton, whom I met in New Orleans about 9 years ago, I have permission to remain another 6 months in Japan, but my status is changed & now I have no connection with the Davenports regarding my stay. You see my time was up but I felt I should do everything possible to stay here as our beloved Guardian wrote me to 'stay as long as possible'.¹⁶

In her 7 October letter to Doris, Agnes wrote that she had moved to yet another new room. Both women were having difficulties and they were praying for each other. Agnes wrote that she did appreciate Doris's prayers for her: 'We all need them, but if we do our part, then there must be a reason for all things. So dear, you may ask that whatever is His will may be.' Though housing may have seemed ephemeral, teaching opportunities always seemed to come. After speaking at a Unitarian Church, she met a man who 'said he had heard of the Baha'i when a boy and had waited 40 years to now learn of it'. Another man said he could not sleep 'because of thinking of the world problems and now he felt he could sleep'.¹⁷

At the end of the year, Agnes was facing the problem of having to yet again renew her visa. She wrote that 'My time is up on February 8, but in my heart I do not feel that it is God's plan for me to leave as there is so very much to be done and God prepared me for this work. Our beloved, Guardian once wrote me: "I feel that your destiny lies in that far-off and promising country where your noble and pioneer services future generations will befittingly glorify and thankfully remember . . ." We must pray for each other . . . this our bounty and what a joy it is!'¹⁸

Agnes's visa was due to expire on 8 February 1952, but she was not worried. She told Doris, 'I am not expecting to leave and that is also in God's hands. Here the ways are so many to work and here is where the Guardian wishes me to be.'¹⁹ On 2 February, she received another letter from Shoghi Effendi, referring to her previous visa renewal: 'He was very happy to hear your visa has been extended, and that you are able to remain longer in Japan . . . He urges you never to feel discouraged, but to go on showering your love on the friends and helping them to a deeper understanding of the Covenant.'[20] Her visa was renewed this time, as well, so she was able to stay until the following September.

In May, the Tokyo Bahá'í community had a new member, Charles W. Smith, a sergeant in the US Air Force. She wrote that 'This week I have been feeling a great joy because God has permitted me to share with a brother who came from the States and had heard of the Faith, but did not have literature or know much. Now he is a new member of our Local Community.' There were also new pioneers, David and Joy Earl. They were sharing Robert Imagire's house. David was there to teach at a university for two years. [21]

Things appeared to be going well for Agnes, but on 21 May, she sent Doris a cryptic note that read: 'I am not so well as most people think, but that is not to be repeated for it does not help, only I would appreciate your dear prayers.' [22] Agnes added no details and the subject did not come up again.

Agnes felt a strong connection with Shoghi Effendi as the infallible mouthpiece of God and his letters always set her path and steadied her aspirations. On 4 July 1952, she wrote:

> To think that on this earth today we can have an unerring Guide and to have him to direct us is God's greatest bounty to us. Our beloved Guardian does not command, but he gives us his loving advice and whatever he directs can always be carried out for it comes from the Unseen Source of Power and Might . . .
>
> What Power is now being released on this earth through our beloved Guardian's decisions! We cannot but feel it and such fragrance comes through the correspondence with those who are striving on earth for His Kingdom. [23]

In July, Agnes received yet another letter from Shoghi Effendi. The letter, written on his behalf by Rúḥíyyih Khánum, stated that 'The Guardian was most happy to learn of the many teaching opportunities which have been coming to you in that land, where you have laboured so tirelessly and so lovingly, and assures you of his loving prayers for you and for those whom you are attracting to the Faith of Bahá'u'lláh.' In his personal note at the end, Shoghi Effendi wrote 'May the Almighty guide your steps, cheer your heart, remove every obstacle from your path, and enable you to enrich the splendid record of your services to His Faith, Your true and grateful brother, Shoghi'.[24]

In September 1952, Agnes attended the Sectional Meeting of the 39th Esperanto Congress of Japan. About 300 participants gathered in Kyoto and, for the first time, one of the meetings was designated for the Bahá'ís. This was arranged by Tokujiro Torii. Agnes attended and presented greetings from the Local Spiritual Assembly of Tokyo. During the Congress, Agnes spoke to the sectional meetings for women, for the blind, and for the Bahá'ís. The *Bahá'í News* account noted that 'The high point of the Congress came when Mr. Torii was called to report on the Blind and Bahá'í sections. As he was guided to the platform, the entire Congress in one accord broke into a prolonged and hearty applause. With his finger tips he read his Braille notes as he spoke in fluent Esperanto. The seeds sown by Mr. Torii, particularly among the blind and those associated with them are now bearing fruit.'[25]

The Holy Year and Ten Year Crusade

On 8 October, Shoghi Effendi announced the first Bahá'í Holy Year. This special year was to mark the Year Nine, which was a reference to the Báb's statement that nine years after His Declaration a new Revelation would appear. The Holy Year, therefore, also marked the centenary of the Revelation received by Bahá'u'lláh in the Síyáh-Chál. Agnes was greatly excited by the Holy Year and the Ten Year Crusade: 'How great are these days! We are living in a Holy Year and the confirmations and Power is released, I feel, as never before.'[26]

Agnes moved to Kyoto on 16 October. She moved for two reasons. First, there were a number of American Bahá'ís in Tokyo at that time and she felt it important that they spread out to other parts of the country if, as the Guardian had requested in the Ten Year Crusade, they were to form their National Spiritual Assembly by 1963. Second, it gave her the opportunity to work closely with Tokujiro Torii. As Agnes noted in a letter to Ray on 23 December, 'It is assured that this is God's plan and it remains for us to assist with His help which is never failing.'[27]

Shortly after the beginning of the Holy Year, Agnes received a letter from the Guardian in which he praised her dedicated service to the Faith: 'The Guardian greatly values your continuous sacrificial services in behalf of the Faith, particularly in Japan. He prays for the success of the efforts of the Friends in Japan, that the Cause may spread rapidly in that country, He will particularly pray for the success of your work in Kyoto. He is hopeful that your contact with the Esperantists in Japan will bring many of them into the Faith.'[28]

Michitoshi Zenimoto

Tokujiro wasted no time in connecting Agnes with receptive souls. In a 23 December letter, she wrote:

> Now I have the great joy of having a spiritual son here, a young student. He has found that for which he has sought. He writes me: 'I must confess, I had not been quiet in my mind till I met you.' . . .
> The name of the student is: Michitoshi Zenimoto. He organized at Doshisha University an association to help the blind students and he is president of it. Mr Torii arranged for me to go to the little room which is set aside for the blind students, to teach them once a week and in this way I met Mr. Zenimoto who is from Hiroshima. All my work here is with the blind or those associated with them and this comes through our dear Mr. Torii's efforts.[29]

Fifteen-year-old Michitoshi Zenimoto had been in Hiroshima on 6 August 1945 when the first atomic bomb was dropped. He and family survived the blast because they lived in 'the shade of the mountain', but he lost many friends. Many Christians were also killed and that brought about a crisis of faith: Michitoshi wondered how could Christians kill other Christians?[30]

In 1952, Michitoshi Zenimoto was a 22-year-old student at Doshisha University, the oldest Christian university in Japan. Michitoshi had enrolled in the Theology Department, but quickly had questions about what they were teaching. When he went to see the Dean, an American missionary, the man repeated several times that 'There is no relief of the soul unless it relies on the Lord Jesus Christ. The salvation is granted only through the Lord Jesus Christ, so we must make Japan a Christian country.' This bothered Michitoshi, so he asked: 'I love and respect my grandfather who has passed away already . . . Was there no salvation for my grandfather?' Instead of answering, the missionary angrily asked, 'Are you really a Christian? Are you a student of the Theology Department? A real Christian wouldn't ask such a stupid question.' Later, the dean cursed him in front of the other students.[31] Here was another crisis of faith. Michitoshi switched from studying theology to studying law.

At that time, blind students were not accepted at any Japanese universities. Michitoshi organized a group called the Doshisha University Blind Student Friendship Association (DUBFA) and soon, the six blind students and up to 80 others were attending its meetings. The blind students wanted to learn conversational English and Michitoshi asked Tokujiro Torii to find an English teacher. Tokujiro contacted Agnes and she came to help them learn. Agnes, however, talked mostly about the Bahá'í Faith and after a while, Michitoshi was the only one still coming.[32]

One day in November, Michitoshi told Agnes about his problems with Christianity. As he recorded, she replied:

'[The] Baha'i [Faith] can clearly answer your troubles'. [She] explained; 'God is one. Buddha and Jesus are the same revealers of the will of God. [Bahá'u'lláh] called both Jesus and Buddha the Manifestations of God. Buddha was one of the Manifestations. No doubt, your grandfather gained salvation, rest and peace in Heaven. Salvation [can be] obtained though the Manifestations at any time and at any place, for God sends his Manifestations to all the people of the world progressively.'

It was a candlelight that stood out in the dark night, indeed!

'If you are interested in Baha'i, I will come to teach you,' she said. 'What time should I come?'[33]

Michitoshi, in his mind, wanted to say, 'Come once a week,' but his heart controlled his mouth and the words he spoke were, 'Every day, please.' So, for 100 consecutive days, with only a short break at Christmas, Agnes went to the University and talked with Michitoshi about the Bahá'í Faith. Even one day when Kyoto was covered with a foot of snow (30 cm) and it was so cold the trains stopped running, she came. Michitoshi didn't think that the 78-year-old Agnes would come, but when he arrived at the University, Agnes was there waiting for him. He asked himself: 'Can I visit someone regularly every day [for] the teaching of Baha'i?' He didn't think so, but there was Agnes doing just that. He then asked: 'What is the love of the Bahá'í Faith?' and noted that 'I always think of this love of Miss Alexander. Thus, Miss Alexander taught me "true love" not by words but by practice.'[34]

Michitoshi faced a dilemma when he returned home for the Christmas break. His mother was a devout Christian and he was afraid that she would view his becoming a Bahá'í as betraying her. Seeking advice, he wrote to Agnes. Her answer proved to be illuminating:

> It has been a great joy for me to have met you and to share with you the Glorious Message for this New Day.
>
> I want you to know that to help and to teach others is my greatest privilege and joy, so you may ask of me whatever you wish. There is so much to share [with you] and so much to tell of our Glorious Faith, but the most essential thing is to be assured in one's heart that Baha'u'llah is the Promised One of all the past religions. He has come to fulfil what Christ and all the Prophets have promised, for this is the Promised Day of God. That is what Christ taught: that we must be 'born again'. To come into the Baha'i Faith is truly to be 'born again'
>
> Can I be of help to you in any way before you go home? I am ready to share or help. What you are doing for the blind is truly worship. The blind are my greatest joy.
>
> To grow spiritually we need to turn our hearts to God in prayer and for this Day we have many prayers written for us. Some have been translated into Japanese . . . If we learn these prayers by heart, then we can say them at any time. That was the first lesson I had was to learn: praying [from the] heart in order to grow and draw near to God through His Prophet.
>
> Today on this earth we have a great gift from God, that is a Guardian who is under God's unerring guidance, Shoghi Effendi, who lives in Haifa, the world Center of our Faith. It is through him we are directed and he is the instrument left to us to guide and direct the Baha'is throughout the world.[35]

When Michitoshi arrived at his mother's home, he told her of his 'change of course' and showed her Agnes's letter. To say the least, it

Agnes with Louise Bosch, one of her closest Bahá'í friends, c. 1948

Left to right: Agnes's cousin Maud Mansfield (nee Baldwin) Cook, Agnes's sister Mary Charlotte Alexander, and Agnes Alexander. Photo probably taken at Lahaina, Maui in 1943

Naw-Rúz 1948 at the home of Mrs Masako. Robert Imagire, who went to Japan in 1947 at the request of Shoghi Effendi, is standing on the left and Daiun Inouye is second left in the front row

*Lt Jacob
Davenport
and Barbara
Davenport with
Agnes Alexander,
1950*

*Robert Imagire, Sachiro
Fujita and Agnes Alexander,
23 May 1950, one of the
first photographs after Agnes
returned to Japan following
World War II*

Agnes Alexander, about 1950

*Agnes Alexander speaking at the Bahá'í Teaching
Conference in Japan, about 1955*

*Pioneers in Japan, 1955. Left to right: children in front: Foad Katirai, Vedad Momtazi
and Farzad Katirai; front row: Robert Imagire, Nehzat Imagire, Ata'ullah Moghbel, Pouran
Momtazi, Revzanieh Katirai; middle row: Yoshiko Morita, Behjat Momtazi, Abbas Momtazi,
Agnes Alexander, Eichu Kim; standing: Philip Marangella, Firouz Mohtadi, Yadullah Rafaat,
Parvis Momtazi, Abbas Katirai, unidentified, Lucille Webster, David Earl, Virginia Hamilton,
unidentified, Mahin Moghbel and Aziz Mohtadi*

The first Local Spiritual Assembly of the Bahá'ís of Kyoto, 1956. Left to right, seated: Jun Koyama, Masazo Odani, Agnes Alexander, Tokujiro Torii, Seiichiro Tsunemi; back row: Shizue Tsunemi, Ito Torii, Yoshiko Morita, Makoto Inaba

The marriage of Isao Sakamoto and Michitoshi Zenimoto, January 1956, the first Bahá'í marriage between Japanese Bahá'ís in Japan

was a tremendous shock to her. But she had always prayed that God would lead her sons according to His Will. Michitoshi told her his 'two Americans' story: 'One was an established dean of the Department of Christian Theology. A ruthless elite scholar who dominated the university. Another was a humble old American lady who rendered her infinite love to a nameless young boy.' His mother asked him to translate Agnes's letter and read it to her. At the end, she said 'If you think that it is the guidance of God, obey it.'[36]

When he returned to the University, he told Agnes about his mother's reaction. She asked if he would arrange for them to meet. In February, Agnes met Michitoshi's mother in Hiroshima:

> My mother was delighted to welcome Miss Alexander and we talked for long hours until midnight . . . [Agnes] stayed at my mother's house over the night.
>
> I have never forgotten what happened that night. [Because of] my poor, broken English, we did not have [the] means to cope with complicated subtle problems. It was truly a mysterious and miraculous event. Both mothers of mine could understand each other fully.
>
> My mother had no ability to speak English. Miss Alexander, too, had none in Japanese. However, they could communicate [with] each other fully. Their 'heart language' was more expressive than the language of tongue of the learn[e]d and more truthful than their word fluency . . .
>
> When Miss Alexander [left] for Kyoto . . . the follo[w]ing morning, my mother told her that her prayer was heard by God and she would entrust me [into] the hand[s] of Miss Alexander. And my mother [said] that she was content with the will of God. [37]

Michitoshi became a Bahá'í in February 1953 and then began attending a fireside at the Toriis' home. It was soon decided that they needed a prayer book in Japanese. Michitoshi wrote, 'We started translating English prayers into Japanese by Mr. Torii's guidance. Word by word, consulting with a dictionary, I found the proper Japanese with a dictionary and suggested [it] to examine [its] compatibility. Starting with the obligatory [prayers] several prayers were translated into Japanese within half a year.' The manuscript was sent to the Tokyo Local Spiritual Assembly for review. In 1955, a committee was formed, consisting of Dr David Earl, an American professor at Yamaguchi University, and an American pioneer, Tameo Hongo, a diplomat working at the Ministry of Foreign Affairs, and Michitoshi, who was working as a journalist. The effort of the Kyoto group resulted in the publication of the *Bahá'í Prayer Collection.*[38]

Ray Wooten remained one of Agnes's primary correspondents and on 5 March 1953 she answered his latest letter. She had connected Ray and Michitoshi:

> I am so happy that you and Zenimoto San are now in correspondence. He gave me a copy of the letter he wrote to you. You are his first American correspondent, that is, Baha'i. He is a very spiritual young man and really from the first was a believer. Now he is full fledged as we have gone over the Will and Testament. Perhaps I wrote you he said I was the first American he had spoken with in English. I feel my greatest work is now to give him all I can before I leave Kyoto to go to Tokyo and then sail from Yokohama on March 30th by way of Honolulu and then on to California and Chicago. God willing we will meet there . . .
>
> Zenimoto San asked me about you as he wanted to know you well. Isn't it wonderful how God guided him to hear of the Faith. He is teaching others already and growing himself. Yesterday he was with me for three hours. It is such a bounty to share with him and I try to help his English. He had learned English through the radio! He had a very spiritual mother who is a catholic but she wrote him to remain here (now is the vacation) and learn all he could of the Faith before I leave . . . What a future he will have before him as he is the first believer of Hiroshima such an important place that has suffered so mercilessly.[39]

Though he now accepted Bahá'u'lláh, Michitoshi still wondered about why God would permit war. On 2 September 1953, he wrote to the Bahá'í World Centre that he was a survivor of the atomic bomb. He was very surprised to receive a reply from the Guardian himself that resolved his dilemma about war. The Guardian's reply, written by Rúhíyyih Khánum, immediately opened his eyes:

Bahá'u'lláh wrote many, many years ago: 'The vitality of men's belief

326

in God in dying out in every land; nothing short of His wholesome medicine can ever restore it. The corrosion of ungodliness is eating into vitals of human society; what else but the Elixir of His potent Revelation can cleanse and revive it?'

This is the ebb of the tide. The Bahá'ís know that the tide will turn and come in, after mankind has suffered, with mighty waves of faith and devotion. The people will enter the Cause of God in troops, and the whole condition will change. The Bahá'ís see this new condition which will take place, as one on a mountain-top sees the first glimpse of the dawn, before others are aware of it; and it is toward that that the Bahá'ís must work.[40]

These words from the Guardian healed Michitoshi's troubled heart. He realized that God did not condone war. Wars were caused by people going against the commands of God.

Two Intercontinental Teaching Conferences

In January 1953, the Asian World Federation Congress held its meeting in Hiroshima and Agnes attended part of the event. She was invited to address one of the sessions and spoke about the Bahá'í plan for world order.[41]

Agnes then went to the Intercontinental Teaching Conference and National Convention in Wilmette, but getting there made her a bit notorious in Japan. She described what happened:

I was taking a steamer to America. I . . . [was] living in Kyoto, and I [boarded the steamer] in Kobe. And then I had a day in Yokohama. And I went up to Tokyo to see the American Consul. There was some business I had to do there. And it was a day that the Crown Prince was sailing. And . . . the streets were lined off. And when I left the American Consul I found that I couldn't go a straight route to take the train. We had to go way round about. And then, when I got to Yokohama, I couldn't go up to the steamers. I always usually did. They were all lined off. And people were only allowed to go a certain distance. And I saw the time was going short. And I had to make the steamer! My things were all on the steamer.

And I tried to get help, and I saw that they were going to take the gangplank up. And then a man offered his cart to take me, and he dashed me up! And the gangplank was taken up, but they put a board down in the baggage hold. And so I went on through the baggage hold! And all the time there was [live] radio. . . because that the Crown Prince going on the steamer – they were telling it. And it went all over Japan, the events that were happening. And then they said, 'Now, an elderly lady is going in the hold!' So, way down in Hiroshima, one of my friends heard this, and she said she thought it was Miss Alexander. So I became quite famous on the steamer.

Well, anyway, that also made me prestige – that I was known on the steamer. And then, of course, I let people know that I was a Bahá'í.[42]

After the Convention, Agnes remained in America for another three months, mostly in California. The spirit of the Ten Year Crusade was evident everywhere. Agnes noted that when Bahia and Robert Gulick were packing to pioneer to Africa, they received a letter from the Guardian with the word '<u>SOON</u>' underlined. [43] The 'soon' was because of Ella Bailey. The Gulicks took Ella Bailey with them in order that her last wish, to pioneer for Shoghi Effendi, could be fulfilled. The 88-year-old's dedication to the Faith resulted in her arriving at her pioneering post in Tripoli, Libya, and then passing away a month later. The Guardian declared her to be a martyr.[44]

Agnes was at Geyserville during the summer, but was preparing to leave for Honolulu on 20 August. The voyage, though, was only the beginning of her travel plans. The previous year, Shoghi Effendi had written to the Bahá'ís in Japan about the New Delhi Intercontinental Teaching Conference in October 1953, saying that he 'would be very happy if some from Japan would attend the Conference, as plans for Japan would be discussed there.'[45] Agnes could never pass up a suggestion from the Guardian – for her it was basically an order. After a couple delays, tickets were purchased to Honolulu on 28 August. She wrote that 'Then I went back to my sister's home and about an hour after a letter from our beloved Guardian confirming it.'[46]

Agnes received her next letter from Shoghi Effendi, this one written by Leroy Ioas on 30 September, before she went to the Conference. It said that 'The beloved Guardian is delighted that you are able to attend the Conference in New Delhi. He attaches the very greatest importance to this Conference, as it will be the first time that eight National Assemblies will have gathered together to work as one unit in the carrying forward of Baha'i work.' [47]

During the New Delhi Conference, many of the early pioneers spoke about their experiences in taking the Faith of Bahá'u'lláh to the far corners of the world. Obviously, that included Agnes. *The Bahá'í World* described her contribution:

> Then Miss Agnes Alexander told the friends that she was in Geneva, Switzerland, when World War I broke out and found herself without luggage and unable to cash her checks. On August 22, 1914, she received a letter from 'Abdu'l-Bahá telling her to go to Japan.
>
> 'Of course,' she said, 'I had no desire but to follow the Master's wish.' She explained how miraculously she was enabled to do so. After 'Abdu'l-Bahá's passing, Shoghi Effendi wrote a beautiful letter to the friends in Japan in which he stated:
>
> 'As attendant and secretary of 'Abdu'l-Bahá for well nigh two years after the termination of the Great War, I recall so vividly the radiant joy that transfigured His face whenever I opened before Him your supplications as well as those of Miss Agnes Alexander. What promises He gave us all regarding the future of the Cause in that land at the close of almost every supplication I read to Him. Let me state straightaway, the most emphatic, the most inspiring of them all. These are His very words that still keep ringing in my ears: "Japan will turn ablaze! Japan is endowed with the most remarkable capacity for the spread of the Cause of God . . ."' [48]

Agnes herself wrote little of the Conference, or at least we have little correspondence by her from this historic event, but in a letter she wrote to Doris in November she said:

> Besides the message from our beloved Guardian which Mr. Remey, as his representative brought to us, the Guardian sent in all four cablegrams. The second one directed all the Hands of the Cause present to disperse after the conference to different parts of the Asian countries and our beloved brother, Mr. Khadem, to Malaya and JAPAN. He has come and gone already, but his spirit will remain with the friends. In all he was nine days in Tokyo and five in Osaka

where there are now three Persian families settled, so darling, things must progress in this wonderful land where God in His bounty prepared me to work.

Here in Tokyo we have another Persian Baha'i who has left his family and come here to serve, Mr. Y.[Yadullah] Rafaat . . . Mr. Rafaat has bought a Japanese house so that it can be a Center in this city; also the brother, Mr. Momtazi in Osaka has done the same. Now already there are two Baha'i centers!

I remained here for Mr. Khadem's visit as there were so many I knew to arrange for him to meet, but now I am going to Kyoto to reside, God willing, although I do not know where I can stay, only for a short time, that is, in a hospital room of Mr. Torii's brother-in-law, a surgeon. But dear ones, pray for me for we can all help each other through our prayers.[49]

Hand of the Cause Zikrullah Khadem tried to meet as many Bahá'ís in Japan as possible personally, and in this Agnes was invaluable.[50]

After Mr Khadem left, Agnes wrote that she had returned to Kyoto and 'I have taken a little room here but do not eat in the hotel. I do what I can in my room and then go to a Japanese restaurant outside.'[51]

Auxiliary Board member

At Riḍván 1954, the Guardian announced the formation of the Auxiliary Boards to aid the Hands of the Cause with their duties of propagation and protection of the Faith. Boards were appointed for Africa, America, Asia, Australia and Europe. Agnes was one of the seven appointed to the Asiatic Board.[52] Her area of service expanded and she received four letters from the Guardian, three of which were about her duties:

The Guardian has been greatly pleased with the manner in which the Faith has been spreading in Japan. He sincerely hopes that during the second year of the Crusade it will spread even more rapidly, and to more centers.

The future of the Faith in Japan is very great. It now depends upon the Bahá'ís to teach, to develop the Faith in a city, and then move on to a new area. If this is continued diligently, it will bring the light of guidance to all parts of Japan in a very short time.[53]

He (the Guardian) was very happy to hear of the progress of the work in Japan; and he greatly appreciates the fact that you have returned once more to that country, so dear to your heart, and where the Master was so eager for you to serve.

He wishes to assure you that he will pray for Mr. Mori, and that before he passes from this world, his spirit may be illumined, and he may come to accept Bahá'u'lláh.

The Guardian was also very pleased to hear that the Momtazis have given their home as a Bahá'í hall and Hazíra, and hopes that this will open the way for the foundation of a firm Spiritual Assembly in the city.[54]

Mr Mori was Tsuto Mori, who was dying. He declared his Faith just before he died. The next letters from the Guardian referred to him: 'He was glad to hear Mr. Mori died a firm Bahá'í and that his funeral was in itself a service to the Faith. He will pray for his soul, and for his dear family.'[55]

Agnes responded to her appointment to the Auxiliary Board in a letter to Shoghi Effendi written in Hiroshima on 12 May 1954. She expressed her joy and thankfulness for the appointment to the Auxiliary Board, gratefully giving credit to her forefathers who carried the message of Christ to Hawaii. She noted that her appointment had given her fresh inspiration to serve.[56]

Agnes's final letter of 1954 from the Guardian again addressed her duties on the Auxiliary Board 'He hopes that, in your capacity as a member of the auxiliary Board of the Hands in Asia, that you will be able to create ever greater unity and enthusiasm amongst the Japanese friends, and the other believers in Japan.'[57]

As a 79-year-old Auxiliary Board member, Agnes now found herself traveling more often and to more places. She and Michitoshi Zenimoto went to Sydney, Australia, sometime in March 1955. Agnes visited Brisbane on the way. Before leaving for Sydney, Agnes moved yet again, though still in Kyoto.[58] On 1 March, the Guardian sent her another letter which said that 'The progress of the Faith in Japan is a source of great joy to the Guardian. It is truly making rapid strides among these keen-minded and receptive people.'[59]

On 16 April, Agnes went to Korea for three weeks at the invitation of 'the boys in the service' to help them with their teaching efforts.[60]

Initially, she had hoped to form a Local Spiritual Assembly before she left, but that proved not to be possible. Upon her return, she noted: 'In time there surely will be an Assembly in Seoul, but not this year.'[61]

Agnes had to make a trip to Honolulu, not for the Faith, but to deal with her house there, which had been much neglected for a number of years. She flew there on 19 June. In a letter to Ramona Brown before her departure, she wrote that she would

> fly to Honolulu where I am needed to see about my house which has been neglected badly. Now is the only time when I feel I can go, and I have the inner guidance that it is His plan which gives me strength. Then I shall be back again to attend the World Religions Conference in Tokyo to which I have an invitation. After that comes the N.T. [National Teaching] Committee meeting and then the All Japan Esperanto Congress in which there is a Baha'i sectional meeting. In September we are having a Conference of Baha'is and some will come from Korea, Formosa and Macau, and perhaps Hong Kong which is not in my assignment. Miss [Charlotte] Linfoot wrote she would come as the N.S.A. representative. It will be a wonderful time. In October for eight days there will be held the first Asian Blind Conference in Tokyo and Mr. Torii is working on the plan. 12 nations will be represented from the Asian countries. Isn't it a wonderful world when you are a Baha'i![62]

In Honolulu, Agnes wrote, 'I left my home in Honolulu to be sold, as I felt I must get back to the work here . . . Of course I shall not be need-ing it, as my work is here & there would be no object to get a home again, but it is necessary that I go to Honolulu in order to dispose of the things . . . these are such important days for the Faith in Japan.'[63] She returned to Japan by the beginning of August.

The next big event was the Tokyo Conference of World Religions in Tokyo, which started the day she arrived in Tokyo from Honolulu. Agnes had an official part in the Conference, and the Baha'is were well represented with three official delegates: David Earl, representing the National Spiritual Assembly of the United States, Philip Marangella, and Agnes. Noureddin Momtazi, the official Baha'i delegate, unfortu-nately was ill and not able to attend. The Conference was divided into several sections and David Earl was elected chairman of the discussion of 'War and Peace', while Philip Marangella chaired the section on 'Religion and Society.'[64]

The following month, on 23–25 September 1955, the Bahá'ís held their first Asia Regional Teaching Conference in the Palace Hotel at Nikko. This was a former summer home of the Japanese Emperor and included the famous Toshogu Shrine and its surrounding temples and was a very popular tourist destination. The Shrine had been built in the 1600s and today is a World Heritage Site. The Conference was jointly sponsored by the Asia Teaching Committee and the Local Spiritual Assembly of Tokyo, its first major project as an administrative body. The primary goal of the Conference was to 'expedite teaching plans that would bring into existence a sufficient number of new assemblies by April 21, 1956, to ensure the election of the National Spiritual Assembly of Japan in 1957'. The second goal was to 'give added impetus to the spread of the Faith in all the nearby countries'. These nearby countries who sent delegates were Formosa, Korea, Macao, Hong Kong, Guam, and the Caroline Islands. Delegates came as well from all parts of Japan.[65] *Bahá'í News* described the event:

An especial bounty was the early arrival also of Mr. and Mrs. Khádem and Miss Talia Haddah, whose loving charm made a deep impression on everyone, Bahá'ís and non-Bahá'ís alike.

A pre-conference public meeting in the Tokyo Ḥaẓíratu'l-Quds drew such a large attendance that there was scarcely one square inch of the entrance way that was not covered by footwear that was removed in Japanese fashion before entering the main room. Here everyone had a foretaste of the spirit that was to prevail in Nikko for the next few days.

The following day almost an entire railway coach was filled with the Bahá'ís who traveled by rail from Tokyo to Nikko through what is perhaps the neatest and most picturesque countryside in the entire world. At the station in Nikko the friends were greeted by large placards bearing the words: 'Alláh'u'Abhá – Bahá'í World Faith – Asia Teaching Conference,' and directions for reaching the hotel . . .

Special mention must be made of the presence and participation of two of the very early pioneers in Japan, Miss Agnes Alexander and Mr. Sachiro Fujita, who spoke often of the high hopes of 'Abdu'l-Bahá and of the Guardian for Japan . . .[66]

Mr Khádem and some of the visiting Bahá'ís remained in Japan for three weeks following the Conference and visited many Japanese cities. In Hiroshima, they met an especially receptive soul:

> In Hiroshima, the city that has suffered so much at the hands of man, Mr. Khádem, Mr. N. Momtazi and Miss Agnes Alexander found, in a meeting with an English conversation club, a young man so enthusiastic that he, too, spent two whole days with them, accepted the Faith completely, visited the Bahá'ís in Kobe a few days later, and returned to open a Bahá'í center in his new home where a dozen or so friends from Kansai and some thirty Hiroshima students heard Mr. Khádem and inaugurated a program of weekly firesides. One of the believers writes: 'Thus, the situation in Hiroshima changed from difficult to very favourable in less than three weeks.'[67]

Also in April 1956, Agnes wrote to Ramona Brown and summarized what she had done after returning from Honolulu:

> After the Religionists Conference I came to Kyoto & attended an Esperanto Congress for two days in Osaka. Then again to Tokyo for the wonderful Nikko Baha'i Conference. Then back here & again to Tokyo for the Far East Blind Conference. So you see how my time was taken up, but all for the glorious Cause!
>
> In Tokyo the last time, I met a glorious Baha'i lady who was returning from two years in Africa where she left 45 believers in Pretoria, Mrs Bula [Mott] Stewart. We will never be separated in heart, & now she is on her way to Hawaii to go to Molokai where there are no Baha'is, as the beloved Guardian asked for at least one Baha'i on each island as part of the Crusade. The Honolulu friends have not dispersed as they were asked to do, but others have gone to Hilo & Kauai. Bula is a brave-hearted radiant Baha'i!
>
> The last of December I returned to Kyoto & have been here in this house ever since, as it was so important that Kyoto have an LSA this year. Now that is assured as there are nine & so my heart is at ease. Two of our Iranian Baha'is [Mr Mohtadi and his wife] made the pilgrimage to Haifa & have brought back wonderful news from our beloved Guardian that Japan will become another Africa, and that now is the time to spread the Faith here. We are to have an

N.S.A. next year. Isn't that wonderful! Whatever is God's Plan can always be fulfilled. Japan will then be the N.S.A. for surrounding countries as Formosa, Macau, Hong Kong, & others which are now red [Communist].[68]

In the same month, Agnes wrote to Doris Ebbert, saying that:

> We have wonderful news concerning Japan. An Iranian couple [Mohtadis] have been in Haifa & our beloved Guardian told them many things. The greatest is that the Faith will now spread in this country & next year we will have a NSA. Here in Kyoto I have been concentrating on the ones who will make the LSA in a few days. There are nine. When we have the NSA, some surrounding countries will be under it as Hong Kong, Macau, Formosa, Hainan, Sakalin Is. These are indeed great days to be living.[69]

Agnes also told Doris about why she had sold her house in Honolulu, saying 'That time is passed & now my life is so important here.'[70]

In September, the Japanese Bahá'ís held a Teaching Conference organized by the National Teaching Committee of Japan in Kyoto. A total of 58 adults and 15 children attended. With the impending election of the first Japanese National Spiritual Assembly the next Riḍván, the Conference's primary agenda was to educate the Japanese Bahá'ís about the Covenant and Baha'i Administration. Agnes presented a talk on 'Teaching in Japan'.[71]

A trip to Taiwan

On 11 and 12 November, Agnes was in Taiwan for their first All-Taiwan Baha'i Teaching Conference held in Tainan. She was delighted to be reunited with the Suleimanis, pioneers to Taiwan she had first met in Shanghai in 1923.[72] Agnes arrived two weeks before the Conference to visit the Bahá'ís and 'brought great inspiration to the friends, both by her presence and her participation in the program, which was designed principally to aid in increasing the understanding of the believers of the institutions of the Faith and of the World Spiritual Crusade'. Reporters for two local newspapers attended a tea at the Conference on the second afternoon and 'learned a great deal from Miss Alexander about the history of the Faith and its teachings. Both promised to publish articles on the Faith in their respective papers.'[73]

Agnes's service as an Auxiliary Board member had changed her focus from the raising up of individual Bahá'ís to raising up Local and National Spiritual Assemblies and inspiring the local Bahá'ís to do the primary teaching. Her duties had taken her to Sydney and Brisbane, Australia, Korea and Taiwan, as well as to major Conferences in Tokyo, Kyoto, Osaka and Nikko. She was being prepared for her next station.

18

HAND OF THE CAUSE OF GOD

1957–1965

On 25 March 1957, Hand of the Cause of God George Townshend died in Dublin, Ireland. The Guardian always replaced a Hand of the Cause with a new Hand, so two days after Mr Townshend's death, Shoghi Effendi sent the following cable to the Bahá'ís of the world:

> Inform Hands and national assemblies of the Baha'i world of the passing into Abhá Kingdom of Hand of Cause George Townshend, indefatigable, highly talented, fearless defender of the Faith of Bahá'u'lláh.
>
> Agnes Alexander, distinguished pioneer of the Faith, elevated to rank of Hand of Cause. Confident her appointment will spiritually reinforce teaching campaign simultaneously conducted in north, south and heart of Pacific Ocean.[1]

Agnes Alexander, an 81-year-old woman living in Japan, received a personal telegram from Shoghi Effendi that appointed the utterly humble Agnes to something inconceivable. The Guardian's telegram to Agnes on 29 March confirmed the cable to the Bahá'í world: 'Gladly announce your elevation rank Hand Cause. Praying further enrichment record historic services. Shoghi Haifa.'[2]

After the initial shock of being given such an amazing honour, Agnes reacted in a very surprising, but for her a very typical, way. In a letter, she wrote:

> Probably you have heard by now that a great new spiritual life has come to me, that is, to be a Hand of the Cause. It is something I could not have dreamed of, but God works in mysterious ways, and

337

this is His Plan, or it could not come, so I leave all and turn to our beloved Guardian, knowing that he will guide me, and if I keep in the right direction, I cannot fail with his prayers. It makes the beloved Guardian seem so much nearer now.[3]

In a letter to Ramona Brown on 12 April, Agnes further explained her feelings at being raised to the rank of a Hand of the Cause:

Two weeks ago I received a Telegram which came from Haifa, through Wilmette. For several days I had had a very great happiness and felt something was happening in the spiritual world. The Telegram at first I was dazed and it took a little time for me to comprehend it for as you can imagine such a thing could never have entered my thought, but it came from the beloved Guardian and under his guidance, so that as I turned to him, I could not fail . . .

It was March 29th, when I received the telegram. When the friends in Japan learned of it such love and telegrams, letters and cards came to me. Truly a great wave of love & unity seemed to be released in this land. How mysteriously God works!

Now I have our beloved Guardian only to 'turn' to and it is such a great bounty which one cannot express. To be close to him and follow his unerring guidance.[4]

To Agnes, if one sincerely tried to serve the Faith, then everything was the Will of God. This allowed her to take everything in her stride – even being elevated to the rank of Hand of the Cause of God.

The Guardian followed up on 14 April with what turned out to be his 94th and final letter to Agnes. Addressing her duties and his support, he wrote:

He is confident that you will discharge your duties as a Hand with the same characteristics of loyalty and devotion, and in the same spirit of service, that you have always shown in your Bahá'í life, and which has entitled you to this great honor.

It will no doubt be a source of encouragement to the believers that they now have two Hands of the Cause, one in the South and one in the North Pacific; and, in view of the remarkable spread of the Faith throughout that whole region, your services will be of much help in stimulating and reassuring the friends, and encouraging them to arise and constantly extend the outposts of the Faith.

He will remember you in the Holy Shrines, and pray that you may be strengthened, guided and blessed in this new form of service to the Cause you love so dearly.

In his own hand, he added, 'May the Almighty, Whose Cause you have served so long, so nobly and so devotedly, shower His manifold blessings upon you, and aid you, now that you occupy so lofty a position in the ranks of the followers of His Faith, to enrich the record of your distinguished and truly historic services to its institutions. Your true brother, Shoghi.'[5]

Agnes's first official duty as a Hand of the Cause was to be the Guardian's representative, along with fellow Hand Jalál <u>Kh</u>ázeh, at the Japanese National Convention on 27–29 April 1957 in Tokyo that elected the first Regional Spiritual Assembly of North-East Asia. This must have been an extremely emotional day for Agnes. Over 40 years had passed since she had first stepped ashore from the steamer in Kobe, Japan. It had been a long and difficult process, but there, just after Riḍván 1957, was the goal of her heart – and she was a member of it in addition to being a Hand:

Without doubt, the Guardian's messages were the highlights of this historic convention. The teaching session which preceded it; the prayers in four languages with which each session opened; the stimulation and inspiration which radiated from the Hands of the Cause, Djalál <u>Kh</u>ázeh and Miss Agnes Alexander; the anointment by the former of 80 believers present with attar of rose sent from the Guardian; the roll call of the delegates; the formation of the new Assembly and the election of its officers; the splendid publicity in Japan's leading newspapers; the thoughtful deliberations, and the presentation of gifts inaugurating the National Fund – all were significant phases of the convention, but it rose to its greatest heights when the two messages from Haifa were read and discussed . . .

There was a special moment of reverence as the Hand of the Cause, Mr. Djalál <u>Kh</u>ázeh, touched each of those present with the attar of rose, saying as he did so that he was spreading the fragrance of love from the Guardian, and also the fragrance of the Cause all over the area.

Then he offered his sincere congratulations to 'the daughter of the Kingdom,' Miss Agnes Alexander, upon her elevation to the rank of Hand of the Cause, and he repeated that part of a Tablet written by 'Abdu'l-Bahá wherein He said of Miss Alexander: 'If she had founded an empire, it would not be as great as this empire, for this is eternal glory.' . . .

The members of the new Spiritual Assembly and the officers whom they elected are: William Maxwell, chairman; Hiroyaso Takano, vice-chairman; Yadullah Rafaat, corresponding secretary; Mrs. Barbara Sims, recording secretary; Noureddin Momtazi, treasurer; Miss Agnes Alexander, Philip Marangella, Ata'ullah Moghbel, and Michitoshi Zenimoto. The election officers elected at the opening session, were Philip Marangella, chairman and Barbara Sims, secretary.[6]

On 5 June, Agnes wrote to Ramona again, telling her the latest news. She noted that since her elevation to a Hand of the Cause 'I have received so many telegrams & let[t]ers from the five continents and all are so happy. In mysterious ways God brings us all together in love!'[7] Agnes then quoted Shoghi Effendi's personal comment at the end of his last letter in awed devotion.

Between 28 and 30 September, Agnes participated in the first Bahá'í summer school held in Korea, though maybe not in the way she had initially expected:

Anticipated by three preceding winter and summer conferences in that same city, the first Bahá'í Summer School of Korea took place in Kwangju, Korea . . . having been called into being by the beloved Guardian in his message to the first Bahá'í Convention of North East Asia as one of the goals of the Six-Year Plan for that area.

Exceeding both in the depth of the teaching offered and in the maturity of the believers attending any previous gathering of Bahá'ís in Korea, the session began on a serious note when early the first day Hand of the Cause of God Agnes Alexander slipped and fell on the stone steps of the meeting place, spraining her ankle. But the prayers of the following morning brought unity as well as healing, and the school continued with an ever-deepening tone.[8]

Agnes, of course, did not mention her injury to any of her correspondents.

The passing of Shoghi Effendi

Agnes's reaction to the passing of the Guardian, her beloved Shoghi Effendi, is either not recorded or is lost. Her reaction to being at that first Conclave of the Hands in late 1957, when they spent a week working out a way to carry the Faith of Bahá'u'lláh forward without an infallible Guardian, we do have – and it is the steadfastness and faith in the Revelation of Bahá'u'lláh that comes through intensely. There were probably tears, but to Agnes, things happened according to the Will of God. She wrote:

> How wonderful it was that from the five continents 26 Hands of the Cause could meet on such short notice in Haifa. Truly a miracle!
>
> Such an assurance I feel that the nine Hands in Haifa are under God's care & protection. This is His Cause and He never leaves His children.
>
> I had felt assured myself that there could not be a Will, as our beloved Guardian had no one he could appoint, and he had told us that the Will and Testament of the Master was for the ages to come. So I had no feeling, as some express it, of shock.[9]

After the Conclave, Agnes wrote up her notes about that amazing week when the host of the Hands of the Cause charted a path to the end of the Guardian's Ten Year Crusade using all the route markers he himself had set:

> It is my great bounty to try and tell you of the wonderful historical Conference which I have attended of the Hands of the Cause of God. As I will not be able to see you all in person soon, I shall try and write.
>
> On November 11th, I had a call from Mr Rafaat in Tokyo to me in Kyoto just after the noon hour stating that a cable had come calling for all the Hands of the Cause to meet in Haifa on November 17th.
>
> This was breath-taking, but dear Mr. Rafaat said he would do everything for me and the next morning I left for Tokyo where it was necessary for me to see the Immigration Office. There in stating the purpose of my visit to Haifa the name of our most beloved

Guardian was given on the papers which had to be made out. Then when I went to the Israel Legation, I was told Americans did not need a visa to go to Israel, but God had a purpose in my visit for the three women in the office heard of the Faith and saw the picture of the Shrine in Haifa, etc.

The next morning at 8 a.m. dear Mr. Rafaat was here to accompany me to the Air France plane for which he had made all arrangements for my ticket. This plane to Tel-Aviv only goes once a week, so it was necessary for me to take it.

At the first stop in Manila, there in the station I met fellow travelers to Haifa, the Hands of the Cause, Mr. Collis Featherstone and Mother Dunn who was accompanied by Mrs. Marjorie Bowes. From there we traveled together in the same compartment. At Karachi a group of Baha'is met us and we had a happy visit with them. Then again in Teheran many Baha'is came to greet us, among whom were three Hands of the Cause who also were going to Haifa, Mr. Khazeh, Mr. Vargha [Varqá], and Mr. Furuthan [Furútan]. It was a great thrill for me to really be in Iran the land of Baha'u'llah! Mr. Khazeh said that 5000 would have come to meet us if they had not been stopped, for things in Iran were not well for the Baha'is at that time. How happy it was that six Hands of the Cause could travel together to Haifa from there!

The next day, Saturday, Nov. 16th, Ruhiyyih Khanum arranged that all Hands should meet at the Shrine of the Bab, after which we entered the Eastern Pilgrim house where she told us of the last days of our beloved Guardian, a very precious account.

Sunday, the 17th, was a free day, but on Monday the memorial gatherings were held in Bahji in the building adjoining the Mansion. Ruhiyyih Khanum conducted the one for the women while the men held a separate meeting. Many tearful Iranian women had gathered all showing their great sorrow. Their prayers were chanted and recited.

On Tuesday, Nov. 19th., the Conference began in Bahji Mansion in the central hall where no one could disturb us. Arrangements were made so that all the men could remain in the Mansion during the seven days of the Conference. Only Mrs. Collins, Mr. Remey, myself, and a few times Ruhiyyih Khanum returned to Haifa for the night. Meals were served in the [b]uilding adjoining the Mansion.

From nine o'clock until afternoon, and sometimes evening, the Conference continued with breaks for luncheon and a few times tea in the afternoon.

The great miracle of the Conference was that the 26 Hands of the Cause had come together from the five continents on such short notices [missing only Corinne True who was too frail to travel to Haifa]. From the U.S. came Mr. Horace Holley and Paul Haney; from England, John Ferraby, the Sec'y. of the N.S.A. of the British Isles, also Hasan Balyuzi, who is an Afnan and related to our beloved Guardian. From Germany came Dr. Hermann Grossmann and Dr. Adelbert Muhlsch[l]egal; from Iran, Gen. Ala'i, Mr. Samandari, Ali [A]kbar Furutan, Mr. Z. Khadem, Ali M. Vargha, Jalal Khazeh; from Italy, Ugo Giachery; from Arabia Mr. A. Q. Faizi; from Indonesia Dr. Muhajir; from Japan, Agnes Alexander; from Africa, Mr. Banani, Enoch Olinga, William Sears and John Robarts. From Australia, Mother Dunn and Collis Featherstone. [The other four Hands served in the Holy Land: Rúḥíyyih Khánum, Mason Remey, Leroy Ioas and Milly Collins.]

Personally I had realized that there could not be a Will as there was no one the beloved Guardian could appoint in his place as Guardian of the Faith, and the Will and Testament of 'Abdu'l-Baha, the beloved Guardian had told us was the guide for the ages to come.

In the central hall of Bahji tables were arranged. At the front table our Beloved [R]uhiyyih, who guided the Conference through to the end, sat with Mrs. Collins on her left and Mason Remey on her right. Next to Mason sat Leroy Ioas, and next to Mrs. Collins sat Mr. [G]iachery. Then on either side of two long tables and at the end of the table, sat all the Hands of the Cause from the five continents.

The first two days of the Conference there was discussion as different ones expressed their ideas or feelings. It had been ascertained that the Beloved Guardian had left no Will. The third day the plan for enlarging the International Council [actually the Hands resident in the Holy Land] to nine members to live in Haifa as recorded in the Will & Testament of Abdu'l-Baha, Par. 19, was decided upon. First, our Beloved Chairman, Ruhiyyih Khanum eliminated from the list of the Hands those who were needed especially where they were located, then from the remaining number through consultation, the five hands were unanimously decided upon. Mr. Khadem to take Mr. Furutan's place in Teheran released him to remain in Haifa. Dear Dr. Muhlschlegel, who has a wife and child to support said he would try to find work in Haifa. Hasan Balyuzi, who has five boys from the age of seven, said he would try and solve his problem, but it might take several months. The other two, Paul Haney and our dear Mr. Khazeh answered the call. Our Beloved Chairman felt that at this time it was most important to have five remain in Haifa, and for those who could not immediately remain substitutes were arranged.

We were not encouraged to take notes during the Conference. Each day we all prayed together in the room where the Glory of God passed away. Such a Conference has never, nor can it ever again be held in the world! Every morning before beginning the Conference we prayed in the most Holy Shrine.

Our most beloved Amatu'l-Baha Ruhiyyih Khanum told us many things which are helpful to know. It was a great sorrow to our Beloved Guardian that he could not make a Will because he had no children and all the Aghsan were Covenant Breakers. This he spoke of many times to Ruhiyyih Khanum. She told us, how in solving problems, he always started with the simplest things. He was guided each day in making the garden by God, step by step. The door of interpretation is closed, she said. Then our wonderful Hand of the Cause, Mr. Samandari said that Baha'u'llah had said the person who tries to interpret is not My follower.

It was suggested that the pilgrims who were expecting to visit Haifa, but now could not, might give the money to help the Faith. Ruhiyyih Khanum told us the Beloved Guardian had answered a pilgrim who asked whether it was better to give the money to the Faith rather than to visit Haifa and he replied that it was meritorious to give the money to the Faith. (We know that at the present time work at the world center has become so important that it would not be possible to have pilgrims, but that time may come again in the future.)

Ruhiyyih Khanum said that the Beloved Guardian wished the Hands and Auxiliary Board Members from Now on to exercise the utmost vigilance and consider it their first duty to guard the Fold, to carefully, with the assistance of the Board Members and in close cooperation with the various Western H[e]misphere NSA's, to watch over the Faith and observe, particularly in the North American continent, the activities of the external & internal enemies and ascertain whenever possible their movements.

Someone said we must remain completely in the framework of the Will & Testament. One of the Hands said that the Institution of the Guardianship exists in the plan and institutions given to us by Shoghi Effendi. The work of the International Council and the Hands has been given us.

Samandari told us that the last message of the Beloved Guardian is his Will. The house for the Hands will be built in Haifa . . . Consultation only about things not written down. The nine Hands appointed to do the work of the Beloved Guardian must have nothing else to do. They must be born again. Our sword is UNITY.

Beloved Friends, I have tried to share a little with you that it may draw us all nearer together and that we may become as one Soul in many bodies![10]

Agnes stayed in the Holy Land until mid-December. Writing to Ramona Brown at that time, she said that 'I hope in a few days to be in Kyoto. I have delayed here, but all is in God's Hands. I expect you have news of the wonderful Conference in Bahjí from others. I wrote for the Friends in these parts. As the Hand of the Cause, Samandari said, our sword is UNITY. This will bring happiness to our beloved Guardian who gave his all for us.'[11]

Moving forward without the Guardian

Much of the Bahá'í world struggled with grief from the passing of the Guardian, but not Agnes. Even though she had always been very close to him, her continuous optimism shone forth:

These are wonderful days we are privileged to live and spread the message! Our Beloved Guardian is now freed from his cares here and is very near to us all. I have felt this more & more recently. As we are commanded in the Will & Testament to 'turn' to Shoghi Effendi, now more than ever we can find strength in this.

As for myself, I KNOW that I am here because it is God's plan. And when He so wills, then the next step will be shown, so I have no care but to 'turn' and do my best to serve.[12]

In January 1956, before the passing of the Guardian, Agnes had been in Osaka to attend the wedding of 25-year-old Michitoshi and 23-year-old Isao Zenimoto. Isao's name, normally a boy's name, meant 'meritorious service' and was given to her before she was born in the old Japanese Samurai tradition by her father, who was hoping for a boy. Michitoshi wrote that:

> Our marriage [was] the first Baha'i ceremony between Japanese believers. At the Feast day (January 18th) in 1956, the wedding ceremony was held at Amagasaki Baha'i Center. The ceremony was so simple. Those who attended were including Miss Alexander, several Iranian pioneers, and our parents and our relatives only.
>
> Later an uncle of my wife used to say 'your marriage ceremony was best of all that I ever attended filled with pure spirits'. He wasn't baha'i [sic] but [was] moved so much. Without a doubt, that atmosphere was created by Baha'is [who] attended. It was really spiritual, indeed.

All the parents were expecting a traditional Japanese wedding, including a traditional bridal dress. The young couple, however, adopted more western dress because 'a New Age had come'. Afterwards, the parents 'blessed us in one voice, "It was the best wedding ceremony we ever saw".'[13]

Now, on her return to Japan following the Conclave of the Hands of the Cause, on New Year's Day 1958 Agnes was staying with Michotoshi and his wife in Osaka. Michitoshi wrote that 'Miss Alexander stayed for a few days with us at my house in New Year holidays. It was really the happiest and the most blessed days for us.'[14]

Agnes's living arrangements were still a problem. On 2 January, she was again house-hunting when the place she had been living was converted for the use of medical patients.[15]

The second set of Intercontinental Teaching Conferences were held in 1958, according to the Guardian's plan. Unlike 1953, Agnes was not just another participant. This time, she was a Hand of the Cause and one of those charged with completing the Ten Year Crusade. She attended the Conferences in Sydney, Australia, between 21 and 24 March and in Singapore from 21 to 29 September. In Sydney, Agnes was joined by Hands Clara Dunn, Mason Remey, Collis Featherstone and Zikrullah Khadem. On the last day of the Conference, Agnes spoke to those gathered at 'the epoch-making Intercontinental Conference in Sydney':

> She told of the potential spiritual brotherhood between Japan and Australia. It was through her inspiration that National Assembly member Michitoshi Zenimoto, a native Japanese who had been a casualty in the atomic blast of Hiroshima, was enabled to accompany her to this Conference. In a letter to Miss Alexander, Hand of the Cause Collis Featherstone had pointed out this realization of the Guardian's wish that someday the Australian and Japanese friends would invite each other to their homes had come true when Mr. Zenimoto became a guest in the homes of friends in numerous Australian communities.[16]

Nine Hands, including Agnes, attended the Conference in Singapore. The Conference had initially been planned for Jakarta, Indonesia, but unwise publicity by a few Bahá'ís on the planning committee created an uproar and the whole thing had to be moved to Singapore.[17] The Conference was held between 27 and 29 September 1958 and Agnes spoke of the development of the Faith in Japan, noting that there were eight local assemblies and the Regional Spiritual Assembly of North East Asia, which embraced six countries. Agnes said that the Guardian had called the National Spiritual Assembly of Japan the spiritual North Pole of the Pacific, and Australia the spiritual South Pole, and had instructed them to work together as the axis for teaching work in the area.[18]

Between the two big Conferences, Agnes lost a mirror, attended the Regional Convention in Tokyo, and participated in the second Japanese Bahá'í Summer School. The mirror was one Agnes left in Hong Kong. She was very detached from most material things, but not all. On 6 April, she wrote to Mamie Seto in Hong Kong about that mirror:

> You will have discovered that I left my hand mirror and two combs for the hair on your bureau.
>
> As I can get along without them for the present just wait until you come here or otherwise. The mirror I have carried with me every where since 1946 when I was in the apartment which had been our dear Imogene [Emogene] Hoagg's in Charleston, S. Carolina. The mirror belongs to dear Imogene so I have an attachment to it.[19]

Agnes's work as a Hand of the Cause and member of the Regional Spiritual Assembly kept her very busy. One of her concerns was maintaining the Local Spiritual Assembly of Kyoto, where she lived. Shortly before Riḍván, a young man declared and the Assembly was assured. But since there were only nine Bahá'ís, it also meant that she would be on that Assembly as well as a Hand and a member of the Regional Assembly.[20]

On 25 April, Agnes and Auxiliary Board member William Maxwell participated in the Convention to elect the Regional Spiritual Assembly of the North-East Pacific. On the final day of the Convention, Agnes talked about the importance of the Intercontinental Conference in Sydney and the spiritual connection between Japan and Australia as the two poles of the Faith in the Pacific.[21]

Between 29 and 31 August 1958, the Japanese held their second summer school at Gohra (now Gora), in the mountains not far from Mt. Fuji. Agnes spoke on the 'The Guardian and the Institutions of the Faith', and then teamed up with Michitoshi Zenimoto to give a talk about 'What is Prayer?'[22]

In mid-October, Agnes went to Taiwan for their three-day summer school in Taipei. The focus of the school was the Bahá'í Administrative Order and Agnes's primary talk was about 'The Will and Testament of 'Abdu'l-Bahá, and the Guardian'.[23]

Agnes's problems with accommodation continued in 1959. Between May and July, she ended up staying in the National Centre in Tokyo. Barbara Sims has written, 'She loved to say her prayers before the sacred cloth sent to the Haẓíratu'l-Quds by the Guardian.'[24]

The travels of a Hand

On 23 June 1959, Agnes wrote to Ramona Brown saying that she had been very busy travelling and that she had attended the annual Japanese conference for the blind:

> The most wonderful thing I can tell you is that I was speaking at the All Blind yearly meeting and our blind Mr. Torii was translating, it was taken by Television and was seen throughout Japan. Also it was taken in the Radio. The talk was short, but God confirmed it and I have felt such a feeling for the 400 blind who had gathered from the different parts of Japan and heard the name 'Baha'i,' for I started

by saying first I had known Mr. Torii for 40 years, and then that I was a Baha'i.[25]

On one trip, she ended up without one of her bags. Bill Smits was apparently to go with her, but at the train station, Agnes mentioned that she would like to have a newspaper, so Bill had run off to find her one. Unfortunately, the train had been about to leave and their car was one of the farthest away from where she left Bill. She barely managed to get to her seat before it left, leaving Bill and her second bag standing on the platform. When she wrote to him about it, she noted, 'I can get along until I go to Tokyo without it. I am waiting for a room in the International House from the 3rd to the 9th [August] when I expect to fly to Honolulu.' Since she wrote Bill's letter on the day before her birthday, she added, 'When the sun goes down, I shall be 84 years old, but the real age is from the time one becomes a Baha'i.'[26] In those years, she was 58.

On 9 August, Agnes flew from Tokyo to Honolulu to 'represent my generation at a family wedding'. From Honolulu, she continued to Berkeley to visit her sister, Mary, who had long been ill. In a letter to Ramona, she wrote that after Berkeley she was going to the annual Conclave of the Hands at the end of October: 'I am going on around the world, and know in my heart that it is the Plan of God for me at this time. So, dear, I shall go from here on Sept. 9th, to Chicago for 5 days, and then fly to London where I will be Sept. 15 to 22nd. From there to Paris for a few days, and then Germany (Frankfurt) from Sept. 29 to Oct. 14, then Rome & Haifa.'[27]

In a story that may have happened while Agnes was visiting Mary in Berkeley, Valera Allen has written:

Agnes was scheduled to speak in Oakland, California and was to be taken to her appointments by some ladies on the San Francisco side of the bay.

The driver of the car neglected to fill her car with petrol and it carried a penalty to stop on the San Francisco-Bay bridge so it was quite serious when the car stopped – out of petrol!

The driver felt very disturbed because of her negligence but dear Agnes said 'Don't be disturbed, my dear, I will say the Remover of Difficulties.' So all the ladies became quiet for the prayer and Agnes after a moment said – 'Thy name is my healing, O my God. . .' All were amused at her saying the healing prayer instead of the remover of difficulties and had a good laugh when she had finished.

But just at that moment a car pulled up behind the parked car and asked 'Are you ladies in difficulties?'

The driver explained with embarrassment but the man laughed and said 'No need to worry, I just happen to have five gallons of gas in my trunk!'

So it was a good lesson for all that God hears and answers the prayers of the pure in heart.[28]

Agnes's travels as far as Paris were apparently uneventful and well scheduled. In London on 19 September, she spoke at a meeting about the early days of the Faith and 'brought vivid pictures of those historic events to her listeners'.[29]

She left London on 22 September for Paris with the plan to continue to Germany on the 29th. But the German visit became a bit problematic. On 20 August, the schedule was that she would reach Frankfurt on 29 August and leave on 14 October. Within that time frame, Anna Grossmann wrote, 'As we plan a N.T. [National Teaching] Conference at Frankfurt Oct 3 & 4, I would suggest that you may after your arrival at Frankfurt Sept. 29, visit the Rheinland (north of Frankfurt) which has two S.A's & two goal cities & be back to Frankfurt for the Teaching Conference. Afterwards you would have time to visit the S.A's in Southern Germany as Heidelberg, Karlsruhe, Stuttgart, Tubingen, Esslingen & others.'[30]

Four days later, Agnes received a change to the plan:

The following itinerary was prepared for you and we hope that it is not too strenuous. You will be met at the airport upon your arrival in Frankfurt on 29 September, at 8:30 p.m., and brought to your hotel after a short consultation on your trip. On September 30 a meeting is scheduled in Stuttgart, and on Oct. one you would return to Frankfurt, where there is a National Teaching Conference on Oct. 3 in the Hazira, and a meeting of the National Delegates on 4 October, which we would ask you to kindly talk to. On 5 October will be a meeting in Bonn, and on 6 October in Dusseldorf. On 7 October you would travel to Hamburg and address the friends there on 8 October, returning on October 9 to Frankfurt to leave on 10 October . . .[31]

Agnes had to remind them that she would be in Germany until the 14th. How they used the extra days is not known. This was a pretty heavy schedule for an 84-year-old woman, but she did not look upon it as an imposition, but as an opportunity to complete the Guardian's request from 1937 'that I might visit all the friends in Germany as in 1937 when he sent me there from Haifa. I was there when the Nazis forbade the Cause.'[32] To Agnes, a request from Shoghi Effendi never went out of date.

Ramona Brown, at that time, was pioneering in Austria, and the two women fervently hoped that they could get together during Agnes's travels in Germany. Their reunion did take place. In a letter to Ramona after her arrival in Haifa, she wrote about her trip onwards:

> It was wonderful that you could have been with me those days! And it surely was God's plan . . .
>
> When I left you & went into the waiting room in the Airport, then I found a lovely Persian young woman who had met me in both London & Paris & went we together until I left her at Televiv as she went to Teheran. At Televiv I found that John F.[erraby]'s plane had been delayed & could not come. BA [British Airlines] late. I heard that Swiss Air would bring the passage[ngers]. After 1½ hours I left by bus for a hotel in Televiv for the night arriving there at 2 a.m., but left a note for John at the Airport. In the morning as I was having breakfast I heard John's voice. He reached a hotel at 3 a.m. & so we came together to Haifa – so it surely was in God's plan that I did not get a place on his plane.
>
> All is beautiful here – the Wards have done a good work in Bahji & it has been lovely seeing them here.[33] [Forsyth and Janet Ward were the custodians of the Shrine of Bahá'u'lláh.]

After the Conclave of the Hands, Agnes returned to Japan via Manila, where she stayed with Luisa Gomez, a staunch Bahá'í she stayed with after a number of the Conclaves. Luisa was the first woman to accept the Faith in Manila.[34] Agnes noted that Luisa 'takes all the Baha'is into her home when they pass through Manila'. From Manila, Agnes went to Hiroshima and stayed with the family of Mr Assassi, who had purchased a house for use as a Bahá'í Centre in that city. Hiroshima was a special place for Agnes:

> We only have to trust for these are wonderful times we are now living in. Here as never before I have been made happy teaching souls who are eager to know and hear more. Hiroshima I feel has a destiny in the Faith above other places in Japan. The suffering of the people here will not be in vain. You asked about the television picture and circumstances. When I heard from Mr. Torii that the 12th annual Conference of the blind associations of Japan was to be held in the city of Matsue . . . I immediately said I would go for I had had a feeling about that city. Mr. Torii as President of all the blind associations of Japan said I could have three minutes to speak. I was the last speaker and although it was three minutes, I brought greater applause then all the other speakers who spoke for many minutes. It was not myself, you well know, but the Power which came from another Source. The television news went throughout Japan. The Japanese are very keen on television and awake to all new inventions. We know from Abdu'l-Baha's words that the future of this country is great, – so what a privilege is mine to be here! There is no religious prejudice in Japan. That makes it very easy to give the Message.[35]

When Agnes arrived back in Tokyo she had to hit the ground running. But that was not a problem for her. In a letter to Ramona, she wrote:

> I am so sorry that I could not answer your dear letter any sooner, but there has been so much for me to do that was necessary, that since I came to Tokyo for our monthly NSA meeting I have not been able to do much writing . . .
>
> I came to Tokyo with the intentions of staying 10 days and writing the story of my trip around the world, but as yet I have done nothing [of writing] and only today have I started on the many letters I had received before coming here. So it is with us Baha'is – we never know just what will happen that we should do, that is, the most important thing . . . But we can feel assured that if we only want to do God's will, then we will be shown the way. . .[36]

Agnes also put things in perspective for Ramona, who was struggling at her pioneer post:

> Your speaking of your family Xmas dinner made me think of one Thanksgiving day in Kyoto when it was raining and gloomy and I went with the Toriis to Nara where I spoke in the School for the Blind with Mr. Torii translating. I spoke of my family gathering on that day, but was it not far more happy that I could instead of being with my family, tell of the coming of the Baha'i Faith to the friends in the school. So it is with us Baha'is. The greatest thing is Teaching someone and when the heart has only that desire, God opens the door. You have experienced it.[37]

In February, Virginia Breaks, the Knight of Bahá'u'lláh for the Caroline Islands, and Helen Carter from Carmel, California, visited Agnes in Kyoto. Virginia asked for prayers because there were no Bahá'ís in the Carolines at that time and Agnes pulled out a quotation from the Guardian which she had written down when in Haifa: 'In every country it is possible to teach the Cause. If you know how to teach, you can find a few receptive souls.'[38]

No matter how much she travelled and worked for the Faith, Agnes always wanted to do more. In a letter to Ramona on 12 March, she wrote, 'I long to go to visit all the Centers here and also in other places which are under our NSA as Hong Kong and Macau, the last place I have never visited and I have a letter asking or begging that I would go there. What a joy it is for us to visit the Baha'is and share with them!'[39]

At Riḍván 1960, Mason Remey declared himself to be the second Guardian. This created disbelief and consternation across the Bahá'í world and gave the Hands of the Cause a huge challenge. Agnes, however, viewed Remey's defection through her own optimistic eyes:

> So many things have happened in our Baha'i world but all things work together for good [that] we can understand in this Cause. Now there is a new unity between all the NSA's in the world and this is something that only God could bring.
>   . . . I heard from Haifa Hands that only about 15 were claiming allegiance to Mason, 10 in France and 5 in the U.S. who were not active Baha'is . . .[40]

About Mason R., really I feel this is the test of God to bring us all closer together and I feel a greater happiness in going to our meeting this year than ever before . . .[41]

During the summer, Agnes went to Sapporo on Hokkaido Island for eight days to visit the Persian pioneer Mr Tehrani. From there, she attended the three-day summer school at Aichi-keninner (near Nagoya) from 19 to 21 August.[42]

Agnes paid very close attention to her inspirations and on 10 October, she wrote to Ramona that she felt that she would go to Africa after the Conclave:

Now the news I have for you is that after the Conclave in Bahji, I shall go to Africa. Last Spring the inspiration about Africa came to me when the Temple was to be dedicated in August and I knew that it was true but it was not for that time. Now it is certain that I am going for the guidance is very strong. I have heard from Valera Allen and also Mr. Hainsworth and they look for my coming. There will be considerable time before the dedication, but Valera wanted me to visit other places. So, dearest, we really move about these days![43]

Three days after this letter, she wrote Ramona another one about Africa: 'As my trip to Africa came, or was decided, so suddenly after I had my ticket to Haifa & return already, it had to be arranged by a dear Baha'i, Mr. Moghbel in Osaka & I did not receive the ticket until I took the plane.'[44]

Agnes left for the Conclave on 15 October,[45] arriving in Haifa on the 17th, having overnighted in Tehran and having the opportunity to meet some of the Bahá'ís there.[46] After the Conclave, Rúḥíyyih Khánum asked her to remain for an additional ten days.[47] At that point, she noted that 'I have no definite plan yet for Africa', but a few days later, she wrote to Ramona:

About Africa. – It seems that NOW is not the time for me to go there. After I had made the plan, and it seemed difficult in making it, on Monday morning, I awakened and the guidance was very clear that I MUST now return to the Far East. I did not want to speak of it to anyone here until I had told our beloved Ruhiyyih Khanum and she has been overwhelmed with work since our Conclave as the Custodians have been meeting every day and also other work besides, so I had only a moment with her and told her. I know that there is no question in my heart and I have been to have my ticket and routing changed. The part of my ticket that I do not use will be refunded to me in Osaka office when I return there, so nothing is lost.

I know that our beloved Guardian told me when I told him of the guidance which comes to me at times with a feeling of joy and is always fulfilled sooner or later. He said it was the Master. And of course I am thankful that God has given me this guidance.[48]

In the same letter, Agnes noted that she was praying for 'our precious Milly Collins who suffers so much'. She wrote that it was 'the least I can do and my privilege as a sister Hand. Really only Milly, Ruhiyyih Khanum and I are the sister Hands who can work at this time.'[49] Agnes never did get to Africa.

On her way home to Japan, Agnes stopped in Hong Kong to visit Mamie Seto, then to Macao and Manila, where she spent a week with Luisa Gomez.[50] Agnes arrived in Manila on 28 November, the day after the conclusion of the Second All-Philippine Teaching Conference. Many of the Bahá'ís stayed after the Conference in order to meet her.[51]

Agnes was in Berkeley, California, in February after her sister, Mary, passed away. Agnes left on 23 February 1961 and spent two weeks in Honolulu. Hawaii had become a US state in 1959 and she happily noted, 'The beloved Guardian said Hawaii was an important place and now, since it is a State, it seems to be going forward,' with many people coming into the Faith.[52]

Agnes returned to Kyoto in the middle of March and found 30 letters awaiting her attention. She also noted, 'When I came back to my room here and looked at my sister's photo on the bureau, I felt distinctly that she would now, from the Other Realm, help me and it is so I am sure.'[53] Mary had never accepted the Faith in life, but certainly knew a lot about it from Agnes.

Agnes participated in the 1961 National Convention after Riḍván and was again elected to the Regional Spiritual Assembly of North East Asia.

On 7 July, Agnes arrived in Korea for 15 'glorious days'. She was in

Seoul for the first two days and spoke at the 9 July Anniversary of the Martyrdom of the Báb. Her translator was Mr Oh Sang Sun, the same man she had met on her first visit to Korea in 1921.[54] Bill Smits had married a Korean lady named Lee and she accompanied Agnes as she travelled from city to city, going as far as Pusan, South Korea (now called Busan), to visit pioneers Mr and Mrs Enger. Agnes stopped in Chunju, where they had a Local Assembly, as well as the goal cities of Taejon and Taegu. In Pusan, she addressed two public meetings. Returning to Seoul, she spent several more days there.[55] She wrote, 'it was so wonderful to witness His help and confirmations! It is a new Day!'[56]

In December, Agnes visited Hong Kong and the Philippines. The Philippines were undergoing a 'remarkable expansion in teaching activity and many declarations'. In a letter, the Custodians wrote, 'It is obvious that this area is now at the portals of mass conversion.'[57]

Agnes was again elected to the Regional Spiritual Assembly at the 1962 National Convention. Information on her activities that year are limited, but she did continue her international travels. In June, she was in Formosa (Taiwan) for 16 'wonderful' days.[58] This was her third trip to the island, and she wrote:

> When we reached the Center in Tainan I could not get over my delight at the lovely Center with flowers surrounding it. I was there for eleven days, each day full. I came to know the Taiwanese people and truly loved them. Now there are quite a number of Bahá'ís in Tainan, five in one family (the Yang family) declared their faith at the same time. The last evening I met the parents for whom I felt a great love. As they were in the country under the Japanese they know the language so we could speak together. They are not Bahá'ís but their children are.[59]

After Taiwan, she returned to Kyoto and moved, again, this time into two small rooms. It was, she wrote, 'much better than before and I am grateful for God's help always'.[60]

On 15 November, Agnes wrote to Ramona about her plans:

> As you know my life is full and happy. I may go to Honolulu to be with the families there at Xmas time, as they have invited me, and also I am asked to the Philippines where the Mass conversion is now

© Sims, *Traces that Remain*

The first Regional
National Spiritual
Assembly of the
Bahá'ís of North-East
Asia, elected in 1957.
Left to right, seated:
Noureddin Momtazi,
Hand of the Cause
Agnes Alexander,
Barbara R. Sims and
Hiroyasu Takano;
standing: Ata'ullah
Moghbel, Michitoshi
Zenimoto, Philip
Marangella, Yadullah
Rafaat and William
Maxwell

Hand of the Cause Agnes Alexander speaking at the North-East Asia Baháʼí Conference in Tokyo, 27–29 April 1957; Charlotte Linfoot is seated on the right

Hands of the Cause Jalál Kházeh and Agnes Alexander at the Tokyo Conference, April 1957 . . .

. . . and sharing a lighter moment

*Hand of the Cause Agnes Alexander and John McHenry III
depart from the first Bahá'í Summer School in Korea*

*Agnes Alexander and Tokujiro Torii with the Headmaster of the School for the
Blind. This photograph was possibly taken at the 12th National Conference for the
Blind, in Matsue, Japan in 1959*

Conclave of the Hands of the Cause of God gathered in the House of 'Abdu'l-Bahá, November 1957.
Agnes Alexander is standing fourth from left

Hands of the Cause at the 1958 Conclave. Agnes Alexander is standing in the front row, centre

Hands of the Cause with members of the International Bahá'í Council (IBC) at Bahjí, possibly in 1961. 1. John Ferraby 2. 'Alí-Akbar Furútan 3. John Robarts 4. Abu'l-Qásim Faizí 5. Mildred Mottahedeh (IBC) 6. Charles Wolcott (IBC) 7. Enoch Olinga 8. Tarázu'lláh Samandarí 9. 'Alí Nakhjavání (IBC) 10. Agnes Alexander 11. Raḥmatu'lláh Muhájir 12. Ugo Giachery 13. Paul Haney 14. Amatu'l-Bahá Rúḥíyyih Khánum 15. H. M. Balyuzi 16. Jessie Revell (IBC) 17. Adelbert Mühlschlegel 18. Ian Semple (IBC) 19. Ethel Revell (IBC) 20 William Sears 21. Lotfullah Hakím (IBC) 22. Sylvia Ioas (IBC) 23. Zikrullah Khadem 24. Leroy Ioas 25. Shuá'u'lláh 'Alá'í 26. Collis Featherstone 27. Jalál Kházeh

National Spiritual Assembly of the Baha'is of North-East Asia, 1962–1963. Left to right, seated: Barbara Sims, Hand of the Cause of God Agnes Baldwin Alexander, Michitoshi Zenimoto, Hiroyasu Takano; standing: Abba Katirai, David Earl, Masazo Odani, Ikuo Mizuno, Noureddin Momtazi

Pioneers and Japanese believers, 1962. Left to right: Ikuo Mizuno, Ata'ullah Moghbel, Agnes Alexander, Hiroyasu Takano, Barbara Sims, David Earl, Philip Marangella, William Maxwell, Masazo Odoni

Agnes Alexander with Ainu Chief Mr Moritake. In Shoghi Effendi 's last letter to Japan, he advised the Baha'is to teach the Ainu so that they would then arise and teach their own people

Agnes Alexander speaking at the Princess Kaiulani Hotel in Honolulu on the eve of the election of the First National Spiritual Assembly of the Bahá'ís of the Hawaiian Islands, 24 April 1964

Agnes Baldwin Alexander, Hawaii's first Bahá'í, honoured by Governor John Burns at the Princes Kaiulani Hotel in Waikiki, 24 April 1964

First National Spiritual Assembly of the Bahá'ís of the Hawaiian Islands. Left to right, seated: Evelyn Musacchia, Velma Sherrill (assisting Agnes Alexander), Hand of the Cause of God Agnes Baldwin Alexander, representing the Universal House of Justice, Lei Chapman, Elena Marsella, Gertrude Garrida; Standing: James Wada, Claude Caver, Hugh Chapman, Jacques Smith, Michael Woodward. Photograph taken 25 April 1964 at the Hawaii Bahá'í National Centre in Honolulu

Agnes Alexander at the Bahá'í House of Worship in Langenhain, Germany, 1964

going so swiftly and even 'head hunters' have accepted the Faith! It would be a glorious experience for me in these days which will never come again to the world, even though I am not young nor very well, but God helps as you also know, otherwise what could we do? [61]

Agnes was 86 that year.

Agnes did go to the family gathering for Christmas and spent three weeks in Honolulu. She told Ramona, 'It was a truly happy time I had in Honolulu with my family at Christmas time when 22 gathered, 2nd, 3rd, 4th and 5th generations from my grandparents. I am the only remaining one of the second generation.' [62]

On 11 March 1963, Agnes flew to Seoul, South Korea. Realizing the limitations of her age, she asked Bill Smits to have someone meet her at the airport and help her transfer to the train for Taegu (now called Daegu), between Seoul and Pusan. [63] The *Bahá'í News* mentioned that:

> Hand Agnes Alexander (in her eighties) made the long journey from Japan during the period of the Fast. Her unforgettable visit to the mass conversion district of Kajo – made possible through the generosity of Auxiliary Board member William Maxwell and by the hospitality of the new Korean believers of Kajo – and her visits to Taegu, Kyongju, Pusan and Seoul, during which time she saw no reason to break the Fast in spite of continuous daily travel, inspired all the believers to reconsecrate themselves to the Guardian's appeal for teaching the Faith as never before. [64]

She returned to Tokyo on 18 March.

The Ten Year Crusade ended with the election of the Universal House of Justice and Agnes was there. Agnes said a prayer before the balloting began. The only response we have from her about that historic event was 'A New Day has dawned! We have elected the Universal House of Justice whose members are as follows: Hugh Chance, Charles Wolcott, H.B. Kavelin & Amos Gibson of the U.S.; Ali Nakjavani, Ian Semple of Scotland, Dr. Lotfullah Hakim, David Hofman & Hushmand Fatheazam of India. Now we all go to London!' [65]

Unfortunately, Agnes left us none of her impressions of either the election of the Universal House of Justice or the Jubilee in London, though she attended both. In a letter to Ramona on 7 June, Agnes first wrote about her overall feelings about being alive at that particular moment: 'Many thoughts have been in my mind. I was always saying I did not want to grow any older, etc. But NOW I know enough to leave all things in God's Hands for He alone knows best.' She continued, 'There is so much to do, but how glorious to have lived at the TIME and seen the Faith go forward as our beloved Guardian said it would.'[66]

Agnes then wrote to Ramona about getting to London for the Jubilee, her journey home and the fact that the Hands had decided that serving as a Hand should preclude serving on any other administrative body:

> I left Frankfurt the day before you were to arrive there. Miss [Anne-liese] Bopp had reserved for me a room in a hotel [in London], but I only stayed one night and then moved to a Pension where 4 of the Honolulu ladies were and it was all very happy. It was near to the Center and there one met so many of the Baha'is . . .
>
> I had to go to Hamburg to take Air France across the North Pole [to return to Japan], and there I had the joy of being with a Persian Baha'i family whom I had stayed with in 1959, for 3 hours. When we went to the Air Port there in the waiting room I met one of the Japanese Baha'is who was also taking Air France, so we traveled together to Tokyo and it was surely God's guidance, for we had a chance to get acquainted. His name is Dr. Hosoda and he & his wife now are in the [Bahá'í] Center in Tokyo. She should have a baby in a few days . . .
>
> As the Hands decided that we should not be members of the NSAs, I resigned and truly it is a joy to be freed, although I must know & keep up with everything concerning the Faith in N.E. Asia. Also this applies to Board members, so dear Mr. Zenimoto is also now freed and we can work together in Japan.[67]

In another letter to Ramona, she wrote, 'It is truly wonderful that we are really living in the time of the U.H. of J.! I feel such a love for them all and had a note which was in answer to mine which truly brought joy to my heart.'[68] On 20 July, Agnes flew to Tokyo where the friends had arranged to celebrate her 87th birthday. When she arrived, the birthday party included 32 of her friends. Agnes barely had time to catch her breath when she flew off to the Philippines, where she spent two 'wonderful weeks' under 'God's guidance'. She wrote that she went into the mountainous area where they were experiencing mass entry in different tribes, noting that there were now about 16,000 Bahá'ís on five different islands.[69]

Returning from the Philippines, Agnes attended the Japanese summer school, where the main topics of discussion were the London Conference and mass conversion. It was also noted that members of the Ainu tribe, native people on the island of Hokkaido, had begun to enter the Faith, and Agnes said, 'This was our Guardian's last wish that these people should come into the Faith.'[70] They were guided into the Faith by pioneer Noureddin Momtazi.

Hawaii elects first National Spiritual Assembly

Agnes went to Hawaii in April 1964 to attend the first Hawaiian National Bahá'í Convention at which they were to elect their first National Spiritual Assembly. She was met at the airport by her niece and her husband, the Gordon Smiths, and her nephew William Alexander and his wife, plus a large group of Bahá'ís, which impressed her relatives. At first, she stayed with the Gordons in Tantalus and then moved to William's home at Kahala.[71]

As a prelude to Hawaii's first National Convention, a public meeting and reception was held in the Princess Kailulani Hotel at Waikiki on 24 April. Duane Troxel was at the public meeting and learned of Agnes's sense of humour: 'I was an usher at the Princess Kaiulani Hotel gathering . . . Myself and another Bahá'í were placing ashtrays on every other chair (smokers abounded in those days) when Agnes came down the aisle with Mrs. Sherrill before the gathering. She paused when she reached me and said with a twinkle in her eye 'What are you going to do . . . take up a collection?'[72]

The *Bahá'í News* described Agnes:

It was December 26, 1901, when a young lady, fresh from a trip to Europe and glowing with a new inner knowledge alighted from a steamer – the first Bahá'í in Hawaii. It was not easy, in those days, for a member of a famous missionary family to speak of a new faith but the courage came and the torch was placed in other hands. The young lady moved on then by direction of the beloved Master to plant the banner of Bahá'u'lláh in Japan.

It was fitting that the young lady, now known and loved through-out the Bahá'í World as Hand of the Cause Agnes Alexander, represented the Holy Land at the historic First National Convention of the Bahá'ís of the Hawaiian Islands.[73]

Agnes's description of the public meeting and reception is a bit more modest:

> Mrs. Velma Sherrill had come representing the N.S.A. of U.S.A. She was one of the speakers also Gov. John Burns and I said a few words. The room was filled and it was a great day for the Faith. My nephew & wife also were present. Later over the television Gov. Burns was seen putting a carnation lei over my shoulders! It was all excellent for the Faith.
>
> The Convention of two days was truly spiritual, more so than any I have ever attended for there was an atmosphere of love. Now Hawaii has an N.S.A. It is wonderful and they are all very fine Baha'is. One of the members told me that at their first meeting there was such a love among them that they did not like to part![74]

On Sunday morning, 26 April 1964, the 19 delegates from the various Hawaiian Islands cast their ballots at the Bahá'í Mid-Pacific Center in Nuuanu Valley for the first National Spiritual Assembly of the Bahá'ís of Hawaii. Agnes said, 'my greatest duty and joy was to be at the Convention in Honolulu. It truly was most happy and the NSA is made up of the different varieties of race found there which makes it especially precious.'[75]

Craig Quick remembered an amazing change that would come over Agnes when she spoke about the Faith. He wrote, 'she always had a beatific smile and twinkling blue eyes. When she started talking about the need to arise and teach the Cause, however, a most amazing change came over her visage. Gone was the gentle smile and the sparkling eyes, to be replaced by a very firm countenance, and eyes that were blazing with the spirit.'[76]

At one point during the Convention, Agnes spoke about how she became a Bahá'í, and set the stage for her talk with a short story:

> It's a very, very wonderful bounty to be here; and I was just thinking,

God uses those who are nothing; and if you are something He cannot use you. And if you know the story of Peter who . . . Christ appointed as a head . . . of His followers. And in Rome in Italy there are these great cathedrals . . . St. Peter's Cathedral. And Peter couldn't read or write! He hadn't any more knowledge then . . . [to wrap] seven packages of food so he would know when the Sabbath Day came. So that is the point. It's only when you're nothing that God can use you.[77]

Agnes spent a month in Hawaii, most of it under the care of her nephew William.

Agnes went to Maui for four days, beginning on 4 May. She wrote, 'My visit on Maui was very happy as I met many of my relatives there and one who was truly interested, Mrs. Walter Cameron, with whom I stayed for four days.'[78]

In mid-August, Agnes was back in the Philippines and shared stories of the first National Convention in Hawaii and the early days of the Faith. On two weekends, she went to teach the Bahá'ís in Muntinlupa, just south of Manila.[79]

After the 1964 Conclave in Haifa, Agnes wrote from Kyoto to both Ramona and Raḥmatu'lláh Muhájir about the Philippines:

> It is very cold here, especially as I am situated and I know that I must go where it is warmer and now I go to Tokyo for two weeks or more and then the guidance is to go to Hawaii for there is much to be done and my time is short now. So darling you can continue your prayers which help me.
>
> Returning from Haifa, I spent a wonderful day and night in Teheran with Mrs. Jane Khamsi who is American born. Her husband I met in Japan and he told me I might stay with her & her four children. Then a week in the Philippines where once again I had the bounty of going to the large prison outside of the city of Manila [Muntinlupa] where there are many Baha'is.[80]

> I always think, with pleasure, of my trips to the Philippines and especially I remember the prisoners.[81]

Hand of the Cause Abu'l-Qásim Faizi remembered a story Agnes told him about one prisoner:

Many prisoners in the Philippines became Bahá'ís and they built themselves a Bahá'í Centre in the prison. When Agnes visited them for the first time she gave some of them photographs of 'Abdu'l-Bahá and the Greatest Name. The second time she met with them a young man came forward and showed her his photograph of 'Abdu'l-Bahá and with great sadness told her that he had killed someone before becoming a Bahá'í, that his trial had finished on that day and that he was going to be executed the following day. Agnes said that she became so very sad, then thought to herself that, thank God, he is going to meet his Lord tomorrow.[82]

From the Philippines, Agnes returned to Kyoto .

Agnes spent several weeks in Tokyo in January 1965. Early in the month, Eugene Schreiber spent the afternoon with her photographing the copies of her letters from 'Abdu'l-Bahá. Later, referring to Agnes, he said, 'What a spiritual giant that woman is! The things Abdu'l-Baha said to her.' On 9 and 10 January, the National Spiritual Assembly met and since the Hands in the recent Conclave had said that the Hands should 'consult and advise' the National Assembly, Agnes attended their meeting, commenting when she felt necessary. When two of the Assembly members planned to go on a teaching trip to Taiwan, Agnes said that Japan was behind other countries and that they should stay in Japan and teach.[83]

Later in January, Aziz and Soraya Yazdi visited Japan and, of course, spent time talking with Agnes. One day after Agnes had gone to her room, the Yazdis, Eugene Schreiber and Barbara Sims sat around talking about her:

> Aziz says she is quite special among the Hands – that she, no doubt has been under the complete protection of Abdu'l-Baha from the very beginning. All of us have known many Hands intimately and we were saying that no doubt we are too close to them to really appreciate their stature and spiritual station but we try to & we think & discuss it. I told Aziz that Agnes doesn't seem to have tests these days such as most of us have and I know many of the Hands have terrible tests. Of course she has certain health problems like all of us do. He said he thinks Abdu'l-Baha has taken care of everything concerning her. She says over & over that she was nothing, therefore God

could use her . . . This attitude of meekness, humility but combined with the intensity of continuing prayer & supplication to be able to be of any service & the sure knowledge that any trace of ego or self-importance will completely end your usefulness. Agnes speaks so often about the power of prayer that there is no force like it in existence. She told the story of how during the big earthquake of 1923 in Tokyo as the earth was shaking she got out the prayer for protection & started to read it and as she did the earth stopped shaking. She turned to her friend (Ida Finch) & said 'You are my witness'.[84]

In February, she returned to Kyoto and by June material life was unfortunately keeping her busy. Though she was now 89 years old, she still lived alone. She wrote to Ramona that 'These days I am kept very busy a great deal with household work as I have no help and in this region there is no place where I can eat out, so you can understand. But God is the ONLY Helper, as we know and He we can depend on in all circumstances.'[85]

Hand of the Cause Abu'l-Qásim Faizi had tremendous respect for Agnes. At one time, he wrote, 'Everyone thinks that because she is elderly she is incapable of doing anything and has no thoughts whereas she is like a mountain. Just think of a person remaining in one place for 50 years or more and on the face of it nothing to show for it . . . She does not delegate any work to anyone, she does everything herself. You have no idea with what difficulty she accepted to let me take her shoes to her.'[86]

The English-language *Mainichi Daily News*, on 11 May 1965, carried an interesting article about Agnes settling in Japan. The correspondent interviewed Agnes at the Bahá'í National Convention and wrote an article that contained an interesting mix of fact and misinterpretation:

For one who, as a young girl, felt that she was the 'Black Sheep' of a devoutly Christian family, Miss Agnes Alexander has traveled a long road.

She grew up to embrace the Baha'i faith and find the kind of meaning in her life that would serve as a taproot of energy in all her days.

Miss Alexander, who will be 90 years old on July 20, was an honored guest at the Baha'i Community Convention held in Tokyo. Honored indeed, for over the last half-century she has been devoting all of her efforts to furthering the faith all over the world . . .

Miss Alexander is the first Baha'i pioneer to become a resident of Japan. 'We don't say "missionary" – that word is past – but "pioneer",' . . . 'Pioneer' seems more accurate in her case, since she braved German torpedo boats in the Indian Ocean to sail to Japan for the first time in 1914 . . .

. . . Miss Alexander heard Miss Ume Tsuda . . . lecture on Japan, and she determined that one day she would go to that country.

Then, the lady who claims she has 'no courage or daring in the least,' was en route to Germany when the First World War broke out. She found herself in Switzerland, the hurricane's eye, with her money in England and her luggage in Germany.

And then the message came from Abdul Baha, the descendant of the Chosen One of the faith: 'The visit to Japan is preferred to everything else.' Nothing could stop her.

'I'll take steerage,' she said to the head of the Japanese steamship company in Marseilles. The ship had been booked for months. But they gave her the best cabin on board. Her trunk was also aboard, the only piece of anybody's luggage to be returned from Germany . . .

And thus the torpedo-threatened voyage began, with all the cabins blacked out at night and passengers too terrified to undress to go to bed, lest disaster strike. Agnes Alexander docked safely in Kobe on November 1, 1914. But on its return voyage across the Indian Ocean the Japanese vessel that had borne her was torpedoed and sunk.

Miss Alexander alternated periods of temporary residency in Japan with trips to the United States, Europe and China to meet with other Baha'is. Her house in Tokyo was destroyed in the great earthquake of 1923.

She always made the annual pilgrimage to the Baha'i World Center in Akka, in the Holy Land . . .

After May 18, she will return to her home in Kyoto, where she lives within easy walking distance of many Baha'i friends.[87]

Agnes was preparing to go to the World Esperanto Congress that was to be held in July in Tokyo, the first time it had ever been held outside Europe. Thinking back, she told Ramona:

Is it not wonderful I came to Japan as an Esperantist and it opened many doors for me. It was in obedience to Abdu'l-Baha's words when speaking in Edinburgh that He said the Baha'is should learn Esperanto that I learned it and through it many doors opened for me in Japan to speak of the Faith. The Esperantists all liked the Baha'i Faith because of the principle of a universal language but the time has not come for them to in truth become Bahai's.[88]

On the morning of 28 July, Agnes went to the World Esperanto Congress in Tokyo. It turned out to be a life-changing event.[89]

19

THE LAST YEARS

1965–1971

Confined to a bed in Japan

Agnes arrived at the International House Hotel in Tokyo on 28 July.
That evening, she slipped and fractured her thigh and her hip. Barbara
Sims, pioneer and member of the National Spiritual Assembly, wrote
about what happened:

> Last Wed night Agnes got a dizzy spell while she was in her room at
> Int. House & fell down – she was in pain & shock I guess & lay on the
> floor for an hour or so – and couldn't move. Finally she banged on the
> adjoining door & the woman in there called the desk. The boy at the
> desk climbed into her room thru the balcony as she had the chain on
> the door. Anyhow, Phil [Marangella] took her to the hospital & they
> Xrayed her & found that her thigh bone was fractured up into the
> hip joint. She will have to stay in the hospital for some time – hard to
> tell how long – at first they said 3 months on her back & now the Dr.
> says she'll mend sooner. This is apparently the first time she had ever
> been in a hospital & she doesn't know how to act. She seems to think
> of it as if it's a hotel where she can 'order' meals, or little things done
> etc. Well, poor Agnes – it's hard on her but fortunately she does not
> have much pain. Occasionally she complains about her leg aching.[1]

Two months later, Agnes dictated a letter to Ramona from her hospital
bed at the University Hospital in Tokyo. As usual, she was optimistic
about the whole thing:

> I am lying in a bed in a hospital in Tokyo, where a Baha'i friend is
> typing for me . . .

I came to Tokyo to attend the World Congress of the Esperantists, which for the first time was held in the Pacific. The first evening after I arrived at International House, I slipped in my bedroom – the result of which was a fractured hip bone. That night July 28, I was brought on a stretcher to a Japanese hospital, where ever since, I have lain on the same bed. Before very long, God willing, I hope to be able to return to the International House here and then when it is best to my little abode in Kyoto but this is all in God's hands and He knows what is best. There must be a reason that I should be here. You may say a prayer for me.[2]

Little did she know that she would never walk again without help and would spend her last six years mostly in a bed. This immobility did grate on her because she knew there was so much to do in connection with spreading the message of Bahá'u'lláh. Because of her confinement, for the first and only time, she referred to herself as a Hand of the Cause in writing:

Beloved Baha'i friends of the Pacific,
    As you probably know, the beloved Guardian, in one of his cables, gave me the assignment, after the passing of George Townshend.

'Agnes Alexander distinguished pioneer faith elevated rank hand cause. Confident appointment will spiritually reinforce teaching campaign simultaneously north south heart pacific ocean.'

I have only quoted this that you might know the responsibility that our beloved Guardian has given me and that I may have your prayers that as one soul in many bodies we may all work for the one great purpose in life. I have been very grateful for your kind messages since I have been in the hospital. A Baha'i friend is typing this for me as I am lying on the bed. Is it not wonderful that we can all work hand in hand helping each other in the great work of His Cause?[3]

All Agnes wanted to do was serve the Cause of God and she was begging the Bahá'ís of the Pacific to pray for her recovery so she could go back to work. On 26 October, Barbara Sims wrote:

At first they said it would be 3 months & now it is nearly that. The leg healed but it has taken her a long long time to get her strength back & she is still very weak. Dr Muhajir came here a week ago & has helped us arrange things. He sent a cable to Ruth Walbridge in the Philippines to come & help take care of Agnes, to be with her after her release from the hospital. Ruth came immediately & goes to the hospital every day & does little things for Agnes . . . I take her little things she wants & needs – little personal things and extra food – she has lost much weight as she's lost her appetite completely – lying in bed for so long. Agnes says it's the first time she has ever been in a hospital & it took her quite a while to get used to the routine. As a matter of fact she never has gotten used to the routine but has changed it to suit herself. She has been taking care of herself all her life & now for the first time she is lying there for weeks. She has been saying since the very first that the fall, the break & being in the hospital was all the Plan of God & she very much resents references in letters which refer to it as unfortunate & when people say they are sorry . . . Dr Muhajir really took care of everything.[4]

Ruth, who later became Ruth Suzuki, was a professional nurse and cared for the 90-year-old Hand of the Cause until after she had returned to Hawaii.[5] She was very impressed by her patient. She wrote:

After receiving a cable from Hand of the Cause Dr. Mohajir, in late September, 1965 requesting me to come to Japan to take care of Agnes I took time to read the Tablets of the Divine Plan because I knew that Agnes' name had been mentioned in one of them. In the one dated August 11, 1916, the beloved Master wrote 'I declare by the Lord of Hosts, that had this respected daughter founded an empire, that empire would not have been so great! For this sovereignty is eternal sovereignty and this glory is everlasting glory.'

Shortly after I had been in Tokyo for a few days with her I mentioned these words to dear Agnes. Her reply I will NEVER forget as I was so impressed with it. She simply said that it was all because of her grandparents taking the message of Christ to the Hawaiian Islands, going by sailing ship around the southern coast of South America in the 1800s. She gave all the credit to her ancestors. There was no hint of 'I'! Her complete humility impressed me so deeply and to this day it still brings tears to my eyes. Her humility was absolute. What an example she is and was! . . .

I have always thought that the Master saw the purity of Agnes' soul and was completely confident in her humility. I think we have all seen how too much praise can lead to the ego stealing away someone from their true destiny of selfless service. I don't think Abdu'l-Baha would have praised her so much as He did in the Tablets of the Divine Plan if there was any question in His mind that she could not handle the honor He bestowed on her. Her humility and purity were such outstanding virtues!![6]

On 13 October 1965, Agnes decided it was finally time to make a will. Her doctor wrote an affidavit attesting to her soundness of mind:

This is to certify that Miss Agnes Baldwin Alexander was under my medical care from 28 July 1965 to 20 December 1965 during which time I visited her at least once a day in the normal duty schedule of the hospital. At the time she signed her last will and testament on 13 October 1965 to which I was a witness she was in sound mind and of attentive memory. In my frequent talks with her on which occasions she referred to her family and friends and explained to me the Baha'i World Faith, she consistently displayed clarity of thinking, good memory, intelligence and kindliness. I have no doubt that she signed her will with complete understanding and approval of its contents. Ryuji Yamamoto Medical Doctor Jikei Idai University Hospital Tokyo.[7]

Agnes never saw her difficulties as anything more than a temporary setback and continued to ask for prayers so that she would be able to return to the action:

I am so grateful dearest for all your prayers and it must be that God has a purpose in this happening. I am not able to write but a dear friend is typing this for me. If it is God's will I hope before long to be able to walk. The friends have all been so loving and kind, so we cannot really say it is bad news. But I do appreciate your love and the love of all the friends and do tell them how much I appreciate it. Perhaps this is one way that God draws us together.[8]

When December came, Agnes was still bed-bound, except now and then when she was taken out into the garden in a wheelchair.[9]

Agnes kept trying to get herself out of bed. The August 1966 news bulletin from the Hands of the Cause of South and East Asia stated that 'Agnes . . . is much improved, "her spirit as radiant as ever" and she is able to move around a little. She is a source of inspiration to all of the friends who come to visit her.'[10] In a letter to Ramona in April, Agnes wrote about her condition:

> Every day I am up & walk a little in a walker & today I have not returned to my bed but have been writing in a chair . . . Such a great day truly we are living in. Here in this hospital I have met many from different parts of the world whom I would not have met if I were in Kyoto.
>
> I must go to Kyoto when I am able as all my things in my two rooms must be cared for. My nephew, Wm. Alexander & niece, Mrs. Mary Smith came from Honolulu for me. They were here a short time. They have arranged for me to go to Honolulu, but at present it is not possible.[11]

Then in late May, Agnes again wrote to Ramona about going to Kyoto 'Before long, God willing, I hope to get to my apartment in Kyoto to clear it out so that I can go to my family in Honolulu, who have a place reserved for me in the new 12 story "Arcadia" built by the place I was born. Nothing is arranged but God will guide in what is best . . .'[12]

On 29 July, Agnes wrote, 'I am not able to walk except with a walker, or help, but it would not help for me to stay longer here. In two days with a nurse helper, I will go to my apartment in Kyoto which I left two years ago expecting to return after a few days. From there, when my belongings are taken out . . . I will leave, God willing, on August 12th by plane with a Bahai friend (I could not go alone) for Honolulu . . .'[13] As eager as she was to go to Kyoto, her frail body would not let her and it wasn't until 31 August that she managed it.

Her talk of going to Kyoto upset Ramona, who was very worried that she not overdo anything, writing, 'Dear Agnes, please be very careful and not overdo and use too much strength if you are in Kyoto. It is so very important for you to keep well as there is no one as precious as you and the world needs you and you are a great inspiration to all of us . . .'[14]

Ruth was finally able to take Agnes back to her apartment in Kyoto. Ruth described it as:

> two small rooms . . . The kitchen was ultra tiny, probably just about 2 feet wide, just a cubby hole in the wall . . . There was a very little sink, maybe about 14 inches by 14 inches, enough space for one hot plate next to the sink and a very small work space between the hot plate and the sink. She shared the bathroom facilities . . . with the other tenants of the building . . . she slept on an air mattress for many years until one of the pioneer families bought her a simple bed . . . She used to wake up in the middle of the night to re-inflate the air mattress because it had a leak.[15]

Ruth helped Agnes go through her papers and sort them. Most were sent to the National Spiritual Assemblies of either Hawaii or Japan. One letter, however, Agnes showed to Ruth: 'It was a letter from May Maxwell telling Agnes that she was pregnant after ten years of childless marriage. May said that she was only telling Agnes the good news but none of the friends in the North American Baha'i community. She . . . would let Mother Nature do that.'[16]

Though confined mostly to a bed, Agnes was not left alone. Hand of the Cause Ṭarázu'lláh Samandarí attended the Japanese Bahá'í summer school and paid her a visit:

> The Baha'is of Japan were greatly favored during August and September of this year when Mr. Samandarí, Hand of the Cause, visited their country for the first time. He visited the four large islands of Japan, speaking before groups in many cities from Sapporo in the north to Nagasaki in the south, also giving public talks and press interviews.
>
> A high point of his visit was a meeting with Miss Agnes Alexander, Hand of the Cause who has been confined to the hospital. To her delight the room was filled with friends, who, in turn, were delighted by their discussion as to which one was the elder. Miss Alexander, who is ninety-one years of age, is older by about three months.[17]

During this time in hospital, Agnes began sending tape-recorded letters to her friends. Those in Haifa responded in kind on 12 March 1966:

[Rúḥíyyih Khánum]: You are so much thought of here. Our love and our prayers are with you much more than you can realize. I need not tell you how I long to see you, how I wish that I could go into your room in the hospital and put my arms around you and hug you and kiss you and tell you how much I love you; and talk to you about our mutual wonderful mother [May Maxwell] and about the work of the Cause that we love so dearly . . .

There are other friends here of yours with me tonight and they are all eager to send a little word to you, so I will stop and send you my deepest, deepest love and I hope to hear from you again soon.

[Dr Lotfullah Hakím]: Dear Agnes, it is so nice to hear that we can talk together from so far away, and I am very happy that you are keeping well and you are having a very nice time with the Friends there. Here tonight at the house are 'Alí and Violette [Nakhjavání]. We are all so happy in talking, even for a few words with you. Wish you all every happiness and joy in heart soul and spirit.

[A.-Q. Faizi]: Dearest Agnes, it was wonderful to hear your voice – your penetrating voice – your words which can keep in our souls and hearts. We all pray that you will be alright again very soon and resume your wonderful [word unclear] in that part of the world . . .

[Violette Nakhjavani]: Alláh-u-Abhá my dear Agnes. You are with us tonight . . . We heard your voice and we often think of you and pray for you and we hope to hear that you have left the hospital soon and you are continuing your wonderful services in Japan and all that area.

['Alí Nakhjavání]: Alláh-u-Abhá. I want to tell you what a wonderful experience it was to sit here next to Rúḥíyyih Khánum and listen to your voice coming from the hospital in Japan. And it made me think of the wonderful services you have done with the Cause of God from the days of 'Abdu'l-Bahá till now. And how the Faith in Japan has now progressed and how you have been a witness to it all these years . . .

[Rúḥíyyih Khánum]: I think of you, Agnes, so often and your radiant spirit and your example and your love is great comfort to me and I know it is to all my fellow Hands and to all the Bahá'ís. It must be very difficult for you lying there in that hospital. You, who are always been so active and so busy – to find yourself incapacitated physically, because of course you never will be incapacitated

Agnes Alexander holding Mari Zenimoto. Her father Michitoshi Zenimoto said that Agnes had 'insisted that I must have a daughter and call her Mary, and she went on to tell me that her dearest friend and spiritual mother, beloved May Maxwell, had had a lovely little daughter whom she named Mary . . . years later a daughter was born to my wife and me. There was no question as to her name, Mari, the Japanese version of Mary' (Sims, Traces that Remain*). Amatu'l-Bahá Rúḥíyyih Khánum (the original Mary) blessed the Zenimoto home with her presence in 1979*

Agnes Alexander, sitting outside the Tokyo Bahá'í Centre, about 1965

Agnes spent two years in Jikei Idai Hospital in Tokyo, where she was visited by fellow Hands of the Cause and by National Spiritual Assembly members who frequently gathered in her room after a meeting. Ruth Walbridge (right) came from the Philippines to care for her

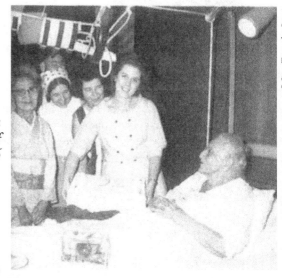

Ruth Walbridge offering Agnes a birthday cake on the occasion of her 91st birthday in 1966

Abu'l-Qásim Faizi and Agnes Alexander at the Bahá'í National Centre in Honolulu in December 1967

In September 1967, Agnes was brought back from Japan to Hawaii by her nephew and was housed in an apartment in the Arcadia Retirement Residence on Punahou Street, Honolulu, which ironically was adjacent to the property on which she was born. This photograph from August 1968 shows Agnes with Mary Tilton Fantom, affectionately known as 'Aunty May'. Mary Fantom became the first native Hawaiian Bahá'í in 1922, and like Agnes, lived out her last days in the Arcadia

On Agnes's 93rd birthday in 1968 two pioneers to Nigeria – Duane and Stephanie Troxel – brought her some gifts on behalf of the Nigerian Bahá'ís . . .

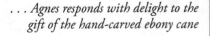

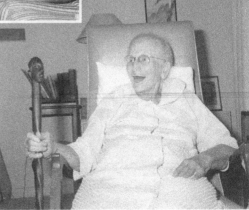

. . . Agnes responds with delight to the gift of the hand-carved ebony cane

Gravestone of Hand of the Cause Agnes Baldwin Alexander. Agnes was interred in the graveyard behind Kawaiahao Church in Honolulu, 'Hawaii's Westminster Abbey'. Many of Hawaii's most distinguished Christian missionaries are buried there

Agnes Baldwin Alexander in Japan, circa 1965

mentally or spiritually. But perhaps as you say this is part of the lesson of life. We never really do know why these things happen to us but all we can do is to realize as they are transient and after all this world and its miseries is not the important one; it is the next world and whatever we have garnered for it so to speak in this world that is the one that really counts. Perhaps we gradually learn this as we get older . . .

[Ethel Revell]: Dear Agnes, we have thought of you so often since your accident and have recently been made so happy to know that you are coming along so well. Just keep up the good work. We think of you and pray for you often. The Hands, in spite of their difficulties, their weaknesses, their ages, nothing stops them from their goals; they have their goals and they pursue them without any cessation. You're one of those. You are the one who is an example to others. Keep up the good work. Alláh-u-Abhá . . .

[Alí Nakhjavání]: My dear Agnes it is real joy and privilege to receive your tapes because it has double blessings for us. It means that Rúhíyyih Khánum comes to our house so that we play the tape to her and the second blessing is hearing your voice. We have always been thinking about you and continue to do so and we hope that you get better and that leave the hospital very soon and go back home and resume your wonderful services to the beloved Faith. God bless you.[18]

By the summer of 1967, after two years at the Japanese hospital, Agnes was accepting that she would never walk again unaided. Since her nephew, William Alexander, and his wife had been able to get her a room in the Arcadia retirement home in Honolulu, she wrote in a letter to Bill and Lee Smits, 'Please say a prayer that I may, if God so wills, be able to go to Honolulu.'[19]

The last years

On 10 September 1967, Agnes arrived back in Hawaii. The Hawaii Bahá'í newsletter, *Light of the Pacific*, announced her arrival:

Hand of the Cause Miss Agnes Alexander returned to her native Hawaii on September 10, 1967.

A large group of friends was on hand to greet her as she was carried from the plane and taken to her apartment. Miss Alexander is living in the beautiful new retirement home, Arcadia, on Punahou St., where her nephew, Will Alexander, also has an apartment . . .

Miss Alexander's name is synonymous with the Faith in Hawaii as it was she who first brought the Message to Maui in 1902.

For many years Miss Alexander has been a venerable influence for the Baha'is and their Faith in Japan and the Orient. Because of her position as a Hand of the Cause she has been able to assist in guiding the formation of the NSA of North East Asia.

We are happy to have our dear Agnes back home once more and pray that God grants her strength and health to be with us for many years.[20]

On 15 August 1968, Duane and Stephanie Troxel and Stephanie's mother, Margery Mugford, visited Agnes. Duane wrote:

As we entered [her room] we saw Agnes seated in a grey high-backed [rocking] chair near the window. Although we knew she had recently celebrated her 93rd birthday her appearance was that of a woman in her mid-70s.

Agnes is very white with high cheekbones and a jaw that juts out very firmly. Her clear blue eyes sparkled as we were introduced. A smile is permanently affixed to her face, otherwise smooth, except for heavy folds of wrinkles in her dimple area that became more pronounced as she drew the slack from her face with a smile.

She remarked that she didn't remember me after we had greeted her with 'Allah'u'Abha.' I explained that I had gone on a picnic with her in 1964 when she was visiting here. She couldn't recall but asked about us. We explained that we were African pioneers and that we carried presents from the N.S.A of West Central Africa for the occasion of her 93rd birthday.

When handed the [walking] cane she remarked sharply, 'Who is the cane for?' with a twinkle in her eyes.[21]

Agnes kept up her correspondence. On 24 September 1968, she wrote to Ramona Brown about her living conditions, 'I have a nice apartment room here & always have someone with me. Here friends come to see

me & sometimes I go out for a ride. I do not go to the dining room
but meals are brought to me. This place is next door to the place where
I was born, now a Christian Science church is built where the home
was.'[22]

The passing of Agnes Alexander

Near the end of December 1970, 18-year-old Elahe Vahdat (now
Young), visited Agnes. She was one of the last visitors and recalled:

> I visited Hand of the Cause Agnes Alexander many times at the
> Arcadia retirement home on Punaho street . . . during the last
> months of 1970 as I lived a walking distance from there. Some-
> times the door to her room would be ajar and sometimes closed. I
> would knock and she would invite me in. Mostly she was in bed and
> sometimes in her wheelchair. Her face was always so radiant. Our
> conversations were not long but her smile was so heart warming and
> she would ask me to say prayers with her which I did.
>
> A few days before her passing when I went to see her I felt that
> it would be best to take my camera and take a picture of her not
> knowing that would be the last picture of her on this earthly plain of
> existence. That day the door to her room was open ajar and I could
> see her sitting in her wheelchair in front of the window looking
> out. I knocked but she did not acknowledge me so I knocked again
> but she did not move. I entered her room and called her name [a]
> couple of times but she did not respond. Standing by her side I saw
> her angelic face illumined and very serene as though her soul was
> visiting the Abha Kingdom. After several minutes she closed her
> eyes and then looked my way and gave me a warm hug inviting me
> to sit next to her. We said prayers, then I asked her if I could take a
> picture with her which she agreed, we hugged again and I kissed her
> on her cheek and left.[23]

That final photo was sent to the Universal House of Justice.

Finally, on 1 January 1971, her soul departed the material plane for
her true abode in the spiritual one. The Universal House of Justice sent
a cable to the Bahá'í world for the passing of the one who had been the
oldest living Hand of the Cause of God:

375

PROFOUNDLY GRIEVE PASSING ILLUMINED SOUL HAND CAUSE AGNES
ALEXANDER LONGSTANDING PILLAR CAUSE FAR EAST FIRST BRING
FAITH HAWAIIAN ISLANDS. HER LONG DEDICATED EXEMPLARY LIFE
SERVICE DEVOTION CAUSE GOD ANTICIPATED BY CENTER COVENANT
SELECTING HER SHARE MAY MAXWELL IMPERISHABLE HONOR MEN-
TIONED TABLETS DIVINE PLAN. HER UNRESTRAINED UNCEASING
PURSUIT TEACHING OBEDIENCE COMMAND BAHA'U'LLAH EXHORTA-
TIONS MASTER GUIDANCE BELOVED GUARDIAN SHINING EXAMPLE ALL
FOLLOWERS FAITH. HER PASSING SEVERS ONE MORE LINK HEROIC AGE.
ASSURE FAMILY FRIENDS ARDENT PRAYERS HOLIEST SHRINE PROGRESS
RADIANT SOUL REQUEST ALL NATIONAL SPIRITUAL ASSEMBLIES HOLD
MEMORIAL MEETINGS AND THOSE RESPONSIBLE HOLD SERVICES
MOTHER TEMPLE[24]

Bahá'í News wrote:

Agnes B. Alexander, who was the oldest living Hand of the Cause
of God and the only Hand mentioned in the Tablets of the Divine
Plan, passed from this world on January 1. Miss Alexander, termed
by 'Abdu'l-Bahá 'the daughter of the Kingdom, the beloved maid-
servant of the Blessed Perfection.' . . .

Agnes Alexander was nearly 96 years old when she passed away.
Her life spanned the closing epoch of the Apostolic Age of the Faith
and the earliest epoch of the Formative Age, saw the erection of
National Spiritual Assemblies in lands where she was once the lone
Bahá'í, and also witnessed the birth of the long-promised era of The
Universal House of Justice. And now at long last Agnes Alexander is
with her beloved Master, 'Abdu'l-Bahá, in the Abhá Kingdom.

Truly Miss Alexander was one of the heroines of the formative
age of the Bahá'í Faith.[25]

Agnes's soul had gone, but her material remains quickly became the
focus of a concentrated effort by the Bahá'ís to forestall the cremation
of her body by her relatives. Agnes's original will, signed in 1965
and witnessed by Hand of the Cause Raḥmatu'lláh Muhájir, John S.
McHenry and her doctor, Ryniji Yamamoto, had stipulated that her
body was not to be cremated, but a codicil added in 1968, after she had
moved to Hawaii, specified that she wanted cremation followed by a

Christian service, with her ashes then interred in the family vault. This led to a week of intense consultation between the National Spiritual Assembly of the Bahá'ís of Hawaii, the Universal House of Justice and the executors of Agnes's will. The executors of the will, her nephew William Alexander and a trust company, were adamant that because of the codicil, it had to be cremation and a Christian service. They also insisted that cremation was necessary because there was no room in the family cemetery for a full burial. The Bahá'ís were just as adamant that Agnes was a Bahá'í and had been for 70 years, and that meant that she should be buried under Bahá'í burial laws.[26]

The Bahá'í effort included letters and phone calls to and from the Universal House of Justice and many meetings with Agnes's nephew William Alexander and the lawyers representing the family. Resolution came about primarily due to a letter sent by the Universal House of Justice which read in part 'You could point out that she was mentioned by 'Abdu'l-Bahá in the Tablets of the Divine Plan 1916, and she was referred to highly by Him, and that literally millions of Bahá'ís in the world have knowledge of this . . .' Their divine infallibility quickly became apparent.[27]

Acting on this guidance, the Bahá'ís took the House's letter along with a copy The Bahá'í World, volume VII, which contained the Tablets of the Divine Plan, and met with William Alexander. William was 'very impressed that the House of Justice would call us regarding the matter'. And when he was shown the references to his aunt in the Bahá'í World volume, he commented, 'She was doing the work of God.' William then set up a meeting with Mr Judd and Mr Roache, lawyers for the trust company. Their initial position was that 'since the Codicil was signed by Miss Alexander nothing could be changed unless we wanted to go to court . . . and we would probably lose . . . He said the codicil was unbreakable and to change it could cost them all their licenses.'[28]

While reiterating their refusal, the lawyers were passing a letter from the Hawaiian National Assembly back and forth without reading it. The Bahá'ís suggested they read the letter and after they had done so, showed them the Bahá'í World volume. After they read the letter and the Bahá'í World, 'Mr Judd sat quietly for a few minutes, visibly impressed, and then commented, with awe in his voice: "She is like a saint to the Baha'is. She is like a Saint."'[29]

After a week of dedicated work by the Bahá'ís, the executors finally relented and everyone realized that Agnes would not have agreed to the breaking of Bahá'í laws. Even the Christian minister agreed, saying that he would not have accepted to do the burial service had he known she was such a dedicated Bahá'í.[30]

To solve the problem of lack of space in the cemetery, Agnes was buried above her mother; the ashes of a brother and a sister had to be moved and reburied by her feet.[31]

Up to the last moment, the Bahá'ís had no idea what part they would play in the burial service, though they had given the minister the prayers and Writings they wished to use. When the minister and two Bahá'ís arrived at the burial site, the minister was obviously impressed with the number of Bahá'ís present and their attitude. At that point, he said to the Bahá'ís, 'Why don't you proceed.' Finally, at 4:30 p.m. on 8 January 1971, Agnes's mortal remains were laid to rest. The minister, after talking about her Christian missionary background, also spoke about her service to the Bahá'í Faith and concluded by saying, 'Although Agnes Alexander spent her life in service to Bahá'u'lláh it did not in any way detract from her reverence and belief in Jesus.'[32]

On 10 January, the Universal House of Justice wrote to the National Spiritual Assembly of Hawaii about their efforts:

> We have a telephonic report from your Chairman that you have been successful in avoiding the cremation of the precious remains of the Hand of the Cause Agnes Alexander and that she will be laid to rest in the family plot of a cemetery adjacent to a church. We note also that the Bahá'ís will have a part in the funeral service.
>
> We regard this as a tremendous victory in view of the circumstances which confronted you, and we are profoundly grateful that your steadfastness and perseverance as well as the prayers of the Hawaiian friends have been rewarded. Please be assured of our prayers of gratitude at the Holy Shrines.[33]

A life well lived

Agnes had two things which guided her life. The first was the direction given both to her personally and to the Bahá'ís collectively by 'Abdu'l-Bahá and Shoghi Effendi. The second was her constant belief that things happen 'if God wills' them to happen.

She was so connected to the spiritual world that she felt 'inspired' to do things, as she felt inspired to go to Japan and then Korea. She believed that these 'inspirations' were her spiritual marching orders, though she was never sure of just when she was to begin marching in the direction of those inspirations. That was where 'if God wills' came in. She knew she was supposed to go somewhere or do something, but not when. And not all of her inspirations came to pass. She never made it to Africa, as she had expected to in 1960. When Agnes was inspired by an idea, she would act on it, just as Shoghi Effendi suggested people should do with prayer. Pray, decide, act. That was her life.

Agnes believed that a suggestion from 'Abdu'l-Bahá or Shoghi Effendi was an order with no expiration date. 'Abdu'l-Bahá suggested that the Bahá'ís should learn Esperanto. Agnes did so to her great advantage in Japan, where knowing the language opened so many doors. And Shoghi Effendi wanted her to visit all the Bahá'í centres in Germany in 1937. She was unable to do so in that year because the Faith was prohibited by the Nazis. So when she went to Germany in 1959, she was grateful that she could finally finish what the Guardian had asked her to do.

Agnes was also the eternal optimist, rarely acknowledging the negative side of things. Even Mason Remey's breaking of the Covenant she viewed as God's way of more closely uniting the Bahá'ís of the world. She radiated love and kindliness everywhere she went and never spoke badly of others. This love mesmerised everyone and she was consequently able to do many things others could not.

Agnes was also the epitome of humility. She accepted being named a Hand of the Cause with surprising calm because she knew that the Guardian was infallibly guided, so it had to be the will of God, her foremost principle.

During her 70 years of service to the Faith of Bahá'u'lláh, Agnes opened Hawaii, Japan and Korea to the Bahá'í Faith, travelled with Martha Root in China and served across the Pacific Ocean as a Hand of the Cause. At the age of 83, she served simultaneously on the Local Spiritual Assembly of Kyoto, the Regional Spiritual Assembly of North East Asia and had her duties as a Hand of the Cause. She never complained.

As Ruth Suzuki wrote, Agnes was 'Japan's real super-hero disguised as a little old lady'. She truly had a life well lived.[34]

APPENDIX

MAY MAXWELL — A TRIBUTE

BY

AGNES B. ALEXANDER[1]

As God granted me the great favour of a deep spiritual love and near-
ness to our most beloved May Maxwell, which extended over 39 years,
I feel I must share this bounty. Words are inadequate to express all that
May has been in my life during these many years.

In Rome, Italy, the Light of the New Day was revealed to me on
November 26, 1900. After that day I was alone for three months with but
one Baha'i prayer. Turning to God for knowledge, day by day the Bible
prophecies of this Day unfolded to me, until at last I felt I must know
others who believed. Looking at some addresses which had been given
me in Rome, on November 26, I found the nearest believer was Miss
May Ellis Bolles, rue du Bac, Paris. From the depths of my longing heart
I wrote asking if she could tell me more of the wonderful Message. The
heavenly letter, which came in reply was so permeated with a divine love
that my heart was filled with assurance. For nearly nineteen years I kept
the letter with my most sacred treasures, until in a fire it was consumed.
The words it contained, though, were forever burned in my heart. She
wrote me that two years before she had the great bounty of making the
pilgrimage to Akka with the first group of American pilgrims, she had
twice seen the Master in visions, and when she met Him, she recognized
her Lord. In the letter she enclosed some prayers and wrote 'Learn them
by heart and say them two or three times daily, then we grow with great
power and spiritually for these prayers are from God'. She bid me come
to my brothers and sisters in Paris and there receive the full Revelation.
With her mother and brother, whose spiritual eyes were not opened to
the glorious Message, she was then living in Paris.

In the spring of 1901, I reached Paris. The first meeting there with beloved May is one of the most precious Memories of my life. She was then very slender and seemed to me like an angel of light. She gave me some pressed violets which had been given her by the master in Akka, and a photograph of our Lord taken when he was a young man in Adrianople. The feelings which came over me as I gazed on the photograph cannot be described. From that day May became my spiritual mother, and through all the years her tender love has been a guiding star in my life.

In Paris May had become the spiritual mother of a group of Americans, many of them students of art and architecture, and some French. They held weekly meetings in the studio of Charles Mason Remey. Accompanying May I attended my first Baha'i meeting. As I entered the room with her someone asked 'Is she a Baha'i?' The reply was, 'Look at her face!' As I looked around the room I saw the same look of peace and light on the faces. They had found their Lord and were at rest. Before the meeting began May retired to a room to pray. There before a photograph of the Master she knelt with forehead to the floor. In that moment I knelt with her and turned in prayer to the Master. An atmosphere of pure light pervaded the Paris meetings so much so that one was transported as it were, from the world of man to that of God. In the spiritual light of those meetings all questions vanished.

May had been chosen by God to be the spiritual mother and first Baha'i to introduce the Cause to the Latin people. Born with great force and energy, she was ill on her bed and couch for two and a half years before she heard the message. She told me in order that God might use her energies for His service, she had first to be laid low. When she heard the message from Lua in Paris in 1898, her whole being became alive with the love of her Lord and service to him, never relaxing until her last earthly moment was spent. At that time there was little printed Baha'i literature besides the Arabic 'Hidden Words' and a book of prayers. While I was in Paris, May received the first copy of the Persian 'Hidden Words'. It was so precious to her that she slept with it under her pillow.

At last the time came when I felt I should return to teach the cause in my home land, Hawaii. A day in June, as I was preparing to leave Paris the next morning a blessed Tablet came to me from the Master in which he wrote, 'Proceed to thy native country.' That night I attended a reception at the Bolles apartment. Carrying the precious Tablet with me my heart was full of joy and assurance. When I said goodbye to May, she accompanied me to the stairs. As I descended, looking back I saw her heavenly eyes follow me. We were not to meet again for many years. May wrote me afterwards that she felt her heart would break at the parting, so tender was the love she bore to all who came under her spiritual influence, a love which the Master said was divine.

For more than twelve years, in far away Hawaii, May's letters like fresh breezes of divine spirit, came stimulating the hearts. All who heard the message there shared in her love and heavenly influence. Thus the foundation of the Baha'i Faith in Hawaii was permeated with her spirit.

In May, 1902, May was married to Mr. W. S. Maxwell, a Scotch-Canadian, and went to live in his home in Montreal, Canada. 'Abdu'l-Baha had written her to devote herself to him until he became illumined and then they would be permitted to visit Akka. Through this marriage Mr. Maxwell came to be the first Canadian Baha'i and May the spiritual mother of Canada. From the purifying fire of tests and temptations she emerged, as 'Abdu'l-Baha wrote 'pure in heart and attracted in soul.' To a number of Baha'is whose husbands were not awakened he wrote advising them to follow the example of Mrs. Maxwell who led her husband to the Cause. To May he wrote. 'Many a leaf was in the utmost attraction, but when united with a man (i.e. when she married) she relaxed, and the fire of her love subsided she became occupied with the earthly world, neglected the divine realm, passionately loved this mortal life and became independent from the divine, eternal life. But as to thee, O thou attracted maid-servant of God, thou art delivered from test and temptation, and naught of the passion and devotion which thou didst have for the Kingdom of God, underwent any change or transformation. This is through the grace of thy Lord, the Clement, the Merciful!'

May once wrote me that some day I would come to their home in Montreal. In the fall of 1913, the dream was realized. May was then the mother of a beautiful child born in 1910 and destined to be the wife of the first Guardian of the Cause. The Maxwell home had become the first Baha'i center in Canada. While I was there, on November 26, the day of the Covenant was celebrated.

After my first sojourn in Japan, I met May at the 1918 Baha'i Convention held in Chicago. She then went around in a wheel chair. Although her health was very delicate, it did not deter her from service to her Lord nor from traveling long distances to serve him. In a talk which she gave during the convention, she seemed like an empty reed through which the spirit spoke. When I mentioned this to May, she told me that she had suffered all the night before, until in reality she had become empty.

In the spring of 1919 before the convention in N. Y. I again visited in the Maxwell home. 'Abdu'l-Baha had written me 'In accordance with the wish of the attracted maid-servant of God to the love of God, Mrs. Maxwell, go thou to Canada and stay there for a time.' The believers in Montreal were as 'Abdu'l-Baha wrote in the Tablet to Canada, 'in the utmost spirituality and attracted from the fragrances of God . . . through the effort of the maid-servant of God, Mrs. Maxwell . . .'

After the Baha'i convention, according to May's wish, I went to Toronto where she came to meet me. There was then in Toronto a few friends whom May had taught in Montreal, and these she gathered around her. On one occasion May's beautiful language greatly impressed me as she talked of the Cause. When I mentioned it to her, she said it was because she was in Canada and the Master had confirmed her to teach there. After ten days I left May to start towards Japan at 'Abdu'l-Baha's request. In Tokyo, on November 26, a blessed Tablet from 'Abdu'l-Baha came to me in which he wrote: 'Thou hast undoubtedly met the attracted maid-servant of God, Mrs. Maxwell, before sailing to Japan, for that maid-servant of God is ablaze with the fire of the love of God. Whom-so-ever meets her feels from her association the susceptibilities of the Kingdom. Her company uplifts and develops the soul.' It was indeed for my own soul's development, that I might better serve his Cause, that God had privileged me to associate with May.

Fifteen years passed before I met May again in 1934. During the interval the Master had ascended. May, who was entirely centered in her Lord, was very ill for a time after his passing. Then in 1923 she went to Haifa with her little daughter and a Canadian maid. It was there the Guardian assisted her to walk and through him she found her Center. She spent seven months in Haifa and then went to Egypt, but again returned. At last Shoghi Effendi bid her to come to America and share the bounty she had received in that Holy Spot. When I met May in 1934, she told me of the glorious experiences of her visit in Haifa. Through beloved May I received new inspiration and insight.

On April 20, 1937, when I reached the Land of Desire, at the invitation of Shoghi Effendi, great was God's bounty to me that there I found my precious spiritual mother. Her daughter was then married to the beloved Guardian, and through this marriage Mr. and Mrs. Maxwell had become members of the Holy Household. How marvelous are the ways of God! Those were never to be forgotten days when we dined together in the presence of the Guardian. In God's plan the way did not open for me to meet 'Abdu'l-Baha, but through His bounty I was privileged to meet the first Guardian at that momentous time. My heart was entirely satisfied when I left Haifa to visit the friends, at Shoghi Effendi's request, and share the impressions and experiences of my stay in the Holy Land.

My last visit with May in her home in Montreal was in December, 1937. She was then conducting a weekly Baha'i study class which was open to the public. It was my privilege to be present at two of these gatherings. Such a spirit pervaded the meetings that the friends and strangers came early and were loath to leave when the hour was over. The lessons were taken from an outline and there were readings from the Holy Utterances which May interspersed with beautiful explanations. This class proved the hunger of people for the Word of God.

While in Evanston, during the 1938 Baha'i convention, I gleaned many precious teachings from May. The day before the convention opened, an informal meeting was held to discuss teaching methods. As it was progressing, May entered and was asked to speak. Her words were like light penetrating through clouds. She said Shoghi Effendi had said America needs most, depth, reverence and humility. She asked what they were going to tell the people, and said to tell them that there is on earth to-day a being through whom the spiritual power flows, that the only hope that can be given is the first Guardian. The world itself she said, is turning to Shoghi Effendi unconsciously. Then she quoted the words from the Revelation of St. John, 'The sun will not set.' She said the American way of speaking was to use many words but to say little, that 'Abdu'l-F[adl] said to take the deepest points first and dwell on them, that we should not speak only to the mind, and that 'Abdu'l-Baha said Unity and such movements are on the mental plain and have not depth. When someone asked if we should speak first of the Guardian, May replied that he had said the Cause is very fluid and we cannot fix it. She then said, 'On this continent we must raise the standard. There is one point of infallibility. We must lose our nationalism and bathe ourselves in the flood which is flowing from Mount Carmel continually.' She said there is a yearning in the public for the Word of God. The convention received great inspiration from May's reading of the 'Notes' taken from Ruhiyyih Khanum in Shoghi Effendi's presence of his words, and sent to the American believers at his request. One morning in the convention, May spoke and told us that the Guardian said every Baha'i should study continually the Will and Testament. She said the foundation of the union of the East and West was consummated by the Guardian and her daughter entering alone the Sacred Shrine of Baha'u'llah, where he chanted two prayers in the presence of God. She spoke of the eight cables which were sent to the National Spiritual Assemblies on that occasion, announcing the marriage, and that the Guardian's cable, replying to one conveying congratulations from the National Spiritual Assembly of the United States and Canada, were these words, 'Institution Guardianship head cornerstone Administration Order.' She told us how the Guardian had said to her, 'Abdu'l-Baha has put all power into my hands.' She asked him, 'Why do you not use it?' and he replied, 'The Baha'is do not let me.' Then May said, 'He is the quickening life in the body of the friends. He is the tangible Point on this earth. The law of the Focal Point exists in every atom of the universe. The Guardian is the Focal Point . . .' She told us how the Guardian asked her, 'How do you pray?' She replied, 'I first turn to you because you are in the body and so am I. You are the tangible point, and when I have made that connection, then I pray to Baha'U'llah and through Baha'U'llah I reach the Almighty Being.' He replied, 'This is exactly correct.'

On another occasion, when speaking informally, May said we have to transcend, first our ego from ancestors, and then our national ego, transcend the one-thousand veils. We grow through struggles. The butterfly if liberated with help is weak. Its strength is in liberating itself. Shoghi Effendi, she said, is the life channel of the House of Justice.

In the spring of 1939 I spent several weeks with May in Evanston, where we enjoyed, as she expressed it, 'sunlit hours of divine companionship.' In interracial work she had supreme courage. Not only did she adhere to the Master's words regarding the complete union of the colored and the white race, but in her life and actions she lived his behests. One morning I was present when she talked with a friend about the race question. A few of her words that morning I wish to share. She said, 'Consciousness of race is a sign of absence of culture. It is a new world Baha'u'llah has ushered us into. He has inoculated us with a new virus. The Master never said we must be careful; we must be wise and cautious. He said if we didn't unite, the negro race would rise up. The world is sunk in ignorance. We must not look at what the world thinks. We are sunk in the sea of imagination.' When I said to May afterwards that it had been a wonderful morning, she asked, 'What did I say?' She was a pure channel used in God's hands. During those weeks in Evanston I entered into Baha'i activity with colored friends in South Chicago. Though physically unable to attend the meetings, May took the deepest interest in the work which she called, 'the Most essential work.'

Several times I was privileged to accompany May to the House of Worship to pray. How joyous she was when she found she could reach the upper floor by an outside stair-way. When she was absorbed in prayer. I felt the invisible connection between her heart and the Center of the Faith, as though space was obliterated and the ideal nearness attained.

The last noon with May in Evanston in June, 1939, a little boy sitting near us came and threw his arms around her neck and kissed her several times. Then a second time he came and repeated it. May said to me, 'This is something mystic.' She did not reciprocate his caresses, as she did not wish his mother to feel jealous. May then told me that the day before she had heard the mother nagging the boy and suggested that children did not like always to be with grown people, and that sometimes we should play with them. The little boy had felt May's mother love without words. The next day I saw the mother and boy having a joyous romp together.

From the time May met her Lord in Akka in 1899, and 'beheld the King in His Beauty,' her whole being was kindled with the divine flame. 'Abdu'l-Baha said to her, 'You are like the rain which is poured upon the earth making it bud and blossom and become fruitful, so shall the spirit of God descend upon you, filling you with fruitfulness and you shall go forth and enter his vineyard.' Her great capacity to weld hearts together and transform the lives of those who came in her path, because she herself was firmly centered in the Center of the Covenant. First in the Master, then in obedience to His Will and Testament, she turned to Shoghi Effendi, the 'sacred branch.' Her nearness and the turning to the Center was the propelling power in her life. Countless are the souls who have been ignited through her divine love. In every land which had the blessing of her presence they are to be found. Into many other countries her spiritual influence penetrated through the letters which she continually poured forth filled with the breath of the love of God, stimulating and encouraging Baha'i teachers in distant lands.

A precious gift from God to May was exquisite speech. One was always conscious that whatever she said was the truth. She had true spiritual humility and reverence which increased as she became a member of the Holy Household. The burning desire of her life was to help establish among the friends a true conception of the administration order and its Guardianship. She possessed great spiritual energy, and though in frail health, devoted her entire being in service to those who came in her path. In a recent letter she wrote, 'You have no idea of the pressure of my life but I am grateful for every moment spent in such service.' She made the supreme sacrifice in the path of the beloved Guardian and has joined the great throng of martyrs gone before. In the infinite World of God her spirit now overshadows us. As Shoghi Effendi cabled, she deservedly won a double crown, the sacred tie as a member of the Holy Household, to which is now added a martyr's death. The greatness of her earthly achievements are hidden with God. In the distant future they will spring with shining brightness.

A thousand loving hearts are now turning toward South America, and Buenos Aires, in longing to attain the spot where our precious mother is laid to rest and there to supplicate her intercession for us all.

BIBLIOGRAPHY

'Abdu'l-Bahá. *Tablets of the Divine Plan*. Wilmette, IL: Bahá'í Publishing Trust, rev. ed. 1993.

— *Will and Testament*. Wilmette, IL: National Spiritual Assembly of the Bahá'ís of the United States, 1944.

— and Shoghi Effendi. *Japan Will Turn Ablaze!* Tokyo: Bahá'í Publishing Trust Japan, 1974, rev. ed. 1992.

Adamson, Hugh. *Historical Dictionary of the Bahá'í Faith*. London: Scarecrow Press, 2006.

Afroukhteh, Youness. *Memories of Nine Years in 'Akká*. Oxford: George Ronald, 2003.

Alexander, Agnes Baldwin. *An Account of How I Became a Bahá'í and My Stays in Paris in 1901 and 1937*. Available at: http://bahailibrary.com/alexander_linard_autiobiography, 1958.

— 'A Bahá'í Enters the Hermit Kingdom', in *World Order* (August 1947), p. 170.

— *Forty Years of the Baha'i Cause in Hawaii: 1902–1942*. Also titled: *Personal Recollections of a Baha'i Life in the Hawaiian Islands*. Honolulu: National Spiritual Assembly of the Bahá'ís of the Hawaiian Islands, 1974.

— *History of the Bahá'í Faith in Japan: 1914–1938*. Osaka: Bahá'í Publishing Trust, 1977. Online edition Barbara Sims, available at: bahai-library.com.

— 'How Abdul-Baha Opened the Door to Korea', in *Reality Magazine* (December 1921), pp. 27–39.

— *How to Use Hawaiian Fruits* (1910).

— *Notes Taken in the Presence of Shoghi Effendi*.

Alexander, Rev. William P. *Mission Life in Hawaii*. Oakland: Pacific Press Publishing Co, 1888.

Allen, Valera. *Memories of Hand of the Cause, Agnes Alexander*. Duane Troxel personal papers.

Bahá'í News. Periodical. National Spiritual Assembly of the Bahá'ís of the United States.

The Bahá'í World: An International Record. Vol. III (1928–1930), Wilmette, IL: Bahá'í Publishing Committee, 1931; vol. IV (1930–1932), Wilmette, IL: Bahá'í Publishing Trust, 1933; Vol. V (1932–1934), Wilmette, IL: Bahá'í Publishing

Trust, 1936; vol. VII (1936–1938), Wilmette: Bahá'í Publishing Trust, 1939; vol. XII (1950–1954), Wilmette, IL: Bahá'í Publishing Trust, 1956; vol. XIV (1963–1968), Haifa: The Universal House of Justice, 1974; vol. XV (1968–1973), Haifa: Bahá'í World Centre, 1976; vol. XVIII (1979–1983), Haifa: Bahá'í World Centre, 1986.

Bahá'u'lláh. *The Kitáb-i-Aqdas: The Most Holy Book.* Haifa: Bahá'í World Centre, 1992.

Collins, William P. *Bibliography of English-Language Works on the Bábí and Bahá'í Faiths, 1844–1985.* Oxford: George Ronald, 1990.

Faizi-Moore, May. *Faizi.* Oxford: George Ronald, 2013.

Fuchs, Lawrence H. *Hawaii Pono.* Honolulu: Bess Press, 1983.

Garis, M. R. *Martha Root.* Wilmette, IL: Bahá'í Publishing Trust, 1983.

Hamilton, Tracy and Healani. *The Passing of Miss Agnes Baldwin Alexander.* Privately printed in Honolulu, 2003.

Harper, Barron. *Lights of Fortitude.* Oxford: George Ronald, 1997.

Hassall, Graham. 'Bahá'í Country Notes: China'. Available at : http://bahai-library. com/hassall_notes_china.

— 'Notes on the Bábí and Bahá'í religions in Russia and its territories', in *Journal of Bahá'í Studies,* vol. 5 (1992), no. 3.

Hassall, Graham; Austria, Orwin. *Mirza Hossein R. Touty: First Bahá'í Known to Have Lived in the Philippines.* 2000. Available at: http://bahai-library.com/hassall_ austria_hossein_touty.

Hopkins, Gerard Manley. *Hawaii: The Past, Present, and Future of its Island-Kingdom.* London: Longman, Green, Longman and Roberts, 1862.

Keller, Rosemary Skinner; Ruether, Rosemary Radford; Cantlon, Marie. *Encyclopedia of Women and Religion in North America.* Indianapolis: Indiana University Press, 2006.

Light of the Pacific. Periodical. National Spiritual Assembly of the Bahá'ís of the Hawaiian Islands.

Macke, Marlene. *Take My Love to the Friends: The Story of Laura R. Davis.* Ontario: Chestnut Park Press, 2009.

Magazine of the Children of the Kingdom. Periodical. Boston, Mass, 191–24.

The Ministry of the Custodians, 1957–1963. Haifa: Bahá'í World Centre, 1992.

Momen, Moojan (ed.). *The Bábí and Bahá'í Religions, 1844–1944.* Oxford: George Ronald, 1981.

Muhájir, Írán Furútan. *Dr Muhajir.* London: Bahá'í Publishing Trust, 1992.

Pfaff-Grossmann, Susanne. *Hermann Grossmann, Hand of the Cause of God: A Life for the Faith.* Oxford: George Ronald, 2009.

Redman, Earl. *'Abdu'l-Bahá in Their Midst.* Oxford: George Ronald, 2011.

— *The Juneau Gold Belt.* Juneau, Alaska: The Gastineau Channel Historical Soc, 2011.

— *Shoghi Effendi Through the Pilgrim's Eye*. Vol. 2: *The Ten Year Crusade*. Oxford: George Ronald, 2016.

— *Visiting 'Abdu'l-Bahá*. Vol. 2: The Final Years, 1913–1921. Oxford: George Ronald, 2020.

Reality Magazine. New York: Reality Publishing Company, Jan. 1921–Dec. 1921.

Remey, Charles Mason. *My Travels Around the World with Howard Struven, 1909–1910*, typewritten account.

Ruhe-Schoen, Janet. *Ransom-Kehler, Keith Bean*, in *The Bahá'í Encyclopedia*, available at: http://www.bahai-encyclopedia-project.org/index.php?view=article&catid=56%3Aa-selection-of-articles&id=73%3Aransom-kehler-keith-bean&option=com_content&Itemid=74.

Rúḥíyyih Khánum, transcript by Duane Troxel and Odmaa Dugersuren of a tape recording of 12 March 1966.

Rutstein, Nathan. *He Loved and Served: The Story of Curtis Kelsey*. Oxford: George Ronald, 1982.

Shoghi Effendi. *Messages to America, 1932–1946*. Wilmette: Bahá'í Publishing Trust, 1947.

— *Messages to the Bahá'í World, 1950–1957*. Wilmette: Bahá'í Publishing Trust, 1971.

— *This Decisive Hour*. Wilmette, IL: Bahá'í Publishing Trust, 1992.

Sims, Barbara. *Taiwan Bahá'í Chronicle: An Historical Record of the Early Days of the Bahá'í Faith in Taiwan*. Tokyo: Bahá'í Publishing Trust of Taiwan, 1994. https://bahai-library.com/sims_taiwan_bahai_chronicle.

— *Unfurling the Divine Flag in Tokyo, An Early Bahá'í History*. Tokyo: Bahá'í Publishing Trust Japan, 1998. Available at: https://bahai-library.com/sims_taiwan_bahai_chronicle.

Star of the West. Periodical, 25 vols. 1910–1935. Vols. 1–14 RP Oxford: George Ronald, 1978. Complete CD-ROM version: Talisman Educational Software/Special Ideas, 2001.

The Bahá'í Encyclopedia Project. National Spiritual Assembly of the Bahá'ís of the United States.

Troxel, Duane. *Agnes Baldwin Alexander and the Origin and Development of the Bahá'í Faith in the Hawaiian Islands: 1900–1913*. Unpublished manuscript.

— Duane Troxel Papers, private collection.

— *Eighty Golden Years: The Bahá'í Faith in Hawaii, 1901–1981*. Honolulu, 1981.

Whitehead, O.Z. *Some Bahá'ís to Remember*. Oxford: George Ronald, 1983.

World Fellowship Magazine. Vol 1, no 6. Montclair, New Jersey, 1924.

Zinky, Kay. *Martha Root: Herald of the Kingdom*. New Delhi: Bahá'í Publishing Trust, 1983.

NOTES AND REFERENCES

Unless otherwise stated, unpublished letters and other documents are in the National Baháʼí Archives of Hawaii or in the US National Baháʼí Archives.

1 Who is Agnes Alexander?

1   G.V. Tehrani, letter to Duane Troxel, dated 4 December 1981.
2   ʼAbduʼl-Bahá and Shoghi Effendi, *Japan Will Turn Ablaze!*, Introduction.
3   ibid.
4   Baháʼuʼlláh, *Kitáb-i-Aqdas*, para. 173, p. 82, and note 183, p. 245.
5   ʼAbduʼl-Bahá, *Will and Testament*, para. 2, p. 3.
6   Shoghi Effendi, *Messages to the Baháʼí World, 1950–1957*, p. 127.
7   ʼAbduʼl-Bahá, *Tablets of the Divine Plan*, p. 42.
8   Troxel, *Eighty Golden Years: The Baháʼí Faith in Hawaii, 1901–1981*.
9   Agnes Alexander, *History of the Baháʼí Faith in Japan*, p. 44.

2 Christianity, Politics and Conquest

1   Fuchs, *Hawaii Pono*, p. 9.
2   Agnes Alexander, *Forty Years of the Baháʼí Cause in Hawaii*, p. 5.
3   William P. Alexander, *Mission Life in Hawaii*, p. 17.
4   ibid. p. 20.
5   Agnes Alexander, *Forty Years of the Baháʼí Cause in Hawaii*, p. 5.
6   Manley Hopkins, *Hawaii*, p. 222.
7   Fuchs, *Hawaii Pono*, pp. 10–13.
8   Manley Hopkins, *Hawaii*, p. 228.
9   Fuchs, *Hawaii Pono*, pp. 15–16.
10   ibid. pp. 10–13, 16–17.
11   ibid. pp. 19, 22.
12   ibid. p. 3–4.
13   ibid. p. 32.
14   ibid. pp. 25, 31–33, 43–44.
15   ibid. p. 46.

3 Agnes Baldwin Alexander: The Early Years

1   William De Witt Alexander, letter to William P. Alexander, dated 16 August 1875.
2   Punahou School, online article available at: http://www.punahou.edu/about/history/index.aspx?Referer=https%253a%252f%252fwww.punahou.edu%252f.
3   Fuchs. *Hawaii Pono*, p. 264.
4   Agnes Alexander, letter to Henry Alexander, dated 7 July 1883.

5   William De Witt Alexander, note from the Hawaiian Mission Children's Society Library taken by Duane Troxel.

6   Agnes Alexander, letter to William De Witt Alexander, dated 6 May 1886.

7   Agnes Alexander, letter to William De Witt Alexander, dated 15 September 1886.

8   Agnes Alexander, letter to Willie Alexander, dated 5 February 1888.

9   Agnes Alexander, letter to Arthur Alexander, dated 15 July 1888.

10 Agnes Alexander, *Forty Years of the Baha'i Cause in Hawaii*, p. 7.

11 Agnes Alexander, letter to Henry Alexander, dated 30 January 1890.

12 Agnes Alexander, letter to Henry Alexander, dated 25 July 1890.

13 Agnes Alexander, letter to Abigail Alexander, dated 3 January 1891.

14 Agnes Alexander, letters to Abigail Alexander, dated 11, 20, and 26 August 1892.

15 Agnes Alexander, letter to Abigail Alexander, dated 20 September 1892.

16 Agnes Alexander, letters to Abigail Alexander, dated 26 September and 18 October 1892.

17 Agnes Alexander, letter to Abigail Alexander, dated 28 July 1893.

18 Agnes Alexander, letter to Abigail Alexander, dated 31 August 1893.

19 Agnes Alexander, letter to Abigail Alexander, dated 11 August 1893.

20 Agnes Alexander, letter to Abigail Alexander, dated 24 August 1893.

21 Agnes Alexander, letter to Mary Alexander, dated 25 November 1893.

22 Agnes Alexander, letter to Mary Alexander, dated 7 February 1894.

23 Agnes Alexander, letter to Mary Alexander, dated 17 April 1894.

24 Agnes Alexander, letters to Mary Alexander, dated 18 and 19 July 1894.

25 Agnes Alexander, letter to Mary Alexander, dated 13 September 1894.

26 Abigail Alexander, letter to Charlotte Alexander, dated 24 June 1895.

27 Agnes Alexander, letter to William De Witt Alexander, dated 9 January 1896.

28 ibid.

29 Dr Sarah Sabour-Pickett, email to the author, 4 October 2016.

30 Agnes Alexander, letter to her parents, dated 5 February 1896.

31 Agnes Alexander, letter to William De Witt Alexander, dated 9 January 1896.

32 Agnes Alexander, letter to Abigail Alexander, dated 14 February 1896.

33 Agnes Alexander, letter to her parents, dated 11 May 1896.

34 Agnes Alexander, letter to William De Witt Alexander, dated 7 July 1896.

35 Agnes Alexander, letter to Abigail Alexander, dated 21 July 1896.

36 Agnes Alexander, letter to Abigail Alexander, dated 7 August 1896.

37 Agnes Alexander, letter to William De Witt Alexander, dated 15 September 1896.

38 Agnes Alexander, letter to William De Witt Alexander, dated 20 September 1896.

39 Abigail Alexander, extracts from her personal journal, p. 21.

40 *The Hawaiian Star*, 2 January 1899.

41 Abigail Alexander, extracts from her personal journal, pp. 23–5.

42 ibid. p. 28.

43 ibid.

44 ibid. p. 29.

4 A Life-Changing Adventure: 1900–1901

1   Emily Baldwin, letter to William De Witt Alexander, dated 26 April 1900.

2   Abigail Alexander, extracts from her personal journal, p. 32.

3   Agnes Alexander, *Forty Years of the Baha'i Cause in Hawaii*, p. 7.

4   Agnes Alexander, letter to her parents, dated 5 November 1900.
5   Agnes Alexander, letter to Abigail Alexander, dated 19 November 1900.
6   Agnes Alexander, letter to her parents, dated 28 November 1900.
7   Agnes Alexander, letter to Mary Alexander, dated 3 November 1900.
8   Agnes Alexander, letter to her parents, dated 28 November 1900.
9   Agnes Alexander, *Forty Years of the Baha'i Cause in Hawaii*, p. 7.
10 Agnes Alexander, transcript of a talk in Menlo Park, CA, 1961.
11 ibid.
12 Agnes Alexander, *Forty Years of the Baha'i Cause in Hawaii*, p. 7.
13 Agnes Alexander, *An Account of How I Became a Bahá'í and My Stays in Paris in 1901 and 1937.*
14 Agnes Alexander, transcript of a talk in Menlo Park, CA, 1961.
15 Agnes Alexander, *Forty Years of the Baha'i Cause in Hawaii*, p. 7.
16 ibid. p. 8.
17 Agnes Alexander, letter to her parents, dated 14 March 1901.
18 Agnes Alexander, letter to her parents, dated March 1901.
19 Agnes Alexander, audio recording of talk at the 1964 Hawaii National Bahá'í Convention.
20 Agnes Alexander, *An Account of How I Became a Bahá'í and My Stays in Paris in 1901 and 1937.*
21 Agnes Alexander, letter to her parents, dated 14 March 1901.
22 Agnes Alexander, *Forty Years of the Baha'i Cause in Hawaii*, pp. 8–9.
23 Agnes Alexander, letter to one of her brothers, dated 28 March 1901.
24 Agnes Alexander, letter to Mary Alexander, dated 28 April 1901.
25 Agnes Alexander, *Forty Years of the Baha'i Cause in Hawaii*, p. 9.
26 Agnes Alexander, letter to her parents, dated 14 April 1901.
27 Agnes Alexander, *Forty Years of the Baha'i Cause in Hawaii*, p. 9.
28 ibid.
29 ibid. p. 10.
30 Agnes Alexander, letter to her parents, dated 8 August 1901.
31 Agnes Alexander, *Forty Years of the Baha'i Cause in Hawaii*, p. 10.

5 Spreading the Bahá'í Faith in Hawaii: 1902–1913

1   Agnes Alexander, *Forty Years of the Baha'i Cause in Hawaii*, p. 10.
2   ibid.
3   Abigail Alexander, extracts from her personal journal.
4   ibid.
5   Elizabeth Muther, letter to Ella Cooper, dated 18 June 1934.
6   'Abdu'l-Bahá, Tablet to Agnes Alexander translated in Chicago on 25 January 1903, quoted in *Forty Years of the Baha'i Cause in Hawaii*, p. 14.
7   Agnes Alexander, *Forty Years of the Baha'i Cause in Hawaii*, p. 13.
8   Abigail Alexander, extracts from her personal journal.
9   Agnes Alexander, *Forty Years of the Baha'i Cause in Hawaii*, p. 13.
10 *US Bahá'í News*, no. 556 (July 1977), p. 5.
11 Agnes Alexander, *Forty Years of the Baha'i Cause in Hawaii*, p. 12.
12 ibid.
13 ibid.
14 Afroukhteh, *Memories of Nine Years in 'Akká*, p. 269.

15 Tablet of 'Abdu'l-Bahá to Mr Yamamoto, quoted in *Forty Years of the Baha'i Cause in Hawaii*, p. 12.
16 Agnes Alexander, *Forty Years of the Baha'i Cause in Hawaii*, p. 13.
17 ibid.
18 Abigail Alexander, extract from her personal journal.
19 William De Witt Alexander, letters to J. S. Emerson of Oxford, England, dated 20 December 1904 and 25 January 1905.
20 Agnes Alexander, letter to 'Dear Folks', dated 25 July 1905, p. 1.
21 ibid.
22 ibid. p. 2.
23 Redman, *The Juneau Gold Belt*, p. 41.
24 Agnes Alexander, letter to 'Dear Folks', dated 25 July 1905, p. 5.
25 ibid. p. 2.
26 It is not known whether this is Mary Baldwin or Mary Alexander.
27 Agnes Alexander, letter to 'Dear Folks', dated 25 July 1905, p. 2.
28 ibid.
29 ibid. pp. 2–3.
30 ibid. p. 3.
31 *Hawaiian Star*, 18 October 1905.
32 Agnes Alexander, unsent letter to 'Abdu'l-Bahá, dated 30 December 1907.
33 Agnes Alexander, letter to 'Dearest Sister', dated January 1908.
34 Agnes Alexander, unsent letter to 'Abdu'l-Bahá, dated 30 December 1907.
35 Agnes Alexander, *Forty Years of the Baha'i Cause in Hawaii*, p. 13.
36 Ada Whitney Weinrich, letter to Agnes Alexander, dated 7 February 1908.
37 Agnes Alexander, letter to Elizabeth Muther, dated 25 August 1908.
38 'Abdu'l-Bahá, Tablet to 'Miss Agnes B. Alexander, Honolulu, Hawaii', 14 August 1909, in 'Abdu'l-Bahá and Shoghi Effendi, *Japan Will Turn Ablaze!*, p. 11.
39 Agnes Alexander, letter to 'Friends', dated 22 November 1908.
40 Agnes Alexander, undated letter to Elizabeth Muther.
41 ibid.
42 ibid.
43 Agnes Alexander, *Forty Years of the Baha'i Cause in Hawaii*, p. 15; Adamson, *Historical Dictionary of the Bahá'í Faith*, p. 98.
44 Agnes Alexander, *Forty Years of the Baha'i Cause in Hawaii*, pp. 15–16.
45 ibid. p. 16.
46 ibid.
47 ibid.
48 Ella Rowland, written commune, in Duane Troxel papers.
49 Gertrude Buikema, letter to Agnes Alexander, dated 10 August 1909.
50 Remey, *My Travels Around the World with Howard Struven, 1909–1910*, p. 59.
51 Agnes Alexander, *Forty Years of the Baha'i Cause in Hawaii*, p. 17.
52 Remey, *My Travels Around the World with Howard Struven, 1909–1910*, pp. 59–60.
53 Agnes Alexander, *Forty Years of the Baha'i Cause in Hawaii*, p. 17.
54 *Hawaiian Star*, 29 November 1909.
55 Remey, *My Travels Around the World with Howard Struven, 1909–1910*, pp. 60–61.
56 Momen (ed.), *The Bábí and Bahá'í Religions*, p. 19.

57 *Honolulu Commercial Advertiser*, 30 November 1909, p. 9.
58 *Hawaiian Star*, 30 Nov. 1909, 4 December 1909, p. 12.
59 Tony Pelle, in *Bahá'í News* (Hawaii), no. 561 (December 1977), p. 5.
60 Remey, *My Travels Around the World with Howard Struven, 1909–1910*, p. 63.
61 *Honolulu Evening Bulletin*, 13 December 1909.
62 Remey, *My Travels Around the World with Howard Struven, 1909–1910*, p. 63.
63 Agnes Alexander, *Forty Years of the Baha'i Cause in Hawaii*, p. 21.
64 Agnes Alexander, letter to Albert Windust, dated 13 March 1910.
65 Whitehead, *Some Bahá'ís to Remember*, p. 189.
66 Duane Troxel, Hawaiian Bahá'í Archives.
67 Hawaiian Archives, Historical Record Card.
68 *The Honolulu Star*, 8 August 1910.
69 Agnes Alexander, letters to Abigail Alexander, dated 11 and 20 August 1910.
70 1910–1923 Honolulu Assembly Record Book, p. 5.
71 *Paradise of the Pacific Weekly*, April 1911.
72 William De Witt Alexander, letter to Rev. W.W. Ferrier, dated 9 October 1911.
73 *Honolulu Advertiser*, undated articles.
74 Agnes Alexander, *Forty Years of the Baha'i Cause in Hawaii*, p. 22.
75 ibid.
76 ibid. p. 23.
77 ibid.

6 Beginning the Great Adventure: 1913

1   Agnes Alexander, *History of the Bahá'í Faith in Japan*, p. 7.
2   'Abdu'l-Bahá and Shoghi Effendi, *Japan Will Turn Ablaze!*, p. 10.
3   Agnes Alexander, *Forty Years of the Baha'i Cause in Hawaii*, p. 24.
4   Agnes Alexander, *History of the Bahá'í Faith in Japan*, p. 8.
5   ibid.
6   'Abdu'l-Bahá, Tablet to Agnes Alexander, dated 31 October 1913, ibid.
7   ibid.
8   Agnes Alexander, *Forty Years of the Baha'i Cause in Hawaii*, p. 21.
9   Agnes Alexander, *History of the Bahá'í Faith in Japan*, pp. 8–9.
10 ibid. p. 9.
11 Agnes Alexander, letter to Mary Alexander, dated 24 May 1914.
12 Agnes Alexander, letter to Mary Alexander, dated 10 June 1914.
13 Agnes Alexander, *History of the Bahá'í Faith in Japan*, p. 9.
14 Agnes Alexander, letter to Arthur Alexander, dated 25 June 1914.
15 Agnes Alexander, letter to Mary Alexander, dated 2 July 1914.
16 Agnes Alexander, *History of the Bahá'í Faith in Japan*, p. 9.
17 Agnes Alexander, letter to Mary Alexander of uncertain date, possibly 5 September 1914.
18 Agnes Alexander, transcript of a talk given in 1961.
19 Agnes Alexander, *History of the Bahá'í Faith in Japan*, p. 9.
20 ibid. p. 10.
21 Agnes Alexander, transcript of a talk given in 1961.
22 Agnes Alexander, letter to Mary Alexander of uncertain date, possibly 5 September 1914.

23 Agnes Alexander, *History of the Bahá'í Faith in Japan*, p. 10.
24 Agnes Alexander, transcript of a talk given in 1961.
25 ibid.
26 Agnes Alexander, *History of the Bahá'í Faith in Japan*, pp. 10–11.
27 ibid.
28 Agnes Alexander, letter to Mary Alexander, dated 4 October 1914.
29 Agnes Alexander, *History of the Bahá'í Faith in Japan*, p. 10.

7 The Japanese Adventure: 1914–1917

1   Agnes Alexander, *History of the Bahá'í Faith in Japan*, p. 12.
2   ibid.
3   ibid.
4   Agnes Alexander, letter to Arthur Alexander, dated 12 November 1914.
5   Agnes Alexander, *History of the Bahá'í Faith in Japan*, p. 12.
6   Agnes Alexander, letter to Arthur Alexander, dated 12 November 1914.
7   Agnes Alexander, *History of the Bahá'í Faith in Japan*, pp. 12–13.
8   ibid. p. 13.
9   ibid.
10 *The Bahá'í World*, vol. XVIII, p. 670.
11 Agnes Alexander, *History of the Bahá'í Faith in Japan*, pp. 13–14.
12 ibid. p. 14.
13 ibid. p. 13.
14 ibid. p. 15.
15 ibid. pp. 14–15.
16 ibid. p. 15.
17 ibid.
18 ibid.
19 ibid.
20 Michitoshi Zenimoto, email to the author, 12 January 2017.
21 Agnes Alexander, *History of the Bahá'í Faith in Japan*, p. 14.
22 ibid.
23 ibid. p. 16.
24 Agnes Alexander, letter with the first page missing, December 1915.
25 Agnes Alexander, *History of the Bahá'í Faith in Japan*, p. 16.
26 Michitoshi Zenimoto, email to the author, 11 January 2017.
27 Garis, *Martha Root*, pp. 69–70.
28 Agnes Alexander, *History of the Bahá'í Faith in Japan*, p. 17.
29 ibid. p. 38.
30 Agnes Alexander, letter with the first page missing, December 1915.
31 Agnes Alexander, letter written to 'Friends', dated 20 August 1915.
32 Agnes Alexander, letter written to Mrs Dugdale Dunn, dated 5 August 1915, in Eric Petersen private papers.
33 Agnes Alexander, *History of the Bahá'í Faith in Japan*, p. 17.
34 Agnes Alexander, letter written to Mary Alexander, dated 1 December 1915.
35 Agnes Alexander, letter written to Mary Alexander, dated 14 December 1915.
36 Agnes Alexander, *History of the Bahá'í Faith in Japan*, p. 18.
37 ibid.

38   Agnes Alexander, letter with the first page missing, December 1915.

39   Agnes Alexander, letter to Mary Alexander, dated 14 December 1915.

40   Agnes Alexander, *History of the Bahá'í Faith in Japan*, p. 18.

41   ibid. p. 19.

42   ibid.

43   ibid.

44   John Esslemont, letter to Agnes Alexander, dated 21 March 1916.

45   Agnes Alexander, letter to 'Bahá'í friends', dated 29 April 1916.

46   Agnes Alexander, letter to Arthur Alexander, dated 3 April 1916.

47   Agnes Alexander, *History of the Bahá'í Faith in Japan*, pp. 19–20.

48   ibid. p. 20.

49   ibid.

50   ibid. pp. 20–21.

51   ibid. p. 21.

52   ibid. p. 20.

53   ibid. p. 21.

54   ibid. pp. 21–2.

55   ibid. p. 22.

56   Tokujiro Torii, in *The Bahá'í World*, vol. IV, p. 490.

57   Agnes Alexander, *History of the Bahá'í Faith in Japan*, p. 23.

58   Agnes Alexander, letter to Bahiyyih Ford, dated 12 June 1943.

59   Agnes Alexander, *History of the Bahá'í Faith in Japan*, p. 23.

60   ibid.

61   ibid.

62   ibid. p. 24.

63   Agnes Alexander, letter to Victoria Bedikian, dated 5 April 1920.

64   Agnes Alexander, *History of the Bahá'í Faith in Japan*, p. 24.

65   ibid.

66   ibid. p. 25.

67   *Star of the West*, vol. VIII, no. 5 (9 June 1917), pp. 54–5.

68   Agnes Alexander, *History of the Bahá'í Faith in Japan*, p. 25.

69   *Star of the West*, vol. VIII, no. 5 (9 June 1917), pp. 55–6.

70   Agnes Alexander, *History of the Bahá'í Faith in Japan*, p. 26.

71   Agnes Alexander, letter to Arthur Alexander, dated 22 February 1917.

72   Agnes Alexander, *History of the Bahá'í Faith in Japan*, p. 26.

73   ibid. p. 26.

74   ibid.

75   ibid. p. 27.

76   ibid. p. 26.

77   ibid. p. 27.

78   Agnes Alexander, 'The New Spirit of Japan', in *Everywoman Magazine* (December 1917), p. 9.

8 Two Years in America: 1917–1919

1   Agnes Alexander, letter to 'Bahá'í friends', dated 4 September 1917.

2   *The Hawaii Advertiser*, 22 August 1917.

3   Hawaiian Mission Children's Society, 66th Annual Report, 1918, p. 15.

4 Agnes Alexander, letter to 'Baháʼí friends', dated 4 September 1917.
5 *The Friend*, October 1917, p. 228.
6 ibid. January 1918, p. 14.
7 Agnes Alexander, letter to Arthur Alexander, dated 22 December 1917.
8 ibid.
9 Agnes Alexander, commemoration for Lua Getsinger, dated 31 December 1917.
10 Agnes Alexander, *History of the Baháʼí Faith in Japan*, p. 28.
11 ibid. p. 27.
12 Agnes Alexander, letter to 'Baháʼí Brother', dated 25 March 1918.
13 Agnes Alexander, letter to 'Beloved Friends', dated 8 May 1918.
14 Agnes Alexander, letter to 'Friends', dated May 1918.
15 See Redman, *Visiting ʼAbduʼl-Bahá*, vol. 2, p. 167.
16 Agnes Alexander, letter to 'Friends', dated May 1918.
17 ibid.
18 See Redman, *Visiting ʼAbduʼl-Bahá*, vol. 2, p. 168.
19 Agnes Alexander, letter to 'Beloved Friends', dated 8 May 1918.
20 ibid.
21 Joseph Hannen, letter to Agnes Alexander, dated 14 June 1918.
22 Agnes Alexander, *History of the Baháʼí Faith in Japan*, p. 28.
23 Macke, *Take My Love to the Friends*, pp. 15, 19.
24 Agnes Alexander, letter to 'Baháʼí Brother', dated 11 October 1918.
25 Agnes Alexander, *Forty Years of the Baháʼí Cause in the Hawaiian Islands*, p. 26.
26 Agnes Alexander, *History of the Baháʼí Faith in Japan*, pp. 30–31.
27 ʼAbduʼl-Bahá, *Tablets of the Divine Plan*, pp. 41, 42.
28 Agnes Alexander, *History of the Baháʼí Faith in Japan*, p. 31.
29 Agnes Alexander, letter to Victoria Bedikian, dated 6 June 1919.
30 Agnes Alexander, *Forty Years of the Baháʼí Cause in the Hawaiian Islands*, p. 26.
31 Agnes Alexander, letter to Ella Cooper, dated 5 June 1919.

9 Return to Japan: 1919–1921

1 Agnes Alexander, *History of the Baháʼí Faith in Japan*, p. 31.
2 ibid.
3 ibid.
4 ibid.
5 ibid. p. 32.
6 Agnes Alexander, letter to 'folks', dated 28 August 1919.
7 Agnes Alexander, letter to Arthur Alexander, dated 18 September 1919.
8 Agnes Alexander, *History of the Baháʼí Faith in Japan*, pp. 32–3.
9 ibid.
10 Agnes Alexander, letter to Arthur Alexander, dated 30 November 1919.
11 Agnes Alexander, *History of the Baháʼí Faith in Japan*, p. 33; see also *Star of the West*, vol. 10, no. 13 (4 November 1919), pp. 246–7.
12 Agnes Alexander, *History of the Baháʼí Faith in Japan*, p. 34.
13 ibid. p. 35.
14 ibid. p. 34.
15 ibid.
16 Agnes Alexander, letter to 'Beloved Friends of God', undated.

17 Agnes Alexander, *History of the Bahá'í Faith in Japan*, p. 34.
18 Agnes Alexander, letter to 'Beloved Friends of God', undated.
19 Hawaiian Mission Children's Society, 68th Annual Report, 1920, p. 25.
20 Agnes Alexander, letter to Arthur Alexander, dated 11 January 1920.
21 S. Saiki, letter to Agnes Alexander, undated.
22 Agnes Alexander, *History of the Bahá'í Faith in Japan*, p. 34.
23 Agnes Alexander, letter to Victoria Bedikian, dated 5 January 1920.
24 Agnes Alexander, letter to Arthur Alexander, dated 3 March 1920.
25 Agnes Alexander, letter to Arthur Alexander, dated 1 February 1920.
26 ibid.
27 Agnes Alexander, letter to Arthur and Mary Alexander, dated 22 February 1920.
28 ibid.
29 Ida Finch, letter to unknown recipient, dated 5 February 1920.
30 ibid.
31 Agnes Alexander, *History of the Bahá'í Faith in Japan*, p. 34.
32 Agnes Alexander, letter to Arthur Alexander, dated 1 February 1920.
33 Agnes Alexander, letter to Arthur Alexander, dated 22 June 1920.
34 Agnes Alexander, *History of the Bahá'í Faith in Japan*, p. 34.
35 Agnes Alexander, letter to Arthur Alexander, dated 1 February 1920.
36 Agnes Alexander, letter to Arthur Alexander, dated 3 March 1920.
37 Agnes Alexander, *History of the Bahá'í Faith in Japan*, p. 34.
38 ibid. p. 37.
39 ibid.
40 Hide Tanaka, letter to 'Abdu'l-Bahá, dated 8 August 1920.
41 Agnes Alexander, *History of the Bahá'í Faith in Japan*, p. 35.
42 ibid. p. 36.
43 Agnes Alexander, in *The Magazine of the Children of the Kingdom*, vol. 1, no. 3 (June 1920), p. 15.
44 Collins, *Bibliography of English-Language Works on the Bábí and Bahá'í Faiths, 1844–1985*, p. 175.
45 Agnes Alexander, letter to Ella Cooper, dated 20 August 1920.
46 Chu Komatsu, letter to unknown recipient, dated 9 August 1920.
47 Agnes Alexander, *History of the Bahá'í Faith in Japan*, p. 34.
48 Agnes Alexander, letter to 'George' (Latimer?), dated 19 August 1920.
49 Agnes Alexander, letter to 'Friends', dated 21 September 1920.
50 Agnes Alexander, *History of the Bahá'í Faith in Japan*, p. 38.
51 Agnes Alexander, letter to 'Friends', dated 21 September 1920.
52 Agnes Alexander, *History of the Bahá'í Faith in Japan*, p. 55.
53 Agnes Alexander, letter to Ella Cooper, dated 19 October 1920.
54 Agnes Alexander, *History of the Bahá'í Faith in Japan*, pp. 38–9.
55 ibid. p. 39.
56 Agnes Alexander, letter to Ella Cooper, dated 28 July 1921.
57 Agnes Alexander, *History of the Bahá'í Faith in Japan*, p. 39.
58 ibid.
59 ibid.
60 ibid. pp. 39–40.
61 ibid. p. 40.
62 ibid.

63   ibid.
64   Agnes Alexander, letter to Ella Cooper, dated 21 October 1920.
65   Agnes Alexander, letter to Arthur and Mary Alexander, dated 13 January 1921.
66   Agnes Alexander, letter to 'Friends', dated 9 February 1921.
67   Charles Mason Remey, letter to Agnes Alexander, dated 29 March 1921.
68   Agnes Alexander, letter to 'Fred' (Lund?), dated 5 July 1921.
69   Agnes Alexander, letter to Ella Cooper, dated 5 August 1921.

10 Korea, China and Japan's Great Earthquake: 1921–1924

1   Agnes Alexander, 'How Abdul Baha Opened the Door to Korea', in *Reality Magazine*, December 1921, pp. 27–8.
2   Agnes Alexander, letter to George (Latimer?), dated 21 May 1921.
3   Agnes Alexander, 'A Bahá'í Enters the Hermit Kingdom', in *World Order*, August 1947, p. 170.
4   Agnes Alexander, *History of the Bahá'í Faith in Japan*, p. 65.
5   ibid.
6   Agnes Alexander, letter to Arthur and Mary Alexander, dated 12 September 1921.
7   ibid.
8   Agnes Alexander, 'How Abdul Baha Opened the Door to Korea', in *Reality Magazine*, December 1921, pp. 29–30.
9   Agnes Alexander, *History of the Bahá'í Faith in Japan*, p. 65.
10   Agnes Alexander, 'How Abdul Baha Opened the Door to Korea', in *Reality Magazine*, December 1921, p. 30.
11   Agnes Alexander, *History of the Bahá'í Faith in Japan*, p. 66.
12   ibid.
13   Agens Alexander, 'How Abdul Baha Opened the Door to Korea', in *Reality Magazine*, December 1921, p. 31.
14   ibid. p. 30.
15   Agnes Alexander, letter to Arthur and Mary Alexander, dated 12 September 1921.
16   Agnes Alexander, 'How Abdul Baha Opened the Door to Korea', in *Reality Magazine*, December 1921, p. 32.
17   ibid.
18   ibid. pp. 33–4.
19   ibid. pp. 34–5.
20   ibid. p. 35.
21   ibid. p. 36.
22   Agnes Alexander, *History of the Bahá'í Faith in Japan*, p. 67.
23   Agnes Alexander, 'How Abdul Baha Opened the Door to Korea', in *Reality Magazine*, December 1921, p. 37.
24   ibid. p. 39.
25   Agnes Alexander, *History of the Bahá'í Faith in Japan*, p. 42.
26   ibid.
27   Agnes Alexander, letter to Arthur Alexander, dated 9 October 1921.
28   ibid.
29   Agnes Alexander, *History of the Bahá'í Faith in Japan*, pp. 42–3.

30 ibid. p. 43.
31 ibid.
32 ibid.
33 ibid.
34 ibid.
35 Agnes Alexander, letter to Arthur and Mary Alexander, dated 29 December 1921.
36 Agnes Alexander, letter to Victoria Bedikian, dated 20 January 1922.
37 Agnes Alexander, *History of the Bahá'í Faith in Japan*, p. 44.
38 Agnes Alexander, letter to Victoria Bedikian, dated 29 March 1922.
39 Agnes Alexander, letter to Victoria Bedikian, dated 8 June 1922.
40 Agnes Alexander, letter to Victoria Bedikian, dated 14 July 1922.
41 Agnes Alexander, *History of the Bahá'í Faith in Japan*, pp. 44–5.
42 ibid. p. 45.
43 *Star of the West*, vol. VIII, no. 3 (28 April 1917), p. 37.
44 Agnes Alexander, letter to 'My dearest Lillian', dated 11 April 1922.
45 Agnes Alexander, letter to 'Lillian', dated 21 July 1922.
46 Agnes Alexander, *History of the Bahá'í Faith in Japan*, p. 56.
47 ibid. p. 58.
48 ibid. p. 57.
49 *Star of the West*, vol. XIII, no. 8 (November 1922), p. 215.
50 Agnes Alexander, *History of the Bahá'í Faith in Japan*, p. 58.
51 ibid. p. 45.
52 ibid.
53 ibid.
54 ibid.
55 Zinky, *Martha Root: Herald of the Kingdom*, p. 10.
56 Agnes Alexander, *History of the Bahá'í Faith in Japan*, p. 46.
57 ibid.
58 See Garis, *Martha Root*, p. 165.
59 ibid. p. 166.
60 Agnes Alexander, *History of the Bahá'í Faith in Japan*, p. 47.
61 ibid. p. 48.
62 ibid. p. 46.
63 Agnes Alexander, letter to 'folks', dated 9 September 1923.
64 'Abdu'l-Bahá and Shoghi Effendi, *Japan Will Turn Ablaze!*, pp. 61–2.
65 Agnes Alexander, letter to 'Friends', dated 1 September 1923.
66 Agnes Alexander, *History of the Bahá'í Faith in Japan*, p. 48.
67 Agnes Alexander, letter to 'Friends', dated 1 September 1923.
68 *Star of the West*, vol. 14, no. 8 (November 1923), pp. 244–5.
69 https://www.britannica.com/event/Tokyo-Yokohama-earthquake-of-1923.
70 *Star of the West*, vol. 14, no. 10 (January 1924), p. 311.
71 Agnes Alexander, letter to 'folks', dated 9 September 1923.
72 Mary Alexander, letter to 'Family and Friends', dated 4 October 1923.
73 ibid.
74 *Star of the West*, vol. 14, no. 10 (January 1924), p. 311.
75 Agnes Alexander, letter to 'folks', dated 9 September 1923.

76 ibid.
77 ibid.
78 Agnes Alexander, *History of the Bahá'í Faith in Japan*, p. 48.
79 *Star of the West*, vol. 14, no. 10 (January 1924), p. 312.
80 Agnes Alexander, letter to Ida Finch, dated 5 October 1923.
81 Mary Alexander, letter to 'Family and Friends', dated 4 October 1923.
82 Agnes Alexander, *History of the Bahá'í Faith in Japan*, pp. 48–9.
83 ibid. p. 52.
84 ibid. pp. 49–51.
85 Agnes Alexander, letter to 'Beloved Friends', dated 23 December 1923.
86 Agnes Alexander, letter to Ida Finch, dated 5 October 1923.
87 Agnes Alexander, *History of the Bahá'í Faith in Japan*, p. 69.
88 *Star of the West*, vol. 14, no. 10 (January 1924), p. 313.
89 Agnes Alexander, *History of the Bahá'í Faith in Japan*, pp. 59, 62–3.
90 ibid. p. 59.
91 ibid.
92 ibid.
93 Mary Alexander, letter to unknown recipient, dated 3 January 1924, p. 4.
94 ibid. p. 5.
95 ibid.
96 Agnes Alexander, *History of the Bahá'í Faith in Japan*, p. 60.
97 ibid.
98 Mary Alexander, letter to unknown recipient, dated 3 January 1924, pp. 6–7.
99 ibid. pp. 7–8.
100 Agnes Alexander, letter to 'Beloved Friends', dated 23 December 1923.
101 Agnes Alexander, *History of the Bahá'í Faith in Japan*, p. 60.
102 Agnes Alexander, letter to 'Friends', dated 23 December 1923.

11 Back in Hawaii: 1924–1927

1   Agnes Alexander, *Forty Years of the Bahá'í Cause in Hawaii*, pp. 37–8.
2   Agnes Alexander, *History of the Bahá'í Faith in Japan*, pp. 52–3.
3   Agnes Alexander, *Forty Years of the Bahá'í Cause in Hawaii*, pp. 35–6.
4   ibid.
5   ibid. p. 37.
6   Letter written on behalf of Shoghi Effendi to Agnes Alexander, dated 5 December 1924.
7   Agnes Alexander, *Forty Years of the Bahá'í Cause in Hawaii*, p. 29.
8   Carole Lombard was a well-known actor in Hollywood who died tragically at an early age. See https://en.wikipedia.org/wiki/Carole_Lombard.
9   Agnes Alexander, *History of the Bahá'í Faith in Japan*, p. 53.
10 ibid. p. 70.
11 Agnes Alexander, *Forty Years of the Bahá'í Cause in Hawaii*, p. 30.
12 *Star of the West*, vol. 16, no. 7 (October 1925), p. 589.
13 *Star of the West*, vol. 17, no. 2 (May 1926), p. 56.
14 Agnes Alexander, *Forty Years of the Bahá'í Cause in Hawaii*, p. 37.
15 Agnes Alexander, *History of the Bahá'í Faith in Japan*, p. 70.
16 Valera Allen, *Memories of Hand of the Cause, Agnes Alexander*, Duane Troxel

personal papers.

17 Agnes Alexander, *Forty Years of the Baha'i Cause in Hawaii*, p. 31.
18 US *Bahá'í News,* no. 19 (August 1927), p. 5.
19 Agnes Alexander, *History of the Bahá'í Faith in Japan*, p. 70.
20 ibid.
21 ibid.
22 ibid.
23 ibid.
24 Agnes Alexander, *Forty Years of the Baha'i Cause in Hawaii*, p. 32.
25 ibid.
26 *The Bahá'í World*, vol. III, p. 85.
27 Agnes Alexander, *History of the Bahá'í Faith in Japan*, pp. 70–71.
28 ibid.
29 ibid. p. 72.

12 Japan and China: 1928–1933

1   Agnes Alexander, *History of the Bahá'í Faith in Japan*, p. 71.
2   Agnes Alexander, letter to 'folks', dated 15 January 1928.
3   Agnes Alexander, *History of the Bahá'í Faith in Japan*, p. 71.
4   Agnes Alexander, letter to 'folks', dated 15 January 1928.
5   Agnes Alexander, letter to Arthur Alexander, dated 27 November 1928.
6   Agnes Alexander, letter to Arthur and Mary Alexander, dated 6 February 1928.
7   Agnes Alexander, letter to Arthur Alexander, dated 27 November 1928.
8   Agnes Alexander, letter to 'folks', dated 15 January 1928.
9   See Redman, '*Abdu'l-Bahá in Their Midst*, pp. 161–2.
10 Agnes Alexander, letter to Arthur and Mary Alexander, dated 6 February 1928.
11 Agnes Alexander, *History of the Bahá'í Faith in Japan*, p. 72.
12 Agnes Alexander, letter to Mary and Arthur Alexander, dated 6 February 1928.
13 Agnes Alexander, *History of the Bahá'í Faith in Japan*, p. 72.
14 ibid. pp. 54 and 72.
15 ibid. pp. 72–3.
16 ibid. p. 73.
17 Momen (ed.), *The Bábí and Bahá'í Religions, 1844–1944*, p. 334.
18 Agnes Alexander, letter to 'friends', dated 22 April 1928.
19 Agnes Alexander, *History of the Bahá'í Faith in Japan*, p. 75.
20 ibid.
21 ibid. pp. 75–6.
22 ibid. p. 76.
23 Agnes Alexander, undated letter to 'Marion' (Holley or Yazdi?), 1933.
24 ibid. p. 74.
25 ibid.
26 ibid.
27 Agnes Alexander, letter to Arthur Alexander, dated 16 July 1928.
28 Agnes Alexander, *History of the Bahá'í Faith in Japan*, p. 75.
29 Agnes Alexander, letter to 'Bahá'í brother', dated 30 January 1929.
30 Agnes Alexander, *History of the Bahá'í Faith in Japan*, p. 75.
31 *Star of the West*, vol. 20, no. 8 (November 1929), p. 250.

32 Agnes Alexander, *History of the Bahá'í Faith in Japan*, p. 77.
33 *Star of the West*, vol. 20, no. 9 (December 1929), pp. 285–6.
34 Agnes Alexander, letters to Arthur Alexander, dated 9 December 1929 and 13 January 1930.
35 Agnes Alexander, *History of the Bahá'í Faith in Japan*, p. 77.
36 'Abdu'l-Bahá and Shoghi Effendi, *Japan Will Turn Ablaze!*, p. 60.
37 Agnes Alexander, letter to Arthur Alexander, dated 21 January 1930.
38 Agnes Alexander, letters to Arthur Alexander, dated 30 July 1930 and 30 October 1930.
39 Agnes Alexander, *History of the Bahá'í Faith in Japan*, p. 77.
40 ibid. p. 78.
41 Agnes Alexander, letter to Arthur Alexander, dated 30 July 1930.
42 Letter written on behalf of Shoghi Effendi to Agnes Alexander, dated 16 January 1930.
43 Agnes Alexander, *History of the Bahá'í Faith in Japan*, p. 61.
44 Agnes Alexander, letter to 'folks', dated 1 September 1930.
45 Agnes Alexander, *History of the Bahá'í Faith in Japan*, p. 61; Hassall, 'Bahá'í country notes: China'.
46 Agnes Alexander *History of the Bahá'í Faith in Japan*, p. 61.
47 Agnes Alexander, letter to Arthur Alexander, dated 30 October 1930.
48 Garis, *Martha Root*, pp. 364–5.
49 Agnes Alexander, *History of the Bahá'í Faith in Japan*, p. 79.
50 *Star of the West*, vol. 22, p. 75.
51 Agnes Alexander, *History of the Bahá'í Faith in Japan*, p. 80.
52 ibid.
53 Agnes Alexander, letter to Emogene Hoagg, dated 24 May 1931.
54 Agnes Alexander, *History of the Bahá'í Faith in Japan*, p. 80.
55 ibid. p. 81.
56 ibid. p. 80.
57 ibid. p. 61.
58 ibid.p. 81.
59 ibid.
60 Ruhe-Schoen, 'Ransom-Kehler, Keith Bean', in *The Bahá'í Encyclopedia*; see also *The Bahá'í World*, vol. V, p. 398.
61 Agnes Alexander, *History of the Bahá'í Faith in Japan*, p. 82.
62 Letter written on behalf of Shoghi Effendi to Agnes Alexander, dated 13 July 1931. National Bahá'í Archives of Japan, Agnes Alexander Papers.
63 Agnes Alexander, *History of the Bahá'í Faith in Japan*, pp. 82–83.
64 'Abdu'l-Bahá and Shoghi Effendi, *Japan Will Turn Ablaze!*, pp. 60–61.
65 Letter written on behalf of Shoghi Effendi to Agnes Alexander, dated 30 October 1931. National Bahá'í Archives of Japan, Agnes Alexander Papers.
66 Letter written on behalf of Shoghi Effendi to Agnes Alexander, dated 22 December 1931. National Bahá'í Archives of Japan, Agnes Alexander Papers.
67 Agnes Alexander, *History of the Bahá'í Faith in Japan*, pp. 83–84.
68 ibid. pp. 83–84.
69 Letter written on behalf of Shoghi Effendi to Agnes Alexander, dated 30 April 1932.

70   Agnes Alexander, *History of the Bahá'í Faith in Japan*, pp. 83–4.
71   ibid. p. 85.
72   ibid.
73   ibid.
74   Hassall and Austria, *Mirza Hossein R. Touty: First Bahá'í Known to Have Lived in the Philippines*; Hassall, 'Notes on the Bábí and Bahá'í religions in Russia and its territories', in *Journal of Bahá'í Studies*, vol. 5 (1992), no. 3.
75   Agnes Alexander, *History of the Bahá'í Faith in Japan*, p. 86.
76   Letter from Shoghi Effendi to Agnes Alexander, dated 16 January 1930.
77   Letter from Shoghi Effendi to Agnes Alexander, dated 26 March 1930.
78   Bahá'í World Centre Research Department, 'Agnes Alexander's correspondence with 'Abdu'l-Bahá and Shoghi Effendi', Memorandum dated 20 May 2019.
79   Agnes Alexander, *History of the Bahá'í Faith in Japan*, p. 78.
80   ibid. p. 61.
81   Bahá'í World Centre Research Department, 'Agnes Alexander's correspondence with 'Abdu'l-Bahá and Shoghi Effendi', Memorandum dated 20 May 2019.
82   Agnes Alexander, letter to Emogene Hoagg, dated 24 May 1931.
83   Agnes Alexander, *History of the Bahá'í Faith in Japan*, p. 82.
84   ibid.
85   Letter written on behalf of Shoghi Effendi to Agnes Alexander, dated 13 July 1931. National Bahá'í Archives of Japan, Agnes Alexander Papers.
86   Agnes Alexander, *History of the Bahá'í Faith in Japan*, p. 82.
87   'Abdu'l-Bahá and Shoghi Effendi, *Japan Will Turn Ablaze!*, pp. 60–61.
88   Letter written on behalf of Shoghi Effendi to Agnes Alexander, dated 30 October 1931. National Bahá'í Archives of Japan, Agnes Alexander Papers.
89   Letter from Shoghi Effendi to Agnes Alexander, dated 22 December 1931. National Bahá'í Archives of Japan, Agnes Alexander Papers.
90   Letter written on behalf of Shoghi Effendi to Agnes Alexander, dated 6 January 1932. National Bahá'í Archives of Japan, Agnes Alexander Papers.
91   Letter written on behalf of Shoghi Effendi to Agnes Alexander, dated 25 January 1932. National Bahá'í Archives of Japan, Agnes Alexander Papers.
92   Agnes Alexander, *History of the Bahá'í Faith in Japan*, p. 86.
93   ibid.
94   ibid.
95   Letter written on behalf of Shoghi Effendi to Agnes Alexander, dated 30 April 1932.
96   Letter written on behalf of Shoghi Effendi to Agnes Alexander, dated 6 October 1932.
97   ibid.
98   Agnes Alexander, *History of the Bahá'í Faith in Japan*, p. 86.
99   ibid. pp. 86–7.
100 ibid.
101 Letter written on behalf of Shoghi Effendi to Agnes Alexander, dated 17 April 1933.
102 Agnes Alexander, *History of the Bahá'í Faith in Japan*, p. 87.
103 ibid.
104 Agnes Alexander, letter to Arthur Alexander, dated 25 May 1933.

13 Hawaii and America: 1933–1935

1 Agnes Alexander, *Forty Years of the Baha'i Cause in Hawaii*, p. 39.
2 Agnes Alexander, letter to Ella Rowland, dated 25 May 1933.
3 Agnes Alexander, *Forty Years of the Baha'i Cause in Hawaii*, p. 40.
4 ibid.
5 ibid. pp. 40–41.
6 ibid. p. 40.
7 ibid. p. 38.
8 ibid.
9 ibid.
10 Letter written on behalf of Shoghi Effendi to Agnes Alexander, dated 5 May 1934.
11 Agnes Alexander, letter to 'Dearest sister', dated 26 May 1934.
12 US *Bahá'í News*, no. 84 (June 1934), p. 4.
13 Letter written on behalf of Shoghi Effendi to Agnes Alexander, dated 8 August 1934. National Bahá'í Archives of Japan, Agnes Alexander Papers.
14 *Bahá'í News*, no. 87 (Sept. 1934), pp. 4–5.
15 Letter written on behalf of Shoghi Effendi to Agnes Alexander, dated 26 September 1934. National Bahá'í Archives of Japan, Agnes Alexander Papers.
16 ibid.
17 'Abdu'l-Bahá and Shoghi Effendi, *Japan Will Turn Ablaze!*, p. 51.
18 Agnes Alexander, letter to Ella Rowland, dated 1 December 1934.
19 Agnes Alexander, *Forty Years of the Baha'i Cause in Hawaii*, p. 41.
20 Agnes Alexander, letter to 'Maudie', dated 24 April 1935.
21 'Abdu'l-Bahá and Shoghi Effendi, *Japan Will Turn Ablaze!*, p. 52.

14 Back to Japan: 1935–1936

1 Agnes Alexander, letters to Arthur Alexander and 'Ella', both dated 16 May 1935.
2 Agnes Alexander, *History of the Bahá'í Faith in Japan*, p. 91.
3 Agnes Alexander, letter to 'Beloved Bahá'í Friends', dated 25 October 1936.
4 ibid.
5 Agnes Alexander, *History of the Bahá'í Faith in Japan*, pp. 91–2.
6 ibid. p. 92.
7 ibid. p. 95.
8 ibid. p. 92.
9 Agnes Alexander, letter to Louise Bosch, dated 9 March 1936.
10 Ruth Randall Brown, letter to 'Friends', dated 12 December 1935.
11 Agnes Alexander, letter to Arthur Alexander, dated 28 December 1935.
12 https://en.wikipedia.org/wiki/February_26_Incident.
13 Agnes Alexander, letter to Arthur Alexander, dated 27 February 1936.
14 Agnes Alexander, letter to Arthur Alexander, dated 11 March 1936.
15 Agnes Alexander, *History of the Bahá'í Faith in Japan*, p. 93.
16 Agnes Alexander, letter to Arthur Alexander, dated 16 August 1936.
17 'Samuel Amalu hoax revealed', http://www.hawaiihistory.org/index.cfm?fuseaction=ig.page&PageID=489&returntoname=Short%20Stories&returntopageid=483.

18 Agnes Alexander, *History of the Bahá'í Faith in Japan*, p. 96.
19 Rutstein, *He Loved and Served*, p. 75.
20 Agnes Alexander, *History of the Bahá'í Faith in Japan*, p. 96.
21 ibid. p. 97.

15 Pilgrimage: 1937

1   Cable from Shoghi Effendi to Agnes Alexander, dated 6 October 1936. National Bahá'í Archives of Japan, Cabinet A2 Drawer A 12.
2   Agnes Alexander, *History of the Bahá'í Faith in Japan*, p. 96.
3   ibid. p. 98.
4   ibid.
5   ibid.
6   ibid.
7   Agnes Alexander, letter to Arthur Alexander, dated 24 March 1937; Agnes Alexander, *History of the Bahá'í Faith in Japan*, p. 98.
8   Agnes Alexander, letter to Arthur Alexander, dated 24 March 1937.
9   Agnes Alexander, *History of the Bahá'í Faith in Japan*, p. 99.
10 Agnes Alexander, letter to Arthur Alexander, dated 24 March 1937.
11 ibid.
12 Agnes Alexander, *History of the Bahá'í Faith in Japan*, pp. 95–6.
13 Agnes Alexander, letter to Arthur Alexander, dated 24 March 1937; Agnes Alexander, *History of the Bahá'í Faith in Japan*, p. 99.
14 ibid.
15 Agnes Alexander, letter to Arthur Alexander, dated 24 March 1937.
16 Agnes Alexander, *History of the Bahá'í Faith in Japan*, p. 99.
17 Agnes Alexander, letter to 'Sister', dated 26 April 1937.
18 Cable from Shoghi Effendi to Agnes, dated 19 April 1937. National Bahá'í Archives of Japan, Cabinet A2 Drawer A 12.
19 Agnes Alexander, *History of the Bahá'í Faith in Japan*, p. 99.
20 ibid. pp. 99–100.
21 ibid. p. 100.
22 ibid.
23 Agnes Alexander, letter to Mary Fantom, dated 19 May 1937.
24 Agnes Alexander, letter to 'beloved Friends in Japan', dated 9 May 1937.
25 Agnes Alexander, *History of the Bahá'í Faith in Japan*, p. 100.
26 Harper, *Lights of Fortitude*, p. 152.
27 Agnes Alexander, *Notes Taken in the Presence of Shoghi Effendi*, p. 4.
28 Agnes Alexander, *History of the Bahá'í Faith in Japan*, p. 100.
29 ibid.
30 ibid.
31 ibid. pp. 98, 100–01.
32 ibid. p. 101.
33 Agnes Alexander, letter to 'beloved Friends in Japan', dated 9 May 1937.
34 Agnes Alexander, *History of the Bahá'í Faith in Japan*, p. 101.
35 ibid.
36 ibid.
37 Agnes Alexander, letter to Mary Fantom, dated 19 May 1937.

38 Agnes Alexander, letter to 'beloved Friends in Japan', dated 9 May 1937.

39 Agnes Alexander, pilgrim note fragment.

40 Agnes Alexander, undated letter to Elma Adolphson (probably late September 1937).

41 Agnes Alexander, letter to Mary Alexander, dated 16 May 1937.

42 Agnes Alexander, letter to 'Martha dearest' (Martha Root), dated 9 July 1937, in *The Bahá'í World*, vol. VII, p. 111.

43 Pfaff-Grossmann, *Hermann Grossmann*, p. 55.

44 Letter written on behalf of Shoghi Effendi to Agnes Alexander, dated 30 June 1937. National Bahá'í Archives of Japan, Agnes Alexander Papers.

45 Agnes Alexander, letter to Martha Root, dated 9 July 1937.

46 Letter written on behalf of Shoghi Effendi to Agnes Alexander, dated 16 September 1937. National Bahá'í Archives of Japan, Agnes Alexander Papers.

47 Agnes Alexander, undated letter to Elma Adolphson (probably late September 1937).

48 ibid.

49 Agnes Alexander, letter to 'Bahá'í Sisters', dated 28 September 1937.

50 Agnes Alexander, letter to 'beloved Honolulu Bahá'ís', dated 12 November 1937.

51 Agnes Alexander, letter to Elma Adolphson, dated 11 February 1938.

52 Letter written on behalf of Shoghi Effendi to Agnes Alexander, dated 23 January 1938. National Bahá'í Archives of Hawaii, Duane Troxel Papers.

53 *Bahá'í News*, no. 115 (April 1938), pp. 5, 7, 8.

54 Agnes Alexander, letter to 'Dearest', dated 30 June 1938.

55 Maxie Jones, letter to Agnes, dated 20 September 1938.

56 Harlan Ober, letter to Agnes, dated 5 August 1938.

57 Agnes Alexander, letter to friend, dated 30 June 1938.

58 *Bahá'í News*, no. 117 (July 1938), p. 5.

59 Letter written on behalf of Shoghi Effendi to Agnes Alexander, dated 7 July 1938. National Bahá'í Archives of Hawaii, Duane Troxel Papers.

60 Harlan Ober, letter to Agnes, dated 13 November 1938.

61 Letter written on behalf of Shoghi Effendi to Agnes Alexander, dated 2 (?) November 1938..

62 Agnes Alexander, *Forty Years of the Baha'i Cause in Hawaii*, pp. 40–41.

63 Letter written on behalf of Shoghi Effendi to Agnes Alexander, dated 15 December 1938. National Bahá'í Archives of Hawaii, Duane Troxel papers.

64 Agnes Alexander, letter to Ella Cooper, sometime in December 1938.

65 Agnes Alexander, letter to Ella Cooper, dated 9 December 1938.

16 Hawaii and America: 1939–1949

1 Agnes Alexander, letter to 'Dearest Sister', dated 12 January 1939.

2 Letter written on behalf of Shoghi Effendi to Agnes Alexander, dated 3 January 1939.

3 Agnes Alexander, *Forty Years of the Baha'i Cause in Hawaii*, p. 44.

4 ibid. pp. 43–4.

5 Letter written on behalf of Shoghi Effendi to Agnes Alexander, dated 22 February 1939.

6 Agnes Alexander, *Forty Years of the Baha'i Cause in Hawaii*, p. 38.

7   Rúḥíyyih Khánum, letter to Agnes Alexander, dated 3 May 1939.
8   Shoghi Effendi, *Messages to America, 1932–1946*, p. 6.
9   Redman, *Shoghi Effendi Through the Pilgrim's Eye*, vol. 2, p. 69.
10 Shoghi Effendi, *Messages to America, 1932–1946*, p. 17.
11 Letter written on behalf of Shoghi Effendi to Agnes Alexander, dated 22 April 1939.
12 Agnes Alexander, letter to 'Dearest', dated 28 March 1939.
13 Agnes Alexander, *Forty Years of the Baha'i Cause in Hawaii*, p. 44.
14 Shoghi Effendi, *Messages to America, 1932–1946*, pp. 20–21; Shoghi Effendi, *This Decisive Hour*, note 34, pp. 140–41.
15 Agnes Alexander, letter to 'Beloved Bahá'í Friends' dated 11 May 1939.
16 Agnes Alexander, letter to May Maxwell, dated 21 June 1939.
17 Rúḥíyyih Khánum, letter to Agnes Alexander, dated 13 May 1939.
18 Agnes Alexander, *Forty Years of the Baha'i Cause in Hawaii*, p. 44.
19 Agnes Alexander, letter to 'Beloved Friends', dated 8 October 1939.
20 ibid.
21 Rúḥíyyih Khánum, letter to Agnes Alexander, dated 25 March 1940.
22 Agnes Alexander, *May Maxwell – A Tribute*, 1940. See Appendix to this book.
23 Letter written on behalf of Shoghi Effendi to Agnes Alexander, dated 13 December 1939.
24 Agnes Alexander, letter to the Honolulu Bahá'í community, dated 16 February 1940.
25 Agnes Alexander, letter to Utie, Kathrine and May, dated 13 February 1940.
26 Charles Mason Remey, letter to Agnes Alexander, dated 19 February 1940.
27 Agnes Alexander, letter to Ella Cooper, dated 26 August 1940.
28 Agnes Alexander, letter to Ella Cooper, dated 6 September 1940.
29 Agnes Alexander, letter to Louise and John Bosch, dated 22 November 1940.
30 Letter written on behalf of Shoghi Effendi to Agnes Alexander, dated 12 March 1941.
31 Agnes Alexander, letter to Ella Cooper, dated 11 August 1941.
32 Agnes Alexander, *Forty Years of the Baha'i Cause in Hawaii*, p. 46.
33 ibid.
34 ibid. pp. 46–7.
35 Letter written on behalf of Shoghi Effendi to Agnes Alexander, dated 14 December 1941.
36 Agnes Alexander, *Forty Years of the Baha'i Cause in Hawaii*, p. 46.
37 Agnes Alexander, letter to Ella Cooper, dated 17 March 1942.
38 ibid.
39 Letter written on behalf of Shoghi Effendi to Agnes Alexander, dated 5 May 1943.
40 Rúḥíyyih Khánum, letter to Agnes Alexander, dated 6 August 1943.
41 Letter written on behalf of Shoghi Effendi to Agnes Alexander, dated 9 March 1945.
42 Letter written on behalf of Shoghi Effendi to Agnes Alexander, dated 11 March 1946.
43 Faizi-Moore, *Faizi*, pp. 180–81.
44 Archives and History Committee of the National Spiritual Assembly of the Bahá'ís of the United States and Canada, May Scheffler (secretary), letter to Agnes Alexander, dated 22 March 1944.

45 Letter written on behalf of Shoghi Effendi to Agnes Alexander, dated 22 July 1944.
46 Josephine Kruka, undated letter to Agnes Alexander (probably about 1945).
47 Agnes Alexander, personal journal for 1946.
48 ibid.
49 ibid.
50 Agnes Alexander, letter to Ella Cooper, dated 29 May 1946.
51 Letter written on behalf of Shoghi Effendi to Agnes Alexander, dated 3 June 1946.
52 *Charleston News and Courier*, 7 June 1946.
53 Agnes Alexander, personal journal for 1946.
54 Redman, *Visiting 'Abdu'l-Bahá*, vol.1, p. 194; Redman, *Shoghi Effendi Through the Pilgrim's Eye*, vol.1, p. 196.
55 Agnes Alexander, personal journal for 1946.
56 ibid.
57 ibid.
58 Agnes Alexander, letter to Arthur Alexander, dated 30 July 1946.
59 Agnes Alexander, personal journal for 1946.
60 ibid.
61 ibid.
62 ibid.
63 ibid.
64 Agnes Alexander, letter to 'Gertrude', dated 25 September 1946.
65 Agnes Alexander, personal journal for 1946.
66 ibid.
67 ibid.
68 ibid.
69 *The Bahá'í World*, vol. 14, p. 338.
70 *The Courier-Journal*, Louisville, KY, 4 December 1946.
71 Agnes Alexander, letter to Arthur Alexander, dated 5 December 1946.
72 Agnes Alexander, personal journal for 1946.
73 ibid.
74 Corinne True, letter to Agnes Alexander, dated 5 May 1947.
75 Letter written on behalf of Shoghi Effendi to Agnes Alexander, dated 28 June 1947.
76 *Yakima Herald-Republic*, Yakima, WA, 17 June 1948.
77 *The Marysville Globe*, Thursday 24 June 1948.
78 *Jamestown (NY) Post-Journal*, 29 October 1948.
79 US *Bahá'í News*, no. 220 (June 1949), p. 7.
80 Agnes Alexander, letter to the Baha'is of Honolulu, dated 17 June 1949.
81 Agnes Alexander, letter to Ella Cooper, dated 28 July 1949.
82 'Abdu'l-Bahá and Shoghi Effendi, *Japan Will Turn Ablaze!*, p. 54.
83 US *Bahá'í News*, no. 216 (February 1949), p. 7.

17 Back in Japan, Again: 1950–1957

1 US *Bahá'í News*, no. 192 (February 1947), p. 3.
2 ibid. p. 4.
3 Shinagawa Girl's School, undated report.

4   Agnes Alexander, letter to Doris Ebbert, dated 20 April 1950.

5   Agnes Alexander, letter to Doris Ebbert, dated 16 July 1950.

6   Agnes Alexander, letter to Doris Ebbert, dated 17 October 1950.

7   US *Bahá'í News*, no. 241 (March 1951), p. 3.

8   Bahá'í World Centre Research Department, 'Agnes Alexander's correspondence with 'Abdu'l-Bahá and Shoghi Effendi', Memorandum dated 20 May 2019.

9   Letter written on behalf of Shoghi Effendi to Agnes Alexander, dated 6 October 1950.

10   Letter written on behalf of Shoghi Effendi to Agnes Alexander, dated 20 November 1950.

11   Redman, *Shoghi Effendi Through the Pilgrim's Eye*, vol. 1, p. 23.

12   Records of Allied Operational and Occupation Headquarters, World War II (Record Group 331) Entry UD 1697-5831. The series is called SCAP; Civil Information & Education Section; Religion & Cultural Resources Division; Special Projects Branch; Religious Research Data, 1945–51, provided by Don Calkins, 14 October 2017.

13   Agnes Alexander, letter to Doris Ebbert, dated 3 January 1951.

14   Agnes Alexander, letter to Doris Ebbert, dated 13 May 1951.

15   Agnes Alexander, letter to Ray Wooten, dated 26 August 1951.

16   Agnes Alexander, letter to Doris Ebbert, dated 26 August 1951.

17   Agnes Alexander, letter to Doris Ebbert, dated 7 October 1951.

18   Agnes Alexander, letter to Doris Ebbert, dated 30 December 1951.

19   Agnes Alexander, letter to Doris Ebbert, dated 12 January 1952.

20   Agnes Alexander, letter to Ray Wooten, dated 11 February 1952.

21   Agnes Alexander, letter to Doris Ebbert, dated 12 May 1952.

22   Agnes Alexander, letter to Doris Ebbert, dated 31 May 1952.

23   Agnes Alexander, letter to Ray Wooten, dated 4 July 1952.

24   Letter written on behalf of Shoghi Effendi to Agnes Alexander, dated 22 May 1952.

25   US *Bahá'í News*, no. 261 (November 1952), p. 7.

26   Agnes Alexander, letter to Ray Wooten, dated 23 December 1952.

27   ibid.

28   'Abdu'l-Bahá and Shoghi Effendi, *Japan Will Turn Ablaze!*, p. 55.

29   Agnes Alexander, letter to Ray Wooten, dated 23 December 1952.

30   Michitoshi Zenimoto, email to the author, dated 23 January 2017.

31   Michitoshi Zenimoto, email to the author, dated 13 January 2017.

32   ibid.

33   ibid.

34   ibid.

35   Agnes Alexander, letter to Michitoshi Zenimoto, dated 22 December 1952 (courtesy of Mr Zenimoto).

36   Michitoshi Zenimoto, email to the author, dated 15 January 2017.

37   ibid.

38   Michitoshi Zenimoto, email to the author, dated 13 January 2017.

39   Agnes Alexander, letter to Ray Wooten, dated 5 March 1953.

40   Letter written on behalf of the Guardian to Michitoshi Zenimoto, dated 5 October 1953 (courtesy of Mr Zenimoto). Also in *Japan Will Turn Blaze!*, p. 102.

41 US *Bahá'í News*, no. 263 (January 1953) p. 9.
42 Agnes Alexander, audio recording from Meno Park, CA, April 1961.
43 Agnes Alexander, letter to Doris Ebbert, dated 1 July 1953.
44 Redman, *Shoghi Effendi Through the Pilgrim's Eye,* vol. 2, p. 55.
45 Agnes Alexander, letter to Doris Ebbert and Olga, dated 4 August 1953.
46 Agnes Alexander, letter to Doris Ebbert, dated 20 November 1953.
47 Agnes Alexander, letter to Doris Ebbert, dated 19 December 1953.
48 *Bahá'í World*, vol. XII, p. 184.
49 Agnes Alexander, letter to Doris Ebbert, dated 20 November 1953.
50 US *Bahá'í News*, no. 275 (January 1954), p. 9.
51 Agnes Alexander, letter to Doris Ebbert, dated 19 December 1953.
52 *Bahá'í World*, vol. XII, p. 40.
53 'Abdu'l-Bahá and Shoghi Effendi, *Japan Will Turn Ablaze!*, pp. 55–6.
54 ibid. p. 56.
55 ibid.
56 Bahá'í World Centre Research Department, 'Agnes Alexander's correspondence with 'Abdu'l-Bahá and Shoghi Effendi', Memorandum dated 20 May 2019.
57 'Abdu'l-Bahá and Shoghi Effendi, *Japan Will Turn Ablaze!*, p. 56.
58 Agnes Alexander, letter to Mamie Seto, dated 29 February 1955.
59 'Abdu'l-Bahá and Shoghi Effendi, *Japan Will Turn Ablaze!*, p. 56.
60 Agnes Alexander, letter to 'Dear Bahá'í Sister', dated 6 April 1955.
61 Agnes Alexander, letter to 'Dear Bahá'í Sister', dated 13 June 1955.
62 Agnes Alexander, letter to Ramona Brown, dated 14 June 1955.
63 Agnes Alexander, letter to Ramona Brown, dated 13 April 1956.
64 US *Bahá'í News*, no. 296 (October 1955), p. 6.
65 US *Bahá'í News*, no. 297 (November 1955), p. 6.
66 ibid. pp. 7–8.
67 US *Bahá'í News*, no. 298 (December 1955), pp. 8–9.
68 Agnes Alexander, letter to Ramona Brown, dated 13 April 1956.
69 Agnes Alexander, letter to Doris Ebbert, dated 17 April 1956.
70 ibid.
71 US *Bahá'í News*, no. 310 (December 1956), p. 3.
72 Sims, Barbara, *Taiwan Bahá'í Chronicle*, p. 17.)
73 US *Bahá'í News*, no. 311 (January 1957), p. 3.

18 Hand of the Cause of God: 1957–1965

1 Shoghi Effendi, *Messages to the Bahá'í World, 1950–1957*, p. 174.
2 Cable from Shoghi Effendi to Agnes Alexander, Bahá'í World Centre, as quoted in her letter to Ramona Brown, dated 12 April 1957.
3 Agnes Alexander, letter to 'May', dated 16 April 1957.
4 Agnes Alexander, letter to Ramona Brown, dated 12 April 1957.
5 'Abdu'l-Bahá and Shoghi Effendi, *Japan Will Turn Ablaze!*, pp. 56–7.
6 US *Bahá'í News*, no. 317 (July 1957), pp. 15–16.
7 Agnes Alexander, letter to Ramona Brown, dated 5 June 1957.
8 US *Bahá'í News*, no. 322 (December 1957), pp. 10–11.
9 Agnes Alexander, letter to Ramona Brown, dated 13 December 1957.
10 Agnes Alexander, Conclave notes, dated 1 December 1957.

11   Agnes Alexander, letter to Ramona Brown, dated 13 December 1957.

12   Agnes Alexander, letter to Bill Smits, dated 31 January 1958.

13   Michitoshi Zenimoto, post on his Facebook page, 19 January 2017.

14   Michotoshi Zenimoto, email to Duane Troxel, 9 January 2017.

15   Agnes Alexander, letter to Bill Smits, dated 2 January 1958.

16   US *Bahá'í News*, no. 330 (August 1958), p. 7.

17   See Redman, *Shoghi Effendi Through the Pilgrim's Eye*, vol 2, p. 213.

18   US *Bahá'í News*, no. 334 (December 1958), p. 3.

19   Agnes Alexander, letter to Mamie Seto, dated 6 April 1958.

20   ibid.

21   US *Bahá'í News*, no. 330 (August 1958), pp. 5, 7.

22   US *Bahá'í News*, no. 335 (January 1959), p. 15.

23   US *Bahá'í News*, no. 334 (December 1958), p. 10.

24   Sims, *Unfurling the Divine Flag in Tokyo*, p. 52.

25   Agnes Alexander, letter to Ramona Brown, dated 23 June 1959.

26   Agnes Alexander, letter to Bill Smits, dated 20 July 1959.

27   Agnes Alexander, letter to Ramona Brown, dated 30 August 1959.

28   Valera Allen, undated story about Agnes.

29   US *Bahá'í News*, no. 349 (March 1960), p. 5.

30   Agnes Alexander, letter to Ramona Brown, dated 20 September 1959.

31   Agnes Alexander, letter to Ramona Brown, dated 24 September 1959.

32   Agnes Alexander, letter to Ramona Brown, dated 20 September 1959.

33   Agnes Alexander, letter to Ramona Brown, dated 29 October 1959.

34   US *Bahá'í News*, no. 348 (February 1960), p. 5.

35   Agnes Alexander, letter to Ramona Brown, dated 15 December 1959.

36   Agnes Alexander, letter to Ramona Brown, dated 22 January 1960.

37   ibid.

38   Agnes Alexander, letter to Ramona Brown, dated 16 February 1960.

39   Agnes Alexander, letter to Ramona Brown, dated 12 March 1960.

40   Agnes Alexander, letter to Ramona Brown, dated 26 June 1960.

41   Agnes Alexander, letter to Ramona Brown, dated 10 October 1960.

42   Agnes Alexander, letter to Ramona Brown, dated 6 September 1960.

43   Agnes Alexander, letter to Ramona Brown, dated 10 October 1960.

44   Agnes Alexander, letter to Ramona Brown, dated 23 October 1960.

45   Agnes Alexander, letter to Ramona Brown, dated 10 October 1960.

46   Agnes Alexander, letter to Ramona Brown, dated 23 October 1960.

47   Agnes Alexander, letter to Ramona Brown, dated 2 November 1960.

48   Agnes Alexander, letter to Ramona Brown, dated 17 November 1960.

49   ibid.

50   ibid.

51   US *Bahá'í News*, no. 359 (February 1961), p. 7.

52   Agnes Alexander, letter to Ramona Brown, dated 20 May 1961.

53   ibid.

54   *Ministry of the Custodians*, p. 305.

55   US *Bahá'í News*, no. 368 (November 1961), p. 2.

56   Agnes Alexander, letter to Ramona Brown, dated 3 August 1961.

57   *Ministry of the Custodians*, p. 327.

58   Agnes Alexander, letter to Ramona Brown, dated 23 August 1962.

59 Sims, *Taiwan Bahá'í Chronicle*, p. 34.
60 Agnes Alexander, letter to Ramona Brown, dated 23 August 1962.
61 Agnes Alexander, letter to Ramona Brown, dated 15 November 1962.
62 Agnes Alexander, letter to Ramona Brown, dated 18 January 1963.
63 Agnes Alexander, letter to Bill and Lee Smits, dated 5 March 1963.
64 US *Bahá'í News*, no. 390 (September 1963), p. 2.
65 Agnes Alexander, letter to 'Beloved Bahá'í Sister' dated 25 April 1963.
66 Agnes Alexander, letter to Ramona Brown, dated 7 June 1963.
67 ibid.
68 Agnes Alexander, letter to Ramona Brown, dated 17 July 1963.
69 Agnes Alexander, letter to Ramona Brown, dated 20 August 1963.
70 ibid.
71 Agnes Alexander, letter to Ramona Brown, dated 20 May 1964.
72 Duane Troxel, personal remembrance.
73 US *Bahá'í News*, no. 400 (July 1964), p. 10.
74 Agnes Alexander, letter to Ramona Brown, dated 20 May 1964.
75 Agnes Alexander, letter to Ramona Brown, dated 3 June 1964.
76 Craig Quick, email to the author, dated 9 December 2016.
77 Agnes Alexander, audio recording from the 1964 Hawaiian National Convention.
78 Agnes Alexander, letter to Lil Hollinger, dated 20 May 1964.
79 US *Bahá'í News*, no. 405 (December 1964), p. 8.
80 Agnes Alexander, letter to Ramona Brown, dated 13 December 1964.
81 Muhájir, *Dr Muhajir*, p. 307.
82 Faizi-Moore, *Faizi*, p. 271.
83 Barbara Sims, personal log book, dated 3 January and 9 & 10 January 1965.
84 ibid. dated 20 January 1965.
85 Agnes Alexander, letter to Ramona Brown, dated 23 June 1965.
86 Faizi-Moore, *Faizi*, pp. 270–71.
87 *The Mainichi Daily News*, 11 May 1965.
88 Agnes Alexander, letter to Ramona Brown, dated 23 June 1965.
89 Agnes Alexander, letter to Ramona Brown, dated 27 July 1965.

19 The Last Years: 1965–1971

1 Barbara Sims, personal log book, dated 2 August 1965.
2 Agnes Alexander, letter to Ramona Brown, dated 22 September 1965.
3 Agnes Alexander, letter to 'Beloved Bahá'í friends of the Pacific', dated 30 September 1965.
4 Barbara Sims, personal log book, dated 26 October 1965.
5 Sims, *Unfurling the Divine Flag in Tokyo*, pp. 52–3.
6 Ruth Suzuki, email to the authors, dated 12 March 2017.
7 Ryuji Yamamoto, Affidavit, 27 April 1966.
8 Agnes Alexander, letter to Ramona Brown, dated 7 October 1965.
9 Agnes Alexander, letter to Ramona Brown, dated 12 December 1965.
10 US *Bahá'í News*, no. 428 (November 1966), p. 12.
11 Agnes Alexander, letter to Ramona Brown, dated 29 April 1967.
12 Agnes Alexander, letter to Ramona Brown, dated 28 May 1967.
13 Agnes Alexander, letter to Ramona Brown, dated 29 July 1967.

14 Ramona Brown, letter to Agnes, dated 6 September 1967.
15 Ruth Suzuki, email to the authors, dated 12 March 2017.
16 ibid.
17 US *Bahá'í News*, no. 429 (December 1966), p. 14.
18 Transcript by Duane Troxel and Odmaa Dugersuren of tape recorded on 12 March 1966.
19 Agnes Alexander, letter to Bill and Lee Smits, dated 9 August 1967.
20 *Light of the Pacific*, no. 29 (September 1967).
21 Duane Troxel, interview with Agnes Alexander, 15 August 1968.
22 Agnes Alexander, letter to Ramona Brown, dated 24 September 1968.
23 Elahe Vahdat Young, email to the authors, dated 5 September 2017.
24 Cable from the Universal House of Justice, dated 4 January 1971.
25 US *Bahá'í News*, no. 480 (March 1971), p. 7.
26 Tracy and Healani Hamilton, *The Passing of Miss Agnes Baldwin Alexander*, pp. 1–3.
27 ibid. pp. 5–6.
28 ibid. pp. 2, 11, 13–14.
29 ibid. pp. 15–18.
30 ibid. pp. 3–23.
31 ibid. p. 20.
32 ibid. p. 30.
33 Letter from the Universal House of Justice to the National Spiritual Assembly of the Bahá'ís of the Hawaiian Islands, dated 10 January 1971.
34 Ruth Suzuki, email to the authors, dated 12 March 2017.

Appendix: May Maxwell – A Tribute, by Agnes Alexander

1 Agnes Alexander, *May Maxwell – A Tribute*, written in 1940.

INDEX

'Abdu'l-Bahá
  and China 69, 167
  and Hands of the Cause 3
  and Japan 2, 5, 47-8, 71, 78, 88, 96,
    110-11, 125, 130, 147-51, 179,
    223, 225, 251, 260, 329, 333, 352
  passing of 58, 162-3
  photographs of 87, 91, 99, 104, 144,
    156, 159, 362
  portrait 241
  Shrine of 221, 263, 270-71
  Tablets 2, 5, 45, 56, 57, 71, 95-6,
    104, 153, 160
    to Agnes Alexander 2, 36, 45, 51,
      53, 72-3, 110-11, 124-6, 130,
      160, 329, 362, 383
    to Japanese believers 47, 137-40,
      145, 146-51, 299, 252, 269
  voice recording 119, 229
  and West, Western believers 29, 41,
    68-70, 72, 81, 207, 258, 305
  Writings and talks
    Paris Talks 100, 182
    Some Answered Questions 103, 127,
      268, 305
    Tablets of the Divine Plan 4,
      125-6, 305, 368-9, 376-7, 383
    Will and Testament 247, 311,
      316, 326, 341, 343, 348, 385,
      386
Abu'l-Faḍl, Mírzá 1, 34, 36, 384
Aden 81-3, 266
Adolphson, Elma 277
Africa, Africans 38, 153, 196, 267, 328,
  330, 334, 343, 354-5, 374, 379
  House of Worship, Kampala 354
Aibara, Susumu 169-71, 173, 204, 234

Ainu tribe, Hokkaido 359
'Akká 28-31, 34, 47, 92, 106, 108, 131,
  180, 232-3, 272-3, 380, 381, 382,
  386
Akita, Ujaku 91, 94, 100, 107-8, 113,
  167
'Alá'í, Shu'á'u'lláh 343
Alaska, Alaskans 49-51, 193, 305
Alexander, Abigail Baldwin (mother of
  Agnes) 6, 11, 24, 25, 41, 43, 72
Alexander, Agnes
  Auxiliary Board member 330-31, 336
  books
    Forty Years of the Bahá'í Cause in
      Hawaii 293, 295-302
    History of the Bahá'í Faith in Japan
      167, 268, 274, 293, 295-302
    How to Use Hawaiian Fruits 64
  Hand of the Cause 2, 337-9, 367,
    379
  histories of Faith in Hawaii and
    Japan 1, 249, 270, 295-7, 299-302
  letters from Shoghi Effendi 2, 180,
    180, 188, 192-3, 196-202, 208-
    11, 213-14, 216-19, 225, 227-9,
    233-40, 242-50, 251-5, 257-8,
    260-61, 275-6, 279, 281-6, 289,
    295, 297-303, 304, 309-11, 315-
    16, 318-21, 328-9, 331, 337-9,
    351, 378-9
  pilgrimage 261-6, 268-74, 275,
    277-9, 286, 293, 296, 298, 384
  radio broadcasts 244, 257, 282, 290,
    293, 301-2
  Tablets from 'Abdu'l-Bahá 2, 36, 45,
    51, 53, 72-3, 110-11, 124-6, 130,
    160, 329, 362, 383

passing and funeral 375-8
  will 369, 376-7
Alexander, Ann (Dickey) (aunt of
  Agnes) 8, 14, 16, 43, 45-6, 54, 117
Alexander, Arthur (brother of Agnes)
  11, 13-14, 19, 75, 101, 112, 117,
  135, 161, 216-17, 241, 243, 251,
  255, 256, 308
Alexander, Charles Hodge (uncle of
  Agnes) 8
Alexander, Ellen (Lottie Ferreri, aunt of
  Agnes) 8, 26, 73-5
Alexander, Emily (aunt of Agnes) 8
Alexander, Henry (brother of Agnes)
  11-14
Alexander, Henry (uncle of Agnes) 8, 25
Alexander, James (uncle of Agnes) 8, 21
Alexander, Mary (sister of Agnes) 11-14,
  16-17, 20-21, 23, 24, 26, 35, 40, 44,
  49, 75, 81, 85, 116-17, 124, 173,
  176-9, 182-7, 284, 309, 349, 355
Alexander, Mary Ann McKinney 7-8
Alexander, Mary Jane (aunt of Agnes)
  8, 21-3
Alexander, Samuel (uncle of Agnes) 8
Alexander, William (brother of Agnes)
  11-14. 23-4, 117
Alexander, William (nephew of agnes)
  359, 361, 373, 377
Alexander, William De Witt (father of
  Agnes) 6, 8, 11, 23, 25-6, 41, 44,
  60-62, 66-7, 72
Alexander, William Patterson 7, 195,
  308
Alexander & Baldwin 9
Allen, Dale 1
Allen, John 196
Allen, Valera 1, 191, 195-6, 349, 354
All-Japanese Religious Conference
  (1928) 211-12
All-Philippine Teaching Conference 355
All-Taiwan Teaching Conference 335
Alu Saad El Din 267
Amalu, Samuel 257-8
America, Americans see United States,
  and individual entries
American continent 287

Arabia 82, 343
Arakawa, Mikae see Komatsu, Mikei
Arcadia retirement home, Honolulu
  373-5, 370
Armstrong, Leonora Holsapple 287
Asahi newspaper 87, 178
Ascona, Switzerland 76
Asgarzadeh, Ziaoullah 181
Ashqabat 219
Ashton, Beatrice 306
Asia Regional Teaching Conference 333
Asian World Federation Congress 327
Aso, President (of Japan Women's Col-
  lege) 131
Assassi, Mr 352
Atami, Japan 176, 216
Atlanta, Georgia 304, 305-6, 313
Augur, George 2, 56, 59, 63-4, 65, 71,
  85-6, 88, 89, 91, 95-6, 99, 103, 108,
  112, 114, 194, 199-200, 201
  Tablets from 'Abdu'l-Bahá 71, 86,
    95-6
Augur, Ruth 2, 55, 56, 59, 63, 65, 71,
  91, 95-6, 99, 105, 194, 199-200
Augusta, Georgia 304
Australia, Australians 193, 194, 221, 224,
  265, 292, 330, 331, 336, 343, 346-8
Austria 351
Auxiliary Board 330-31, 336, 344, 348,
  357

Báb, the 61-2, 220, 270, 307
  Bayán, the 61
  Declaration of 91, 112, 139, 167,
    221, 321
Martyrdom of 356
prayer of 79
  Shrine of 194, 270-71, 342
Bagdadi, Zia 123, 304
Bahá'í
  Holy Year 321
  House of Worship
    (Mashriqu'l-Adhkár)
    Kampala 354
    Wilmette 62, 67, 68, 101-2, 126,
      151, 157, 165-6, 246, 232,
      266, 291, 295, 304, 386, 376

National Conventions 1, 4, 68, 102, 120, 122-5, 245, 246-7, 278, 279, 289, 290, 291, 294, 297, 298, 303-4, 309-10. 327-8, 339-40, 347-8, 355-6, 359-61, 363, 382-3, 384-5

Bahá'í News 4, 222, 246, 280, 311, 321, 333, 357, 359, 376

Bahá'í Prayer Collection (in Japanese) 326

Bahai Scriptures 194

Bahá'í World, The 106, 200, 265, 266, 269, 279, 285, 329, 377

Bahá'í World Centre 261, 326, 364

Bahjí 235, 239-40, 244, 253, 270, 294, 342-3, 345, 351

Mansion of 235, 239-40, 253, 342, 272-3

Bahá'u'lláh 13, 29, 40, 52, 56, 61, 69, 70, 77, 88, 91, 93, 100, 103, 104, 112, 113, 118, 130, 140, 148, 153, 156, 162, 169, 196, 199, 209, 210, 211, 214, 216, 221, 228, 232, 248, 249, 269, 272, 274, 286, 289, 290, 292, 307, 321, 323, 324, 326, 331, 341, 342, 344, 359, 376, 378, 385

Cause, Faith, Message, Teachings of 2, 58, 85, 88, 114, 137, 143, 168, 169, 174, 188, 197, 204, 232, 234, 238, 246, 262, 287-8, 313, 316, 321, 329, 337, 341, 367, 379

Shrine of 233, 239, 244, 271-3, 294, 351, 385

World Order of 3, 172, 269-70, 288-9, 294, 386

Writings 94, 100, 136, 144, 146, 227, 316, 326

Gleanings 268

Hidden Words 29, 42, 71, 85, 89, 91, 94, 100, 109, 142, 146, 233, 268, 381

Kitáb-i-Aqdas 3

Kitáb-i-Íqán 245, 268, 305

Seven Valleys 143, 196

Bahá'u'lláh and the New Era 101, 103, 182, 233-40, 252-4, 266, 285, 305, 313

Bailey, Anna 48

Bailey, Ella 328

Baker, Dorothy 38

Baldwin, Abigail (Alexander) 6, 11, 24, 25, 41, 43, 72

Baldwin, Barbara 244

Baldwin, Charles 6

Baldwin, Charlotte 6

Baldwin, David 6

Baldwin, Douglas 6

Baldwin, Dwight, Rev. Dr and family 6

Baldwin, Emily (Whitney) 6, 14, 25, 44, 245

Baldwin, Harriet 6

Baldwin, Henry 6

Baldwin, Kathrine 170, 190, 194, 199, 206, 245, 286, 292, 296

Baldwin, Mary 6

Baldwin, Samuel (cousin of Agnes) 170

Balyuzi, Hasan 343-4

Banání, Músá 343

Batavia, Java 243

Bayán, the 61

Bay City, Michigan 293

Beckwith, Ethelwynn 290

Bedikian, Victoria 165-6, 181, 297

Beecher, 'Mother', Ellen 38

Beijing (also Peiping, Pekin, Peking), China 167-8, 174-5, 181-3, 187, 189, 219, 293

Benedict, Mrs 307

Bentley family 26-7

Berkeley, California 19, 22-4, 128, 166, 197, 246, 266, 296, 308-9, 349, 355

Spiritual Assembly of 282, 284

Bethlen, Aurelia 2, 64, 85

Beverly, Mass. 306-7

Bible 11, 13, 29-30, 34, 55, 67, 92, 290, 380

Daniel 34

Gospels 159

Malachi 30

Revelation 30, 384

Bidwell family 305

Bishop, Helen 277

blind, School(s) for the 89, 105-6, 170, 207, 353

Blomfield, Lady 207
Bolles, May *see* Maxwell, May
Bolles, Jeanne 181
Bolton, Stanley, Mr and Mrs 292
Bopp, Anneliese 358
Bosch, John 38, 247, 297
Bosch, Louise 1, 38, 118, 247, 255, 262, 297
Boston, Mass. 6, 120, 129, 141, 277, 306
Bowes, Marjorie 342
Braille 269
    English 89
    Esperanto 89, 105-6, 109-10
    Japanese 107, 114-15, 131, 152, 252-4, 262, 321
Breaks, Virginia 353
Breakwell, Thomas 196
Brewer, John 309
Brisbane, Australia 331, 336
Brooklyn, New York 73-4, 100
Brooks, Elizabeth 307
Brown, Ramona 332, 334, 338, 340, 345, 348, 349, 351-4, 356-8, 361, 363-4, 366, 370, 374
Browne, E. G. 61
Bryn Mawr College 221
Buddha, Buddhists 207, 323
    in Hawaii 191
    in Korea 157, 159, 182
    in Japan 87-8, 90, 102-3, 114, 136, 194, 195, 211, 220, 226, 233, 255, 259, 263-4, 283, 323
    in Malaysia 266
    in United States 197
Buenos Aires, Argentina 293, 387
Buffalo, NY 307
Buikema, Gertrude 59
Burma (Myanmar), Burmese 59, 171, 220, 221
Burns, John, Governor 360
Busan (Pusan, Fusan), Korea 154, 356, 357

Cairo, Egypt 243, 266
California 12, 17, 19, 38-9, 48, 71, 85, 97, 116-20, 126, 127-8, 138, 166, 187, 189, 195, 197, 221, 258, 266, 279, 281-2, 284, 285, 297, 326, 328, 349, 353, 355
    University of, at Berkeley 19, 22-4
Calkins, Don 316
Cameron, Mrs Walter 361
Camp Azalea, California 21, 120
Canada, Canadians 45, 125, 194, 212, 306, 382-3
    National Spiritual Assembly (US and Canada) 194, 224, 255, 385
Canton, China 143-5, 169, 187, 224
Canton Times 144-5, 182-3
Caravan of the East 314, 315-17
Carmel, California 353
Carmel, Mount 31, 180, 385
Caroline Islands 333, 353
Carter, Helen 353
Castle & Cook 9
Casulli, Mme 80-81, 93
Chan, Mo 264
Chance, Hugh 357
Charleston, South Carolina 304-5, 347
Chen, Kai Tai 169
Chen, P. W. 182-3
Chengtu, Szechuan 168-9
Cheyne, T. K. 107
Chicago, Ill. 28, 39, 59, 62, 87, 120-21, 126, 127, 138, 246, 258, 278-9, 290-91, 303, 308-9, 310, 317, 326, 349, 382, 386
    House of Worship, Mashriqu'l-Adhkár (Wilmette) 62, 67, 68, 101-2, 126, 151, 157, 165-6, 246, 232, 266, 291, 295, 304, 386, 376
Chieh-Ming, Deng 183
China, Chinese 1, 9, 24, 50, 143-5, 162, 165, 167-9, 173, 181-9, 194, 199, 203, 207, 218-20, 221, 223, 224, 236, 285, 308, 364, 378 *see also individual entries for cities and people*
Chinese Legation 144, 163
Chinese Women's Association 167-8
Christ (Jesus) 7, 13, 29-30, 35-6, 42-3, 45, 51, 66-7, 95, 103, 111, 123, 154, 159, 300, 322-3, 324, 331, 361, 368, 378

Christianity, Christians 6-7, 26, 40, 42, 46-7, 51, 56, 62, 67, 88, 90, 104, 106, 114, 129, 131, 136, 139, 145, 155, 157, 159, 161, 172, 173, 182, 183, 190-91, 210, 211, 217, 221, 232, 255, 270, 272, 322-5, 363, 377-8 *see also* missionaries
Christian Science Church 65, 375
Christmas 14. 49. 88. 98. 117. 151. 163. 170. 187. 213. 220. 255. 259. 323-4, 357
Chugai Nippo newspaper 103
Chundokyo Society, Seoul 157-8
Chunju, Korea 356
Cleveland, Ohio 307-8
Cleveland, Grover, US President 10, 16
Cobb, Stanwood 265
Coles, Helen Ellis 34
Collins, Amelia 342-3, 355
Colombia 251
Colombo, Sri Lanka 79, 266
Columbus, Ohio 304-5
Communism, Communist 103, 171, 209-11, 220, 335
Conference on World Religions, Tokyo 332-3
Confucius 184, 189
Conte, Charlotte 127
Cook, Captain James 6, 8
Cook, Inez (Greeven) 207
Coombs, Genevra 55-6, 63
Coonradt, Mary 63-4
Cooper, Ella Goodall 1, 24, 41, 59, 118-20, 127, 222, 251, 297, 299, 304, 311
Cornell, John 310
Cornell University 224
Covenant-breaking 104, 121-2, 135-6, 307, 314, 316, 344, 353, 379
Crosby Club, Tokyo 316
Cuba 187, 303

Datte, Mr 157-8
Davenport, Jacob and Barbara 311, 313-14, 316, 319
Dawn-Breakers, The 305
Denton, Miss 134-5, 137, 263

D'Evelyn, Dr 123
Disciples of 'Abdu'l-Bahá 200
Dixon, Charlotte 28-31, 38
Dodge, Philip and Mrs 83, 85, 90
Dole, Stanford 10
Doshisha University, Japan 322-3, 325
Blind Student Friendship Association 323
Drevet, Mrs 207
Dreyfus-Barney, Hippolyte 2
Dreyfus-Barney, Laura 1, 2
Dublin, Ireland 337
Dublin, New Hampshire 205
Dugdale Dunn, Mrs 95
Dugersuren, Admaa ix
Dunn, Clara, 287, 342-3, 346
Dunn, Hyde 287

Earl, David and Joy 320, 326, 332
Ebbert, Doris 305, 313-14, 318-20, 329, 335
Eddy, Mary Baker 65-6
Edinburgh, Scotland 365
Edisto Island, South Carolina 305
Eito, Miss 229
Ejiri, Japan 105, 108, 114
Eleele, Kauai 192
Enger, Mr and Mrs 356
Eliot, Maine 37-8
Emery, Della 307
Emery, Ralph 310
England, English 6, 34, 69, 72, 84, 95, 100, 102, 104-5, 134, 139, 156, 181, 196, 207, 221, 223, 230, 267, 276, 343, 364
English language 23, 34, 46-7, 51, 86-8, 91-3, 102, 105, 107, 111, 113, 115, 119, 134, 137, 141, 144, 151, 154, 156, 157, 159-60, 162-3, 170-71, 186-7, 206, 212, 216, 217, 221-3, 257, 275, 312, 323, 325-6, 334, 363
Ernst, Mrs 127-8
Eroshenko, Vasily 79, 89-91, 99-100, 103, 105
Esperanto 73-4, 79, 89-90, 97-9, 100, 102, 105-6, 109, 111, 115-16, 129, 146, 153, 161, 167, 170-71, 173,

183, 190-91, 209-10, 230-32, 233, 244, 265, 321
Braille 89, 105-6, 109-10
Esperanto Association of North America 124
Japanese Congresses 174, 179, 218, 230-31, 321, 332, 334
Japana Esperantisto 100
Kasitaj Vortaj (Hidden Words) 109
La Orienta Azio 89
Universal Esperanto Association 79, 89
World Esperanto Congress, Tokyo 364-5, 367
Espinosa, Pedro 290
Esslemont, John 100-01, 146, 192, 219, 233-8, 252-3, 272
Bahá'u'lláh and the New Era 101, 103, 182, 219, 233-8, 240, 252-4, 266, 285, 305, 313
Evans, Mr 187
Evanston, Illinois 291, 294, 304, 308-9, 384, 385-6
Everywoman magazine 114

Faizi, Abu'l-Qásim 302, 343, 361-2, 363, 372
Fantom, Mary 64, 190, 245, 269, 273, 296
Far East weekly 91, 104
Far East Blind Conference 332, 334
Farmer, Sarah 37-9
Farrington, Wallace 190, 203
Fatheazam, Hushmand 357
Featherstone, Collis 342-3, 346, 347
Ferrier, Rev. W. 66
Ferraby, John 343, 351
Ferreri family 26-7
    Ellen (Lottie) Alexander 8, 26, 73-5
    Guilio 26, 73-75, 275
    Hale 26-7
    Imogene 26-7
Finch, Ida 129-31, 134-6, 141, 144, 150, 163, 166, 173-6, 178, 181, 230, 363
Fisher, Valera *see* Allen, Valera
Fisk, Mrs 307

Fitzgerald, Georgy 280, 309
Fletcher, Miss 65
Florence, Italy 32, 35
Forni, Mme 76
Ford, Alexander Hume 207
Ford, Bahiyyih 107, 306-7
Ford, Dorothy 305
Ford, Harry 306
Formosa 228, 332, 333, 335
Forsgrene, Hilda 298
Fort Wayne, Indiana 307
France, French 32, 77, 80-81, 102, 124, 127, 161, 173, 187, 207, 276, 353, 381 *see also* Marseilles, Paris
French language 15, 16, 20, 80-80
Frankfurt, Germany 349-51, 358
Frankland, Kathryn 166, 258, 307-8
Fraser-Chamberlain, Isabel (Soraya) 84, 108
Freitas, Elinor 74
Friend, The 116
Fuch, Lawrence H. 10
Fujita, Sachiro 138, 145, 165, 174, 181, 188, 258-60, 263, 268, 271, 308, 312, 313, 315, 333
Fukuda, Kenji 161, 163
Fukusawa, Kazu 140
Fukuta, Kikutaro (Fukuata San) 92-6, 99, 101-2, 107-8, 110, 113, 128, 141, 206, 227
Fulton, Miss 98
Furukawa, Yuri 229, 237, 238, 241 *see also* Mochizuki, Yuri
Furútan, 'Alí-Akbar 342-4

Garden of Light magazine 152
Garis, Mabel 183
Geneva, Switzerland 77-9, 84, 89, 203-4, 207, 329
Genoa, Italy 26, 74
Georgetown, South Carolina 305
Germany, Germans 32, 35, 75-81, 116, 130, 212, 364
    Bahá'ís in 75, 193, 265, 268274-6, 308, 343, 349-51, 358, 379
German language 233
Getsinger, Edward 1, 34

Getsinger, Lua 1, 34, 117-18, 381
Geyserville, California 21, 38, 118, 120,
     130, 247, 275, 280, 296-7, 328
Giachery, Ugo 343
Gibraltar 74
Gibson, Amoz 357
Ginanfu (Chin-ch'eng), China 183
Glendale, Arizona 279
Gobineau, Count 61
Goldman, Charles and Julia 242, 277
God Passes By 300, 301
Goodall, Edwin 41
Goodall, Ella see Cooper. Ella
Goodall, Helen 24, 39, 41, 45, 48-9
Gomez, Luisa 351, 355
Gordon, Mrs (in Kyoto) 134
Gordon Smith family 359
Graham, Augusta 62, 65
Grant, Mr 255
Greatest Holy Leaf 162, 181, 238, 270,
     271
Great Kanto earthquake (1923), Japan
     174-81, 191, 204, 226, 363, 364
Greece, Greeks 80-81
Green Acre, Maine 37-8, 104-5, 118,
     124, 143, 275, 277, 306-7
Greenville, South Carolina 305
Gregory, Gayne 193
Gregory, Louis 181
Grosfeld, W. E. M. 243-4
Grossmann, Anna 350
Grossmann, Hermann 265, 271, 343-4
Grundy, Julia M. 91, 92
     Ten Days in the Light of Akka 91, 92,
          106, 131
Guam 333
Gulick, Bahia and Robert 328
Guppy, Miss 204-5, 216, 255, 257

Haddad, Anton 34, 36
Haddah, Talia 333
Hagiwara, Kimiko 140
Haifa, Israel 59, 138, 147, 159, 174,
     179-80, 181, 188, 192, 193, 219,
     221, 236, 242, 243, 258-9, 262,
     264-75, 277-8, 281, 284, 286, 290,
     293, 295-6, 298, 307, 324, 334, 335,
     337-8, 339, 341-5, 349, 351, 353-4,
     361, 371, 383-4
Haiku, Maui 14-15
Hainan 335
Hainsworth, Philip 354
Hakim, Lotfullah 357, 372
Hale, Mr 291
Haleakala volcano 14-16, 272
Hamada, Tomojiro 170
Hamburg, Germany 350, 358
Hamilton, Mass. 306
Hands of the Cause 3, 329, 330, 338-9,
     341-3, 353, 370
     Conclave(s) 341-5, 349, 351, 354,
          361, 362
     Custodians 355, 356
     see also individual entries
Haney, Mariam 181
Haney, Paul 343-4
Hangchow College, Shanghai 187
Hannen, Joseph 110, 124
Hannen, Pauline 76
Harmon, W. W. 121
Hataya, M. 173
Havana, Cuba 303
Hawaii Advertiser 116
Hawaiian Islands 1, 4, 6-7, 34, 60, 126,
     190, 194, 203, 242, 246, 249, 270,
     274, 277, 285-6, 295, 297-8, 308-9,
     360, 368, 376, 334, 355, 381-2
     Bahá'ís in 2, 4, 35, 41-3, 45-9, 52-3,
          54-68, 71, 116, 128, 170, 190-91
     Agnes Alexander's history of 293,
          295-302
     Archives 4, 248-9
     Light of the Pacific magazine
          373-4
     National Convention (1964) 1, 4,
          359-61
     National Spiritual Assembly 194,
          359-60, 371, 377-8
     Christian missionaries to 1, 6-10, 12,
          14, 26, 28, 35, 56, 60, 171, 195,
          308, 331, 359, 368, 378
     House of Nobles 9
     Republic of 10
     royal house 6, 9-10, 14, 17, 24, 25, 161

Supreme Court 194
Hawaii (Big Island) 6, 17, 23-4, 35,
    46, 58-61, 64, 116, 189, 190, 292,
    297, 309 *see also* Honolulu
Kauai 56, 192, 195, 246, 334
Lanai 6
Maui 6, 12, 45-6, 170, 190, 245-6,
    286, 374
    Baldwin High School 311
    Spiritual Assembly 190
Molokai 6, 334
Hawaiian Mission Children's Society
    116, 133
Hawaiian Star newspaper 62
Healdsburg, Calif. 21, 120
Hearst, Phoebe 24
Henri, Monsieur 33
Heritage Project of the National Spir-
    itual Assembly (US) ix
Hidden Words 29, 42, 71, 85, 89, 91, 94,
    100, 109, 142, 146, 233, 268, 381
Higher Normal School(s), China 168-9
Hilo, Hawaii 18, 191, 334
Himmler, Heinrich 275
Hirohito, Emperor 214, 220-21
Hiroshima, Japan 89, 97-8, 258, 313,
    322, 325-6, 327-8, 331, 334, 347,
    352
Ho, Chien Yung 167-8, 185
Ho, Mr 163
Hoagg, Emogene 1, 34, 305, 347
Hoar, William 1, 34, 37
Hodgson, Dorothy 69, 102, 104
Hofman, David 357
Hokkaido, Japan 230-2, 151, 312-13,
    354, 359
Hokkai Times 231
Holley, Horace 200, 285, 315, 343
Holley, Marion (Hofman) 211, 277
Holy Land 2, 69, 77, 140, 151, 158-9,
    174, 224, 228, 244, 261-4, 268, 277,
    279, 285, 343-5, 360, 384 *see also*
    'Akká, Bahjí, Haifa, Jerusalem
Hong Kong 79, 81-2, 219, 2665, 332-3,
    335, 347, 353, 355-6
Hongo, Tameo 326
Honolulu, Hawaii 7-10, 12, 14-15, 16,

18, 24, 40, 72-3, 83, 114, 116-17,
    126, 128, 157, 187, 189, 190, 194-5,
    199-200, 203, 206-7, 216, 220, 222,
    241-2, 285-6, 298, 332, 349, 355-7,
    370
Arcadia retirement home 373-5, 370
Bahá'ís in 34, 40-41, 48-9, 54-68,
    70, 71, 74, 91, 116, 193-6, 242-6,
    248-9, 277, 278, 292-3, 295-6,
    299, 302, 310, 334
    and 'Abdu'l-Bahá 68-70, 96, 104,
        126, 130
    Bahá'í Centre 298-9
    Incorporation 299
    passing of Martha Root 292-3
    Spiritual Assembly 64-8, 246,
        248-9, 289
    Unity Calendar 67-8, 79, 89
Central Union Church 286
Punahou School 12-13, 18, 33, 49,
    258
Punahou Street 374
Honolulu Advertiser 67, 116, 191-2
Honolulu Commercial Advertiser 61-2
Honolulu Evening Bulletin 62
Honolulu Star-Bulletin 64, 191, 244
Honshu Island, Japan 151, 154, 218,
    263
Horioka, Goro 313
Hosoda, Dr 358
Hungary 64
Hustace, Isabel 257

Imagire, Robert 313, 320
Imaoka, N. 234
Ioas, Leroy 246, 328, 343
Ioas, Sylvia 246
India 59, 69, 77, 224, 301, 357
Indians 38, 50-51, 91, 101, 266
Indian Ocean 81, 364
Inouye, Daiun 102, 136, 179, 194, 224,
    235, 237, 252, 259, 264, 273, 283,
    312-13
Inouye, Saeno 190-91
Institute of Pacific Relations 194, 199,
    207
Intercontinental Teaching Conferences

327-9, 346-8

International Friendship Association, Korea 157

Iran, Iranian 220, 221, 224, 298, 334-5, 342, 343, 346 *see also* Persia

Ireland 15, 337

Ishigura, Yoshio 173

Islam 61-2

Israel 342

Italy 24, 26-8, 32, 38, 73-5, 76, 118, 275, 343, 361, 380

Ito, Sempo 217, 221, 223, 229, 234

Iwahashi, Mr 233

Jack, Marion 269, 287, 305

Jakarta, Indonesia 347

James, Lillian 126

Jamestown, NY 307, 310

Jamir, Michael 306, 312

Japan, Japanese
  and 'Abdu'l-Bahá *see* 'Abdu'l-Bahá
  Bahá'ís in *see individual entries*
  National Spiritual Assembly of the Bahá'ís 321, 333, 335, 347, 362, 366, 371
  and Shoghi Effendi *see* Shoghi Effendi

Japan Advertiser 111-12, 222

Japan Times 220

Japanese Women's Peace Society 171

Japan Women's College (University) 107, 131, 142, 223

Java 221, 243

Jerusalem 267, 271-2
  Church of the Holy Sepulchre 272
  Mosque of Omar 272

Jessup, Rev. H. H. 66

Jesus *see* Christ

Jinan (Tsinan), China 183, 189

Johnson, Abby Frances 56-9, 62-3, 64

Jones, Maxie 279-80

Jordan, David Starr 192

Kadota, Shozo 313

Kahala, Hawaii 359

Kaichika, Miss 96

Kai Tai Chen 169

Kaiulani, Princess 22
  Hotel, Waikiki 359

Kajo, Korea 357

Kalakaua, King 9, 13

Kamehameha, King 6

Kamichika, Ichi 87, 108-9

Kanazawa, Japan 218

Kansai, Japan 334

Kantara 267

Kappus, Fred 307

Karuizawa, Japan 94, 142

Kataoka, Y. 229, 230, 262

Kavelin, H. Borrah 357

Kawai, Michi 221

Kealakekua, Hawaii 190

Keio University, Japan 169-71, 223

Keller, Helen 269

Khadem, Zikrullah 329-30, 333-4, 343-4, 346

Khamsi, Jane and family 361

Khan, Ali-Kuli 1

Kházeh, Jalál 339, 342-4

Kilohana Art League 62-3

Kilauea volcano 64

Kim, E. 153

Kinney family 278

Kirchner, Luella 121-2, 136

Kitáb-i-Aqdas 3

Kitáb-i-Íqán 245, 268, 305

Knights of Bahá'u'lláh 196, 353

Knobloch, Alma 4, 75, 126

Knobloch, Fanny 153
  Tablet from 'Abdu'l-Bahá 153-4

Knudsen, Margaret 58

Kobe, Japan 79, 82, 83-4, 102, 163, 173, 177, 179, 181-2, 187, 189, 193-4, 224, 226, 235, 259, 264, 327, 334, 339, 364

Kodaira, Rev. 221

Komatsu, Mikae Arakawa (Chu) 138, 141, 162, 166, 259, 251

Kona, Hawaii 190-91, 278

Koran *see* Qur'án

Korea, Koreans 1, 153-60. 162. 163. 165. 168. 181-2, 189, 194, 199, 223, 304, 308, 331-2, 333, 336, 355-6, 357, 379

Bahá'í summer school, first 340-41
International Friendship Association
    157
    see also Seoul
Kruka, Josephine 303
Kumagae, Mr 129
Kunz, Anna 158
Kurita, Mr 155-7
Kuwaki, Genyoku 266
Kyongju, Korea 357
Kyoto, Japan 83-4, 85, 96, 98, 129, 134,
    166, 170, 172, 224, 259, 263, 265,
    272, 312, 314, 321-3, 326-7, 330-31,
    334-6, 341, 345, 353, 355-6, 361-4,
    367, 370-71
    Spiritual Assembly of the Bahá'ís 2-3,
    334, 335, 348, 379

Lahaina, Maui 6
Lake Como, Italy 75
Lake Maggiore, Italy/Switzerland 75
Lake Nojiri, Japan 212-13, 218
Langier, C. Fisher 65
La Orienta Azio 89
Latimer, George 70, 246
Lawrence, Emma 305
Leach, Bernard 87
League of Nations 203-4, 207
Leipzig, Germany 75
Lexow, Berthalin 33
Leyland, Mrs 59
Light of the Pacific 373
Lihue, Kauai 192, 195
Liliuokalani, Queen 9-10, 13, 16
Lindsey family 307
Linfoot, Charlotte 332
Ling, K. C. 173
Little, Frances 97-8
Little Rock, Arkansas 310
Liu, Fung-Ling 224
Lo, Y. S. 173
Locarno, Switzerland 75-6
Lombard, Carole 193
London, England 27, 778-9, 100, 107,
    142, 181, 223, 268, 275-6, 349-50,
    351
    Japanese Embassy 264

Jubilee (1963) 357-9
Los Angeles, California 193, 279, 280,
    309
Louhelen Bahá'í School 275, 277, 279-
    81, 291, 293, 304, 306-7
Louisville, Kentucky 307-9
Lucerne, Switzerland 26, 75
Lunt, Alfred 122

Macao, Macau 332, 333-5, 353, 355
MacNutt, Howard 2
Mac Phee K 305
Madeira 74
Magazine of the Children of the Kingdom
    140-41
Mainichi Daily News 363
Makawao, Maui 14, 190, 245, 272
Makiki Heights 6, 13
Malaysia 266, 329
'Maluhia' 6, 117
Manchuria 256
Manila, Philippnes 342, 351, 355, 361
Marangella, Philip 332-3, 340, 366
Marques, Laura 74
Marseilles, France 78-80, 160, 187, 364
Masujima, Dr R. 206-7, 213, 220, 223,
    257, 263, 295
Mathews, Loulie 249
Mathewson, Mr 135
Matsuda, H. 229, 230, 238
Matsushima, Japan 104
Maui, *see* Hawaiian Islands
Maxwell, Emma 195
Maxwell, Mary *see* Rúḥíyyih Khánum
Maxwell, May Bolles 1, 4, 72-3, 120,
    123-6, 130, 196, 247, 266, 268-71,
    290, 293-4, 303, 269-70, 371, 372,
    376, 380-87
Maxwell, Sutherland 269-70, 277, 382
Maxwell, William 340, 348, 357
Mayer, Richard 120
McAlpin Hotel, New York 125
McBride Sugar Plantation, Kauai 192
McCandless, Doris 307
McCormick, Margery 306
McHenry, John S. 376
McVeagh, Charles and Fanny 205

Meiji, Emperor 161
Mexico 290
Michigan 258, 279-80, 293, 296, 306
Milan, Italy 26, 74-5, 78, 275
Mills, Mountfort 207
Milwaukee 290
Mimura, H. 262
Misawa, Sanzo 91, 163, 179, 193-4, 259
missionaries
    in China 185, 187, 203
    in Hawaiian Islands 1, 6-12, 14, 26,
        28, 35, 56, 60, 171, 308, 359, 378
        Kauai 56, 195
    in Japan 97-8, 142, 155, 157, 212,
        230, 322-3
Mochizuki, Yuri (Furukawa) 113, 119,
    125, 128, 129, 140-41, 143, 145,
    146, 161, 13, 181, 205-6, 229, 237,
    262
Moghbel, Ata'ullah 340, 354
Mohtadi, Mr and Mrs 334-5
Molokai see Hawaiian Islands
Momtazi, Noureddin and family 330-
    32, 334, 340, 359
Montclair, New Jersey 124, 166
Monte Verità, Ascona 76
Montreal, Canada 72-3, 120 1225, 126,
    277, 382-4
Mori, Haruko 137-8, 140, 146, 163
    Tablets from 'Abdu'l-Bahá 140, 146
Mori, Rev. J. 221
Mori, Tsuto 331
Moscow, Russian Federation 89
Mosque of Omar, Jerusalem 272
Mount Fuji, Japan 106, 173, 176-7,
    199, 206, 214-16, 314, 348
Mugford, Margery 374
Muhájir, Raḥmatu'lláh 343, 361, 368,
    376
Muhammad, Prophet 62, 67, 81, 111
Muhammadans, Muslims 85, 182, 267
Mühlschlegel, Adelbert 343-4
Munírih Khánum 270
Muntinlupa, Philippines 361
Murakami, Otoe 140, 163, 179, 229
Muther, Elizabeth 41-2, 44-7, 53-4,
    56-7, 63, 64-5, 68, 197, 296, 297

Nagano, N. 172
Naganuma, Antoinette 217, 221, 229
Nagasaki, Japan 203, 371
Nagoya, Japan 105, 172, 354
Naimi, Philip 267
Naito, Akinobu 86, 92
Nakamura, Mr 105-7
Nakanishi, Mr S. 229
Nakhjávání, 'Alí 357, 372, 373
Nakhjavani, Violette 372
Nanjing (Nanking), China 185-6, 189
Nara, Japan 353
Nasu, Dr Shiroshi 199
Naruse, Jinjo 107, 131, 142, 223
Naw-Rúz 112, 207, 208, 229-30, 264,
    286, 289
Netherlands, Dutch 243, 251
New Bedford, Mass. 7
New History Society 314-17
New Tide magazine 99, 167
New Zealand 194, 221
New York 2, 23, 38, 73-4, 84, 88, 93,
    98, 125, 160, 179, 181, 207, 277-8,
    290, 306-7, 310, 317
Niagara Falls 127, 306
Nichi Nichi 102
Nicholson, Lillian 83-4
Nikko, Japan 233, 333-4, 336
Nitobe, Dr Inazo 207
Noguchi, E. 173
Norway 303
Noto, Tomonaga 128
Nuuanu Street Bahá'í Centre, Hawaii
    199

Oahu College 18, 24
Oahu Prison 62
Oakland, California 12, 17, 19-20, 39,
    41, 48-9, 126, 221, 246, 258, 349
Ober, Elizabeth 306-7
Ober, Harlan 280-81
Oberlin University, Ohio 23
Obon ceremony 226
Odaka, Mr 85
Odashina, Mr 231
Oh Sang Sun 153, 156-60, 182, 356
Okayama, Japan 174, 179

Oklahoma City 279
Okuma, Count 172
Olinda, Maui 14-16
Olinga, Enoch 343
Omaha, Nebraska 127
Ono, Kenjiro 131, 143, 145-6, 160, 173
    Tablets from 'Abdu'l-Bahá 146, 149,
    173
Onuma, Hokkaido 230-32
Oomoto religion 172, 210, 231
Osaka, Japan 84, 129, 172, 194, 329-30,
    334, 336, 346, 354-5
    Bahá'í Centre 346
    Spiritual Assembly 331
Osaka Mainichi newspaper 221
Otani, Chief Abbot Sonyu 195
Otis, Alice 49, 54, 56
Ouskouli, Husayn, and family 219, 264
Owen, William 46

Pacific Heights 40, 41, 48
Pacific peoples, region 2, 173-4, 194-6,
    298, 310
    Bahá'ís in 48, 338, 347-8 355, 379
Paia, Maui 14-15
Palestine 34, 194, 207, 221, 261, 267
Pao, S. J. Paul 144, 182-3
Pan-Pacific Union 195, 206
Paradise of the Pacific Weekly 65-6
Paris, France 26-8, 32, 35, 79, 268
    Bahá'ís in 28, 30, 32-4, 55, 63, 69,
    275-6, 295, 349-51, 380-81
Paris Talks 100, 182
Pearl Harbor 62, 256, 298
Peiping, Pekin, Peking, China *see* Beijing
Peiping Women's Teachers College 167
Persia, Persian 59, 61, 65-7, 104, 150,
    165, 218-19, 225, 232, 298, 330,
    351, 354, 358 *see also* Iran
Persian language 31, 146, 188, 227,
    233, 236, 381
Peter, Saint 34, 361
Philippines, Filipino 128, 194, 232,
    3535-6, 358-9, 361-2, 368
Phoenix, Arizona 279
Piedmont, California 118, 126, 130
Pinang, Malaysia 266

Pinson, Josie 305
Pittsburgh Post 171
Platt, Orol 193
politics 14, 16, 153-4, 168
Portland, Maine 37
Portland, Oregon 247
Port Said, Egypt 79-81, 266
Portuguese 74, 233, 245-6
Powell, Rufus and Mrs 73, 181
Pretoria, South Africa 334
Princess Kaiulani 24
Princess Kaiulani Hotel, Waikiki 359
Punahou School 12-13, 18, 24, 33, 49,
    258
Punahou Street, Honolulu 374-5
Pusan (Busan, Fusan), Korea 154, 356,
    357
Pye, Miss 207

Quaker(s) 100, 192, 207
Quick, Craig 360
Qur'án (Koran) 67, 110, 111, 139
Qurratu'l-'Ayn (Ṭáhirih) 147

Rabbani, Hussein 272
Rafaat, Yadullah 330, 340-42
Randall, Harry (William) 107, 123, 307
Randall Brown, Ruth 255
Ransom-Kehler, Keith 221, 235
Raven, Mr 187
Remey, Mason 2, 33, 37, 59, 60, 63, 70,
    121, 136, 151, 192, 263, 296, 307,
    329, 342-3, 346, 353, 379, 381
Revell, Ethel 373
Rexford, Orcella 193
Riḍván, Garden of, Holy Land 272
Robarts, Ella 141
Robarts, John 343
Rochester, NY 307
Rockefeller, John D. 155
Roh, Mr 158, 182
Rolpa, Mrs 265
Rome, Italy 26-9, 335, 38, 349, 361, 380
Root, Martha 1, 93-5, 99, 108, 120-21,
    124, 142, 167-8, 170-73, 181-7, 189,
    204, 206, 212, 218-20, 223-4, 275,
    287, 290, 292-3, 298, 307, 379

Rosenberg, Ethel 1, 34
Rowell, Teresina 263
Rowland, Ella Louise 58-9, 63-5, 197, 243, 251
Rowland, Virginia 58, 63
Rugge, Mary 306
Ruhe, David and Margaret 305
Rúḥíyyih Khánum 73, 266, 269, 271, 273, 287-8, 291-2, 293, 300, 309, 315, 320, 326, 342-4, 354-5, 372-3, 382-4, 385
Rúmí, Siyyid Muṣṭafá 220
Russell, Sigurd 63
Russia, Russians 51, 79, 89-91, 101-2, 103, 130, 171, 233

Sabet, Habib and Bahiyyih and family 298
Sabour-Pickett, Sarah 19
Sadako, Empress 94
Sagami Gulf, Japan 176, 216
Saiki, S. 133-4, 136, 150
    Tablet from 'Abdu'l-Bahá 150
Saito, Viscount 155-6, 256
Sakalin Island 335
Sakatani, Baron 220
Sakurai, Mr 5-7, 91, 204-5
Samandarí, Ṭarázu'lláh 343-5, 371
Sandwich Islands 6
San Francisco, California 24, 39, 49, 59, 64, 68, 117, 126, 127, 166, 192, 221, 246, 279-80, 298, 303, 309, 349
Sapporo, Japan 231, 312, 354, 371
Sasaoka, Tamigiro 129
Sawada, Keiji 170, 173, 229
Scepler, Mrs 307
School(s) for the Blind 89, 105-6, 170, 207, 353
Schreiber, Eugene 362
Scott, Mr 83, 85
Sears, William 343
Seattle, Washington 51, 107, 178, 310
Security for a Failing World 265-6
Seikei Gakuyen school 265, 268
Semple, Ian 357
Seoul, Korea 154-60, 181-2, 189, 332, 356-7

Chosen Hotel 154
Chundokyu Society 197-8
First Bank 156
Severance Hospital 160
Seoul Press 154
YMCA 160
Seto, Anthony 194, 197, 290
Seto, Mamie 193, 194, 197, 199, 249, 347, 355
Seven Valleys 143, 196
Seven Year Plan
    First 287
    Second 303
Shanghai, China 59, 85, 144, 169, 176, 183, 186-7, 189, 219, 220, 232, 234, 236, 264-5, 293, 335
    Hangchow College 187
    Shangtung Christian College 183
Sharp, Adelaide 270-72
Shastri, Dr and Mrs 127
Shaw family 45, 64-5, 218
Sherrill, Velma 359, 360
Shibusawa, Viscount 154-5
Shigenobu, Okuma, Premier 94
Shik Fan Fong 169
Shinagawa Girl's School 312
Shinshu sect (of Buddhism) 195
Shintoism 90, 114, 211
Shoghi Effendi, Guardian of the Bahá'í Faith 264, 266, 268-90, 274, 279-80, 290-92, 299, 300-01, 318, 320, 324, 343, 345, 380
    and 'Abdu'l-Bahá 5
    and Agnes Alexander
        histories of Faith in Hawaii and Japan 1, 249, 270, 295-7, 299-302
        letters to 2, 180, 180, 188, 192-3, 196-202, 208-11, 213-14, 216-19, 225, 227-9, 233-40, 242-50, 251-5, 257-8, 260-61, 275-6, 279, 281-6, 289, 295, 297-303, 304, 309-11, 315-16, 318-21, 328-9, 331, 337-9, 351, 378-9
        pilgrimage of 261-6, 268-74, 275, 277-9, 286, 293, 296, 298, 384

and Auxiliary Boards 330-31, 344
and Bahá'ís in:
America 222, 224, 247, 277,
279281-2, 287-8, 290, 298,
300, 303, 384-5
Hawaii 242-6, 285-6, 334, 355,
359
Japan 5, 163-5, 173-4, 229, 232,
247-9, 251, 253-4, 257, 260,
262, 283, 304, 309, 311, 313,
315-16, 319-22, 326-31, 333,
334-5, 339-40, 347-8
Mexico 290
and Emperor of Japan 214, 220
Guardianship 273-4, 385, 387
and Hands of the Cause 2, 3, 225,
329, 337, 344, 367, 379
Holy Year 321
passing 3, 341-5
Seven Year Plans 287, 303
on teaching 353, 357, 359
Ten Year Crusade 3, 196, 321, 328,
341, 346, 357
Writings
A Pattern for Future Society 305
God Passes By 300
Shōwa (Hirohito), Emperor 214,
220-21
Siam (Thailand) 103, 105
Sims, Barbara 340, 348, 362, 366-7
Singapore 79, 221, 265-6, 396-7
Six-Year Plan (North-East Asia) 340
Skelton, Lane 315, 319
Smith, Abby 41, 46, 48
Smith, Charles W. 320
Smith, Clara 163
Smith, Clarence 35, 40-41, 45 48 56, 63
Smith, Frances 310
Smith, Mary 370
Smith, Sila 190
Smith, William Owen 46
Smits, Bill 349, 356-7, 373
Smits, Lee 356, 373
Sohrab, Ahmad 167, 314-18
South Africa 153
South Bend, Indiana 307
South Carolina 304-5

Spiritual Assemblies
Local 202, 229, 244, 336
Berkeley, California 282-4
Chicago 121
Chunju, Korea 356
in Germany 193, 275-6
Haifa 174, 180, 181
in Hawaii 190, 245, 246
in Japan 201-2, 208, 213, 229-9,
241, 269, 333, 347
in Korea 332
Honolulu 64-5, 67-8, 246, 248-9,
289, 310
Kyoto 2-3, 334, 335, 348, 379
Maui 190, 245
Osaka 331
Seoul 332
Tokyo 229-30, 232, 241, 254,
312, 321, 325, 331, 333
National 329, 336, 337, 353, 358,
376, 385
Hawaii 194, 359-60, 371, 377-8
Japan 321, 333, 335, 347, 362,
366, 371
United States ix, 194, 300, 332,
360
United States and Canada 194,
224, 255, 280, 385
Regional
of North East Asia 3, 335, 339-40,
347, 355-6, 374, 379
of West Central Africa 374
Sprecklesville, Maui 190, 286
Stanford University 192
Star of the East 145-8, 153, 161-2
Star of the West 76, 83, 111, 124, 145-6,
169, 222, 265
Steer, Mrs 62
Stewart, Bula Mott 334
Stewart, Frances 306-7
Struven, Howard 2, 59, 63
Stuttgart, Germany 76-8, 79, 275, 350
Suez Canal 266
Suguki, Mrs (Miss Lane) 83
Suhou (Soochow), China 186, 189
Suleimani, Suleiman and family 219,
264, 335

Sumatra 251, 266
Sutherland, Mita 58, 63-4
Suzuki, Mr 178
Suzuki, Ruth Walbridge x, 368, 379
Sweezey, Mrs 196
Switzerland 26, 32, 75-6, 329, 364
Sydney, Australia 292, 331, 336, 346-8
Szechuan province, China 168-9

Tablets of the Divine Plan 4, 125-6,
  305, 368-9, 376-7, 383
Tachibana, T. 119
Taegu. Korea 356, 357
Taejon, Korea 356
Tainan, Taiwan 335-6
Taipei, Taiwan 348
Taiwan 219, 335-6, 348, 356, 362
Takahashi, F. 97, 173, 256
Takamatsu, Prince 313
Takano, Hiroyaso 340
Takao, Kenichi 90, 99
Takao, Yuri 140, 166
Takeshita, Kanae 166, 229
Tanabata custom 226
Tanaka, Hide 139, 141
Tanaka, Miss 87, 94, 99
Tanaka, Mr 179, 312
Tanakamuru, E., 173
Tehran, Iran 270, 354
Tehrani, Mr 354
Ten Days in the Light of Akka 91, 92,
  106, 131
Ten Year Crusade 3, 196, 321, 328, 341,
  346, 357
Theosophical Society 182
Thailand (Siam) 103, 105
Tianjin (Tientsin), China 183, 189
Thompson, Juliet 241
Thompson, J. Wesley 190
Thompson, Leona 190, 278
Thorpe, Ruth 307
Tinsley, Mrs 307
Tobey, Mark 87
Tokushima, Shikaku Island, Japan 170
Tokyo, Japan
  Agnes Alexander in 2, 85-114,
    128-52, 160-81, 201-2, 204-41,

  251-63, 313-221, 332, 334,
    361-2, 364-70
All-Japanese Religious Conference
  (1928) 211-12
American Embassy 171, 220
Bahá'ís in 85-7, 91, 92-6, 99-102,
  105, 107-8, 111-15, 119, 128,
  131, 137-42, 145-51, 161-2, 166-
  71, 173, 179, 208, 217, 221, 224,
  225-6, 229-30, 254, 260, 263,
  311, 312-13, 320-21, 330, 333
  Ḥaẓíratu'l-Quds (Bahá'í Centre)
    333, 348, 358
  National Conventions 339-40, 363
  Spiritual Assembly 201-2, 208-9,
    213, 229-30, 232, , 241, 254,
    312, 321, 325, 333
Conference on World Religions
  332-3
Crosby Club 316
earthquake (1923) 174-81, 191, 204,
  363, 364
English Speaking Society 171, 223
Esperantistis 79, 89-91, 97, 99-100,
  111, 124, 161, 170, 171-2, 210-
  11, 364-5, 367
Far East Blind Conference 334
Good Relations Club 207
Imperial Court, Household 84, 220
Imperial Hotel 129, 131-5, 144
Imperial University 199
International House Hotel 366-7
Japan Women's College (University)
  107, 131, 142, 223
JOAK radio station 220
Pan-Pacific Union 195, 206
Schools for the Blind 106, 170, 207
School of Music 255
Station Hotel 128
Tsuda English School 138, 161, 171
Unitarian Church 90, 108, 319
Universities 170-71, 199, 211, 223-4,
  320, 326
University Hospital 366-7, 369
YMCA 217, 223
YWCA 314, 318
Torii, Akira 224, 252

Torii, Ito 105, 108, 109, 114-15, 131, 166, 224-7, 253, 259, 263, 273, 325, 353
Torii, Tokujiro 105, 108. 109. 114-15, 119, 125, 128, 131, 145, 149-50, 152, 155, 163, 166, 173, 179, 224-7, 228, 235, 252-4, 259, 260, 263, 312, 314, 321-3, 325, 330, 332, 348-9, 352-3
    Tablets from 'Abdu'l-Bahá 150, 252
Torikai, Kenzo 107
Toronto, Canada 124, 126, 310, 383
Touty, Hossein 219, 232, 264-5
Townshend, George 3, 337, 367
    The Promise of All Ages 305
Tribune Herald, Hilo 191
Trieste, Italy 275
Tripoli, Libya 328
Troxel, Duane x, 1, 3-4, 359, 374
Troxel, Stephanie 374
Tsao, Dr and Mrs Yun-Siang 182, 219, 234, 285
Tsing Hua University, China 182
Tsing, Lieut. K. 182
Tsuchowfu, China 185, 189
Tunis, Tunisa 128
Turner, Jessie 64, 97
True, Corinne 56, 84, 304, 309, 343
Tsuda, Ume 72, 364
Tsuda English School, Tokyo 138, 161, 171

Uchigasaki, Rev. 90
Uluniu Women's Club, Waikiki 243
Unitarian Church (Japan) 90, 108, 314, 319
United States
    Bahá'í National Archives x, 300, 302
    Board of Commissioners for Foreign Missions 6
    Consuls, Consulates 77, 79-80, 327
    Embassy, Tokyo 96, 130, 171, 178, 220
    Government 9-10, 178
    National Spiritual Assembly of the Bahá'ís ix, 194, 300, 332, 360
Universal House of Justice 3, 4, 279, 305, 357, 358, 375-6, 377-8, 385

Urbana, Illinois 124
Urushi, Masako 313

Vahdat (Young), Elahe x, 375
Vail, Albert 124, 126, 181
Varqá, 'Alí-Muḥammad 220, 342-3
Vassar College 223, 266
Venice, Italy 28, 32, 35
Vladivostok 127, 232
volcanos
    Haleakala, Maui 14-16 15-17
    Kilauea, Hawaii 17-18, 64
    Mt Asama, Japan 94
Voss, Daisy 286, 311

Waikiki 6, 17, 44, 49, 200, 243, 359
Waite, Louise 63, 91, 131, 137
Walbridge (Suzuki), Ruth x, 368, 379
Walker, Mrs 62
Wallis, William 53-4
Ward, Forsyth and Janet 351
Waseda University, Japan 107, 172, 216
Washington DC 59, 124, 128, 190, 192
Watanabe, Tadashi 230-2, 263, 271
Watson, Albert Durrant 124
Waung, C. W. 183
Waung, H. C. 168, 173
White, Adeline Mary 64, 68-9
Whitney, Ada 12, 18, 23, 51-3, 54
Whitney, Emily 25
Whitney, Ethel 23
Whitney, Henry 25
Whitney, Mary and John Morgan 12, 15, 23
Whyte, Frederick 207
Whyte, Jane 207
Wilcox, Emma 258
Wilhelm, Roy 94, 129, 136, 179, 181, 199, 277
Wilkins, Mary 307
Wilkinson, Miss (Mrs) 166, 1886
Williams, Roy 160
    Tablet from 'Abdu'l-Bahá 160-61
Wilmette, Illinois
    Bahá'ís in 291
    House of Worship, Temple 68, 232, 266, 295, 304

National Bahá'í Convention(s) 246, 290, 298, 327
Intercontinental Teaching Conference (1953) 327-8
Wilson, Lucy 307
Wilson, Roberta 310
Windust, Albert 63
Wolcott, Charles 357
Wooten, Ray 318-19, 321, 326
World Esperanto Congress, Tokyo 364-5, 367
World Order magazine 305
World War
  First 76, 121, 207, 329, 364
  Second 302, 312-13
Wright, Lorraine 313
Wu, T. Z. 186
Wuchang, China 168

Yahyá, Mírzá 61
Yakima, Washington 310
Yamada, Hiroshi 172
Yamagata, Mr 154
Yamamoto, Kanichi 45-8, 54, 56, 128, 296
Yamamoto, Ryniji, Dr 369, 376
Yamashita, Bryan 128
Yanagi, Mr 153-4
Yanai, Yamaguchi province, Japan 258-9, 312
Yang family, Tainan 356
Yang, H. L. 163
Yasuda, Y. 172
Yawata, N. 173

Yazdi, Ahmad 80-81, 266-7
Yazdi, Ali 266
Yazdi, Aziz and Soraya 362
Yentai (Chufoo), China 184, 189
YMCA
  Berkeley 197
  China 223
  Honolulu, Hawaii 24
  Rochester, NY 307
  Seoul, Korea 156, 159-60
  Tokyo, Japan 99, 217, 223
YWCA
  Honolulu, Hawaii 249
  Tokyo, Japan 314, 318
Yokohama, Japan 79, 85, 90, 93, 99-100, 112, 1114, 128-9, 170-71, 176-7, 179, 182, 187, 189, 199, 204, 222, 224, 251, 326-7
Yomiuri newspaper 128
Yoshida, Kinichiro 264
Yoshihito, Emperor 94
Young Hotel, Honolulu 60, 63
Yu, Daniel 183
Yúnis Khán 47
Zenimoto, Isao 346
Zenimoto, Michitosi 322-7, 331, 340, 346-8, 358
Zia Khánum 271

CPSIA information can be obtained
at www.ICGtesting.com
Printed in the USA
BVHW030317190722
642003BV00002B/4

9 780853 986478